Safeguarding children's dignity has become a ma
Within the pages of this book, one is presented wi
tation of inspiring life stories that highlight simi
differences. Written by a diversified authorship, with writers from countries across Asia, Africa, and South America, this book is very enriching. Although the reader's typical eagerness to learn more is toppled by a strong sense of sadness for the many hardships endured by children all around the world, the book carries a great message of resilience and hope. Each of the authors carry the reader in their way through the realities of Christian and non-Christian communities in various cultures. I see in this work an opportune journey to explore what is happening to children and their inalienable right to live in peace and dignity, in our increasingly complex, harsh, and cruel global world.

Hiba Al-Jamal
Director, SKILD,
Smart Kids with Individual Learning Differences Center,
Mansourieh El Maten, Lebanon

This book honors children by enlarging our view of their vulnerabilities, strengths, and contributions and offering creative strategies for protecting, learning from, and collaborating with them. The volume brings together highly respected faith leaders from diverse contexts in the Majority World and is divided into eight chapters that address urgent challenges children are facing worldwide. Chapters are both sobering and inspiring because they carefully examine multiple dimensions of the suffering and agency of children and provide practical strategies and biblical and theological foundations for hope and positive change. The chapters speak powerfully and effectively to the church worldwide by incorporating insights from a range of sources, including the Bible, theologians past and present, the social sciences, policies and best practices of secular and faith-based organizations, national and international reports and agreements regarding child well-being, and the stories and experiences of children themselves.

Marcia J. Bunge, PhD
Professor of Religion and the Drell and Adeline Bernhardson Distinguished Chair,
Department of Religion, Gustavus Adolphus College, Minnesota, USA
Extraordinary Research Professor, North-West University, South Africa

As I reflected on this book, I was deeply conscious that the book is being released at a time when the world is haunted by the images out of Ukraine – a weeping child carrying a stuffed teddy bear walking to "nowhere." It is reported that there have been more than 1.5 million children who have fled the country and more than 75,000 children becoming refugees every day (over 50 children every minute). As the global powers skirt around the issues involved in this war, are the children paying the price for someone's deeply overgrown ego and the helplessness of the nations? Will the church in obedience to her God be able to say with conviction, "I have seen violence done to the helpless, and I have heard the groans of the poor [children]. Now I will rise up to rescue them" (Psalm 12)?

God's Heart for Children is in many ways a search for an answer to this desire to see God and the church act. This book locates itself stubbornly on the margins alongside vulnerable children. It places the child as the "lens" for developing perspectives on humanitarian issues and framing a counter narrative to challenge the adult-centric flawed paradigms dominant in the humanitarian space. The book weaves a fine tapestry with simple stories of children, reflections on theological motifs, and the rich experiences of authors drawn from all across our nations.

Jayakumar Christian
Former National Director World Vision India,
Chennai, India

When we worked two decades ago on the collective project of a biblical framework to understand God's heart for children, our hope was that a new generation of practitioners and theologians would take on the assignment to help Christians with a sound biblical theology of ministry to and with children. *God's Heart for Children* is just the fulfillment of a dream that was planted in our hearts back then. I'm blessed to know that this new generation of scholars and practitioners have taken on the value of children in the mission of God and they have done it with passion, depth, and commitment to both children and God's word.

Gustavo Crocker, PhD
General Superintendent,
Church of the Nazarene, USA

As the church seeks to participate in God's mission, and does so "to, for, and with children," volumes like this one make for essential reading and remind us that the church participates in God's mission "as" children as well. This wide-ranging and rich collection of essays by authors from around the globe illustrates why it is so important to take context seriously in our theological reflection, and why we need one another – children and adults – to discern how to live and speak as faithful disciples of Jesus today.

Tim J. Davy, PhD
Lecturer and Head of Research and Consultancy,
All Nations Christian College, Ware, UK

God's Heart for Children: Practical Theology from Global Perspectives is a practical, contextual, and contemporary resource for any Christian organization working with children, mainly focusing on children at risk. It is great to see such important theological reflections, case studies, and contributions from across the globe, which is particularly exciting for me, especially in relation to our work across Asia.

Prabu Deepan
Regional Director for Asia,
Tearfund, Sri Lanka

Over a decade on from the original *Understanding God's Heart for Children*, this edition of *God's Heart for Children* draws out important voices from around the world in helpfully constructive ways. Hearing the contextual theological and biblical responses to both the issues statements and case studies is particularly enlightening. With strong experienced voices, the children who are at the center of this book are seen and heard. Thank you for doing this so respectfully and honorably. Their resilience against all the odds is awe-inspiring, and yet so often the authors call upon the church at large to learn, reflect, and do better.

The discussion questions at the end of each chapter are helpful to pause, reflect, and put it into our contexts, looking through familiar lenses. Combined with this is a very helpful Scripture reference index and many extended footnotes as well as bibliography. Do read the author bios, they are inspirational people!

This digest of contemporary issues facing children today is a study compendium for all students, churches, and missions as they seek to do no harm, to combine efforts to build God's kingdom, and to see children in their context, honoring them, and giving a hope and a future.

I am going to keenly encourage all my students and faculty at All Nations Christian College to engage with this excellent compendium. Thank you very much each and every author, editor, and support team. Let's get this out to a global audience who need to read it too!

Andy Dipper
Principal & Chief Executive,
All Nations Christian College, Ware, UK

God's Heart for Children challenges us to examine how we perceive children: do we see the same value, the same dignity, and the same potential that God sees in them? Do we consider them as prepared by God to participate in his work and actively contribute to his kingdom? And how can we help them overcome what keeps them from fulfilling their God-given calling? Experts from different regions of the world allow us to hear the voices of children by telling their stories. With profound theological insights, unsettling facts and statistics, and deeply relatable testimonies, the authors give a face to the issues children experience in various cultures and contexts. The book also provides proven practical steps on how the church can effectively respond. It is a valuable resource for anyone who works with children and desires to see them flourish in accordance with God's will.

Rebecca Goropevsek, DMin
Coordinator, Children's Network,
World Evangelical Alliance, New York, USA

I was deeply influenced in my work in the Christian development sector by the 2007 publication of *Understanding God's Heart for Children*. The perspectives it presented shaped my understanding of the centrality of children, and especially children at risk, in community-based work informed by a Christian perspective.

I was therefore delighted to receive this new edition with its global voices and contextual approach. It is a valuable resource for individual and group study to inform action that reflects God's heart for children. I recommend this book highly, not only for those working directly with children, but for all those seeking to understand the importance of children in God's mission. My hope and belief is that this book will fuel thinking and action that will substantially increase the flourishing of all children and especially of those currently living in very difficult circumstances.

Deborah Hancox, PhD
Micah Global International Coordinator,
South Africa

God's Heart for Children: Practical Theology from Global Perspectives provides a seven-point roadmap of a kingdom approach to our responsibility to fulfil God's mandate to, for, and with children. Situating contextual theologies from the Majority World as the basis for reflection and praxis, the authors have diligently provided a biblical foundation for a missional, intergenerational, and a holistic spiritual formation of inclusion of children in the congregational community and society. This is a must-read book by all undergraduate level students of theology and ministry, as well as children at risk practitioners such as those leading ministries and organizations.

Malinda N. Harrahs, PhD
Deputy Vice Chancellor – Academic Affairs,
Scott Christian University, Kenya

This is a broad, yet deep, exploration of children and their value in the eyes of God. It is hard-hitting, yet rich in what it offers to us all. Throughout the contributions we are reminded that our knowledge and understanding of the lived experience of children around the world is only of use if it is strengthened by our own proactive efforts to be a part of the change that is so needed. This lived experience of children is the lens through which we can begin to come close to and feel the pain in the heart of God. It is powerful and humbling to be encouraged to reflect on the fact that Jesus always elevated and dignified children. As you read this book, you will be challenged, stirred, and perhaps led to resist the urge to look up (at adults) and instead to look down (at children) to see where justice must find its foundations.

Justin Humphreys
Chief Executive,
Thirtyone:eight, UK

In *God's Heart for Children*, an excellent group of diverse scholars and practitioners have come together to give us a book that will not only persuade us that God cares for children but also show us how to work with God to raise up children who will be a generation that will follow Christ. With the continued growth of Christianity around the world, the median age of Christians is falling fast. Thus, the subject of this book ought to be a concern for all Christians thinking about the church's existence, both today and in the future. It comes with great recommendation for all Christians involved in the ministry, especially those involved with families and children.

Harvey Kwiyani, PhD
CEO of Global Connections, UK

Ever looked at a night sky full of stars? Or listened to the lark sing overhead? God created life to be good, happy, fun, and beautiful. The longer I travel with the Lord, the more I realize his desire to reveal the beauty and wonder of what he has made.

One of those great goodnesses is surely the quiet happy hum of great children's ministry: community groups – mostly churches – caring, nourishing, educating, and challenging children to become all they should be. Places run by leaders dedicated to teach the next generation the right ways of God; children keen to learn more about who God is, how he has put things together, and who he wants them to be and become.

Those leaders will treasure this book full of depth, experience, challenge, and insight. Enjoy it. Apply it. Buy it and share it.

Patrick McDonald
Founder of Viva, UK

Three themes run vividly through this global vision of childhood – dignity, *ubuntu* (community), and hope – underpinned by an honest theology that acknowledges that community can be toxic as well as sustaining, that hope springs not just from rights but essentially from spiritual well-being, and that the child has dignity not as a subject, but rather as an agent of the kingdom of God.

Rev. Canon Mark Oxbrow
President, Feed the Minds, UK

This is a book that puts children at the center of God's heart and God's mission. It is written by an experienced cohort of global theologians and practitioners who desire to see children renewed and restored by God's love. The writers tackle contemporary themes that affect children the most severely, such as bonded labour, climate change, homelessness, and migration. You will be informed, challenged, and changed by reading these articles, and you will never look at children in our world the same way again.

Cathy Ross, PhD
Leader, Pioneer Mission Leadership Training, Oxford, UK
Lecturer in Mission, Regents Park College, Oxford, UK

God's Heart for Children is an incredible book that will help readers grasp the intricate value of children in God's sight. I believe this book, through its profound message and in-depth theological responses on the various critical global issues on children, will have a great impact on how we perceive children and motivate us to value and transform children's lives after God's own heart.

Aashima Samuel
National Director,
Evangelical Fellowship of India Children at Risk, India

The milestone of this volume is the diversity of its voices. While prior contributions to theology that attend to children have unavoidably or inadvertently centered on Western perspectives and experiences, this volume stubbornly proclaims that understanding children as Christians can – and must – be done outside of the West, and done well. The authors in this book challenge, arrest, and chide all of us to do better, to learn better, and to listen better in order to hear the voice of the Holy Spirit while we attend to the strident tones and eager whispers of the children in our midst.

David Scott, PhD
Assistant Professor of Intercultural Studies and Children at Risk,
Associate Dean of the School of Mission and Theology,
Fuller Theological Seminary, California, USA

This is a diverse treasury. At times, the content will horrify you and shatter your peace of mind – it was a false thing anyway. The threats to vulnerable girls and boys in this age are varied, ever-present, and rapidly escalating. We need the wisdom in this book. It gives principles to help individuals, families, communities, and churches to understand the intersecting risks and vulnerabilities that threaten children, and to respond with the love, courage, and the indignation of Christ. Some threats to children are new; others have been with us since the beginning . . . The fingerprints of God are on this book. I am glad it was written and pray it will help us all better value, protect, and nurture vulnerable children, families, and childhoods.

Camilla Symes
Senior Director, Transformational Development,
World Vision International, UK

God's Heart for Children

God's Heart for Children

Practical Theology from Global Perspectives

Edited by Rosalind Tan, Nativity A. Petallar, Lucy A. Hefford

Foreword by Douglas McConnell

Published 2022 by Langham Global Library
An imprint of Langham Publishing
www.langhampublishing.org

Langham Publishing and its imprints are a ministry of Langham Partnership

Langham Partnership
PO Box 296, Carlisle, Cumbria, CA3 9WZ, UK
www.langham.org

ISBNs:
978-1-83973-275-1 Print
978-1-83973-692-6 ePub
978-1-83973-693-3 Mobi
978-1-83973-694-0 PDF

British Library Cataloguing-in-Publication Data
A catalogue record for this book is available from the British Library

ISBN: 978-1-83973-275-1

Cover & Book Design: projectluz.com

Contents

Foreword

Taking my grandson to school today was a precious moment in time. I remember taking his mother to school as if it were yesterday. I could even see my mother's smiling face as she took me to school. One of the joys of aging is the freshness of memories of family. Our ability to remember is foundational to who we are as human beings. It is also a critical element in being people who love God. The book of Deuteronomy states it well,

> *But take care and watch yourselves closely, so as neither to forget the things that your eyes have seen nor to let them slip from your mind all the days of your life; make them known to your children and your children's children. (Deut 4:9 NRSV)*

Seeing, hearing, and sharing are actions incumbent on God's family. For the people called to love and care for children, the focus is ensuring that the children see, hear, and experience God's love in their daily lives. It is faith in action. It is also obedience to the great commandment, "to love the Lord your God with all your heart, and with all your soul, and with all your mind . . . love your neighbor as yourself" (Matt 22:37–38 NRSV).

The myriad of problems facing children today challenges us to discern what God wants for them at any moment in time. It is not as though a single course or even a complete degree can synthesize everything there is to know about children. Instead, it requires a much more vigilant approach. The phrase "all the days of your life" provides a clue to understanding God's heart for children. It is a disciplined practice of seeing, hearing, and sharing. Mission alongside children is not only a calling; it is a life sentence!

As Patrick McDonald, founder of Viva, often said, "children are human beings, not human becomings." Children are to be in the midst of us. Their value is limitless in God's heart, requiring the most disciplined commitment from those called to serve with children. The individuals and organizations associated with Viva exemplify the discipline needed for practical work with children. A testimony to this standard of practice occurs when we meet adults who testify to God's love learned from an individual or organization associated with the network Viva represents. We also find it in the depth of insight shared in this latest book, *God's Heart for Children: Practical Theology from Global Perspectives.*

Through association with Viva over the past three decades, I observed the maturation of theology and practice within the network. This volume, skillfully edited by Rosalind Tan, Nativity Petallar, and Lucy Hefford, brings together the insights from scholars and practitioners globally. They explore the seven statements of the biblical framework, plus significant engagement with creation care.[1] The subtitle *Practical Theology from Global Perspectives* is critical as it accurately identifies the authors' concerns for addressing practical questions from the perspective of faith in action. This book contributes significantly to the literature on work with children at risk in all its dimensions.

The twenty-first century is full of crises that swamp even the most effective work with children. Poverty, exploitation, climate change, and countless other macro-level problems pull our focus to the overwhelming problems facing children today. As we move forward in the faith so attested to in this book, religious historian Martin Marty offers a surprising thesis for our study of children. "The provision of care for children will proceed on a radically revised and improved basis if instead of seeing the child first as a problem faced with a complex of problems, we see her as a mystery surrounded by mystery."[2]

This mystery takes on theological significance in the alignment of children and the kingdom of God. In response to the disciples' question of who is the greatest in the kingdom, Jesus places a child in their midst and says, "Truly I tell you, unless you change and become like children, you will never enter the kingdom of heaven." And sending us even deeper into the mystery of the child, Jesus added, "Whoever welcomes one such child in my name welcomes me" (Matt 18:1–5 NRSV).

The individuals, organizations, and churches represented in this book embrace the mystery of what we see, hear, and share in God's heart for children.

Douglas McConnell
Fuller Theological Seminary, California, USA

1. Douglas McConnell, Jennifer Orona, and Paul Stockley, eds., *Understanding God's Heart for Children: Toward A Biblical Framework* (London: Authentic Publishing and World Vision, 2007).

2. Martin Marty, *The Mystery of the Child* (Grand Rapids, MI: Eerdmans, 2007), 1.

Acknowledgments

This publication is like a beautiful, multicolored quilt sewn together by people who love God and love children. Each piece is diligently crafted to tell a story of real encounters. Imagine the hours put into the many stitches, the time taken to make decisions on colors and designs. This publication is a *visio divina*. The images and words form our prayer to invite God to speak to us.

Hence, we want to thank the people who have made this experience possible.

To the contributors who have diligently crafted their unique pieces of work. Without you, there would be no quilt. Thank you for your willingness to write amidst busy schedules and your patience as we worked through the drafts.

Thank you to Doug McConnell and the Tyndale House Foundation for their generosity. Thank you to Dave Scott, Marcia Bunge, Glenn Miles, and Angus Crichton for their guidance.

To Langham Publishing, especially to Luke Lewis, Isobel Stevenson, and Vivian Doub, for believing in this work. Thanks too to Lyndsay Marshall for providing us with the index.

To the Viva family for all of your support and help: to Anna Barker and Brian Wilkinson for getting this project off the ground, Mark Stavers and the whole leadership team for releasing us to pursue the vision, Andrew Dubock for providing help, Lucy Cox and Charlotte Pearson-Miles for proofreading and editing, and Tony Houghton for his speedy translation from Spanish.

To the organizations that are represented in this publication, thank you for supporting this initiative.

To our family, friends, and colleagues at work who gave us space and time to do our writing and editing, thank you for your understanding.

We the editorial team are grateful to God who led us through different challenges, inspired us through his Spirit to see deeper truths, and provided good health to complete this project.

Soli Deo Gloria!

Rosalind, Nativity, and Lucy
2022

Preface

This book is a sequel to the former *Understanding God's Heart for Children: Toward a Biblical Framework.*[1] Based on Viva Network's 2005 Cutting Edge conference, the 2007 publication delved into the theological foundation for ministry to, for, and with children at risk by tracing the biblical narrative from Genesis to Revelation. Practitioners, teachers, and theologians develop seven key themes that provide an overview of a kingdom approach describing our responsibility to, for, and with children.

Our goal in convening this new book has been to diversify the authorship of the former *Understanding God's Heart for Children* to ensure that we hear African, Asian, and Latino perspectives on practical theologies of children more clearly. Furthermore, we set out to update the practitioner contributions and case studies to reflect issues which children-at-risk are facing in 2022, including adding a new chapter entitled "Engaged in Creation Care."

As a result, *God's Heart for Children* considers contextual theologies from the non-Western world as the basis for reflection and praxis. To our knowledge, this approach has not been used in a publication about children at risk to date. Hence, we hope that it will be a vibrant and meaningful tool to guide dialogue and improve practice, especially when practitioners are informed and shaped by contextual theology. The Bible, Lausanne Occasional Papers on children at risk, and the Cape Town Commitment have acted as our guideposts.

This is not the end, but merely the beginning. Much more should and *must* be written on contextual theologies of children and childhood so that organizations who minister to, for, and with children can do so in ways that are informed by the full spectrum of *God's Heart for Children* – a spectrum we cannot have the privilege of seeing unless we involve people from every tribe, tongue, and nation in the conversation.

Rosalind, Nativity, and Lucy
2022

1. Douglas McConnell, Jennifer Orona, and Paul Stockley, eds., *Understanding God's Heart for Children: Toward A Biblical Framework* (London: Authentic Publishing and World Vision, 2007).

List of Abbreviations

BCEs	basic ecclesiastical communities
CFS	child friendly space
COMAR	Commission for Attention to Refugees, Mexico
CRANE	Children at Risk Action Network
CRC	Convention on the Rights of the Child
CTC	Cape Town Commitment
EES	environmental and economic sustainability
GHG	global greenhouse gas
HCD	Holistic Child Development
IPCC	Intergovernmental Panel on Climate Change
IDPs	Internally Displaced Persons
IJM	International Justice Mission
IOM	International Organization for Migration
MDGs	Millennium Development Goals
NGOs	Non-Government Organizations
PMA	Pathein Myaungmya Association
RENAP	Registro Nacional de Personas
RHP	Refugee Highway Partnership
UCZ	United Church of Zambia
UN	United Nations
UNICEF	United Nations International Children's Emergency Fund
UNODC	United Nations Office on Drugs and Crime
WCC	World Council of Churches
WHO	World Health Organization
WWO	World Without Orphans

1

Created in Dignity

Every child is created in dignity as fully human and is individually valued by God. Making dignity an "experiential reality" for children is a theological mandate to which we are bound to respond.

Global Critical Issue:
Getting to the Root of the Problem

Jan Grobbelaar – South African

Introduction

This article poses a fundamental and probing question: How do we view children? Or more importantly, do our views of children affirm the God-given dignity of all children? Do the ways in which legislators and policymakers, the church and different agencies serving children, the academics doing research, and the societies in which they are living view children, both girls and boys, as dignified human beings created by God? Nearer to ourselves, we also must ask do the ways in which we as Christians view children in our daily lives affirm their God-given dignity?

Why is it necessary in 2022 to ask these questions? Maybe the following words of Dominic Wyse give a clue for answering them: "The way that we view children in general is directly linked to the way we deal with them practically and specifically."[1] The implication is that all of our practices regarding children are always caused and shaped by our views of children. When people do not think about children in ways that affirm their human dignity, children can experience exploitation and indignity at the hands of adults.

One example of this exploitation is descent-based slavery passed down the maternal line in contexts like the Sahel belt of Africa, as in the case of Moulkheir from Mauritania who grew up working as a slave for a family. She tells her story:

> My mother worked for them before me and my children . . . all grew up working for the family too. Two of my girls are the daughters of the master's eldest son. He said he would behead me if I ever told anyone they were his. When I had my fourth child, a baby girl, the family wouldn't let me take her out to the fields

1. Dominic Wyse, "Interdisciplinary Perspectives: The Demonization of Childhood," in *Childhood Studies. An Introduction*, ed. Dominic Wyse (Malden: Blackwell, 2004), 211.

> with me. I came home one day and found that the baby had been left out in the sun all day. She had died and her body was being eaten by ants. I had to bury her myself, with my hands; it felt like I was burying an animal instead of my child.
>
> One day they sent me to another home. My new master was a colonel. . . . Later . . . he decided he would marry my eldest daughter. . . . She was very young. She cried and cried. Well, he called it marriage, but there was no dowry, no ceremony, nothing. It was just a way to abuse her.[2]

Every day, girls under the age of eighteen are forced into early childhood marriages. In Nigeria and Niger, the *wahaya* practice by which children are sold as unofficial "fifth wives" for sexual and domestic exploitation still exists.[3] In Romania a ten-year-old girl

> was sold by her parents to be "married" to a seventeen-year-old boy with a contract specifying that she bear two children. The girl gave birth at the age of 12 and was warned by a doctor not to have any more children because of the risk to her health. This led the boy's parents to try to reclaim the money they paid for "breach of contract."[4]

In Afghanistan, Nilab was married at the age of thirteen to a married man with three children. Nilab experienced the wedding party as childhood play and did not understood what it meant to become the man's life partner. "From the first day of Nilab's marriage, her husband and in-laws wanted her to become a prostitute. When Nilab attempted to escape her in-laws' house to her grandparents, they forced her to return to her in-laws' house."[5]

Another experience of indignity which children face can be seen in the lives of children who are forced to beg every day for food and money in the streets of many West Africa citics. These *talibé* children, generally boys between the ages of five and fifteen, study in Quranic schools *(daaras)* and live in extremely dirty conditions without sufficient food and medical care. They are usually exposed to physical abuse like beating and whipping, being chained

---

2. "Moulkheir, Mauritania," Anti-slavery (n.d.), https://www.antislavery.org/impact/stories/moulkheir/.

3. "Behind Closed Doors: Child and Early Marriage as Slavery," Anti-Slavery (n.d.), 5, http://www.antislavery.org/wp-content/uploads/2017/01/behind_closed_doors_child_marriage_as_slavery.pdf.

4. "Behind Closed Doors," 7.

5. "Behind Closed Doors," 6–7.

and bound, as well as sexual abuse. In 2019 it was estimated that more than 100,000 *talibé* children begged an average of five to eight hours a day on the streets of Senegal.[6]

Our Views of Children in Our Daily Lives

The question of our views of children and childhood is not a mere academic one. It is a question which is in many ways connected to our daily lives. Our views of children influence our behavior toward them. Therefore every person must ask themselves, do the ways I talk about children and to them, how I act toward them or not, what I expect from them or not, and how I guide them and live with them affirm their God-given dignity?

Under the influence of psychological and educational developmental theories, many adults tend to see children as incomplete, less developed persons that will only become full human beings somewhere in the future. Children are viewed as pre-adults rather than as dignified fellow human beings in the here and now. This is an adult-centered view of development in which adulthood becomes normative for being a full human being. The result is that some adults tend to see children as totally dependent on them, irrational and incapable, inferior and always subordinate to their power and authority, irresponsible, and without any agency. These are the views that contribute to the exploitation of children as indicated above.

These views also contribute to the development of a "savior complex" among some adults who want to save the children from what they perceive to be factors endangering their lives. Although these humanitarian actions are usually undertaken with good intentions, they sometimes perpetuate indignity because these outsider saviors lack respect for children, their own agency, and the cultural circumstance in which they are growing up. This issue raises the question, do the outsiders really save the children? It is not easy to answer this question. In some situations are positive results, but as is well documented, aid from the West to Africa has also caused problems. In many other contexts, the outcomes seem to be even more negative. Perhaps the following story of the lion and the gazelle can help us to find an answer.

6. "Anti-Slavery International and RADDHO submission to the Human Rights Committee, 127th session (14 October 2019 – 8 November 2019): Fifth periodic report of Senegal," Anti-Slavery (September 2019), https://www.ecoi.net/en/file/local/2018876/INT_CCPR_CSS_SEN_37129_E.docx.

The lion came home with a gazelle kid that was covered in blood and barely breathing, stating that he had saved it from the crocodiles. For days, the animals discussed this incident. Some of them could not believe that a lion would save a gazelle kid. Some thought this event was the beginning of a new order of harmony between all animals. The hyena opined that a lion will always be a lion, and as soon as he became hungry, he would eat the kid. Another was convinced that the mother gazelle was negligent, and others wished they could grow up among the lions. The fox asked for the appointment of a committee to investigate everything while he took care of the kid. At last, they submitted the problem to the wise grandma elephant. After closing her eyes for a long time, she finally said,

> "Did the lion save the kid?
> The answer is hidden in the forests of time
> Grazing with the kid's ancestors
> Grazing with its offspring
> You may ask the kid to guide you there
> But you will need wisdom and patience
> For it cannot talk to you today."[7]

Did the lion really save the kid? Concerning Africa's children, Johannes Malherbe points out that although most outsiders coming to Africa to help "save" Africa's children "presented themselves as the lion saving the kid from the crocodiles,"[8] as "with most hunters' tails, one should suspect that the lions told only part of the story and liberally embellished it to suit their purposes."[9] After all, it is "the assumed right of the lion – 'to the victor belongs the spoils', which includes the right to write the history!"[10]

The Rights of Children

As an effort to enhance the dignity of children, much interest and action has been focused over many years on children's rights. It is therefore no surprise that in the *Understanding God's Heart for Children* publication of 2007, Dave Scott identifies human rights for children as the global critical issue concerning

7. Johannes Malherbe, *Saved by the Lion? Stories of African Children Encountering Outsiders* (Mogale City: About Children, 2012), 1–2.

8. Malherbe, *Saved by the Lion*, 2.

9. Malherbe, 3.

10. Malherbe, 4.

the confirmation of the human dignity of all children.[11] He suggests that "the use of rights language and the leverage that comes with it can be very helpful in ensuring God's purposes in children's lives are achieved, and that governments and institutions of society provide an environment in which children are not denied this opportunity."[12]

Scott's arguments are still valid. But the important question is this: has the emphasis on the rights of children, as well as the use of rights language, really affirmed the human dignity of children? In some contexts, children's rights make a difference, even transforming some societies or some pockets in them[13] as experienced for example in Ethiopia[14] and the Democratic Republic of Congo.[15] In other African contexts, children's rights are not accepted, valued, or applied because of a variety of factors.[16] For example implementation measures are deficient, or people do not have knowledge of the legal protections available.[17] Or certain groups of children like those with special needs[18] or street children[19] are neglected or ignored. But the lack of progress cannot be attributed only to mere practicalities. Behind the issues are views of children that do not confirm their God-given dignity.

---

11. Dave Scott, "Critical Issues: Theological Dignity and Human Rights for Children," in *Understanding God's Heart for Children*, eds. Douglas McConnell, Jennifer Orona, and Paul Stockley (Colorado Springs: Authentic, 2007), 23–35.

12. Scott, "Critical Issues," 23.

13. Nicola Ansell, "The Convention on the Rights of the Child: Advancing Social Justice for African Children," in *Children's Lives in an Era of Children's Rights: The Progress of the Convention on Children's Rights in Africa*, eds. Afua Twum-Danso Imoh and Nicola Ansell (London, New York: Routledge, 2014), 312.

14. Tatek Abebe and Tamirat Tefera, "Earning Rights: Discourses on Children's Rights and Proper Childhood in Ethiopia," in *Children's Lives,* eds. Imoh and Ansell, 87–110.

15. Géraldine André and Marie Godin, "Children's Rights in The Democratic Republic of Congo and Neoliberal Reforms: The Case of Mines in the Province of Katanga," in *Children's Lives*, eds. Imoh and Ansell, 112–36.

16. Ansell, "Convention," 312.

17. Emilie Secker, "Barriers to the Effective Implementation of the UN Convention on the Rights of the Child in the Niger Delta in Nigeria," in *Children's Lives*, eds. Imoh and Ansell, 243–64.

18. Jacque O'Riordan, et al., "Accessing and Participating in Education in Lesotho: Children in the Early Years with Special Needs," in *Children's Lives*, eds. Imoh and Ansell, 223–42.

19. Lorraine van Blerk, "Progressing Street Children's Rights and Participation in Policy: Evidence from South Africa," in *Children's Lives*, eds. Imoh and Ansell, 266–86.

Labeling Children

One way of degenerating children is to label them. Simplistic labels such as child soldiers, child prostitutes, child laborers, refugee children, migrant children, child asylum seekers, homeless children, and street children can be reductive and contribute toward striping children of their dignity. It is true that some of these labels are used as descriptive terms, especially in the academic world, but some people have negative thoughts toward these groups when they use or hear these labels. For example the labels migrant children, child asylum seekers, and refugee children are used by some people to emphasize that "these children are not like us; we do not like them; they are outsiders who do not belong here." In some contexts, such labels promote hatred and contribute toward acts of xenophobia.

One way of degenerating children is to label them.

The sad consequence of all labels is that they usually lead to stereotyping, as if all children to whom a specific label is attached are the same. For instance when we label children as vulnerable, we usually stereotype them

> either as victims of other people, social structures or government institutions, or we see them as transgressors who deserve their situation. And it is not only our thoughts about them that are influenced in this way, but also our attitudes and actions towards them, their situations and other role players in their contexts.[20]

In the emerging literature on children and childhood in the Global South, it seems that authors from the Global North are excessively concerned with the social problems children experience, especially related to work and family life. One of the results is that people in the Global North do not know or understand much about the total contexts of children and childhood outside their own life sphere and often view the children of the Global South in one-sided ways that lead to stereotyping.

Consequently, some of these groups of children were and are seen as less human or as having diminished human dignity. They are submitted to paternalistic activities from the "other world" which seldom acknowledge and incorporate their own agency. In studies on children and childhood, it seems that "the challenge of depicting and analysing how childhood is shaped by

20. Jan Grobbelaar, "The Plight and Vulnerability of Children Living in South Africa and the Calling of the Church," in *Childhood Vulnerabilities in South Africa: Some Ethical Perspectives*, eds. Jan Grobbelaar and Chris Jones (Stellenbosch: Africa Sun Media, 2020), 15.

other social identities, including 'race', class and gender, has not been actively taken up within the contemporary sociology of childhood; the childhoods of white and middle-class children have remained the central subject of the sociology of childhood."[21]

The Interconnectedness of Children and Their Community

When studying childhood in Africa, we ought always to view children in terms of their interconnectedness with other people as an expression of the African worldview of *ubuntu*, as verbalized in the saying, "a person is a person through other people,"[22] or "I am because we are."[23] Several African proverbs such as – "A letter is half as good as seeing each other" (Swahili); "It is through people that we are people" (Swazi, Swaziland); "A person is a person because of neighbors" (Tumbuka, Malawi); "Mountains never meet, but people do" (Gusii and Kamba, Kenya; Sukuma)[24] – emphasize this same idea. The wide acceptance of *ubuntu* and interconnectedness illustrates that humanness on the African continent is the life vibe of African people.[25] To live, as a child or adult, is to participate in communion with other people, "a continual becoming more of a person through one's interaction with others."[26] In this regard Desmond Tutu declares, "We need other human beings for us to learn how to be human . . . For us, the solitary human being is a contradiction in terms. . . . I need other human beings in order to be human. The completely self-sufficient human being is subhuman."[27]

We ought always to view children in terms of their interconnectedness with other people as an expression of the African worldview of *ubuntu*.

Therefore the upbringing of African children is an effort of the

21. Karen Wells, *Childhood in a Global Perspective* (Cambridge: Polity, 2015), 3.

22. Hanneke Stuit, *Ubuntu Strategies: Constructing Spaces of Belonging in Contemporary South African Culture* (New York: Palgrave Macmillan, 2016), 2.

23. John S. Mbiti, *African Religions and Philosophy* (New York: Anchor, 1970), 141.

24. Joseph Healey and Donald Sybertz, *Towards an African Narrative Theology* (New York: Orbis, 1996), 107.

25. Johann Broodryk, *Africa Is Best* (Waterkloof: uBuntu School of Philosophy, 2010), 45–46.

26. Augustine Shutte, *UBUNTU: An Ethic for a New South Africa* (Pietermaritzburg: Cluster, 2004), 12.

27. Desmond M. Tutu, *God Is Not a Christian: Speaking Truth in Times of Crisis* (London: Rider, 2011), 21–22.

whole community, which is expressed in African proverbs such as "One knee does not bring up a child" (Sukuma) and "One hand does not nurse a child" (Swahili).[28] African childhood cannot be understood in individualistic ways without considering children's embeddedness in their extended family, clan, and community. African children lose their identity and are robbed of their God-given dignity if their umbilical cord with their extended family, clan, and society is severed. Extreme examples of this severing include trafficking and smuggling children, forcing children to become soldiers, and enslaving children. Discussing and formulating understandings of children and childhood in the African context without taking into consideration the formational influence of the interconnectedness of children and their communities in Africa is to ignore an important factor in their identity formation. To view African children with an individualistic anthropology which separates them from each other and the social systems in which they are living is to rob them of their human dignity. Therefore it is always better to use "children" rather than "a child" when studying childhood in the African context.

African children lose their identity and are robbed of their God-given dignity if their umbilical cord with their extended family, clan, and society is severed.

Concluding Remarks

In creating a just world for children, the human dignity of all children should be confirmed and restored in our views of children and in our daily living together with them. New understandings of children and childhood should be developed not only in childhood studies, but also in all other disciplines involved in studying children by studying from the ground up with the children within their different contexts. With this approach the agency of children, not as the possession of a self-present knowingness but as the product of social relations supported across the arrangements of human and non-human actors, should be taken seriously in knowledge production. In this regard, theologies of childhood[29] have to play an important decolonizing role by searching for better ways of understanding and expressing the human dignity of all children.

28. Healey and Sybertz, *Towards an African*, 113–14.

29. See Jan Grobbelaar and Gert Breed, eds., *Theologies of Childhood and the Children of Africa* (Cape Town: AOSIS, 2016).

The human dignity of children is connected to the fact that human beings are created in the image of God. The challenge before us is this: how do we view and live with children with this significant principle in mind?

Bibliography

Abebe, Tatek, and Tamirat Tefera. "Earning Rights: Discourses on Children's Rights and Proper Childhood in Ethiopia." In *Children's Lives in an Era of Children's Rights: The Progress of the Convention on Children's Rights in Africa*, edited by Afua Twum-Danso Imoh and Nicola Ansell, 87–110. London, New York: Routledge, 2014.

André, Géraldine, and Marie Godin. "Children's Rights in The Democratic Republic of Congo and Neoliberal Reforms: The Case of Mines in the Province of Katanga." In *Children's Lives in an Era of Children's Rights: The Progress of the Convention on Children's Rights in Africa*, edited by Afua Twum-Danso Imoh and Nicola Ansell, 112–36. London, New York: Routledge, 2014.

Ansell, Nicola. "The Convention on the Rights of the Child: Advancing Social Justice for African Children." In *Children's Lives in an Era of Children's Rights: The Progress of the Convention on Children's Rights in Africa*, edited by Afua Twum-Danso Imoh and Nicola Ansell, 312–35. London, New York: Routledge, 2014.

"Anti-Slavery International and RADDHO submission to the Human Rights Committee, 127th session (14 October 2019 – 8 November 2019): Fifth periodic report of Senegal." Anti-Slavery (September 2019), https://www.ecoi.net/en/file/local/2018876/INT_CCPR_CSS_SEN_37129_E.docx.

"Behind Closed Doors: Child and Early Marriage as Slavery." Anti-Slavery (n.d.). http://www.antislavery.org/wpcontent/uploads/2017/01/behind_closed_doors_child_marriage_as_slavery.pdf.

Broodryk, Johann. *Africa Is Best*. Waterkloof: uBuntu School of Philosophy, 2010.

Grobbelaar, Jan. "The Plight and Vulnerability of Children Living in South Africa and the Calling of the Church." In *Childhood Vulnerabilities in South Africa: Some Ethical Perspectives*, edited by Jan Grobbelaar and Chris Jones, 1–32. Stellenbosch: African Sun Media, 2020. https://doi.org/10.18820/9781928480952.

Grobbelaar, Jan, and Gert Breed, eds. *Theologies of Childhood and the Children of Africa*. Cape Town: AOSIS, 2016. http://www. dx.doi.org/10.4102/aosis.2016.tcca02.01.

Healey, Joseph, and Donald Sybertz. *Towards an African Narrative Theology*. New York: Orbis, 1996. Kindle edition.

Imoh, Afua Twum-Danso, Michael Bourdillon, and Sylvia Meichsner. "Introduction: Exploring Children's Lives Beyond the Binary of the Global North and Global South." In *Global Childhoods beyond the North-South Divide*, edited by Afua Twum-Danso Imoh, Michael Bourdillon, and Sylvia Meichsner, 1–10. Cham: Palgrave Macmillan, 2019.

Malherbe, Johannes. *Saved by the Lion? Stories of African Children Encountering Outsiders*. Mogale City: About Children, 2012.

Mbiti, John S. *African Religions and Philosophy*. New York: Anchor, 1970.

"Moulkheir, Mauritania." Anti-slavery (n.d.). https://www.antislavery.org/impact/stories/moulkheir/.

O'Riordan, Jacqui, James Urwick, Matemoho Khatleli, Stella Long, Grace Ntaote, Florence Nyakudya, and Nthabeleng Maketala. "Accessing and Participating in Education in Lesotho: Children in the Early Years with Special Needs." In *Children's Lives in an Era of Children's Rights: The Progress of the Convention on Children's Rights in Africa*, edited by Afua Twum-Danso Imoh and Nicola Ansell, 223–42. London, New York: Routledge, 2014.

Oswell, David. *The Agency of Children: From Family to Global Human Rights*. Cambridge: Cambridge University Press, 2013.

Scott, David. "Critical Issues: Theological Dignity and Human Rights for Children." In *Understanding God's Heart for Children: Toward a Biblical Framework*, edited by Douglas McConnell, Jennifer Orona, and Paul Stockley, 23–35. Colorado Springs: Authentic, 2007.

Secker, Emilie. "Barriers to the Effective Implementation of the UN Convention on the Rights of the Child in the Niger Delta in Nigeria." In *Children's Lives in an Era of Children's Rights: The Progress of the Convention on Children's Rights in Africa*, edited by Afua Twum-Danso Imoh and Nicola Ansell, 243–64. London, New York: Routledge, 2014.

Shutte, Augustine. *UBUNTU: An Ethic for a New South Africa*. Pietermaritzburg: Cluster, 2004.

Stuit, Hanneke. *Ubuntu Strategies: Constructing Spaces of Belonging in Contemporary South African Culture*. New York: Palgrave Macmillan, 2016.

Tutu, Desmond M. *God is Not a Christian: Speaking Truth in Times of Crisis*. London: Rider, 2011.

Van Blerk, Lorraine. "Progressing Street Children's Rights and Participation in Policy: Evidence from South Africa." In *Children's Lives in an Era of Children's Rights: The Progress of the Convention on Children's Rights in Africa*, edited by Afua Twum-Danso Imoh and Nicola Ansell, 266–86. London, New York: Routledge, 2014.

Wells, Karen. *Childhood in a Global Perspective*, 2nd ed. Cambridge: Polity. 2015. Kindle edition.

Wyse, Dominic. "Interdisciplinary Perspectives: The Demonization of Childhood." In *Childhood Studies: An Introduction*, edited by Dominic Wyse, 205–12. Malden: Blackwell, 2004.

Biblical and Theological Response:

Affirming Children's Dignity as a Theological Vision and Mandate

Jessy Jaison – Indian

Introduction

Despite winning the much coveted first prize in a national arts competition, Lena,[30] the beautiful six grader, returned gloomy and depressed. To the teacher who enquired about the matter, Lena replied rather apathetically, "Ma'am, do you think awards and achievements would mean anything to the poor kids whose parents are alcoholics?" Lena was coming to terms with the life of indignity that she was "destined" to live. From the sparkles, applause, colors, limelight, and celebrations, she's landed suddenly at her run-down home. In her shack, what matters is not prizes but more hands to work and find the next meal.

Children's experience of their God-given dignity calls for our urgent attention, even in the church. Discussions of children's dignity and related concerns are too often relegated by the church and the academy to the extreme margins of our interests. Higonnet says that our discourses on children are "too dangerous and too safe, too difficult and too silly . . . good only for second rate minds and perhaps for women."[31] This is a matter of attitude. This attitude controls our responses and behaviors. We may have to admit that, "Understanding the situation of children and youth in the world is a major blind spot in

Children's experience of their God-given dignity calls for our urgent attention, even in the church.

30. Not her real name.

31. Anne Higonnet, *Pictures of Innocent: The History and Crisis of Ideal Childhood* (New York: Thames and Hudson, 1998), 13–14.

Christian mission."[32] Only by a divine intervention on human minds and hearts can the church and the world capture a redeemed vision for the child. In recent years we have witnessed a rapid conscientization and development in voicing out for children, yet the road ahead may be longer and more tiresome than we imagine.

Endless discussion can be had on Christian beliefs about children's God-given dignity. The difficult thing to do, however, is to put these beliefs into practice because children's needs are multilayered and their situations are complex. In the first edition of *Understanding God's Heart for Children*, Douglas McConnell in his article "God Creates every Unique Person as a Child with Dignity" coherently states that children enter this world with the unique capacity to be in relationship with God, humankind, and creation.[33] While his chapter focuses on dignity in God-ordained relationships, this article discusses how important it is to see this theological mandate reflected in the experiences of a child. This vision presupposes that we move from knowledge to living. Grobbelaar above states how vital it is to review our subjective concepts and abstractions of children against their daily experiences. In the first part of this article, we explore the concept of "dignity," discussing children's intrinsic worth as image bearers, fully human, crowned with glory and honor, and valued by Creator God. Second is a discussion on the enduring deprivation of dignity experienced by Indian Dalit (lower caste) children and the forms of grave violations of human dignity they experience.[34] Christians have a mandate to be intentional in shaping the experiential reality of the children entrusted to us. This article admits that families, churches, and societies often fall short of God's vision to provide children with this "experiential reality" of dignity.[35] The attempt here is however not to theologize experience, rather to emphasize experiential

Christians have a mandate to be intentional in shaping the experiential reality of the children entrusted to us.

32. Bryant L. Myers, "State of the World's Children: Critical Challenge to Christian Mission," *International Bulletin of Missionary Research* 18, no. 3 (July 1994): 98.

33. Douglas McConnell, "God Creates Every Unique Person as a Child with Dignity," in *Understanding God's Heart for Children*, eds. Douglas McConnell, Jennifer Orona, and Paul Stockley (Colorado Springs: Authentic, 2007), 13–22.

34. See James Massey, ed., *Indigenous People: Dalits: Dalit Issues in Today's Theological Debate* (Delhi: ISPCK, 1994).

35. Jesudason Jeyaraj, ed. *Children at Risk: Issues and Challenges* (CFCD Bangalore: ISPCK, 2009).

reality as the means by which children make sense of God and the world around them.

The Impacts of Creation and Fall

The English word "dignity" comes from the Latin *dignitas* which means "worthiness."[36] In certain cultures it connotes a genuine pride in being a valuable, esteemed person. The implication is that each child is worthy of honor and respect for who he or she is and not what he or she can do. The dignity of children refers to the value of their existence and their unique self as fully human, worthy of flourishing through meaningful experiences, and agents of transformative influence in the world in which they live. Dignity cannot be earned or taken away. It only needs to be realized and affirmed. We recognize that the justice systems, human rights policies, economic structures, power structures such as media and communication, caste divisions, gender assumptions, and religious affiliations all impact the dignity of a child. Grobbelaar's exposition of children being in a world created by adults and stereotyped and labeled calls us to revisit the conceptual frames that have enslaved us for too long and kept us from valuing the dignity of children.[37]

Dignity is reflected in the care, service, and respect a child receives. Children's understanding of their dignity is affected by how they view themselves – their self-concept. Dignity is God-given. As God is invisible, children develop their sense of worth primarily from the dignity that those around bestow on them.

> Children develop their sense of worth primarily from the dignity that those around bestow on them.

Child as the Divine Image Bearer

The dignity of human beings is at the core of biblical revelation. So is the dignity of the child who is fully human. Dignity as a theological motif holds in balance two things: the God-given intrinsic worth as the divine image bearers and the lived experiences within the family and community that ensure children as fully human and worthy of flourishing. Human dignity originates in the fact that

---

36. "dignity," *Merriam Webster.com Dictionary*, https://www.merriam-webster.com/dictionary/dignity.

37. See page 12 above.

God created human beings in God's own image and likeness,[38] and they are of infinite value to God, created to fulfill his unique purposes. When referring to a child as a person with dignity, we signify her or his unique self and valuable existence; we affirm that the child is worthy of rights and responsible living and is not a means for others to reach their ends. God-given dignity endorses that a child has the potential to meaningfully experience and influence the environment and the society in which she or he is living.

Fully Human and Individually Valued

Critically, children are not less human than adults. McConnell affirms, "To be a child is to be fully human."[39] The relational dimensions he expounds in his chapter correspond with what John Stott established on human dignity.[40] The inherent worth of people, be they children or adults, is built on the Christian belief that (1) they are created in the image of God; (2) they are created to love and worship God; and, (3) they are created to partner with the creation and revelation of God. According to Grudem,

> Every single human being . . . has the status of being in God's image and therefore must be treated with dignity and respect that is due to God's image-bearer. This has profound implications for our conduct toward others. . . . If we ever deny our unique status in creation as God's only image-bearers, we will soon begin to depreciate the value of human life, will tend to see humans as merely a higher form of animal, and will begin to treat others as such. We will also lose much of our sense of meaning in life.[41]

Scripture envisions persons as responsible and responsive beings in dynamic relationship with the Creator God rather than as individualistic, anthropocentric, autonomous beings as in Marxism or the rationalism of the Enlightenment-era advocate. That humans are special and distinct among the creatures can be seen in God's solemn announcement that brought humans to existence (Gen 1:26), God's affirmation that they are created in his own image and likeness (Gen 1:27), and God's commissioning of humans in a preeminent

38. W. Sibly Towner, "Children and the Image of God," in *The Child in the Bible*, ed. Marcia J. Bunge (Grand Rapids, MI: Eerdmans, 2008), 321.

39. McConnell, "God Creates," 22.

40. John Stott, *Issues Facing Christians Today*, rev. ed. (Delhi: GLS, 2005), 173–75.

41. Wayne Grudem, *Systematic Theology* (reprint Hyderabad: G. S. Books, 2017), 450.

position of dominion over creation (Gen 1:28–30). While animals may be killed, humans are not to be killed because of the image of God they bear (Gen 9:1–7). The terms "image" and "likeness" bear profound meanings as "represent and resemble."[42] A child is a whole person who bears this image and likeness of God and is crowned by God with glory and honor (Ps 8:5).

Keeping the Balance

The dignity of children is a theological motif. The detrimental fall of humans in sin (Gen 3) generated distorted views about fellow beings and hampered all aspects of human existence and relationships. Ever since the fall, children's dignity has had to be argued for, acquired, and protected. In the ceaseless endeavor to restore dignity, however, children turn out to be the last priority because of their inability to speak for themselves. When sin marred humanity, it marred the following generations too; yet in the divine design and vision every new child signifies hope and promise to humanity. All through the Bible we see God's amazing plan of redemption in which children are integral.

To expound on the divinely accorded dignity of children, we need to guard the hermeneutic from losing sight of the effects of the fall that marred human identity. Intellectual classifications of children as less human or less mature or less able have been a fault in our stories, traditions, language, and mindset. It is true that children are growing, and they err and need guidance and protection. Yet none of these issues alter their status as humans created in dignity. It was after the fall that God declared, "Whoever sheds human blood, by humans their blood shall be shed; for in the image of God has God made mankind" (Gen 9:6). Stott explains the continuity as fully human before and after birth through the cases of Jeremiah and Paul. From the fetus stage a child is "the already and the not yet."[43] Therefore the family, church, and society have to remind themselves that any amount of dignity that is accorded to an adult should be equally accorded to a child.

Intellectual classifications of children as less human or less mature or less able have been a fault in our stories, traditions, language, and mindset.

42. N. W. Porteous, "Image of God," in *The Interpreter's Dictionary of the Bible*, vol. 2, 683, quoted in Jose Kuttianimattatthil, *Theological Anthropology* (Bangalore: Theological Publications in India, 2013), 96.

43. Stott, *Issues Facing Christians*, 362.

Our theological thinking needs to hold a balanced perspective of a child's dignity and vulnerability. Overly leaning to either side will only lead us to a flawed perception of God's heart for children. Bunge has addressed this issue extensively through themes elucidating the complexity of biblical understandings of children. Her articulation of "the inherent paradoxes of being a child" presents to us four sound directives that are biblically and theologically based:

> Children are *fully human and made in the image of God yet also still developing and in need of instruction and guidance.*
>
> Children are *gifts of God and sources of joy yet also capable of selfish and sinful actions.*
>
> Children are *vulnerable and in need of protection, yet also strong and insightful.*
>
> Children are *metaphors for immature faith and childish behaviour and yet models of faith and sources of revelation.*[44]

Such a rounded view can only do the intended good in our doing of theology. Theological positions from the either-or ends of *childishness* and *childlikeness* might find this view challenging.[45] In Towner's words, "Human beings are not 'mini-gods' or 'miserable offenders,' wholly incapable of good. From childhood onward, they are God's creatures and chosen partners in the work of creation."[46] The practical irony has been the dichotomy of the theory and experience of dignity. Let's see how the caste segregations in India defect children's experience of their dignity.

---

44. Marcia J. Bunge, "Biblical Understandings of Children and Childhood: Resources for the Church and Mission Today," in *Now and Next*, eds. Siga Arles, Dan Brewster, Chik-Bu Kok, Rosalind Tan, and Keith J. White (Malaysia: Compassion International, 2011), 30, emphasis added.

45. Childishness in the thought of Thomas Aquinas signifies the ignorance and irrationality of children, while childlikeness in the thought of Rahner and Schleiermacher connotes "spiritual perfection." See Cristina L. H. Traina, "A Person in the Making: Thomas Aquinas on Children and Childhood," in *The Child in Christian Thought*, ed. Marcia J. Bunge (Grand Rapids, MI: Eerdmans, 2001), 128.

46. W. Sibly Towner, "Children and the Image of God," in *The Child in the Bible*, ed. Marcia J. Bunge (Grand Rapids, MI: Eerdmans, 2008), 323.

Exploring Dalit Children's Experience[47]

We in the world of ideas can posit countless claims on children's rights and participation while still ignoring what a child in front of our own eyes is experiencing. Childhood experiences are crucial; they have to be central to our theological vision. The tragic plight of the Dalit children's lived reality in caste-affected countries like India may be a worthy point of reflection, as this poem of Dalit protest expresses:

> Mother, you used to tell me
> When I was born
> Your labor was very long.
> The reason, mother,
> The reason for your long labor:
> I still in your womb was wondering
> Do I want to be born –
> Do I want to be born at all
> In this land?
> —L. S. Rokade *To Be or Not To Be Born*[48]

Insulted and injured, the Dalit writer combated the caste-based divisive forces in this Dalit poetry. A corresponding reflection is made by Shiri's reference to the "wounded psyche."[49]

Dignity in Self-Perception

What a child experiences and the feelings and perceptions that a child derives from these experiences matter.[50] Though born in a royal line, Mephibosheth viewed himself as a "dead dog" based on his life experiences (2 Sam 9:8). Relationships or non-relationships give children experiences. Among

47. "T 00-005: Total Population, Population of Scheduled Castes and Scheduled Tribes and their proportions to the total population," Office of the Registrar General & Census Commissioner, India (Census of India 2011), https://censusindia.gov.in/Tables_Published/A-Series/A-Series_links/t_00_005.aspx. See also M. Azariah, "The Church's Healing Ministry to the Dalits," in *Indigenous People: Dalits*, ed. James Massey (Delhi: ISPCK 1994), 322.

48. L. S. Rokade quoted in J. H. Anand, "Dalit Literature is the Literature of Protest," in *Dalit Solidarity*, eds. Bhagawan Das and James Massey (Delhi: ISPCK, 1995), 181.

49. Godwin Shiri, *Dalit Christians: A Saga of Faith and Pathos* (Nagapur: National Council of Churches in India, 2012), 8–9. With the mounting levels of untouchability in schools and harassment in the society, Dalit children develop what has been termed a "wounded psyche."

50. See Bill Prevette, "Child Theology and the Reflective Practitioner," in *Repairer of Broken Walls* (Bangalore: CFCD, 2014), 156.

philosophers were those who saw the world of everyday experience as the primary ground of perceiving something. True perception or learning is defined as "continual reorganisation, reconstruction and transformation of experience."[51] John Dewey believed that it is only through experience that humans make sense of their world and only by using that experience can they maintain and better themselves, which is why childhood experiences are vitally significant in the process of development.

Drawing on the Divine Rendering

Children are integral partners in the covenantal frame of God's action plan with Abraham, Isaac, and Jacob. God rescued both Isaac and Ishmael when they were children.[52] God cared for children in spite of their vulnerabilities; he heard the cry of Ishmael and offered protection to the threatened Isaac. God attended to his children in spite of their social stature. His divine provision of the spring of water rescued Ishmael and a provided ram rescued Isaac. Any form of indignity of children dishonors God. God honors and promotes children.

In a culture where children were not welcomed or considered, Jesus welcomed the little ones (Matt 19:14) and counted them with dignity in his business. Timeless theological reminders to us are the radical directives of Jesus such as "do not hinder [the children]" (Mark 10:14), "change and become like little children" (Matt 18:3), and "whoever welcomes one such child in my name welcomes me" (Matt 18:5). In that day, wisdom was associated only with adults, but the prayer of Jesus in Luke 10:21 challenges that paradigm. From an unnoticed, unimportant presence, the boy in the multitude becomes a partner with Jesus by sharing his provisions to feed them (John 6:5–13). In all of these situations, Jesus does not merely confess dignity, but takes tangible, experiential initiatives in real time in the community. We envision the child standing in the midst to have dignity as God's agent and message, and not as a passive, helpless recipient of our sympathy.

---

51. John Dewey, *Democracy and Education* (1916, reprint New York: Macmillan, 1960), 51.

52. Terence E Fretheim, "God Was with the Boy (Gen 21:20): Children in the Book of Genesis 3–23," in *The Child in the Bible*, ed. Marcia J. Bunge (Grand Rapids, MI: Eerdmans, 2008), 8–15.

Realizing Dignity in Family, Church, and Society

The vision of dignity for children I present recognizes five practical dimensions: provision, protection, promotion, participation, and partnership. These are to be progressive and all-encompassing the family, church, and the society.

Provision: In the story of the boy Isaac, God reveals himself as Jehovah Jireh, the God who provides (Gen 22:1–14). Stafford analyses *the poverty wheel* in which children suffer economic, health, social, educational, and spiritual poverty.[53] Adults are responsible to provide children with supplies for physical sustenance but also their holistic needs for love, security, significance, identity, and discipline.

Protection: The story of Ishmael shows how God sustained the life of a child in answer to the cry of a desperate mother. Protecting children from every form of ridicule, harassment, bonded labor, and abuse – physical, mental, social, sexual, emotional, and spiritual – is the responsibility of adults. Jesus said, "See that you do not despise one of these little ones. For I tell you that their angels in heaven always see the face of my Father in heaven" (Matt 18:10). While provision and protection are foundational in letting the child realize dignity, still more is required.

Promotion: Children's dignity needs to be intentionally guided and guarded. The adult tendency to mock and ridicule children needs to change. God distinctively promoted the young David in the Old Testament and the young Timothy in the New Testament. The promotion of children as divine agents and speakers is also evident in the accounts of Samuel, and others. Timely motivation and due recognition are integral.

Participation: Children are authentic parts of the community, be it a family, church, or society. Samuel had to be in a community larger than his family to develop into God's will for him; God made Eli the high priest listen to the boy Samuel, and Naaman the general listen to the little servant girl, and the disciples listen to a boy with some provisions (1 Sam 3; 2 Kgs 5:1–14; John 6:5–13). The participation of children takes intentionality and vision.

Partnership: From participation, children of God can grow into active partners in God's agenda in the world, a strategic vision every family and church should possess. God shared his agenda with youngsters like Samuel and David. God uses the resources of children to make his kingdom flourish –

53. Wess Stafford, *Too Small to Ignore* (Colorado Springs: WaterBrook, 2005). Also see Luis Bush, *The 4/14 Window: Rising up a New Generation to Transform the World* (Colorado Springs: Compassion, 2009), 56–57.

like the sling David held as a youth, and the five small loaves and two fish the boy held.

Jan Grobbelaar's liberationist hermeneutical objective in child theology invites us to walk further from the spheres of new knowledge of God to a new way of living with children *Coram Deo*,[54] and then have new stories to share.[55]

Summary

Dignity is the God-bestowed worth on each child who is a divine image bearer and agent. While God's image in humans was not fully destroyed by the fall, it has still skewed and twisted the ways we view and relate to children. From the ageless sociopolitical and theological discussions that pay lip service to the dignity of children, every day we open our eyes to see the painful indignities that children encounter in their families, churches, and neighborhoods. A balanced biblical position views a child as a person of dignity and as one in need of intentional care, protection, and instruction. The church is called to break out from the cells of theoretical theology to stand on the ground of children's experience, where dignity is still a mirage for the majority. Children in our world are waiting for someone like Jesus who will respond with grace and courage to raise them as dignified partners in the kingdom of God. To provide, protect, promote, participate, and partner – there is no better model than Jesus Christ, no better resource than the Bible, and no better ground than the church, if only we open our eyes to see.

The church is called to break out from the cells of theoretical theology to stand on the ground of children's experience, where dignity is still a mirage for the majority.

Bibliography

Anand, J. H. "Dalit Literature is the Literature of Protest," In *Dalit Solidarity*, edited by Bhagawan Das and James Massey, 177–84. Delhi: ISPCK, 1995.

Arles, Siga, Dan Brewster, Chik-Bu Kok, Rosalind Tan, and Keith J. White, eds. *Now and Next*. Malaysia: Compassion International, 2011.

---

54. Jan Grobbelaar, *Child Theology and the African Context* (London: CTM, 2012), 18.

55. Walter Brueggemann, *Belonging and Growing in the Christian Community*, ed. Elizabeth McWhorter (Louisville: General Assembly Mission Board, PCUSA, 1979), 31.

Azariah, M. "The Church's Healing Ministry to the Dalits." In *Indigenous People: Dalits: Dalit Issues in Today's Theological Debate*, edited by James Massey, 316–23. Delhi: ISPCK, 1994.

Brueggemann, Walter. *Belonging and Growing in the Christian Community*, ed. Elizabeth McWhorter. Louisville: General Assembly Mission Board, PCUSA, 1979.

Bunge, Marcia J. "Biblical Understandings of Children and Childhood: Resources for the Church and Mission Today." In *Now and Next*, edited by Siga Arles, Dan Brewster, Chik-Bu Kok, Rosalind Tan, and Keith J. White, 15–34. Malaysia: Compassion International, 2011.

Bunge, Marica J., ed. *The Child in Christian Thought*. Grand Rapids, MI: Eerdmans, 2001.

Bush, Luis. The 4/14 Window: Rising up a New Generation to Transform the World. Colorado Springs: Compassion International, 2009.

"Dalits' Access to Education." IDSN briefing paper (n.d.). http://idsn.org/wp-content/uploads/user_folder/pdf/New_files/Key_Issues/Education/DALIT_EDUCATION_IDSNbriefingpaper.pdf.

Dewey, John. *Democracy and Education*. 1916. Reprint New York: Macmillan, 1960.

"dignity." *Merriam Webster.com Dictionary*, https://www.merriam-webster.com/dictionary/dignity.

D'Souza, Joseph. *Dalit Freedom: Now and Forever*. Andhra Pradesh: Dalit Freedom Network, 2004.

Fretheim, Terence E. "God was with the Boy (Gen 21:20): Children in the Book of Genesis 3–23." In *The Child in the Bible*, edited by Marcia J. Bunge. Grand Rapids, MI: Eerdmans, 2008.

Grobbelaar, Jan. *Child Theology and the African Context*. London: CTM, 2012.

Grudem, Wayne. *Systematic Theology*. Reprint Hyderabad: G. S. Books, 2017.

Higonnet, Anne. *Pictures of Innocent: The History and Crisis of Ideal Childhood*. New York: Thames and Hudson, 1998.

Ilnisky, Esther, and Karen Moran. "The Littlest Prayer Warriors." In *Children in Crisis: A New Commitment*, edited by Phyllis Kilbourn, 169–78. Monvovia, California: MARC, 1996.

Iqbal, Mohammed. "Dalit children narrate heart-wrenching tales at public hearing." *The Hindu* (2 January 2018). https://www.thehindu.com/news/national/dalit-children-narrate-heart-wrenching-tales-at-public-hearing/article22347238.ece.

Jayaharan, John. "Untouchability and Dalit Children." In *Children at Risk: Issues and Challenges*, edited by Jesudason Jeyaraj, 251–60. Bangalore: CFCD-ISPCK, 2009.

Jeyaraj, Jesudason, ed. *Children at Risk: Issues and Challenges*. CFCD Bangalore: ISPCK, 2009.

Jeyaraj, Jesudason, Rosalind Tan, Shiferaw Michael, and Enrique Pinedo, eds. *Repairer of Broken Walls*. Bangalore: CFCD, 2014.

Kuttiyanimattathil, Jose. *Theological Anthropology: A Christian Vision of Human Beings*. Bangalore: Theological Publications in India, 2013.

Lim-Tan, Rosalind. *Child Development and Functioning*. Malaysia: HCDI, 2009.

Massey, James, ed., *Indigenous People: Dalits: Dalit Issues in Today's Theological Debate*. Delhi: ISPCK, 1994.

McConnell, Douglas. "God Creates Every Unique Person as a Child with Dignity." In *Understanding God's Heart for Children: Toward a Biblical Framework*, edited by Douglas McConnell, Jennifer Orona, and Paul Stockley, 13–22. Colorado Springs: Authentic, 2007.

Myers, Bryant L. "State of the World's Children: Critical Challenge to Christian Mission." *International Bulletin of Missionary Research* 18, no. 3 (July 1994): 98–102.

Prevette, Bill. "Child Theology and the Reflective Practitioner." In *Repairer of Broken Walls*, edited by Jesudason Jeyaraj, Rosalind Tan, Shiferaw Michael, and Enrique Pinedo, 151–66. Bangalore: CFCD, 2014.

"Report of the UN Secretary-General: A Life of Dignity for All." We Can End Poverty: Millennium Development Goals 2015, United Nations (September 2013). https://www.un.org/millenniumgoals/pdf/SG_Report_MDG_EN.pdf.

Shiri, Godwin. *Dalit Christians: A Saga of Faith and Pathos*. Nagapur: National Council of Churches in India, 2012.

Stafford, Wess. *Too Small to Ignore*. Colorado Springs: WaterBrook, 2005.

"T 00-005: Total Population, Population of Scheduled Castes and Scheduled Tribes and their proportions to the total population," Office of the Registrar General & Census Commissioner, India (Census of India 2011), https://censusindia.gov.in/Tables_Published/A-Series/A-Series_links/t_00_005.aspx.

Towner, W. Sibly. "Children and the Image of God." In *The Child in the Bible*, edited by Marcia J. Bunge, 307–23. Grand Rapids, MI: Eerdmans, 2008.

Traina, Cristina L. H. "A Person in the Making: Thomas Aquinas on Children and Childhood." In *The Child in Christian Thought*, edited by Marcia J. Bunge, 103–33. Grand Rapids, MI: Eerdmans, 2001.

White, Keith. *Theological Foundations for Holistic Child Development*. Malaysia: HCDI/Compassion, 2009.

Yadav, Archana. *Social Dimension of Child Labor: Dalit Children in Hazardous Industries*. New Delhi: Indian Social Institute, 2007.

Case Study:
Restoring Dignity to Children in Bonded Labor

Adnan Azhar Sandhu – Pakistani

A Day with Chandhu

We loaded the truck with games and gifts. Going from village to village, we planned to engage with children through our local church's "Games and Fun" activity programs. On this particular day we planned to spend time with children who were in bonded labor at the brick kilns.

The sun was still rising, chasing away the darkness of the night, when we arrived at the brick kiln. We began setting up the props and tables to prepare for the games and be ready before the first risers among the children began to arrive. I strolled around the brick kiln alongside Mr. Arshad, a local helper, trying to locate a more significant, wider area for playing soccer and holding three-legged races.

Then my eyes stopped, startled at a surprising sight. It was around 7:00 a.m. on a cold morning, and there sat a boy around five years old making bricks out of the mud. I could easily see his work skills, how he was molding the big loaf of mud into a brick with his little hands in no time at all. I thought of going over to talk to him. As I was considering this, he had already molded five more bricks. My mind was running a hundred miles an hour at the sight of this barefoot child, wearing no proper clothes on such a cold morning, working in the damp. My own children were probably still in their beds under a cozy blanket, soon to wake up for school. My curiosity peaked. I wanted to meet this boy. I took few steps toward him. By this time, he had already produced a few more bricks.

He soon saw me coming toward him. I noticed fear on his face, and he paused in making the bricks. His eyes monitored my footsteps. I stopped for a moment then walked toward him again. This time the little boy stood up in great fear, as if he saw a monster, and he ran quickly in the opposite direction. He was soon out of my sight.

I was shocked and perplexed by what had just happened. I had never scared someone in such a way in all the years we had been engaging children.

My face must have evidenced my thoughts, because Arshad began to explain to me what had just happened and shared the boy's story.

Arshad told me that the boy's name is Chandhu, and he is five years old. He ran away thinking that I might be the new manager who was going to punish him physically. His father and his uncles had been badly beaten up by the brick kiln caretakers numerous times, so he has a fear of new people. Hearing this shattered my heart. I sat down near the ground where Chandhu had just been very skillfully making the bricks. I could feel tears in my eyes, and I wanted to scream as loud as possible, so that all would know Chandhu's pain that I now felt.

Arshad reminded me of the agenda that we had planned for the day. I stood up and came to the spot where the rest of the team was excited to begin "Games and Fun." But in my heart, I didn't feel like playing games and having fun. Not when Chandhu was hurting so badly. Hiding my expression, I gave them a thumbs up to kick off the event. The games started, but these children had never played any kids' sports. They had no idea what to do with the soccer ball or how to throw a Frisbee. We asked if they were happy, and we encountered silence. Not a single smile. This word, "smile," hit them like a foreign language.

We decided to show them how to play sports which had always worked with other kids. But here it was almost lunch time, and we were still struggling to teach them how to play and laugh. Only a few of the kids were brave enough to smile and play. We didn't give up. My eyes were looking for Chandhu, whom I didn't see that day. I was imagining him hiding behind me, playing and jumping with us. His innocent image was a constant fixture in my mind.

Everyone was quiet on the way back home at the end of our day. I could see mixed emotions on their faces. I broke the silence by asking, "How was your day?" Everyone gazed at me as if I was mocking them, as if we hadn't just had the same experience. But I wanted to see what they would say. Some mentioned how tough the day had been. Others said it was the best experience. It was indeed as sad as it was a happy day for us.

I continued to ponder about those kids, and especially Chandhu. I went to meet Arshad after a few days. It seemed he already knew the purpose of my visit. Without wasting words in asking how I was doing, he immediately jumped right into the real topic. He explained that Chandhu's family and many other families are living in cramped quarters by the brick kiln. These families were already living in poverty and have no way of securing income. They are provided a loan by a brick kiln owner before they start work, but the loan immediately goes into debt. Now they are trapped in the kiln and are forced to work for an entire season without being paid their wages. They don't know if they have worked off their debt or not. As the brick kiln owner keeps no records, they are often paid less at the end of the season.

The brick kiln owner pays the molders per piece of bricks made. The entire family works together, but only the male head of the family is paid. The women are not paid at all. Brick molders also receive a rate below the minimum wage for each brick made, which is well below what workers earn if they are paid minimum wages on a time-based system. Therefore these families get their children to help them make more bricks to make at least minimum wage. Hence, this payment system encourages child labor.

The Indignity of Powerlessness

Chandhu's life clearly explains how poverty deprives him of a dignified life and the privileges associated with that life – deprives him of the dignity he deserves. He is so powerless that he does not even dare to speak for himself and stand against his family's injustice. If we imagine him living in a wealthy family for a moment, he would be wearing expensive clothes and shoes. He would come out of a car in style, and no one would dare insult him or raise a voice on him. Instead, he would be treated with respect and dignity. How inhuman is it that poverty takes away fundamental rights, social status, and dignity? Moreover these children, whom God created to be dignified, have become tools for earning income.

Their upbringing has badly impacted their psyche. They are humiliated almost every day, but they have no sense of humiliation or insult. To them, their experience is just the norm of life. When we asked them if they were happy, they were utterly silent because they were not familiar with happiness and joy.

Every person in this world has been created by God with dignity. Every child is created in God's image and enters in this world with the unique capacity to be in relationship with God, humankind, and creation. We take dignity to mean being respected for who we are and what we believe in.

The word "dignity" means that every child deserves to be respected and honored for who she or he is. A child's dignity cannot be earned or taken away. The Bible tells us that God created humans in his own image and likeness. All human

"Dignity" means that every child deserves to be respected and honored for who she or he is. A child's dignity cannot be earned or taken away.

beings have an absolute value to God. Therefore children are human and have the same value to God as adults.

Many people are concerned about the children around us. As Marcia Bunge writes, we often wonder –

- Are they being raised with love and affection?
- Are they receiving a good education?
- Are they in a safe environment in their homes and schools?
- Are they being exposed to good role models?
- Do they have a sense of meaning and purpose in their lives?
- Will they contribute in positive ways to society?
- In the church we ask, will our children have faith? Will they live out that faith in service and compassion toward others?[56]

Massive Enslavement in Brick Kilns

A Special Report, published February 2018 by Gospel for Asia, reports the following:

> One estimate presents the dire situation of the brick kiln workers: as many as twenty-three million workers are enslaved in one hundred thousand functioning brick kilns in Asia. One third of those enslaved are children who are forced to work an average of nine to twelve hours per day doing the worst form of child labor under international law. Work is the priority. Health and education are not. All brick molders come from marginalized families, communities, and social groups. At least a third of all brick kiln workers are paid less than their country's minimum wage, which is the equivalent of $0.28 an hour in US dollars. Workers at nearly 90 percent of the kilns only have access to polluted, untreated groundwater. Men, women, and children live in filthy, overcrowded quarters.[57]

Child work and child labor are different concepts. Child work refers to activities performed by a child that are not harmful, but may contribute to the healthy development of the child. According to the International Labour

56. Bunge, Marcia J. "Children, the Church, and the Domestic Church: Supporting Parents in the Task of Nurturing the Moral and Spiritual Lives of Children." *New Theology Review* 14, no. 3 (2001), 5–16.

57. https://missionsbox.org/news/children-families-slavery-brick-kilns/.

Organization, child labor refers to "work that is physically, mentally, socially, or morally dangerous and harmful to children."[58]

When children are living in bonded labor, they never understand that there is life outside this shell they are stuck in. Moreover in that outside life, they will not be forced to do physical labor which they cannot do. God did not make them to suffer from this mental and physical crisis. Childhood hardships also impact their physical growth. When she becomes a mother, a bonded labor girl will give birth to a weak child and face consequences to her own health.

Children in bonded labor are almost cut off from society. In other words, their presence goes unnoticed. They have no right to influence their environment, nor are they influenced by the environment around them. They are powerless to speak for their rights or to express their desires. Growing up in bonded labor, these children have no access to new clothes, shoes, proper food, or medical care. They do not get to watch TV, play sports, or listen to music.

It is highly contemptible that an estimated 218 million children as young as five years old are employed, and that at least 152 million are in forced child labor according to basic facts about child labor published by the Child Labor Coalition.[59]

The facts also expose several other startling realities about child labor:

- "Children under the age of twelve perform up to a fourth of all hazardous child labor.
- Almost half of all forced child laborers are between the ages of five and eleven.
- More than 134 million children in forced labor are in Africa, Asia, and the South Pacific."[60]

As Lou Guthelil wrote in 2019: "If the 218 million child laborers founded a country of their own, it would be the fifth largest in the world, surpassing the entire population of Pakistan."[61]

If the 218 million child laborers founded a country of their own, it would be the fifth largest in the world, surpassing the entire population of Pakistan.

58. https://www.ilo.org/moscow/areas-of-work/child-labour/WCMS_249004/lang--en/index.htm.

59. https://stopchildlabor.org/ Accessed 14 March 2022.

60. https://www.gfa.org/special-report/child-labor-today/ Accessed 14 March 2022.

61. https://www.gfa.org/special-report/child-labor-today/ Accessed 14 March 2022.

Best Practices in Response to Children in Bonded Labor

Individuals, organizations, and governments are doing a lot of good work to redeem brick kiln workers and their families from this vicious cycle of bondage. However, these initiatives need to be brought together to develop synergies. Ever since I met Chandhu, I felt obligated to do something for him and the other kids living in bonded labor to restore their dignity. I have launched an advocacy and awareness site on every platform on which I have had an opportunity. I have reached out to churches, Christian organizations, and NGOs, and the organizations that are already working among children have shown interest in extending their vision to support the bonded labor children. Moreover, Christian organizations involved in alleviating poverty and promoting human rights have joined us to support these afflicted children.

Underprivileged Schools – We have reached out to three organizations that are working in education programs. They were primarily focused on establishing school systems in small towns. When we shared with them the vision to begin schooling in Chandhu's village, they happily agreed to work with us. Before starting this school, it was essential to get authorization from the brick kiln landlord and management; otherwise, the consequences could be drastic. After a few meetings with the owner and manager, they gave us permission on one condition: the school would not impact their brick production. Our partner organizations decided to start a two hour school. In this two hour window, a teacher visits these children to teach them how to sit in a classroom, how to read and hold a pencil and write on paper. There is no class system. All age groups sit in one big group, and the purpose is to prepare them all for proper schooling. There is no proper school building; they meet under a tree or the open sky. Through this primary education, the children are learning their fundamental rights. This model became an example to other organizations who also started schools for children from the brick kilns. In some places, these organizations are still struggling to get authorization.

Sports Events – I did not stop here with the school. I extended this vision with different sports ministries and movements. I encouraged our partner organizations to provide essential sports gear and equipment for these kids. Sports and games are essential to add some fitness and entertainment to their lives. Six different Christian ministries and organizations are now working with us. Some are organizing full day and half day sports events, providing soccer balls, bats, socks, shoes, clothes, and bags for these children. There is still much work to be done, as we cannot hold these events in several places. We need more Christian organizations to join us in this mission.

School Bags – The next thing we needed for these children was school bags. At our request, a local Christian ministry that provides gift boxes and school bags to needy children and families gave us school bags filled with books, notebooks, basic hygiene products, and Christian literature. These school bags have been distributed to the brick kiln children. However, many more need to be distributed and more organizations involved.

Gift Boxes – A couple of Christian organizations distribute gift boxes to children during Christmas time. We approached and asked them to send gift boxes for these children and winter clothes including jackets, shoes, socks, caps, and gloves. Chandhu, who was bare foot and had no warm clothes can now wear shoes and warm clothes.

Medical Camps – The families living by the brick kiln lack proper medical care, or rather have no medical care. They cannot afford doctors' fees and other medical expenses. So we reached out to a Christian NGO that works in medicine and asked them to hold medical camps for these families. This particular area needs much work as most of the brick kiln families are still unreached.

Spiritual Education – The spiritual nurture of bonded children is essential to help them understand God's purpose for their lives. In a joint venture, a few organizations developed some wordless Christian books so these children can easily comprehend the material.

Debt Redemption – Last but not least is paying off debts. We are working with a Christian organization that does this noble work of redeeming these families from their debts. They have recently paid a family's debts, pulled them out of the brick kiln bondage, and relocated them to another place in the country. This organization helped this family to start a new career which is bondage free.

These best practices can surely make a big difference in the lives of these people, and their children can breathe freely.

Some Recommendations

1. Build the Capacity of the Workers: There is a dire need for persons in both the private and government sectors to learn to increase monitoring to ensure adherence to the land and labor laws. The skill sets of people currently in the related departments of most Christian organizations and ministries need to be evaluated to determine if they have the right behavioral and technical competencies to perform their jobs. Training needs to be provided for the staff in these departments so they can perform their duties appropriately.

2. Educate the Stakeholders: It is important for the people to know their rights and also their responsibilities. Once they have a better understanding of these, it will be easier for them to claim their rights and rightfully perform their duties as well.

3. Increase Coordination: A lot of good work is being done; however, all initiatives need to be brought together to develop synergies. The role of community groups such as churches should also be enhanced because their input on how to improve the capacity and processes currently employed at various levels and departments is key. Christian NGOs have a role to play in promoting standards of working, and their involvement at the planning level is key to ensure their input is incorporated in the yearly plans for rescuing children from child and bonded labor.

4. Reengineer the Processes: The current processes are inadequate. A complete overhaul is required to ensure that the children – created in dignity – have every right and privilege to lead their lives even in a place which is very different from ours. Christian NGOs, ministries, and churches should carry out inspections to ensure that the educational, technical, medical, health, and safety needs of such children are met and that they have every opportunity to express themselves, explore their talents, and apply their skills anywhere in the world. A strict system of checks and balances should be in place. These inspections need to be well defined, and sample areas should be reinspected by superior staff to ensure compliance. Awareness, sympathy for the downtrodden, care for the well-being of the poor, and benevolence are some of the virtues which can play a major role in restoring the status of these children and enthrone them in the seats for which they were originally created. When these values become prevalent, the law becomes a secondary option.

Conclusion

Chandhu's story does not stop here. We decided not to leave these families as orphans because we are part of one big family in Christ. We go to visit them more frequently and listen to their stories. It did not take us much time to figure out how we can help them. With the help of partners and individuals, we have paid off the debts of a few families and have taken them out of their bondage.

Chandhu is now studying in class six, and he is a bright student. He can now read the Bible. Hopefully he understands that God made him an equal human being and that he feels the dignity and purpose of his life. Chandhu's presence is noticed, and he can influence the society around him. He does not have to make bricks with his father anymore, though he loves helping him in other household chores. Chandhu is inspiring his siblings and other children living near him, and many of those children have now started going to school with him. He will not just appreciate the restored dignity but will be an activist for the dignity of other children.

Bibliography

https://stopchildlabor.org/ Accessed 14 March 2022.

https://www.ilo.org/moscow/areas-of-work/child-labour/WCMS_249004/lang--en/index.htm Accessed 30 March.

https://missionsbox.org/news/children-families-slavery-brick-kilns/ Accessed 30 March 2022.

https://www.gfa.org/special-report/child-labor-today/ Accessed 14 March 2022.

Bunge, M. "Children, the Church, and the Domestic Church: Supporting Parents in the Task of Nurturing the Moral and Spiritual Lives of Children," *New Theology Review* 14, no. 3 (2001), 5–16.

Discussion Questions for Chapter 1

1. In your own context, how are children seen and treated in the community's daily life?
2. How can local churches affect national policies on how children are seen and treated?
3. How can marginalization of children be avoided in all facets of community life?
4. What are some best practices in your own local context that resonate with the concepts identified in this case study?
5. How can you foster dignity in your own ministry or organization?

2

Placed in Families

God's plan has always been to place children in families so they are provided with a safe and protective environment. He extended this opportunity to the whole community of faith so that no child is left "outside the door."

Global Critical Issue: Children Outside the Door

Rosalind Tan – Malaysian

Introduction

The phrase "children placed in families" can immediately trigger the notion that these children are without families and need to be placed in homes, or that they are privileged to experience supportive family life. Both are possible scenarios. The first edition of *Understanding God's Heart for Children* focuses on the critical issue of children's need for a family and parental love in a systematically broken world.[1] In this sequel and chapter, we pick up from where Katharine Putman left off and further explore the phenomenon of a children-at-risk group who have not experienced parental love and being placed in families. This discussion on the global critical issues pertaining to children placed in families starts at a particular location and culture. It then expands to other geographical regions to identify similar groups of children facing the same predicament. While there are limitations to the scope and particularities, the different identified contexts and cultures give a global view of the subject. Hopefully, you will come away with a deeper understanding of the children's situations, empathize with their struggles, and be more determined to advocate on their behalf.

Outside the Door

Our story begins in a Chinese community. In a dialogue on cultural perspectives of children and childhood, I approached a Chinese language translator for

1. Katharine Putman responds to Marcia Bunge's reflections on a biblical and theologically informed perspective of the parenting vocation. Putman discusses the impact of sin on family relationships and their effect on child development. Putman proposes Bunge's "ten best practices" as a way forward for parents to demonstrate God's love to children. Katharine Putman, "Children's Need for Parental Love in a Systemically Broken World," in *Understanding God's Heart*, 66–75; Marcia Bunge, "The Vocation of Parenting: A Biblically and Theologically Informed Perspective," *Understanding God's Heart*, 53–65.

the term "children at risk." She thought for a long while and replied, "Eer . . . the term is 有危险的儿童 (which means children who have danger or risk situations), but I don't think it aptly translates the urgency. A more appropriate term would be 'children outside the door' (门外的孩子)." Her words provoked me to think deeper. The term "children outside the door" refers to minors aged sixteen years and under who are without family protection, left to fend for themselves, and open to risk situations. The term is familiar to the Chinese community where the translator lives, and she explained it from a local cultural perspective. In Chinese culture, the family unit is highly valued, and children are born "inside the door." All children are born into a household. They have a biological father and mother, regardless of whether the parents acknowledge the child. A child also has a larger family of grandparents, uncles, aunties, and cousins. The household (or clan) is where a child belongs. This belonging gives the child a name, an identity, and roles and purposes in community life.[2] The adults are responsible for protecting and nurturing the child. If for some reason a child is not wanted or acknowledged by the household, this child will be ushered "outside the door," or in other words, the child will be given up for adoption, neglected, or abandoned. A child outside the door is nobody's child. The term can also refer to older children who are disowned by their parents and hence disassociated from the family. To my translator friend, it is unthinkable that any family would choose to leave a defenseless child outside their door. But the reality is that it happens.

Outside in Different Cultures

Not all children outside the door are deliberately abandoned. Some children are orphans, that is, children who have lost both parents and are homeless. The United Nations Children's Emergency Fund (UNICEF) estimates that globally there are 153 million orphans, with the highest number in sub-Saharan Africa and South Asia.[3] This figure is conservative and does not include "social orphans," that is, children with one or both parents still alive but unable to provide for the child. These parents have either neglected the child or abandoned the child to the streets.[4] Children outside the door could also mean displaced minors, or child refugees traveling alone due to forced

2. See "The Importance of Family Acceptance," Families for Life (n.d.), https://familiesforlife.sg/discover-an-article/Pages/The-Importance-of-Family-Acceptance.aspx.

3. "Children's Statistics: UN Data on the Plight of Children," SOS Children's Villages (n.d.).

4. "Global Homelessness Statistics," Homeless World Cup Foundation (2020).

migration and war. In 2019, the UN Children's Fund reported that there are 12 million children in this category, traveling alone and later repatriated as asylum seekers. While the exact number is not available, many of these children are in transit refugee camps or institutional care.[5]

While the main contributing factor to children outside the door seems to be parental or household neglect, there are children who have deliberately chosen to stay outside the door. These children prefer to live on the streets, perhaps away from a dysfunctional family structure, domestic violence, or physical, emotional, or sexual abuse. Being outside the door is a personal decision to safeguard themselves from domestic harm and to protect their mental well-being. Children is this situation are found both in impoverished societies and in affluent communities where family units are slowly disintegrating and children are being neglected.[6]

In an East Asian country, the phenomenon of "unwanted children" or "not preferred" children surged under the enforcement of a one child policy. Children born with special needs or of the female gender were often abandoned in preference for healthy male offspring. In the Philippines, the children outside the door are called the *batang kalye* (street kids). There are an estimated 250,000 homeless children in Manila alone; the figure is as high as one million nationwide.[7] *Batang kalye* are often called "Rugby children" – not because they play rugby but because they sniff Rugby glue to dull their hunger and physical pain. In India, there are an estimated 29.6 million *Lawaaris bache*, literally unclaimed children.[8] These children are orphans or have been abandoned by their parents. They are divided into different subgroups according to their location and description. An example of *Lawaaris bache* are the "railway children," the

Being outside the door is a personal decision to safeguard themselves from domestic harm and to protect their mental well-being.

5. "Children without Appropriate Parental Care," Child Rights Connect (20 March 2019).

6. Ann Mooney, Chris Oliver, and Marjorie Smith, "Impact of Family Breakdown on the Children's Wellbeing," Institute of Education, University of London (June 2019).

7. Joshua Meribole, "The State of Homelessness in the Philippines," The Borgen Project (2 July 2020).

8. Shreya Kalra, "Why India's adoption rate is abysmal despite its 30 million abandoned kids." *Business Standard* (30 October 2018).

vagabonds and child beggars who wander in groups from station to station.[9] Another group is the "without home children" who make their dwellings along pavements, in bus stations, and under flyovers or bridges. Some of them frequent shelters by night but return to the streets in the daytime. In Egypt, the children outside the door are called the *atfal bala ma'wa* (children without a home). They are usually orphans or are forced into street living because of abandonment, deteriorating home conditions, or extreme poverty. These children are marginalized and survive on the streets by begging, selling trinkets and tissue paper, or cleaning car windscreens.[10] In 2016, the Egyptian government made provision for the *atfal bala ma'wa* to return to their families or to be placed in institutional care.[11] In Latin America, children outside the door are called the *chicos / chicas de la calle*. They are the children *of* the street, minors "living in urban areas and who call the street their principal home, assuming they no longer live in their familial residence. The street is the central environment from which they develop and obtain social skills."[12]

Outside during the COVID-19 Pandemic

During the COVID-19 pandemic in 2020, the cliche of "stay home and keep safe" mocked the children outside the door. They had no home to stay safe in, let alone talk about social distancing, wearing a face mask, washing hands, or sanitizing. The irony is that they were all at home – on the streets. How could they keep safe?

Al Jazeera reported that in Indonesia, most shelters or drop-in centers were closed during the lockdown. The centers that were open were overcrowded.[13] Thus, many children were unable to find refuge during this time of need. In Senegal, the United Nations Office on Drugs and Crime (UNODC) worked alongside local authorities to locate the families or next of kin to reunite the

---

9. "#StoriesfromtheField – How Our Intervention Helped Biswanath and His Family During Lockdown." Railway Children (September 2020).

10. Hager Harabech, "Egypt Homeless, Street Children Hit Hard By Pandemic Scourge." *Barron's* (22 July 2020).

11. Harabech, "Egypt Homeless, Street Children."

12. Hilary E. O'Haire, "Living on the Streets: The Street Children of Brazil," *Inquiries* 3, no. 4 (2011).

13. Jessica Washington, "For Indonesia's street children, coronavirus means more danger," *Al Jazeera* (24 July 2020).

children on the streets with family members.[14] When family or kinship homes were not available, these children were placed in transit shelters or "alternative homes." In Egypt, physical violence and abuse of vulnerable homeless children decreased due to mandatory social distancing and public fear of contacting the COVID-19 virus.[15] Hunger and starvation posed a more significant threat to children outside the door during the pandemic than the virus did.

There are "positive" reports of how the COVID-19 pandemic has helped to turn situations around for some children. Enforced mandatory social distancing to "flatten the curve" disrupted child exploitation activities. The enforced lockdown in several countries reduced child labor, human trafficking, and child-sex tourism.[16] Generally, most countries did their part in food distribution, but thousands of invisible children outside the door are still unreached.[17]

From Outside to Inside the Door

While the children outside the door may be scattered in different regions worldwide, they all face similar physical, social, emotional, and developmental challenges. For their daily meals, most of them steal, beg, rummage in garbage bins for throwaways, depend on food kitchens, or buy food with whatever little they have. For physical safety, they cluster in "street family groups" watched over by the big brothers or street warlords. Children outside the door often suffer from malnutrition and skin diseases. Socially, they are looked down upon, bullied, and ostracized.[18] Psychologically, these children daily fight for survival. They face uncertainties, are often afraid, and struggle with feelings of being unwanted and unworthy.

However, most children outside the door are also street-smart and have found ways to cope and "manage" their lives on the streets. Empirical observations attest that although integrating into family life again after life on the street is not without its challenges, these children do desire a safe environment with permanent, loving caregivers. This research supports the

14. "UNODC supports Senegal to get street children home during the COVID-19 Pandemic," United Nations Office on Drugs and Crimes (June 2020).

15. "Egypt's street children face poverty, pandemic," *The Arab Weekly* (15 July 2020).

16. "Impact of COVID-19 Pandemic on Trafficking in Persons: Preliminary findings and messaging based on rapid stocktaking." United Nations Office on Drugs and Crimes (n.d.).

17. Geeta Pandey, "Coronavirus: The children struggling to survive India's lockdown," *BBC News Delhi* (11 April 2020).

18. O'Haire, "Living on the Streets."

hierarchy of needs theory that love and belonging are foundational building blocks of a person's well-being and development.[19] This theory echoes my translator friend's thoughts that all children should be nurtured by a family.

The call to place the children outside the door in families is in their best interest to ensure a safe and nurturing space for them to experience normal and healthy child development and relationships. "The right to family life (for children) is enshrined in the national, international, and regional human rights law."[20] A supportive family environment is the first place where children learn to love and be loved. Family life is also where they learn social values and deal with relational dynamics in a safe and protective space. The qualities of a healthy family life for children contribute to healthy adult behavior. This behavior, in turn, will significantly impact society at large. Being placed in a home with a nurturing family environment allows children to experience positive behavior patterns, observe ways to make wise decisions, and imitate appropriate adult modeling. A home also gives children individuality, which is essential for mental health and social belonging. Hence, one practical approach to addressing the issue of children outside the door is to support and strengthen the family unit.[21] The process can include family life education, emphasizing good nutrition, making health services available, and helping families to be financially self-sufficient.

The qualities of a healthy family life for children contribute to healthy adult behavior.

This article also affirms the role of institutional care for children without families and homes. Institutional care can be an alternative when a child is without parents and where kinship, foster, or adoptive homes are not available. Institutional or residential care designed with a family structure concept can invoke relational dynamics similar to natural family life.[22] One concern about institutional care is that children who grow up in long-term institutional care are at risk of physical, emotional, and social harm.[23] This claim is supported by "research evidence on the impact of institutional care on brain growth,

19. See Saul McLeod, "Maslow's Hierarchy of Needs," *Simply Psychology* (29 December 2020).

20. "Children without Appropriate Parental Care."

21. "Strengthening Family Care," Better Care Network (2019).

22. "Transitioning to family care for children," World Without Orphans.

23. "Children in alternative care: Growing up in an institution puts children at risk of physical, emotional and social harm," UNICEF (4 June 2021).

attachment, social behaviour, and cognitive development."[24] When young children lack regular parental care or reliable adult care, they are at a higher risk of developing attachment disorders and experiencing delays in development. The United Nations Convention on the Rights of the Child (UNCRC) recognizes parental roles and supports the need for a family environment for child development (Articles 5–9, 16, 18, 24, 27–29). Articles 20–21 state that children should not be in prolonged homeless situations and are entitled to protection and assistance.[25]

Conclusion

Even as cultural and sociopolitical trends redefine the family unit, a supportive family whether kinship, foster, or adoptive is essential for holistic childhood development and wellness. We used the Chinese contextual idiom "children outside the door" to reflect on children in at-risk situations. Children outside the door include orphans, displaced minors, child refugees traveling alone, street children without homes, and abandoned children. While this idiom is context and culture specific, the phenomenon is global. The discussion highlights similar situations of children in different parts of the world who are left outside the door and are called by different terms. Regardless of context and culture, all children outside the door display similar physical and socioemotional characteristics and face almost similar environmental challenges.

Human rights movements and faith-based organizations have done much to advocate for these children. Homeless or abandoned children have been placed with kinship, foster, or adoptive families. These families are provided with counseling services and taught entrepreneurship skills to cope with their financial constraints. Therefore, the idea of orphans, homeless, or abandoned children placed in families is a realistic possibility. This approach can be an answer to unfavorable long-term institutional care. In other chapters of this book are creative ideas for how we can minister to these children. To this end, we advocate for "children outside the door" to be brought inside and be family.

---

24. Rebecca Johnson, Kevin Browne, and Catherine Hamilton-Giachritsis, "Young Children in Institutional Care at Risk of Harm," Research Gate.net (February 2006).

25. "Convention on the Rights of the Child," United Nations Human Rights Office of the High Commissioner (2 Sept 1990). https://www.ohchr.org/en/professionalinterest/pages/crc.aspx.

Bibliography

Bunge, Marcia J. 'The Vocation of Parenting: A Biblically and Theologically Informed Perspective'. In *Understanding God's Heart for Children: Toward a Biblical Framework*, edited by Douglas McConnell, Jennifer Orona, and Paul Stockley, 53–65. Colorado Springs; London: Authentic : Published in partnership with World Vision, 2007.

"Children in alternative care: Growing up in an institution puts children at risk of physical, emotional and social harm." UNICEF (4 June 2021). https://www.unicef.org/protection/children-in-alternative-care.

"Children's Statistics: UN Data on the Plight of Children." SOS Children's Villages (n.d.). https://www.sos-usa.org/our-impact/focus-areas/advocacy-movement-building/childrens-statistics.

"Children without Appropriate Parental Care." Child Rights Connect (20 March 2019). https://www.childrightsconnect.org/working_groups/children-without-parental-care/.

"Convention on the Rights of the Child." United Nations Human Rights Office of the High Commissioner (2 Sept 1990). https://www.ohchr.org/en/professionalinterest/pages/crc.aspx.

"Egypt's street children face poverty, pandemic." *The Arab Weekly* (15 July 2020). https://thearabweekly.com/egypts-street-children-face-poverty-pandemic.

"Global Homelessness Statistics." Homeless World Cup Foundation (2020). https://homelessworldcup.org/ homelessness-statistics/.

Harabech, Hager. "Egypt Homeless, Street Children Hit Hard By Pandemic Scourge." *Barron's* (22 July 2020). https://www.barrons.com/news/egypt-homeless-street-children-hit-hard-by-pandemic-scourge-01595417408.

"Impact of COVID-19 Pandemic on Trafficking in Persons: Preliminary findings and messaging based on rapid stocktaking." United Nations Office on Drugs and Crimes (n.d.). https://www.unodc.org/documents/Advocacy-Section/HTMSS_Thematic_Brief_on_COVID-19.pdf.

"The Importance of Family Acceptance." Families for Life (n.d.). https://familiesforlife.sg/discover-an-article/Pages/The-Importance-of-Family-Acceptance.aspx.

Johnson, Rebecca, Kevin Browne, and Catherine Hamilton-Giachritsis. "Young Children in Institutional Care at Risk of Harm." Research Gate.net (February 2006). https://www.researchgate.net/publication/ 7436610_Young_Children_ in_Institutional_Care_at_Risk_of_Harm.

Kalra, Shreya. "Why India's adoption rate is abysmal despite its 30 million abandoned kids." *Business Standard* (30 October 2018). https://www.business-standard.com/article/current-affairs/why-india-s-adoption-rate-is-abysmal-despite-its-30-million-abandoned-kids-118103000218_1.html.

McConnell, Douglas, Jennifer Orona, and Paul Stockley, eds. *Understanding God's Heart for Children: Toward a Biblical Framework*. Colorado Springs: Authentic, 2007.

McLeod, Saul. "Maslow's Hierarchy of Needs." *Simply Psychology* (29 December 2020). https://www.simplypsychology.org/maslow.html.

Meribole, Joshua. "The State of Homelessness in the Philippines." The Borgen Project (2 July 2020). https://borgenproject.org/homelessness-in-the-philippines/#:~:text=Homeless%20children%20are%20among%20the,parents%2C%20poverty%20or%20sexual%20exploitation.

Mooney, Ann, Chris Oliver, and Marjorie Smith. "Impact of Family Breakdown on the Children's Wellbeing." Institute of Education, University of London (June 2019). https://dera.ioe.ac.uk/11165/1/DCSF-RR113.pdf.

O'Haire, Hilary. "Living on the Streets: The Street Children of Brazil." *Inquiries* 3, no. 4 (2011). http://www.inquiriesjournal.com/articles/506/living-on-the-streets-the-street-children-of-brazil.

Pandey, Geeta. "Coronavirus: The children struggling to survive India's lockdown." *BBC News Delhi* (11 April 2020). https://www.bbc.com/news/world-asia-india-52210888.

"#StoriesfromtheField – How Our Intervention Helped Biswanath and His Family During Lockdown." Railway Children (September 2020). https://railwaychildren.org.in/blog/2020/09/.

"Strengthening Family Care." Better Care Network (2019). https://bettercarenetwork.org/library/strengthening-family-care/strengthening-family-care.

"Transitioning to family care for children." World Without Orphans. https://worldwithoutorphans.org/resources/resource/transitioning-to-family-care.

"UNODC supports Senegal to get street children home during the COVID-19 Pandemic." United Nations Office on Drugs and Crimes (June 2020). https://www.unodc.org/unodc/en/frontpage/2020/June/unodc-and-partners-support-senegal-to-get-street-children-home-during-the-covid-19-pandemic.html.

Washington, Jessica. "For Indonesia's street children, coronavirus means more danger." *Al Jazeera* (24 July 2020). https://www.aljazeera.com/news/2020/07/24/for-indonesias-street-children-coronavirus-means-more-danger/.

Woodhead, Martin, and Liz Brooker. "A sense of belonging." Early Childhood Matters (November 2008), 3–6. https://earlychildhoodmatters.online/wp-content/uploads/2019/06/ECM111-2008_Enhancing_a_sense_of_belonging_in_the_early_years.pdf.

Biblical and Theological Response:
Kinsman-Redeemer: Welcoming Children Outside the Door

Nativity A. Petallar – Filipino

Introduction

When my daughter was about three years old, she witnessed the birth of a precious baby named Sam. She asked me, "Mama, did Nanay[26] Minnie eat Baby Sam?"

I asked back, "Why?"

She replied, "Why was Baby Sam inside her tummy?" The wonder which the birth of a child affords is not just something my daughter experienced. Many adults, too, are moved by a profound sense of awe at the birth of a child. Sam is now nine, safe and cared for by her family, living out her God-given potential in a beautiful way. This is God's heart for all children. Not all children grow up like Sam. Millions of vulnerable children across the globe suffer the consequences of being "outside the door," neglected and uncared for.

In the first publication of *Understanding God's Heart for Children*, the biblical reflection on being placed in families deals with the vocation of parenting. Bunge emphasizes that biblical parenting is a sacred task.[27] This sequel chapter extends the discussion to highlight the biblical and theological perspectives of children being placed in families. This response includes a Filipino contextual theology on the understanding of children and some implications for children outside the door. The reader is invited to look closely into the world of children who have no supportive family and feel God's heart for these precious ones.

26. "Nanay" is a Filipino word for mother in addition to "Mama." Filipino children call other mothers "Nanay" especially if they feel very close to that person.

27. Marcia Bunge, "The Vocation of Parenting: A Biblically and Theologically Informed Perspective," in *Understanding God's Heart for Children: Toward a Biblical Framework*, eds. Douglas McConnell, Jennifer Orona, and Paul Stockley (Colorado Springs: Authentic, 2007), 53.

Biblical and Theological Perspective of Children Being Placed in Families

The birth of a child into a family is a means of grace.[28] God instituted the family to be his instrument of grace. Bartel and Grabowski observe,

> The Bible is full of families, births, love stories and family crises. This is true from its very first page, with the appearance of Adam and Eve's family with all its burden of violence but also its enduring strength (cf. Gen 4) to its very last page, where we behold the wedding feast of the Bride and the Lamb (Rev 21:2; 21:9).[29]

Every child who comes into the world, regardless of the circumstances, is a gift from the Maker. As Olson simply says, "They're a blessing because the Lord says they are."[30] "This 'biblical plan for the home' is a divine blueprint for family life culled from the pages of Scripture."[31]

In the global critical section of this chapter, Rosalind Tan indicates that across the Global South, many children are displaced, left to fend for themselves by systems that are working against their well-being. Despite the efforts of the United Nations, children are still left outside the door.

Marjorie J. Thompson observes, "It is virtually impossible to overestimate the importance of the family to a child's total development. The basic foundation of character and development of personality that occurs within the home covers all the bases: physical, emotional and spiritual."[32] Deuteronomy 6:4–8 provides guidelines for parents on how to rear their children toward a godly life. Deuteronomy 6 shows a holistic paradigm of child rearing involving the

---

28. Clyde A. Holbrook, *The Ethics of Jonathan Edwards: Morality and Aesthetics* (Ann Arbor: University of Michigan Press, 1973), 3. John Wesley defined "means of grace" as "outward signs, words, or actions, ordained of God, and appointed for this end, to be the ordinary channels whereby he might convey to men, preventing, justifying, or sanctifying grace." John Wesley, *The Sermons of John Wesley: Sermon 16*, ed. Darin Million, Wesley Center Online (1999). While it is true that people who do not believe in God may not perceive that the gift of a child is God's way of showing his faithfulness, their view does not change the fact that a child is one of the channels through which God shows his favor to the world. This situation poses a challenge to Christians everywhere to spread the good news of salvation so others will be brought into the knowledge of the grace of the Lord Jesus Christ (2 Pet 3:18).

29. Sarah Smith Bartel and John S. Grabowski, *A Catechism for Family Life: Insights from Church Teaching on Love, Marriage, Sex, and Parenting* (Washington, DC: Catholic University of America Press, 2018), 238.

30. Dan Olson quoted in Emily Hunter McGowin, *Quivering Families: The Quiverfull Movement and Evangelical Theology of the Family* (Minneapolis, MN: Fortress Press, 2018), 129.

31. McGowin, *Quivering Families*, 171.

32. Marjorie J. Thompson, *Family, the Forming Center*, rev. ed. (Nashville, TN: Upper Room Books, 1996), 20.

sensory faculties. Verse 7 says, "Talk about [these commandments] when you sit at home" (auditory); verses 8–9, "Tie them as symbols on your hands and bind them on your foreheads. Write them on the doorframes of your houses and on your gates (visual); and verse 7, "Talk about them . . . when you walk along the road, when you lie down and when you get up" (kinesthetic). This method is educating the whole child. This is God's heart for children. God's design is to work through the everyday relationships of parents and children to provide children with experiences that prepare them for faith.[33] Deuteronomy 6 capitalizes on the everyday relationships of family members to bring about obedience to God's will. Polycarp, the first century Christian martyr who was considered to be a disciple of John wrote, "our wives also, to walk in the faith that hath been given unto them . . . and to train their children in the training of the fear of God."[34] Furthermore, John Wesley considered children as "immortal spirits whom God hath, for a time, entrusted to your care, that you may train them up in all holiness, and fit them for the enjoyment of God in eternity."[35] These statements also imply teaching on the proper attitude toward children – to keep them in families and not to abandon them.

Jesus Christ Was Placed into a Family

Jesus was placed into a particular family and went through the process of human development, just like any other child in Israel at the time. Luke wrote, "Jesus grew in wisdom and in stature and in favor with God and all the people" (Luke 2:52 NLT). Joseph and Mary had other children (Matt 13:55; Mark 6:3; John 7:3; 1 Cor 9:5), and these individuals comprised the human family of Jesus. In a special kind of way, this human family of our Lord was part of his environment of "growing." Mary and Joseph participated in God's divine plan

---

33. David Seamands, *Healing Grace: Let God Free You from the Performance Trap* (Wheaton, IL: Victor, 1988), 46. Ted Ward says that in the Old Testament, parents were responsible for the spiritual and moral growth of their children. Through family experience children learn many of the most important values; the family is a strong shaper of values. See Ted Ward, *Values Begin at Home* (Wheaton, IL: Victor Books, 1984), 19.

34. Polycarp 4:2. Polycarp, *The Epistle of Polycarp*, quoted in Lawrence Richards, *A Theology of Children's Ministry* (Grand Rapids, MI: Zondervan, 1983), 37.

35. John Wesley, "Sermon 94: 'On Family Religion,'" in *The Works of John Wesley*, 1872. In order to provide families with the tools for religious education in the home, Wesley published *Lessons for Children* in 1746, which was a curriculum comprised of two hundred lessons on the Old Testament. The introduction to *Lessons for Children* included "A Short Catechism for Children," which was twelve lessons on God, creation and the fall of humanity, redemption, the means of grace, hell, and heaven. See Colleen R. Derr, "John Wesley and the Faith Formation of Children: Lessons for the Church" (diss., Regent University, 2013), 115.

of saving the world. They protected the child when in danger – going all the way out for the child. Jesus was not left outside the door. Joseph and Mary provided an example of how parents are to do everything they can with God's help to keep children safe and nurtured so they thrive. In God's providence, they provided an environment where Jesus grew, fulfilling the Lord's purpose for their lives.

God Places Children in Families for a Purpose

God has placed children in homes so they have space, training, discipline, nurture, and the relationships they need to thrive. God mandates the parents to provide this space for every child (Deut 11:19; Ps 78:4; Prov 22:6; Eph 6:1–4; Col 3:21; 1 Tim 5:4, 8; Heb 12:7). God places children in homes for spiritual nurture. Faith development does not happen overnight. In the family, faith is first sensed, is born, and is nurtured.[36] When my daughter was about three or four years old, she saw a huge billboard depicting a man and a big fish. She blurted out to me, "Look Ma, Noah and the big fish!" In the same manner when my son was six years old, he proudly showed me something he made in the application to the "Feeding of the 5,000" (Luke 9:10–17). He said, "Ma, this is my drawing. God made fish and cookies with His bare hands." My children "knew" their Bible stories, but their young minds were not able to quite get their facts straight, let alone fully internalize these accounts into their own belief system. They need an adult to guide them. Westerhoff advocates that faith is developed through ritual, experiences, and action of the environment.[37] Children thrive spiritually when they are exposed to these kinds of stimuli and are given the opportunity to participate. In the Old Testament, children were part of the annual feasts and other religious observances of the whole community. The "home-sized" groups that met in New Testament times are examples of communal events where children observe and learn. These community and family gatherings provide intergenerational avenues for learning, fellowship, and worship.

God places children into families for fellowship. In the Old Testament, Psalm 133:1 says, "How good and pleasant it is when God's people live together

36. Richards, *Theology of Children's Ministry*, 180.

37. John H. Westerhoff, *Will Our Children Have Faith?*, rev. ed. (Harrisburg, PA: Morehouse, 2000), 53–65. Elsewhere he says, "No matter where you look in our Judeo-Christian heritage it is the parents who have the prime responsibility to bring up their children in the faith." John H. Westerhoff, *Bringing Up Children in the Christian Faith* (Minneapolis, MN: Winston, 1980), 7.

in unity!" The King James Version uses the term, "brethren" instead of "God's people." The author of this psalm calls the tribes *brethren* since the tribal leaders whose names they bear were sons of one father.[38] In the New Testament, Paul warns believers, "Anyone who does not provide for their relatives, and especially for their own household, has denied the faith and is worse than an unbeliever" (1 Tim 5:8). Everyone is created for fellowship and nurturing. The need for dialogue and openness with another person may be satisfied within the family – a place where every person emerges with all of their individuality and uniqueness.[39] Respect is a key ingredient to this fellowship.

Filipino Contextual Theology and Children Being Placed in Families

For Filipinos, a family is a sacred trust from God and children are *biyaya ng Diyos* (blessings from God). Like for many Asians and Africans, the Filipino concept of family is not just children saying, "Father and Mother I Love You" (FAMILY), but the ties are extended to first, second, third, even fourth cousins, distant aunts and uncles, and yes, even the next-door neighbor can be considered a *ka-pamilya* (family member). Filipino relationships are familial.[40] Children can live in their parent's house forever and vice versa, though not without problems. Research was conducted on how Filipinos view home, and it revealed that a home is not just a place in which we live (*nakatira*), but a place we return to (*uwian*).[41] One of the respondents in this research indicated that more than memories, a *tirahan* (home) is a shelter; an *uwian* provides security, "a feeling one can stay on, one can come home, go home, every day," a place to "find solace in, but of having someone who will listen to you, who offers a shoulder to cry on, or who's ready to boogie with you as you bring home good news."[42]

38. Theodore of Cyrus, *The Fathers of the Church: Theodore of Cyrus, Commentary on the Psalms, 73–150* (The Catholic University of America Press, 2010), 311.

39. Józef Stala, and Jadranka Gamaz, "The Family Communio Personarum and Upbringing," *The Person and the Challenges* 8, no. 1 (2018): 51.

40. F. Landa Jocano, *Filipino Social Organization: Traditional Kinship and Family Organization Anthropology of the Filipino People III* (Metro Manila: PUNLAD Research House, 1998), 62.

41. Michael L. Tan, "Coming Home, Going Home," *Sunday Inquirer Magazine* (23 November 2008), 5.

42. Tan, "Coming Home," 5.

For many Christians in the Philippines, the family is a sacrament.[43] God uses tangible symbols and realities that enable us to know him, feel his presence, and see him actively working in us and for us.[44] One can experience these symbols and realities inside the home. A traditional Filipino family has an "altar" in the home where children participate in daily prayers. "The Christian family is a communion of persons, a sign and image of the communion of the Father and the Son and the Holy Spirit."[45] To belong to a family is a means of grace and an image of the unity of the Triune God. To be a channel of God's goodness and mission to the world is sacramental. Jose de Mesa explains that the Christian family is not merely a functional unit that contributes to the building up of the basic ecclesiastical communities (BCEs), for it is more basic than BCEs and is the foundational setting of mission.[46] The family can be an instrument of propagating God's mission in the world. The theology of the Filipino family is anchored upon the characteristics of Filipinos as *maka-Diyos* (for God or pro-God), *maka-tao* (for people or pro-people), and *maka-pamilya* (for family or pro-family).[47] Children are expected to look after their parents when the latter get old. This expectation is ingrained in the Filipino psyche. Fulfilling this duty in the family reflects a person's sense of being *maka-Diyos*.

To belong to a family is a means of grace and an image of the unity of the Triune God.

43. The Episcopal Commission of the Philippines defines sacrament as a "performative word events that make present the spiritual reality they express." Episcopal Commission on Catechesis and Education, *Catechism for Filipino Catholics* (CBCP, 1 July 1997): 1521; cited in Maria Victoria G. Bernabe and Jennie Vee F. Pesa, "The Filipino Family, Sacramental Presence of God Today," 22.

44. Bernabe and Pesa, "Filipino Family," 22.

45. Catechism of the Catholic Church, 2205. https://www.vatican.va/archive/compendium_ccc/documents/archive_2005_compendium-ccc_en.html.

46. Jose de Mesa, "Re-Rooting Mission in the Family," *Mission Studies* 19, no. 1 (2002): 149. Cited in Levy Lanaria, "The Filipino Family – Lights and Shadows Challenges to the Domestic Church," *Asian Horizons* 7, no. 2 (June 2013): 237–60, 328. De Mesa is a respected Filipino lay theologian.

47. As per DepEd Order No. 8, s. 2015 on page 20, IV, being *mak-Diyos* and *maka-tao* are some of the core values that the Filipino child should learn. *Maka-Diyos* means being godly or religious or expressing one's spiritual beliefs. *Maka-tao* means to be sensitive to individual, social, and cultural differences. See Mark Anthony Llego, "DepEd Core Values Indicators: Concrete Manifestation," Teacherph, https://www.teacherph.com/deped-core-values-indicators-concrete-manifestation/.

Filipino Theology and Children "Outside the Door"

The Philippines is still considered to be the top Christian country in Asia and fifth in the world.[48] However despite being "Christian," this country is beset with innumerable social problems related with online sexual exploitation of children, child sexual abuse, child trafficking, HIV and AIDS, and other issues.[49] The Filipino theology of the family as a sacrament and a representation of the Triune God and of children being blessings from God all disappear as crime after crime against children are perpetrated. Where is the value of *malasakit* (concern/compassion) when there are about two-hundred and fifty thousand to one million street children (*batang kalye*) in the Philippines?[50] Rosalind Tan writes in the global critical section in this chapter about "Rugby boys."[51]

Another challenge facing the Filipino family is children with special needs. Many families hide them away for different reasons. Some families do not know what to do with a child who has a disability, so hiding them is their first recourse. Some families are ashamed to show their "disabled" child. Stigma is still present even though the government, UNICEF, and NGOs are trying to convince the public that disability is not a curse or a punishment, but rather an opportunity for the family to experience the different "able-ness" of a particular child.[52] Indeed these are hard realities facing these children.

How should we respond to this challenge? The Plenary Council of the Philippines warns of "family unity based solely on ties of flesh and blood," and consequent "insensitive to the greater demands of the common good."[53] Our response should be in obedience to loving God and loving neighbor (Mark 12:30–31). The call to Filipino families is to discover the "vision of the new family" and to set aside the "skewed relational features of the native

The call to Filipino families is to discover the "vision of the new family".

48. Lawrence de Guzman, "Philippines Still Top Christian Country in Asia, 5th in World," *Philipine Daily Inquirer* (21 December 2011).

49. University of the Philippines Manila, The University of Edinburgh, Child Protection Network Foundation and UNICEF Philippines, *A Systematic Review of the Drivers of Violence Affecting Children in the Philippines* (Manila: UNICEF Philippines, 2016), 2.

50. Agence Francaise De Developpement; see also "Street Children at Risk," Hope.org.ph. http://www.hope.org.ph/street-children-at-risk.html.

51. See page 39 above.

52. Don Jaucian, "Breaking the Stigma on Filipino Children with Disabilities," CNN Philippines Life (3 March 2017).

53. Plenary Council of the Philippines, 582, cited in Bernabe and Pesa, "Filipino Family," 22.

kinship system."[54] Nolan challenges every Filipino that "familial provincialism" should be replaced by an inclusive solidarity which embraces all as brothers and sisters.[55] A number of individuals are heeding this call. In many parts of the country, government, non-government, and faith-based organizations are working hand in hand to care for street kids, orphans, victims and survivors of child trafficking and online sexual exploitation, and unwanted children.[56] The need is great, and these organizations can only do so much. But there is hope.

God's Plan for Redeeming Children "Outside the Door": Implications for Care of Children at Risk

Sin breaks family relationships. The Old Testament is witness to the evil effects when families are broken by polygamy (Gen 16:1–16; 17:18–26), favoritism and jealousy (Gen 37:3–4, 18–27), hatred (Gen 4:3–5, 8), deceit (Gen 37:31–35), lust and revenge (Gen 34:1–31), rebellion, etc. Today, sin continues to break relationships. In the Philippines, many parents pimp their own children to sexual predators online.[57] China has millions of "floating" or migrant children.[58] Syria has thousands of refugees, and across the globe, millions of children suffer in silence. Many of the world's governments are corrupt and their justice systems are slow and almost immobilized against multifaceted systems of crime, syndicates, etc. Globally, innumerable children are outside the door in terms of healthcare, spiritual nurture, and home life. Is this God's heart for children? No! A thousand times no!

God has a plan to redeem children who are outside the door. The pages of Scripture echo with God's love for the vulnerable. In reflecting on the Scriptures, Martin writes, "God is particularly concerned for those whose status in social and economic matters makes them most vulnerable in human

54. Albert Nolan, *Jesus Before Christianity* (Quezon City: Claretian, 1999), 143–52, 163–71; cited in Lanaria, "Filipino Family," 259.

55. Nolan, *Jesus Before Christianity*, 73.

56. A number of organizations are working to, for, and with children. Some of the networks are the Child Rights Network (https://childrightsnetwork.ph/who-we-are/), the Philippine Children's Ministries Network (https://www.thepcmn.org/), the Catholic World Missions (https://catholicworldmission.org/help-the-children/), and All God's Children (https://allgodschildren.org/intervening-for-orphans/where-we-work/philippines/). The Department of Social Welfare and Development (DSWD, https://www.dswd.gov.ph/) is working with NGOs to alleviate the suffering of children who are at risk.

57. Russell Goldman, "Parents who Pimp their Children," *ABC News* (8 October 2007).

58. "National Survey Report on the Situation of Left-Behind Children and Migrant Children in China," All-China Women's Federation (2013), https://unesdoc.unesco.org/ark:/48223/pf0000266050.

affairs. *Yahweh* is known as the special protector of these needy ones who are orphans and widows and a special blessing is given to their human preservers."[59]

Niebuhr emphasizes that proper Christian love "meets the needs of the other without concern for the self," reaffirming agape love "as the highest possibility of human existence."[60] Karl Rahner's theological anthropology asserts that love of God can never be separated from love of neighbor.[61] God's judgment of those who do not heed his commands for proper relationships with people in need of protection is quite severe: "Do not take advantage of the widow or the fatherless. If you do and they cry out to me, I will certainly hear their cry. My anger will be aroused, and I will kill you with the sword" (Exod 22:22–24; see also Mal 4:6).

Kinsman-Redeemer: A Model for Responding to Children Outside the Door

The call to reach out to others in need is not just for pastors or practitioners who minister to, for, and with children in crisis but is a call for every Christian. The audience of Moses's discourse in Deuteronomy 6 was the whole community of Israel, not just the elders, but the whole congregation. The listeners also included some foreigners who had journeyed with them. And God's injunction to teach includes them all. In the story of Ruth, we are introduced to the concept of the kinsman-redeemer (Ruth 4:1–12). Boaz acted as Ruth's kinsman-redeemer and rescued her and Naomi from a life of helplessness. Down the bloodline of Boaz came the Messiah who also acted as kinsman-redeemer for us all. The Hebrew term designates a male relative who delivers or rescues (Gen 48:15–16; Exod 6:6) or redeems property (Lev 27:16–25) or a person (Lev 25:47–55).[62] The Hebrew term *goel* is also used, meaning to deliver or redeem.[63]

---

59. Ralph P. Martin, *James, Word Biblical Commentary* (Waco, TX: Word Books, 1998), 52.

60. Reinhold Niebuhr, *The Nature and Destiny of Man: A Christian Interpretation*, Library of Theological Ethics (Louisville, KY: Westminster John Knox, 1996), 295; see also Kelly Conor, "The Anonymous Theology of Modern Family," *Journal of Religion and Popular Culture* 26, no. 3 (Fall 2014): 342.

61. Karl Rahner, "Reflections on the Unity of the Love of Neighbor and the Love of God," in *Theological Investigations 6: Concerning Vatican Council II* (Baltimore, MD: Helicon, 1969), 231–49.

62. Stephen J. Bramer, "Kinsman-Redeemer," *Baker's Exegetical Dictionary of Biblical Theology* (Grand Rapids, MI: Baker Books, 1996).

63. Arthur L. Breslich, "goel," *International Bible Encyclopedia* (1915), https://www.biblestudytools.com/dictionary/goel/.

F. F. Bruce elucidates, "Yahweh . . . is repeatedly called his people's gōʾēl, their kinsman-redeemer; [who] brings . . . [the] deliverance of his people."[64]

Christopher Hunt comments, "In Hebrew culture, even before Mosaic law codified the practice (Deut. 25:5–10), it was understood that if a man died leaving a widow without a son (to be his heir and provide for his mother) the man's nearest male relative (usually a brother) would marry the widow to provide for her and produce an heir for his deceased relative."[65] Although the concept of kinsman-redeemer largely involves property and family lineage, we can extend it in the faith community to include rescuing a child outside the door and placing that child in a secure place where he or she is treated as part of the family. God's original plan was for children to be placed in families. But sin broke this blueprint, and the world is in a real mess. Only the love of Christ expressed through the hands and feet of believers can redeem children to be incorporated into the family of God.

Although the concept of kinsman-redeemer largely involves property and family lineage, we can extend it in the faith community to include rescuing a child outside the door and placing that child in a secure place where he or she is treated as part of the family.

Summary

God's original plan was to place children in families. Being "inside" the love of a family is a means of grace and ideally provides avenues for children's holistic development. The Filipino contextual theology of family as a sacred trust, a sacrament, and a setting for God's mission is an ideal paradigm of what it means to place children in a supportive family. However as presented in the global critical section of this chapter, Filipino and many other children across the Global South are "outside the door." One of the ways that the Christian family can incorporate these children into the family of God is to act as

64. F. F. Bruce, "'Our God and Saviour': A Recurring Biblical Pattern," in *The Saviour God. Comparatives Studies in the Concept of Salvation*, ed. S. G. F. Brandon (Manchester: Manchester University Press, 1963), 51–66.

65. Christopher Hunt, "Boaz: A Story of God's Providence and Redemption," Groundwork (9 August 2018).

kinsman-redeemers – rescuing these children from the dangers outside and inviting them to come into the blessedness of Christ's love.

Bibliography

Agence Francaise De Developpement, https://www.afd.fr/en/actualites/breath-hope-street-children-philippines.

All-China Women's Federation, "National Survey Report on the Situation of Left-Behind Children and Migrant Children in China" (2013), https://unesdoc.unesco.org/ark:/48223/pf0000266050.

Bartel, Sarah Smith, and John S. Grabowski. *A Catechism for Family Life: Insights from Church Teaching on Love, Marriage, Sex, and Parenting*. Washington, DC: Catholic University of America Press, 2018. https://muse.jhu.edu/book/61423/.

Bernabe, Maria Victoria G., and Jennie Vee F. Pesa. "The Filipino Family, Sacramental Presence of God Today." Ateneo de Manila University. https://www.ateneo.edu/sites/default/files/Fourth%20Summer%20Output%20-%20ARTICLE%20%202%29%20Family%20as%20Sacrament%20of%20God%27s%20Presence.docx.

Bramer, Stephen J. "Kinsman-Redeemer." *Baker's Exegetical Dictionary of Biblical Theology*. Grand Rapids, MI: Baker Books, 1996. https://www.biblestudytools.com/dictionaries/bakers-evangelical-dictionary/kinsman-redeemer.html.

Breslich, Arthur L. "goel." *International Bible Encyclopedia* (1915). https://www.biblestudytools.com/dictionary/goel/.

Bruce, F. F. "'Our God and Saviour': A Recurring Biblical Pattern." In *The Saviour God: Comparatives Studies in the Concept of Salvation*, edited by S. G. F. Brandon, 51–66. Manchester: Manchester University Press, 1963.

Catechism of the Catholic Church, 2205. https://www.vatican.va/archive/compendium_ccc/documents/archive_2005_compendium-ccc_en.html.

Conor, Kelly. "The Anonymous Theology of Modern Family." *Journal of Religion and Popular Culture* 26, no. 3 (Fall 2014): 338–352.

Goldman, Russell. "Parents Who Pimp Their Children." *ABC News* (8 October 2007). https://abcnews.go.com/US/story?id=3691604&page=1.

Guzman, Lawrence de. "Philippines Still Top Christian Country in Asia, 5th in World." *Philipine Daily Inquirer* (21 December 2011). https://globalnation.inquirer.net/21233/philippines-still-top-christian-country-in-asia-5th-in-world#ixzz6aFSITBAn.

Holbrook, Clyde A. *The Ethics of Jonathan Edwards: Morality and Aesthetics*. Ann Arbor: University of Michigan Press, 1973.

Hunt, Christopher. "Boaz: A Story of God's Providence and Redemption." Groundwork (9 August 2018). https://groundwork.reframemedia.com/blog/boaz-a-story-of-gods-providence-and-redemption.

Jaucian, Don. "Breaking the Stigma on Filipino Children with Disabilities." *CNN Philippines Life* (3 March 2017). https://cnnphilippines.com/life/culture/2017/03/03/lotta-sylwander-interview-unicef.html.

Martin, Ralph P. *James. Word Biblical Commentary*. Waco, TX: Word Books, 1998.

McConnell, Douglas, Jennifer Orona, and Paul Stockley, eds. U*nderstanding God's Heart for Children: Toward a Biblical Framework*. Colorado Springs: Authentic, 2007.

McGowin, Emily Hunter. *Quivering Families: The Quiverfull Movement and Evangelical Theology of the Family*. Minneapolis: Fortress, 2018.

Mesa, Jose de. "Re-Rooting Mission in the Family." *Mission Studies* 19, no. 1 (2002): 139–49.

Niebuhr, Reinhold. *The Nature and Destiny of Man: A Christian Interpretation*. Louisville, KY: Westminster John Knox, 1996.

Nolan, Albert. *Jesus Before Christianity*. Quezon City: Claretian, 1999.

O'Murchu, Diarmuid. *Christianity's Dangerous Memory: A Rediscovery of the Revolutionary Jesus*. Quezon City: Claretian, 2012.

Polycarp. *The Epistle of Polycarp*. Translated by J. B. Lightfoot. 150 AD. http://www.earlychristianwritings.com/text/polycarp-lightfoot.html.

Rahner, Karl. "Reflections on the Unity of the Love of Neighbor and the Love of God." In *Theological Investigations 6: Concerning Vatical Council II*, 231–49. Baltimore, MD: Helicon, 1969.

Richards, Lawrence. *A Theology of Children's Ministry*. Grand Rapids, MI: Zondervan, 1983.

Robinson, Bernadette. "The Welfare and Education of Left-Behind Children in Western China." In *Educational Development in Western China*, edited by J. CK. Lee, Z. Yu, X. Huang, E. HF. Law, 97–119. Rotterdam: SensePublishers, 2016. https://doi.org/10.1007/978-94-6300-232-5_5.

Seamands, David. *Healing Grace: Let God Free You from the Performance Trap*. Wheaton, IL: Victor Books, 1988.

Stala, Józef, and Jadranka Gamaz. "The Family Communio Personarum and Upbringing." *The Person and the Challenges* 8, no. 1 (2018): 45–57. http://dx.doi.org/10.15633/pch.2424.

Tan, Michael L. "Coming Home, Going Home." *Sunday Inquirer Magazine* (23 November 2008). https://pdfcookie.com/download/the-filipino-family-lights-and-shadows-challenges-to-the-domestic-church-eyv879kogl1l.

Theodore of Cyrus. *The Fathers of the Church: Theodore of Cyrus, Commentary on the Psalms, 73–150*. Washington, DC: Catholic University of America Press, 2010.

Thompson, Marjorie J. *Family, the Forming Center*. rev. ed. Nashville: Upper Room Books, 1996.

University of the Philippines Manila, The University of Edinburgh, Child Protection Network Foundation and UNICEF Philippines, *A Systematic Review of the Drivers of Violence Affecting Children in the Philippines*. Manila: UNICEF Philippines, 2016.

Ward, Ted. *Values Begin at Home*. Wheaton, IL: Victor Books, 1984.

Wesley, John. "Sermon 94: 'On Family Religion.'" In *The Works of John Wesley*, 1872. WordsOfWesley.com.

———. *The Sermons of John Wesley: Sermon 16*, edited by Darin Million. Wesley Center Online (1999). http://wesley.nnu.edu/john-wesley/the-sermons-of-john-wesley-1872-edition/sermon-16-the-means-of-grace/.

Westerhoff, John H. *Bringing up Children in the Christian Faith*. Minneapolis: Winston, 1980.

———. *Will Our Children Have Faith?* rev. ed. Harrisburg, PA: Morehouse, 2000.

Case Study:
A City without Orphans

Faith Kembabazi and Patrick Byekwaso – Ugandan

In 2017, two sisters ages two and six were rescued from the street with their mother. The children were given temporary care with a member of Viva's Ugandan network CRANE (Children at Risk Action Network). The workers in CRANE passionately believe that children belong in safe and loving families. While the children were cared for by CRANE, their mother, aged twenty-one, was enrolled in a crisis rehabilitation center and given counseling by another CRANE member. A third organization gave her vocational training. She was offered a package to start a business, but she couldn't take it on because her life was chaotic. She returned to the streets to work in the sex trade, and it was deemed too high a risk to put the children back in her care.

After six months of trying to find any next of kin, efforts turned to finding a foster family. A couple recruited from one of the network churches agreed to be foster parents so the sisters could remain together, but they needed economic empowerment to be able to feed two extra mouths. So their piggery and goat-keeping work was boosted. The children have been in the care of this foster family for close to two years now. They have bonded well with the family and community and are happy to belong to the family. The older girl is in school, while the younger one is yet to start school.

Uganda: A Nation with Many Children

Uganda is known for having one of the youngest populations in the world today. Estimates from the 2014 National Census indicate that over 56 percent of Uganda's population of 34.6 million are under the age of eighteen.[66] Furthermore, more than 52 percent are under the age of fifteen.[67] In this context

66. "The National Population and Housing Census 2014: Main Report," Uganda Bureau of Statistics (2016).

67. "Program: National Strategy," Ministry of Gender, Labor and Social Development, Uganda (2022).

of a young population, poverty, HIV/AIDS, teenage pregnancy, child abuse, and family breakdown lead many parents to leave their children in institutional care or abandon them to a life on the streets. Although it is not known exactly how many children in Uganda are living outside of family care, several studies estimate that currently a population of over fifteen thousand children live on the streets and over forty thousand live in residential care facilities such as children's homes.[68] The conditions for children living on the streets are very unpleasant and force them to fight constantly in order to survive.

Causes of Family Separation

The separation of children from their families can be the result of many causes, including the death of one or both parents, abandonment, displacement due to armed conflict, trafficking, or simply the inability or unwillingness of the family to provide care. The roots of separation of children from their families can also be found in behavior problems, relationship difficulties, abuse, and neglect. Separation is also caused by larger systemic issues such as poverty, conflict, natural disasters, and HIV/AIDS.[69]

The roots of separation of children from their families can also be found in behavior problems, relationship difficulties, abuse, and neglect.

One other issue which CRANE identifies as sometimes contributing to children living outside of family care is that adults in positions of responsibility are not enacting their duty of care. Starting from the family to the government, people and institutions charged with the responsibility of caring for and protecting children are not. Due to this lack, we have seen an increase in the vulnerability of child orphans as well as in the number of abandoned children and children living on the street.

We have known for a while that the best place to raise children and for them to thrive is in the family setting and not in an institution or on the streets where they are faced with all types of impediments. In particular, these children outside parental care are exposed to many forms of abuse and exploitation.

68. "Program: National Strategy."

69. "Strengthening Family Care," Better Care Network (n.d.).

About CRANE

CRANE is a network of over 140 organizations, schools, and churches across Kampala who work in collaboration to see to it that children are safe, well and thriving in God's plan as they fulfill their God-given potential. Today through CRANE's work, hundreds of thousands of children across multiple categories have been supported, nurtured, encouraged, and helped to grow. This city-wide network allows member organizations, schools, and churches to maintain individual autonomy while providing a solid platform for joint action. Whole communities and cities are transformed as a wide spectrum of civil society players collaborate to achieve an outcome. As a network, CRANE is empowered to fill the gaps in the Christian response to caring for children.

We have known for a while that the best place to raise children and for them to thrive is in the family setting and not in an institution or on the streets where they are faced with all types of impediments.

Best Practices for Family Reintegration

In response to this issue and since 2010, CRANE's family reintegration programmed has reunited more than one thousand children who were previously living in childcare institutions or on the streets with families. CRANE works at four levels in relation to street children: prevention, rescue, restoration, and resettlement. Here is a description of these levels:

1. Prevention includes all efforts carried out to prevent children from ending up on the street or in childcare institutions. Prevention is done by working with churches and other network members to protect marriages and preserve families. Families are supported by church leaders and family mentors to stay together and to provide a loving and safe home for children. Key messages on promoting family preservation, on positive parenting, and on creating safe relationships are agreed upon with church leaders. These messages are then shared widely on multiple media forums using high quality visual messaging and tools. In some communities, family support groups are created to promote family preservation and fight poverty using group saving schemes.

2. Rescue includes all efforts to take children off the streets or out of circumstances where they face a high risk of abuse. Trained social workers support the children who have been separated from their families by making sure they receive appropriate help. Some children are referred by the police, while other children are rescued through outreach activities and drop-in centers where they receive trauma counseling.

3. Restoration includes counseling and all forms of support that is provided to rescued children to prepare them for a home. Where necessary, a child will be referred to a specialist for counseling and psychosocial support. At this point, children can be taken through either fast-track catch-up education or vocational training depending on their age and how long they have been out of school. Usually older children who have been away from home for a long time are better helped through vocational training which prepares them to start a decent job and make an honest living. Family tracing is also carried out at this stage. Priority is always given to finding either a child's birth family or a next of kin. Social workers carry out family assessments to find out the suitability of the family to receive the child. They also work with the family to address any issues that might have caused the child to leave home, which can include forgiveness and reconciliation between the family and the child. When kin relations cannot be found, a family who can offer foster care for the child and possibly later on adopt her or him is sought.

4. Resettlement involves all the work of supporting children who are settled into families. This work is done through collaboration with churches and other stakeholders in the community where the child is resettled so that the proper links are in place to support the child in living and thriving in the family and being safe in the society. In these communities, CRANE is also fighting the social stigma in some sectors of society regarding children who have lived on the streets.

CRANE is working toward Kampala being a city without orphans by undertaking advocacy work at the government level as well as with various childcare institutions and key denominations and church groups in the city, arguing that a family home is a better place for a child than an institution such as an orphanage. CRANE's work with childcare institutions involves training which teaches the staff of the network members how to conduct family reintegration successfully for both the family and the child. Staff who go through this training learn how to trace a child's family, provide counseling, and ensure that the home situation is safe for the child in the long term.[70]

CRANE works strategically to strengthen member institutions by leading a coordinated approach in conjunction with the police to rescue unaccompanied children from the streets. CRANE also works with churches

---

70. Liz Cross, "Working Together to Provide Family Based Care," Viva (10 April 2018).

to provide emergency homes as well as foster and adoptive families. At the governmental level, CRANE works with professionals such as social workers and police officers to better ensure the safety of children who are found living on the streets. Significantly in March 2017, CRANE invited forty-four senior leaders from across Kampala to a high-level roundtable discussion between government ministers, senior denominational church leaders, CEOs, and state authorities addressing the issues of orphans across the city.[71]

The Role of Christians in Supporting Families

Churches and other Christian-based organizations should be working in collaboration to prevent family separation by strengthening and supporting families so they can stay together. This support should be aimed at addressing the different causes of family breakdown and how to create an environment where children are safe, loved, and cared for. This support can take the forms of promoting positive parenting, encouraging safe and healthy relationships in families, and facilitating marriage enrichment and economic empowerment among other interventions.

It is also important to remind Christians of the biblical value of raising children in families and God's heart for the fatherless. Through this effort, key messaging that is contextually relevant should be developed and passed on to various church congregations in addition to being broadcast through various forms of media. Bible studies should be developed and support groups created in church communities. Through these and other similar efforts, kinship care can be encouraged for children whose relatives are found, along with foster care leading to adoption for children whose biological families are not found or are not able to provide the appropriate care they need.

Church communities can be encouraged to form a support community for children and families under foster care so that the parents are supported and children know that they are welcome in the community of faith. Supporting children to live in families and preventing unnecessary family separation are not endeavors that one organization or church can do alone, but rather need to be done through collaboration because each group has unique strengths and contributions to make for the unique needs of children and families.

71. "City Without Orphans," Viva Network (n.d.).

Processes to Enable Children to Live in Families

In ideal situations, three key processes need to happen to enable children live in families.

1. **Prevention**: Strengthening families to help children remain in families, both biological and foster families.
2. **Rescue Separated Children**: Short-term, emergency-based care where possible in families or emergency transition institutions.
3. **Reuniting families**: Transitioning children currently in residential care to long-term family care.

The biblical book of Ruth gives us a splendid story of a kinsman-redeemer, Boaz who, after the failure of the closest relative to take Ruth under his wings, redeems her and offers her an opportunity to be protected from abuse, exploitation, and marginalization (Ruth 4:1–10). He also gives her the ability to protect family property and extend the family name. This account is a shadow of the gospel story in which Jesus Christ gives himself "as a ransom for many" (Matt 20:28), taking on the punishment that was meant for us. As Christians who embrace the redemption Christ offers us, we also ought to follow in his footsteps and offer orphans and children separated from their families the protection and opportunities they need to thrive in God's plan. This way of following Jesus can be very costly at the start, but the long-term rewards cannot be compared to the cost.

In Kampala city, CRANE network members are working together to prevent family separation while childcare institutions are working with local authorities to rescue children from the streets and churches are recruiting families who can take on children who are in need of foster families. The beauty of a being part of a network is that we can all join hands and use our areas of strength to supplement each other rather than giving the appearance that we are competing with each other.

The Challenge to Place Children in Families

CRANE's work to support children is guided by Christian values as laid out in the Bible. There we witness God's love for these children and other vulnerable groups expressed in various ways, see children welcomed into the community of faith, and find examples of key lessons for the faith (see for example Matt 18:1–5; Luke 2:22–40; 18:15–17).

God's design is for children to be born and raised in the context of a family. No other institution in the Bible has been given the mandate to care for, protect, and love children like the family. The Bible shows us through exhortation and example that in the family children are to be welcomed as gifts from God (Ps 127:3–5) and nurtured to love God and live for him (Deut 6:4–9; Col 3:21).

The Bible further calls on the community of faith to carry and reflect God's heart for orphans who need a family to embrace, care for, and protect them, similar to what God does when he welcomes us into his family through the redeeming work of Jesus Christ (Pss 68:5–6a; 82:3; Rom 8:15; Gal 4:4–5; Eph 1:4–5). We serve children best if we either support them in connecting with their biological family, a near kinship relative, or a foster family who will love, care for, and protect them.

We serve children best if we either support them in connecting with their biological family, a near kinship relative, or a foster family who will love, care for, and protect them.

Bibliography

"City Without Orphans." Viva Network (n.d.). https://www.viva.org/wp-content/uploads/2017/10/Family-strategy-grid.pdf.

Cross, Liz. "Working Together to Provide Family Based Care." Viva (10 April 2018). http://blog.viva.org/2017/04/10/working-together-to-provide-family-based-care/.

"The National Population and Housing Census 2014: Main Report." Uganda Bureau of Statistics (2016). https://www.ubos.org/wp-content/uploads/publications/03_20182014_National_Census_Main_Report.pdf.

"Program: National Strategy." Ministry of Gender, Labor and Social Development, Uganda (2022). http://ovcmis.mglsd.go.ug/home.php?linkvar=CSI%20Trend%20Analysis&&action=Reports.

"Strengthening Family Care." Better Care Network (n.d.). https://bettercarenetwork.org/library/strengthening-family-care/strengthening-family-care.

Discussion Questions for Chapter 2

1. Within your own context, what are the challenges that children outside the door face?
2. How is the church responding to their needs?
3. What is your opinion on the biblical concept of kinsman-redeemer?
4. Is this concept of kinsman-redeemer practiced in your community?
5. List some practical ways for your ministry to incorporate children outside the door.

3

Cared for in Community

God gives children to communities as a gift to welcome and nurture. A healthy community is a place where its residents create a safe and healthy environment for the children amongst them.

Global Critical Issue:
It Still Takes a Village to Raise a Child

Amberbir Tamire Habtemariam – Ethiopian

In Chapter 3 of the first edition of *Understanding God's Heart for Children*, Jennifer Orona begins her article with the famous African saying, "It takes a village to raise a child," and looks at it from a Western perspective.[1] In this edition I use the same phrase, except I will be looking at it from an African perspective. The saying is globally well-known, but in many parts of Africa, the practice is slowly fading. In this chapter, I argue that if this issue is not addressed, the saying will end up as an old one which the elders share as a childhood experience, a practice that is relegated to the "good ole' days" when everyone in the village played a part in raising the next generation.

The Child and the Village

Indeed, as I look back to those "good ole' days" in the village environment, I see what looks like a togetherness of views, mutual responsibility, well-established hierarchical structures, and a sense of security in which the children felt safe and protected. The family together with the neighbors encouraged, cared for, and disciplined the children. The village was a nursery bed where the culture was communal and relational, imbued with a desire to teach the children rightly. In response, the children were to receive the parental nurture and the elders' guidance and to be responsible for their actions. When the children grew to be working adults and started earning income, they were to show responsibility for not only their parents but also their neighbors. This response is a way of giving back from generation to generation and a way of showing appreciation.

Traditionally, a community is understood as people who live in a specific geographical area and among other things share similar beliefs, customs,

1. Jennifer Orona, "The Role and Responsibilities of Children and their Communities," in *Understanding God's Heart for Children: Toward a Biblical Framework*, eds. Douglas McConnell, Jennifer Orona, and Paul Stockley (Colorado Springs: Authentic, 2007), 97–108.

interests, and language. In Amharic, one of the Ethiopian dialects, we use the word *mahibereseb* (ማህበረሰብ) to denote the concept of community life. *Mahibereseb* is literally translated as "the association of human beings," and describes a group of people in social relationship who interact and share values. Another word that denotes community living is *ubuntu* (humanness and commonness). "Ubuntu is an African philosophy that says people exist in community, not isolation. We are human because of our interconnectedness with other humans. . . . It is an attitude of faithfulness and commitment to the group above success of the individual."[2] In an *ubuntu* culture, children are encouraged to express themselves and meaningfully participate in village life to experience shared values and identity.

Ubuntu is an African philosophy that says people exist in community, not isolation. We are human because of our interconnectedness with other humans.

In a traditional African village, children are considered to be an important and integral part of community life, literally an extension of the adults. This practice and guideline for child nurture and education can be said to be similar to that in Deuteronomy 11:19, "Teach [these commands] to your children, talking about them when you sit at home and when you walk along the road, when you lie down and when you get up." In an African village, children are encouraged to participate in many of the communal cultural practices and celebrations. The adults instinctively nurture children as part of their collective responsibility. These villagers seek to protect the young ones from any harmful activities, chastise adult culprits, and isolate the children from those who may harm them.

The African village was a place where children learned culturally acceptable social etiquette and cultural values and inherited the shared stories from their elders. In most African communities, stories were told over campfires in the cold evenings. This was how the children learned the history, traditions, and values of their forefathers and mothers and the clan elders in the village. These involvements gave the children their identity as Africans, and they learned to be proud of their heritage. As part of their responsibilities and from an early age, the children were given distinct tasks to support the village well-being. For instance, the children were given the task of caring for the young

2. Dennis Kilama, "Christians in Community: Redeeming the Concept of Ubuntu" https://africa.thegospelcoalition.org/article/redeeming-ubuntu/.

sheep, goats, or chickens under the watchful eyes of the village elders. Since the African village was agrarian, the children were also taught to plant and grow food, mostly for family consumption. When it came to handing down craftmanship and life skills, the community served as a school by mentoring the young ones. The adults were deliberate in their attempts to transfer culture, life skills, and relational etiquette to the children through implicit and explicit teaching and modeling.

The Child and the City

In this age of globalization and urbanization in which the working adults and young people are moving away from the villages and into the cities, the responsibility of childcare in traditional institutions such as the family, village, and community is being challenged. Often left behind are the elderly and the very young children. While city life has much to offer in terms of progress, there is also the overarching concern of the rise of individualism and consumerism. In most developed social societies, a sense of altruism and a culture of volunteerism and caring for the needy is in decline. Coupled with the growing wealth disparity in some cities, the plight of vulnerable children is worsening. They are left to fend for themselves due to parental absence or assigned to institutional care. As a result this group of children are raised with an attitude of entitlement and little sense of social responsibility and community. Busy parents often outsource their childcare responsibilities to institutions, and older children are left to care for themselves as parents work long hours and have little time left for the children after a hard day's work.

In the progress of industrialization, urbanization, and globalization, the African village concept of community care and nurture is fast eroding as people become overly engrossed in their individual pursuits, and the fast speed of modern life does not provide enough time for strong relationships and deep reflections. The ideas and practices of *mahibereseb* and *ubuntu* are gradually lost in the fast lanes of urbanization. This lack of supportive social structures is having an increasingly negative impact on the development of children. More so in the city, the children need a responsible and caring community to support their physical, mental, social, and emotional well-being. Without proper parental or wise guidance from a more mature member, the children are open to all types of influences, both positive and negative.

Challenges for Urbanized Children in Africa

The current trends of social disintegration and loss of cohesion in community life, coupled with wealth disparity and moral degradation have brought misery to the lives of many children, especially those who are vulnerable. Below I raise two major challenges experienced by the children in Ethiopia: child abuse and neglect and uncontrolled media exposure.

Child Abuse and Neglect

Child abuse and neglect top the list as indicators of a dysfunctional family and community. How child abuse and neglect are globally understood varies because what is considered to be child maltreatment is socially constructed by the local culture and setting. The World Health Organization (WHO) defines child abuse or maltreatment as "all forms of physical and/or emotional ill-treatment, sexual abuse, neglect or negligent treatment or commercial or other exploitation, resulting in actual or potential harm to the child's health, survival, development or dignity in the context of a relationship of responsibility and, trust or power."[3] Globally an estimated 95 million children experience abuse annually, with the highest rates reported in Africa than on any other continent.[4] Schools, playgrounds, hospitals, and even places of worship have become grounds for child abuse.[5]

Uncontrolled Media Exposure

It has become a common phenomenon that children and youths are being discipled by social media through the screen of their televisions or other electronic devices. In Africa (and I presume in most parts of the world), the television, while being a significant socializing agent, is also a "childcare" device. Parents who want time for themselves are finding that digital screens are great ways to entertain their children. Media has become the forefront agent in forming the children's culture, and this childhood culture is becoming less and less characterized by the important and active aspect of social relationships.

---

3. "Child Maltreatment" World Health Organization (2022), https://apps.who.int/violence-info/child-maltreatment/.

4. UNICEF. UNICEF; New York: 2014. "Hidden in plain sight: a statistical analysis of violence against children."

5. Victor Selengia, Hanh Nguyen Thi Thuy, and Declare Mushi. 2020. "Prevalence and Patterns of Child Sexual Abuse in Selected Countries of Asia and Africa: A Review of Literature." *Open Journal of Social Sciences* 08 (09): 146–60.

Instead, the shift is toward a more passive association with television, computer games, and other electronic devices. Digital obsession can affect the physical health of children, limits and taints the development of their imagination and creative minds, and negatively affects their social development.[6] Children who are constantly exposed to media advertisements are prone to develop a consumeristic attitude. This attitude in turn can motivate hedonistic pursuits and individualism which is an antithesis of the African community lifestyle. Also a study on consumerism shows that children who are involved in consumer culture exhibit more depression and elevated anxiety, possess lower self-esteem, and suffer from psychosomatic problems.[7]

Conclusion

In the summary of *Hardwired to Connect*, a seminal research report by the Commission on Children at Risk and published by Institute for American Values, the high levels of depression, anxiety, conduct disorder, and other related mental health problems in children are directly related with a lack of connectedness to other people.[8] The study highlights the importance of having a strong community that supports the well-being of children and concludes that "meeting these basic needs for connections is essential to health and to human flourishing"[9] A healthy and caring community is a place that mediates and practices shared history, beliefs and values, life skills, and equity and upholds social structures such as the family unit. A healthy community is a place where people value, protect, and nurture children and childhood so that they will be able to realize their potential as people. In following the trends of globalization and urbanization, in which people from the villages are compelled to migrate to the cities to find work, earn their living, enroll in institutions of higher learning, and so forth, the concept of a village should not be totally lost.

In response to the challenges of globalization, urbanization, and marginalization, I believe that Christians have the answer. The local church can be the new village. Although the congregation may not all come from the

---

6. I. D. Silva, "Demographic and social trends affecting families in the south and central Asian region," in *Major Trends Affecting Families: A Background Document* (New York: United Nations, 2003).

7. J. A. Hill, "Endangered Childhoods: How consumerism is impacting child and youth identity," in *Media, Culture and Society* (April 2011), 348–62.

8. Commission on Children at Risk, *Hardwired to Connect: The New Scientific Case for Authoritative Communities* (New York: Broadway Publications, 2003), 3.

9. Commission on Children at Risk, *Hardwired to Connect*, 44.

same geographical area, strong threads still tie them together – the shared history of the gospel; shared faith, beliefs and values; shared faith practices; and a commitment to raise generations that testify to the working of the risen Lord in our midst. Indeed, the African saying that it takes a village to raise a child still stands, and that village is the local church!

Bibliography

Commission on Children at Risk. *Hardwired to Connect: The New Scientific Case for Authoritative Communities*. New York: Broadway Publications, 2003.

Hill, J. A. "Endangered Childhoods: How consumerism is impacting child and youth identity." In *Media, Culture and Society*, 348–62. April 2011.

Kilama, Dennis. "Christians in Community: Redeeming the Concept of Ubuntu" https://africa.thegospelcoalition.org/article/redeeming-ubuntu/ (Accessed 14 March 2022).

Orona, Jennifer. "The Role and Responsibilities of Children and their Communities," in *Understanding God's Heart for Children: Toward a Biblical Framework*, eds. Douglas McConnell, Jennifer Orona, and Paul Stockley (Colorado Springs: Authentic, 2007), 97–108.

Selengia, Victor, Hanh Nguyen Thi Thuy, and Declare Mushi. "Prevalence and Patterns of Child Sexual Abuse in Selected Countries of Asia and Africa: A Review of Literature." *Open Journal of Social Sciences* 08, no. 09 (2020): 146–60. https://doi.org/10.4236/jss.2020.89010.

Silva, I. D. "Demographic and social trends affecting families in the south and central Asian region." In *Major Trends Affecting Families: A Background Document*, 45–77. New York: United Nations, 2003.

UNICEF. UNICEF; New York: 2014. "Hidden in plain sight: a statistical analysis of violence against children."

World Health Organization ("Child Maltreatment" 2022), https://apps.who.int/violence-info/child-maltreatment/.

Biblical and Theological Response: *Ubuntu*: Conceptualizing Community for Children in the African Context

Roseline Olumbe – Kenyan

Introduction

In this chapter, I explore a biblical understanding of community in caring for children and highlight the lapses of communities in this obligation. Children grow and thrive within a supportive and caring community. Urie Bronfenbrenner conceptualizes that children grow and develop within an ecology that has a direct impact on them.[10] He argues that there are five systems within this ecology namely, microsystem, mesosystem, exosystem, macrosystem, and chronosystem.[11] Each of these systems has a direct impact on the developing child – whether the child interacts with it directly or otherwise. Specifically, the microsystem which includes home, school, church, and immediate neighborhood is the primary system in which the child receives nurture. The mesosystem involves the interactions that take place between the various microsystems. These systems broadly reveal that childhood nurture not only takes place at home but in the community at large. The resulting outcomes of these interactions can be positive or negative based on the prevailing circumstances in the ecology. Likewise, the child actively interacts with these ecological systems and creates a similar impact. Based on these ecological principles, the environment within which children grow and develop has a direct impact on them, and if appropriate will lead to positive outcomes. The effectiveness of this environment is dependent on the members of the community where the child grows and develops.

10. Urie Bronfenbrenner, ed., *Making Human Beings Human: Bioecological Perspectives on Human Development* (Thousand Oaks, CA: SAGE, 2004).

11. Urie Bronfenbrenner, *The Ecology of Human Development: Experiments by Nature and Design* (Cambridge: Harvard University Press, 2009).

A community is essential for the socialization of children. Although children receive their primary care and support from families, a community is critical for providing life and practical lessons. Children learn moral values and expectations for behavior from the community within which they live. In some cases where family structures have failed, children can receive their primary care and nurture from the community. This type of situation calls for community members to have intentional interactions with the children that enhance positive outcomes.

This type of situation calls for community members to have intentional interactions with the children that enhance positive outcomes.

The African community by nature is known for being communal and lays emphasis on togetherness. It was the famous bishop Desmond Tutu who envisioned *ubuntu* as an integral part of African culture. *Ubuntu* is the principle of caring for each other and the spirit of mutual support. Johann Broodryk argues that *ubuntu* is based on the values of humaneness, caring, sharing, respect compassion, and similar values that enhance the happiness and quality of life among members of the community.[12] *Ubuntu* denotes that our humanity is reflected in our relationships with others.[13] It underscores the importance of consensus which requires a conscious effort to make peace with one another for enhanced community cohesiveness.[14] Mary Thamari in her research found that the nature of reciprocity in community provides a strong sense of social obligation for mutual support in times of instability.[15] Such expressions of *ubuntu* are central to the African community and provide children a context in which to learn the value of being humane. Such values are not necessarily taught in the classroom; however, they are learned within the community as children interact with their peers and adults.

---

12. Johann Broodryk, "Ubuntu African Life Coping Skills: Theory and Practice," in *CCEAM Conference 12–17 October 2006* (Lefkosia, Cyprus: Knowledge Resources, 2006).

13. Dirk J. Louw, "The African Concept of Ubuntu and Restorative Justice," in *Handbook of Restorative Justice: A Global Perspective*, ed. Dennis Sullivan and Larry Tifft (New York: Routledge, 2008), 161.

14. Louw, "African Concept of Ubuntu," 162.

15. Mary Thamari, "Femininity, Gender Relations and Livelihood Vulnerabilities in Southwestern Kenya" (diss., University of Birmingham, 2019).

Children: A Community or Individual Responsibility?

In most African communities, collective responsibility is emphasized and appreciated as a way of life. The way children are treated provides a sense of communal responsibility. This way of thinking embodies the phrases "we are because you are" and "your child is my child" which are enshrined in *ubuntu* philosophy.[16] This life philosophy signifies the importance of a community in which members are committed to the care and support of one another. Additionally, *ubuntu* underscores the fact that children belong to all members of the community, and as a result every member should be responsible for the children's welfare. I remember that in my childhood days, any adult could discipline a child without parental consent. If the report of misbehavior reached the parents, the child would be further disciplined. A collective responsibility in child rearing was enhanced by all. However, this attitude has significantly changed in postmodern culture both in rural and urban areas. Care and nurture have become solely a family affair as opposed to communal.

A caring community is important and significant to the well-being of the children and other members, prompting unity and increasing caretaking and caregiving.[17] Children born within such communities enjoy these benefits and become care receivers from the members of the community. However, fear and mistrust among community members has increased due to emergent cases of child abuse and exploitation. Parents have become more cautious of neighbors and strangers, and this attitude hinders community collaboration and support.

A child is valued and treasured by all in the African context, and community responsibility in caregiving is envisioned. According to John Mbiti, an individual does not and cannot exist alone, but corporately.[18] Traditionally, a child is secluded for a period of time after birth and later exposed to the community. During this introduction to the community, the baby's hair is shaved as a sign of purification, separation, and newness.[19] The child's integration into the community is marked with a celebration as a sign of joy which involves feasting, dancing, rejoicing, and congratulating the mother and family. This celebration is a sign of joy but also a renewal of the life of the community.[20] These activities acknowledge that a child is valued by the

---

16. C. Engelbrecht and M. I. Kasiram, "Original Research: The Role of Ubuntu in Families Living with Mental Illness in the Community," *South African Family Practice* 54, no. 5 (2012): 441.

17. Engelbrecht and Kasiram, "Original Research," 445.

18. John S. Mbiti, *Introduction to African Religion* (Nairobi: East African Educational Publishers, 1991), 92.

19. Mbiti, *Introduction,* 92.

20. Mbiti, 92.

community and is officially integrated into the community. The child belongs to the community and is to be nurtured in this context.

Since a child is dependent on the community for care and nurture, the community must make, create, or produce the individual, for the individual depends on the corporate group.[21] The centrality of the community in making an individual cannot be understated. Mbiti argues that existence of a person is dependent on the community, and the individual can only say, "I am, because we are; and since we are therefore I am."[22] In Mbiti's visualization the existence of human beings, in this case children, is fully dependent on the community where they exist. The functionality of the community is dependent on the members within it and vice versa. Harmony of individuals within the environment is therefore critical, but individuals must also enhance the harmony of the environment or community within which they live. I see this harmony from a biblical lens and thus worthy to embrace. The creation account in Genesis 1 describes the goodness of creation and the harmony within it. It is recorded, "God saw all that he had made, and it was very good" (Gen 1:31). Clearly, God made everything good, and as human beings we must strive to achieve the goodness of creation but also enhance our responsibility for stewarding this creation (Gen 1:28).

Clearly, God made everything good, and as human beings we must strive to achieve the goodness of creation but also enhance our responsibility for stewarding this creation.

Biblical Reflection on Childcare in Community

In reflecting on the place of children in the Bible, we develop a proper understanding of their existence according them their rightful place in the community. Several passages in the Bible provide insights into who children are, and these passages should form the basis for our understanding and acceptance of children.

21. Michael Onyebuchi Eze, "What Is African Communitarianism? Against Consensus as a Regulative Ideal," *South African Journal of Philosophy* 27, no. 4 (January 1, 2008): 386–99.

22. John Mbiti quoted in Maulana Karenga, "Black Religion," in *African American Religious Studies: An Interdisciplinary Anthology*, ed. Gayraud S. Wilmore (Durham; London: Duke University Press, 1989), 141.

Children are Gifts from God to Families

Children come to us as gifts from God and are placed in families. From Psalm 127:3, we gain an understanding of children as gifts from God. From the passage, we read, "Children are a heritage from the LORD, offspring a reward from him." This verse reveals the special aspect of children as purely a gift from God to parents. Any gift giving activity requires a giver, receiver, gift, and occasion.[23] In the case of children, God is the giver, children are the gifts, parents are the receivers, and birth is the occasion. Gifts are not predetermined by the receivers; the giver determines what gift to give and when to give that gift. God thus gifts parents with children of different natures, genders, sizes, colors, and abilities.

Vinita Ambwani notes that the giving of gifts is a social, cultural, and economic phenomenon that happens across different divides of life including cultures and socioeconomic levels.[24] Giving of gifts happens within a context, and one needs to understand the context. Within the African context, the receiver of a gift has very few options in regard to what gift will be received and what to do with the gift. Rejecting a gift is culturally offensive. The receiver of the gift is expected to accept it with joy even if they do not like the gift. I came to understand a different aspect of gifts during my stay in England. I was given a chance to select the kind of gift I wanted. In addition, I was given the option to reject a gift if it was contrary to my cultural orientation. Today, I see the same aspects in my own community though not equally the same. The receiver of a gift can propose what gift to be bought; however, the receiver does not reject a gift.

When I think of children as gifts from God, I think in terms of an African who has very little option to select or reject a gift. Therefore, children as gifts from God are to be accepted, enjoyed, and treasured. Parents and the entire community must seek to shepherd children's growth and development, advocate for their welfare, and provide for their needs. Discrimination and rejection of children with special needs or different abilities should be rejected in all of their forms. Nurturing children is in itself a cyclic reproduction of *ubuntu* because when children are well nurtured, they in turn reciprocate by nurturing others when that time comes. Shipton Parker's research in Kenya

---

23. Jackie R. Clarke, "Different to 'Dust Collectors'? The Giving and Receiving of Experience Gifts," *Journal of Consumer Behaviour* 5, no. 6 (2006): 533–49.

24. Vinita P. Ambwani, "Examining Gift-Giving Motives in a Cross-Cultural Context" (diss., Carleton University, Ottawa, 2014).

revealed the value of exchange between generations as symbolic of "borrowing and lending" or passing along important community values.[25]

Children Need Nurture and Guidance

The nurture of children is significant for their proper growth and development. Having grown in a context where farming was critical for food production and sustenance, I saw what needed to be done for better production. It demanded many hours of tilling the land, planting, weeding, and tending the crops. A great investment of time and money was spent on the farms so that the produce would be good and sustain the family. In the same way, investing in the nurture of children is critical for their positive outcomes. Proverbs 22:6 states, "Start children off in the way they should go, and even when they are old they will not turn from it." This passage directly gives parents the responsibility to provide their children with a solid spiritual foundation in the early years whose impact will be realized in their old age. A solid foundation is critical for children, which calls on parents to be present, supporting, and modeling to children the expected Christian lifestyle. Glenn Myles posits that, "Shema, the Hebrew confession of faith, was to be impressed on children 'when you sit at home, and when you walk along the road, when you lie down and when you get up (Deut 6:4–9).'"[26] Teaching and nurturing children to enable the passing on of values is significant in the Bible. Doing so demands a lifestyle commitment from parents and community members to nurture the children.

Special Care for Children at Risk

Care for orphans is well outlined in the Bible, and structures were established to protect orphaned children. Psalm 68:5 declares God to be "A father to the fatherless, a defender of widows." Furthermore Psalm 82:3 calls on people to "Defend the cause of the weak and fatherless; uphold the cause of the poor and oppressed." These verses indicate a commitment to the welfare of orphans and their relatives taking them in as family. This practice ensures that children as vulnerable members of the community receive care. Christians ought to

25. Parker MacDonald Shipton, *The Nature of Entrustment: Intimacy, Exchange, and the Sacred in Africa* (New Haven: Yale University Press, 2007).

26. Glenn Miles, "The Development of Children in Their Families and Communities," in *Celebrating Children: Equipping People Working with Children and Young People Living in Difficult Circumstances Around the World*, ed. Glenn Miles and Josephine-Joy Wright (Carlisle: Paternoster, 2006), 33–39.

be engaged in caring and protecting orphans, the poor, and the vulnerable. Zechariah 7:10 states, "Do not oppress the widow or the fatherless, the foreigner or the poor." Children are by nature vulnerable, and their vulnerability is intensified when they are orphaned, homeless, or poor. Vulnerable children lack both social and financial security to meet their developmental needs. God in his plan made provisions for the care of children who encounter these vulnerabilities. The community is mandated to take care of and provide for their essential needs. In Leviticus 19:9–10 is the command "When you reap the harvest of your land, do not reap to the very edges of your field or gather the gleanings of your harvest. Do not go over your vineyard a second time or pick up the grapes that have fallen. Leave them for the poor and the foreigner. I am the LORD your God." Allowing those who are poor to glean helps them find food for survival.

In traditional African communities, the extended family system provides a safety net for caring for orphans and poor children. In some communities in Kenya, orphaned children are provided for and live in a family environment. Although Kenya has seen a mushrooming of charity institutions for orphans and vulnerable children, there are problems with this method of nurture. Two examples are the disadvantages of living in crowded institutions and child abuse.[27] These concerns have led to a deinstitutionalization program that is promoting family-based care instead of orphanages.

Children Need Protection

Child abuse is a global problem that leads to adverse health, educational, and behavioral outcomes that have lifelong negative consequences on children. Furthermore, abuse has destructive effects on children in every country and affects families and communities from generation to generation.[28] In light of these abuses and the resultant effects on children, protection and safeguards are needed for the children's positive development. Protection of children refers to measures and structures to prevent and respond to abuse, neglect, exploitation,

27. Paula Braitstein, et al., "Child Abuse and Neglect in Charitable Children's Institutions in Uasin Gishu County, Kenya: A Challenge of Context," in *Child Maltreatment in Residential Care*, ed. Adrian V. Rus, Sheri R. Parris, and Ecaterina Stativa (Cham, Switzerland: Springer International AG, 2017), 337–56.

28. Susan Hillis, et al., "Global Prevalence of Past-Year Violence Against Children: A Systematic Review and Minimum Estimates," *Pediatrics* 137, no. 3 (1 March 2016).

and violence affecting children.[29] Protection of children is a Christian mandate, and there is need to advocate for the safety of children in the community. James 1:27 describes true religion as creating a safe environment for women and children, specifically the widow and the orphan. God is concerned with the safety of children and the vulnerable; therefore we should be concerned about the safety of children. Advocating child protection is a calling not only for professionals but for all Christians.

Children as Part of a Community

In the Old Testament, we see corporate solidarity and children as part of the community in various contexts. For instance, children participated in community activities: 2 Chronicles 20:12–13 states that when the Israelites were challenged by their enemies, they stood before the Lord to seek for help. All of the people including the children and young ones stood before the Lord. Verse 13 reads, "All the men of Judah, with their wives and children and little ones, stood there before the LORD." Children were involved in the community prayer for deliverance. Further, Deuteronomy 30:1–3 reveals that God is not only concerned about the uprightness of adults; he is also concerned about the uprightness of children. This concern is not an afterthought in the community of Israel but central to their community life. Children were involved in all activities that enable them to observe what adults do and to ask questions regarding some of the godly practices and gain knowledge. For instance as the Israelites prepared to depart from Egypt, God commanded them to annually celebrate the Passover, and when their children asked them about the festival, they had the opportunity to explain God's deliverance (Exod 12:21–27). Integrating children in all of their faith activities enhanced social learning through observing what their parents and other adults did and helped children learn the origins of their faith. Hence, our engagement of children in all of our activities will enhance their learning within the social contexts of our day-to-day activities.

Community as a Fiery Furnace or Safe Space?

Although children have a special place in the community, there is great concern for their well-being because across the globe, children have become victims of

29. "Save the Children's Definition of Child Protection," Child Rights Resource Centre (10 December 2007).

violence and exploitation at home, in school, and in the community, the specific environments that are meant to protect them.[30] Global statistics indicate that many children face the risks of abuse and neglect. Estimates indicate that every year, one out of two children ages two to seventeen experience some form of violence; one third of students between ages eleven and fifteen have been bullied by peers; and 120 million girls have suffered some form of sexual violence before twenty years of age.[31] Further, studies indicate that one in three children experience emotional violence; while one in four children live with a mother who experiences intimate partner violence.[32] These statistics reveal that community is no longer a safe place for children.

Evidence indicates that a number of children in the African continent suffer. Allan Pence and his colleagues note that, "Of the children who are born, 65 percent will experience poverty, 14 million will be orphans affected by HIV/AIDS, directly and within their families, and one third will experience exclusion because of their gender or ethnicity."[33] The plight of African children calls for a communal response to provide them with a more conducive space in which to grow and thrive. These issues indicate that the community has become a furnace for children as opposed to a safety net. The community must provide a safe space and a welcoming heart to all children.

The community must provide a safe space and a welcoming heart to all children.

Protecting children is at the heart of God, and Christians need to be part of child protection. The Bible calls for protecting girls from being sold as slaves (Exod 21:7–11), protecting them from physical injuries (Exod 21:12, 18–19, 23–24), protecting them from rape (Deut 22:25–26); protecting them from prostitution (Lev 19:29); protecting them from divorce (Deut 22:13–15); protecting them from being sacrificed (Lev 18:21); and protecting them from discrimination

30. *A Review of Laws, Policies and Programmes for Elimination of Child Labour and Violence against Children in Kenya* (Nairobi, Kenya: African Network for the Prevention and Protection Against Child Abuse and Neglect and Global March Against Child Labour, 2018).

31. *Global Status Report on Violence against Children 2020* (Geneva: World Health Organization, 2020).

32. "A Familiar Face: Violence in the Lives of Children and Adolescents" (New York: United Nations Children's Fund, 2017); see also Marije Stoltenborgh, et al., "The Universality of Childhood Emotional Abuse: A Meta-Analysis of Worldwide Prevalence," *Journal of Aggression, Maltreatment & Trauma* 21, no. 8 (1 November 2012): 870–90.

33. Alan Pence, Judith Evans L, and Marito Garcia, "Introduction," in *Africa's Future, Africa's Challenge: Early Childhood Care and Development in Sub-Saharan Africa*, ed. Marito H. Garcia, Alan Pence, and Judith Evans (Eugene, OR: World Bank, 2008), 2.

(Gal 3:26–29).[34] Since protecting children is a biblical requirement, no child should be exposed to risks of abuse.

Conclusion

Children are precious and need to be cared for and protected by the community. Although there have been many cases of abuse and exploitation of children, protecting them should be at the forefront. *Ubuntu* as an African philosophy of humanness, caring, compassion, and respect should penetrate the community and enhance the positive values that promote care for children. When the children receive this kind of care, they will in turn transmit these values to the next generation. Care and compassion are not only African virtues but also biblical concepts. God calls his people to display true religion which includes caring for orphans and widows (Jas 1:27).

Bibliography

Ambwani, Vinita P. "Examining Gift-Giving Motives in a Cross-Cultural Context." PhD diss., Sprott School of Business, Carleton University, Ottawa, 2014. https://curve.carleton.ca/system/files/etd/28dbeb19-3e6b-4298-868c-1168ca1db7d3/etd_pdf/5126dc5a059632e6176f2206d545496d/ambwani-examininggiftgivingmotivesinacrosscultural.pdf.

Braitstein, Paula, Samuel Ayaya, David Ayuku, Allison DeLong, and Lukoye Atwoli. "Child Abuse and Neglect in Charitable Children's Institutions in Uasin Gishu County, Kenya: A Challenge of Context." In *Child Maltreatment in Residential Care*, edited by Adrian V. Rus, Sheri R. Parris, and Ecaterina Stativa, 337–56. Cham, Switzerland: Springer International AG, 2017. https://ecommons.aku.edu/eastafrica_fhs_mc_intern_med/164.

Bronfenbrenner, Urie. *The Ecology of Human Development: Experiments by Nature and Design*. Cambridge: Harvard University Press, 2009.

Bronfenbrenner, Urie, ed. *Making Human Beings Human: Bioecological Perspectives on Human Development*. Thousand Oaks: SAGE, 2004.

Broodryk, Johann. "Ubuntu African Life Coping Skills: Theory and Practice." Paper delivered at CCEAM Conference 12–17 October 2006, Lefkosia, Cyprus, 2006. https://documents.pub/document/ubuntu-school.html.

34. Jesudason B. Jeyaraj, "Biblical Perspectives on Children and Their Protection," in *Children at Risk: Issues and Challenges*, ed. Jesudason B. Jeyaraj (Delhi: ISPCK/CFCD, 2009), 1–31.

Clarke, Jackie R. "Different to 'Dust Collectors'? The Giving and Receiving of Experience Gifts." *Journal of Consumer Behaviour* 5, no. 6 (6 December 2006): 533–49. https://doi.org/10.1002/cb.201.

Engelbrecht, C., and M. I. Kasiram. "Original Research: The Role of Ubuntu in Families Living with Mental Illness in the Community." *South African Family Practice* 54, no. 5 (2012): 441–46.

Eze, Michael Onyebuchi. "What Is African Communitarianism? Against Consensus as a Regulative Ideal." *South African Journal of Philosophy* 27, no. 4 (1 January 2008): 386–99. https://doi.org/10.4314/sajpem.v27i4.31526.

"A Familiar Face: Violence in the Lives of Children and Adolescents." New York: United Nations Children's Fund, 2017.

"The Framework for the National Child Protection System in Kenya." Nairobi: National Council for Children Services (NCCS), 2011.

"Global Status Report on Violence against Children 2020." Geneva: World Health Organization, 2020. https://www.who.int/teams/social-determinants-of-health/violence-prevention/global-status-report-on-violence-against-children-2020.

Hillis, Susan, James Mercy, Adaugo Amobi, and Howard Kress. "Global Prevalence of Past-Year Violence Against Children: A Systematic Review and Minimum Estimates." *Pediatrics* 137, no. 3 (1 March 2016). https://doi.org/10.1542/peds.2015-4079.

Jeyaraj, Jesudason B. "Biblical Perspectives on Children and Their Protection." In *Children at Risk: Issues and Challenges*, edited by Jesudason B. Jeyaraj, Chris Gnanakan, Thomas Swaroop, and Phillips Prasad, 1–31. Delhi: ISPCK/CFCD, 2009.

Karenga, Maulana. "Black Religion." In *African American Religious Studies: An Interdisciplinary Anthology*, edited by Gayraud S. Wilmore, 271–300. Durham; London: Duke University Press, 1989.

Louw, Dirk J. "The African Concept of Ubuntu and Restorative Justice." In *Handbook of Restorative Justice: A Global Perspective*, edited by Dennis Sullivan and Larry Tifft, 161–73. New York: Routledge, 2008.

Mathews, Ben, Rosana Pacella, Michael P. Dunne, Marko Simunovic, and Cicely Marston. "Improving Measurement of Child Abuse and Neglect: A Systematic Review and Analysis of National Prevalence Studies." *PLOS ONE* 15, no. 1 (28 January 2020): e0227884. https://doi.org/10.1371/journal.pone.0227884.

Mbiti, John S. *Introduction to African Religion*. Nairobi: East African Educational Publishers, 1991.

Mercer, Joyce Ann. *Welcoming Children: A Practical Theology of Childhood*. Des Peres, MO: Chalice Press, 2005.

Miles, Glenn. "The Development of Children in Their Families and Communities." In *Celebrating Children: Equipping People Working with Children and Young People Living in Difficult Circumstances around the World*, edited by Glenn Miles and Josephine-Joy Wright, 33–39. Carlisle: Paternoster, 2006.

Pence, Alan, Judith L. Evans, and Marito Garcia. "Introduction." In *Africa's Future, Africa's Challenge: Early Childhood Care and Development in Sub-Saharan Africa*, edited by Marito H. Garcia, Alan Pence, and Judith Evans. Eugene, OR: World Bank, 2008.

"A Review of Laws, Policies and Programmes for Elimination of Child Labour and Violence against Children in Kenya." Nairobi: African Network for the Prevention and Protection against Child Abuse and Neglect (ANPPCAN) and Global March Against Child Labour, 2018. http://www.anppcan.org/wp-content/uploads/2014/11/Review-on-laws-policies-and-programmes-on-VAC.pdf.

"Save the Children's Definition of Child Protection." Child Rights Resource Centre (10 December 2007). https://resourcecentre.savethechildren.net/library/save-childrens-definition-child-protection.

Shipton, Parker MacDonald. *The Nature of Entrustment: Intimacy, Exchange, and the Sacred in Africa*. New Haven: Yale University Press, 2007.

Stoltenborgh, Marije, Marian J. Bakermans-Kranenburg, Lenneke R. A. Alink, and Marinus H. van IJzendoorn. "The Universality of Childhood Emotional Abuse: A Meta-Analysis of Worldwide Prevalence." *Journal of Aggression, Maltreatment & Trauma* 21, no. 8 (1 November 2012): 870–90. https://doi.org/10.1080/10926771.2012.708014.

Thamari, Mary. "Femininity, Gender Relations and Livelihood Vulnerabilities in Southwestern Kenya." PhD diss., University of Birmingham, 2019.

The United Nations Convention on the Rights of the Child. Dublin, Ireland: Children's Rights Alliance, 2010. http://www.childrensrights.ie/sites/default/files/submissions_reports/files/UNCRCEnglish_0.pdf.

Case Study:
Church and Village as Community

Saw Law Eh Htoo – Myanmarese

The Situation

One rainy day, I rode my motorcycle to meet with the churches in the Pathein area on their child development programs. While passing through a village, I saw three children playing near a rain gutter by a driveway. So I mentioned to the community leaders at the meeting that it is very dangerous for the children to do so. It was here that I heard the story of four siblings.

Due to the scarcity of jobs in the village and income too low to support her family, a teenage girl, just like other teenagers in the village, went to find work in the city. The promises of a glittering life and a good paying job soon faded for these teenagers who endure physical abuse by employers, exploitation of their labor, sexual assault, and emotional trauma. In hindsight, it seems that these are the normative problems faced by young people who migrate to the city for work.

To get out of this abusive cycle, the teenage girl married a man from a different religion, race, and social background. They were happy and returned to her village to start a new life. But after the birth of her fourth child, the husband got tired of the family. He left his family in the village and never came back. At that time the eldest girl was nine years old, and the others were a seven-year-old girl, a three-year-old boy, and a newborn baby boy. As the mother had to work on the farm every day to earn a living, she could not sufficiently be home for her children. Sadly, the newborn baby died due to lack of care. Depressed and traumatized by her home situation, the young mother abandoned her three children and once again left the village for the city.

Since then, the three siblings have lived by themselves. The elder girl takes care of her two younger siblings. She cooks, washes, and manages the house matters. The gutter beside the driveway in front of their house is a water source for them during the rainy season. There is no doubt that three children under the age of ten living and surviving by themselves without adult care in the house will surely have serious health, educational, economic, and social problems.

While the mother sometimes sent a monthly allowance to the relatives to help buy food, the amount was not sufficient. At times, the children rummaged through the scraps left by others or depended on the goodwill handouts of the villagers. The situation was indeed very serious in view of child kidnapping as the children had no protection against unscrupulous people in the area.

The Advocate

Pathein Myaungmya Association (PMA) is a Karen Baptist organization under the Myanmar Baptist Convention. Of the fourteen departments, the Christian Religious Education Department works for the holistic development of children and youths under the association churches. To support better and more wholesome development of children and youths in 302 churches, the PMA religious department develops, publishes, and distributes Sunday school lessons, relevant books, and literature in the Karen language, our mother tongue. PMA also collaborates with other organizations of similar vision and mission for the spiritual growth and needs of their children and youths. Together they provide training and evaluation and advocate for more effective teaching, training, social outreach, and ministry in these churches.

The village where the woman and her children live is about twenty-four kilometers (fifteen miles) from Pathien city and situated along the Ayeyarwaddy region in the southern part of Myanmar. This village has a population of only 260 people and was relocated because the government converted the former site into an industrial zone. The village has been adopted into the PMA community. In my context, the word "community" refers to the villages in the vicinity and environment where a PMA church is located. This particular village is not as developed as the other villages around it. Moreover, all of these communities have a common situation – most children and youths are no longer worshiping in the church because they have moved to big cities with their parents or migrated to another country to earn a living. As a result, the churches have fewer children and youths. In a number of families, the parents are working in the cities and have left their children to live with their grandparents, uncles, and aunts in the village.

The Community's Responsibility

As stated above, the word, "community" refers to villages in the vicinity and environment where a PMA church is located. Since the mother was not able to take responsibility for the children and had abandoned them, the community took up the role of caregiver. Members of the local church and other concerned individuals made an effort to address the children's needs such as fixing up the house, ensuring they have an adequate food supply, and financially providing the school fees and uniform for the second girl who was enrolled in a government school. The community also helped the youngest, a three-year-old boy, to attend a preschool that was operated by a PMA church. The preschool teachers were assigned to take extra care of the boy. The church leaders also asked the children's neighbors to be more alert and watchful of the children's situation.

Since the mother was not able to take responsibility for the children and had abandoned them, the community took up the role of caregiver.

On one occasion, the community leaders consulted each other and considered sending the children to an orphanage run by the PMA. However, the leaders could not get the mother's approval, and the children did not want to go. They were determined to stay together, no matter how dire the situation. As the eldest girl did not go to school, she was able to accompany her younger brother to the PMA preschool and take care of him. There the teachers let her learn with preschool children. They gave her the extra attention and taught her how to read and write. Even though she did not have the opportunity to learn at a government school, she could read and write basic words in her language.

Articles 20 and 27 of the United Nation Convention on the Rights of Children (UNCRC), state the following in cases where children are deprived of a family:

> Article 20: 1. A child temporarily or permanently deprived of his or her family environment, or in whose own best interests cannot be allowed to remain in that environment, shall be entitled to special protection and assistance provided by the State.
>
> 2. States Parties shall in accordance with their national laws ensure alternative care for such a child.
>
> 3. Such care could include, inter alia, foster placement, kafalah of Islamic law, adoption or if necessary placement in suitable institutions for the care of children. When considering solutions, due regard shall be paid to the desirability of continuity in a child's upbringing and to the child's ethnic, religious, cultural and linguistic background. . . .

> Article 27: 1. States Parties recognize the right of every child to a standard of living adequate for the child's physical, mental, spiritual, moral and social development.
>
> 2. The parent(s) or others responsible for the child have the primary responsibility to secure, within their abilities and financial capacities, the conditions of living necessary for the child's development.
>
> 3. States Parties, in accordance with national conditions and within their means, shall take appropriate measures to assist parents and others responsible for the child to implement this right and shall in case of need provide material assistance and support programmes, particularly with regard to nutrition, clothing and housing.
>
> 4. States Parties shall take all appropriate measures to secure the recovery of maintenance for the child from the parents or other persons having financial responsibility for the child, both within the State Party and from abroad. In particular, where the person having financial responsibility for the child lives in a State different from that of the child, States Parties shall promote the accession to international agreements or the conclusion of such agreements, as well as the making of other appropriate arrangements.[35]

Children are in risk situations when they are deprived of their rights to basic needs such as clean water, food, health care, housing, protection, and emotional nurture. In a developing country like Myanmar, where governmental structures are not able to cope with the demands of children's basic rights, the responsibility to care for these children falls on the community. The local church is the association of members who are cooperating and working for the prosperity and well-being of their community. The government recognizes the social work and arrangements of the local church to intervene on their behalf.

The local church is the association of members who are cooperating and working for the prosperity and well-being of their community.

The community looked for solutions to ensure the long-term well-being of these

35. "Convention on the Rights of the Child," United Nations Human Rights Office of the High Commissioner (2 Sept 1990). https://www.ohchr.org/en/professionalinterest/pages/crc.aspx.

three siblings. In the end, they made a decision that seemed best for all. The community leaders consulted the family members, and the children are now living with their grandparents. These children are still being supported financially and with supplies, and the arrangement is safer and more secure for these children. This is only a short-term solution as the grandparents are advanced in age. But for now, the community leaders think this is the best solution.

Dreaming of What Could Work

As I consider the life experiences of these three siblings, I dream of what could happen to make the local church into a living witness for Christ in a community of different faith. Perhaps churches could do the following:

1. Invite the community leaders, regardless of their faith, to meet, talk, and pray together as a community and to seek God's wisdom on how to best care for children and youths in need.
2. Lead the way and set up a model foster family care unit example of how locals can care and reach out to nurture and support children at risk.
3. Invite other Christian organizations to work with the community to provide educational facilities and centers to help children and youths in personal and skills development and to disciple them to be useful citizens of the country.
4. Support the development of families through training that nurtures and disciples the younger generation to testify to God's work in their lives.
5. Provide literacy programs for older members in the family so they can identify with and support the young children in their studies.
6. Seek opportunities for the adults to be gainfully employed in ways that ensure the family is financially stable.
7. Develop an intervention program to support children who are found to be at risk in whatever situation. This program could include child protection, health and nutrition, learning life skills, and trauma counseling for children who are abused, abandoned, or orphaned and are developmentally delayed.

8. Connect with government agencies to ask them to provide some form of healthcare for the children and expectant and young mothers.
9. Initiate a community center or location staffed by concerned individuals with whom the villagers can consult.
10. Work with the school leadership to keep them informed of the students from the particular village and notified if there are behavioral or learning concerns.

As I write, I am moved to say that the time is now! There should not be a "perhaps."

In the case study, the community leaders got together and decided the best solution for the three siblings. Their decision was a short-term solution and a reprieve for the mean time. The community leaders still have to make arrangements for long-term care. While help can be sought from outside organizations, it is the community that can and should be relied on for the long run. Hence, the local church must come together with the villagers and build a good support system or framework for children who cannot receive sufficient parental care.

Theologically, the body of Christ is a community. Culturally and contextually specific in Myanmar, "community" includes the villagers who are neighbors. God's story is not just about what God has done for us as individuals, but also about what he has done for others, and they include the whole village. In the tradition of my country from the religious point of view, church members are dependent on the local church to help them when they are in need, and the local church stands by its members in times of need. In the same way, the children who are God's gifts not only to their parents but also to the community will look to the church for support. It is the godly duty of the local church, and the church at large, to respond to their cries. These children are members of a community from birth, and they will play various and complex roles within it. In addition, they will grow up to be not only sons and daughters, but also husbands, wives, friends, neighbors, and citizens.[36] In responding to the children in need, we are actually discipling a nation.

God's story is not just about what God has done for us as individuals, but also about what he has done for others, and they include the whole village.

36. Marcia J. Bunge, "Historical Perspectives on Children in the Church," in *Toddling to the Kingdom*, ed. John Collier (London: The Child Theology Movement, 2009), 102.

Conclusion

On a Sunday in April 2019, I attended the youngest boy's preschool completion program. He was six years old. Three years previously, he and his siblings faced a grim future after being abandoned by their parents. During the worship service, the children made their presentations, and the three siblings sang this song:

Jesus Loves Me

Jesus loves me, this I know
For the Bible tells me so
Little ones to Him belong
They are weak, but He is strong
Yes, Jesus loves me
Yes, Jesus loves me
Yes, Jesus loves me
The Bible tells me so.

How wonderful would it be if all the children in our communities could sing this song. More specifically, that they could sing it with conviction and add another stanza,

Jesus loves me this I know
For my community tells me so
Little ones they love and care
Give them hope, the gospel share
Yes, Jesus loves me
Yes, Jesus loves me
Yes, Jesus loves me
My community tells me so.

Bibliography

Bunge, Marcia J. "Historical Perspectives on Children in the Church," in *Toddling to the Kingdom*, ed. John Collier 102. London: The Child Theology Movement, 2009.
"Convention on the Rights of the Child," United Nations Human Rights Office of the High Commissioner (2 Sept 1990). https://www.ohchr.org/en/professionalinterest/pages/crc.aspx.

Discussion Questions for Chapter 3

1. How can the famous African saying "It takes a village to raise a child" be understood from a biblical perspective? Are there examples from Scriptures that support this communal practice? Discuss.
2. Is the concept of *ubuntu* applicable to other contexts? What are its perceived advantages and disadvantages?
3. Many churches in Myanmar are consolidating their efforts to be a "living witness for Christ in a community of different faith" for children who have been abandoned by their parents. Can this practice be replicated in your own context? In what specific ways?

4

Advocated by Society

Society has a God-given responsibility to advocate for the well-being of children and families. Advocating for children and childhood surmounts to advocating for the sacredness of human life.

Global Critical Issue: Hubs of Light

Menchit Wong – Filipino

Patrick McDonald, founder of Viva,[1] tells of a vision he had while working with a local mission for street kids in South America. In his own words, Patrick saw

> a picture of a globe at night, majestically spinning in its expanse, but somehow "dark," . . . Then suddenly a few pin pricks of light sprang forth. Small, frail, insignificant. Then more. Then they started connecting in hubs of light, wheels of light covering an area. The light or atmosphere with each step somehow changed and got incrementally stronger, brighter.[2]

Patrick knew the vision was from God. It was God's response to his question, "What is the plan? How, Lord, do you hope to meet the needs of these children?" The vision represented a mass mobilization of congregations catalyzed into action, connected into networks, and equipped to a common standard. The vision was of community-based work that is concerted, comprehensive, and credible. Patrick McDonald saw that vision more than twenty years ago. Today, the vision is a reality. These networks, glowing as hubs of light, are connected across continents to shine as beacons of advocacy for children at risk.

Defend the Cause of Children

Advocacy as described in the Bible is pleading for or speaking up for and defending the cause of children. As we will read further in this chapter, what

1. Viva is an international children's charity who are passionate about releasing children from poverty and abuse. Viva has partnerships with thirty-eight local networks in twenty-seven countries around the world to ensure that children are safe, well and able to fulfil their God-given potential.

2. Patrick McDonald, interview, Berkley Center for Religion, Peace and World Affairs, Berkley, January 12, 2009. https://berkleycenter.georgetown.edu/interviews/a-discussion-with-patrick-mcdonald-founder-viva.

we seek is advocacy that goes beyond being spokespersons. Defending the cause of children is an all-embracing, holistic mission.[3]

- It is mission ***for*** children, meaning standing on their behalf to promote their dignity and rights, aware of their vulnerability and lack of power among adults.
- It is mission ***to*** children, meaning meeting their needs for holistic growth and providing opportunities to become all that God has purposed them to be.
- It is mission ***with*** children, meaning inviting, engaging, and supporting them in their purpose as active participants (not passive beneficiaries) in the work of God's mission.

Then and Now

In the first issue of the book *Understanding God's Heart for Children*,[4] the authors of the critical issues section of the chapter on "Well-being in Society," Ravi Jayakaran and Paul Stockley, cite reasons for the failure of society to fulfill its God-given responsibility. Society has a biblical mandate to provide for the well-being of children which includes ensuring their full participation in promoting their well-being, protecting them, and keeping them safe. To address children's deprivation, exclusion, and vulnerability, the Jayakaran and Stockley propose a framework of actions that the church make to fulfill this God-given responsibility. Their recommended key actions are the following: (1) Become conscious of the mandate to collaborate with institutions for health care, shelter, access to social services, safe drinking water, information, and safety; (2) Spread awareness and mobilize to advocate for access on behalf of the poor; (3) Identify high-risk areas where children are deprived, excluded, or vulnerable; and (4) Play the role of salt and light in society to influence the people in authority to act on behalf of the poor.

It is now more than ten years since the book *Understanding God's Heart for Children* was published. How has society addressed the issues and needs

3. For a deeper understanding and reflection, see Desiree Segura-April, Susan Hayes Greener, Dave Scott, Nicolas Panotto, and Menchit Wong, "Mission with Children at Risk: Lausanne Occasional Paper 66," Lausanne Movement Consultation on Children at Risk, Quito, Ecuador, 17–19 November 2014.

4. Ravi Jayakaran with Paul Stockley, "Well-being in Society: Critical Issues: Society Has a God-Given Responsibility for the Well-Being of Children and Families," in *Understanding God's Heart for Children: Toward a Biblical Framework*, eds. Douglas McConnell, Jennifer Orona, and Paul Stockley (Colorado Springs: Authentic, 2007), 131–36.

of children? This article revisits and reflects on the progress that has been made. It highlights a few global milestones of society in general and of the global evangelical church as a principal partner of society in advocating for the well-being of children.

Intentional Global Collaboration

One of the hallmarks of child advocacy in the last ten or fifteen years has been a resounding commitment all over the world to collaborate on behalf of children. International organizations such as the United Nations and faith-based networks and organizations and national governments and civil societies have recognized the truth that working interdependently, not independently, will help us comprehensively address the needs and vulnerabilities of more than 2.2 billion children. Let us revisit these milestones of global collaboration.

The United Nations Millennium Development Goals

The former United Nations general secretary Ban Ki-moon said that the United Nations Millennium Development Goals (UN MDGs) "generated new and innovative partnerships, galvanised public opinion and showed the immense value of setting ambitious goals."[5] Furthermore, the 2015 report on fulfilling the MDGs is a strong testimony to the power of intentional and committed global collaboration among international and local organizations, governments, civil society groups, and faith-based organizations. The UN MDG report in 2015 presented significant accomplishments that directly impact the protection and well-being of children including –

1. Eradicating extreme poverty and hunger[6]
2. Achieving universal primary education
3. Reducing child mortality[7]
4. Combating HIV/AIDS, malaria, and other diseases[8]

---

5. Ban Ki-moon in "The Millennium Development Goals Report 2015," United Nations (July 2015).

6. "The State of the World's Children 2019: Children, Food and Nutrition: Growing Well in a Changing World." UNICEF (October 2019).

7. "State of the World's Children 2019."

8. "Goal 3: Ensure healthy lives and promote well-being for all at all ages," United Nations Sustainable Development Goals (n.d.).

The Evangelical Church as Champion for Children

International organizations such as the United Nations have esteemed the role of religious organizations in advocating for the well-being of children and families. The values of churches and religious communities including peace, justice, social equality, and dignity of all persons are the same pillars that shaped the Convention on the Rights of the Child (CRC). Moreover, religious communities have deeply respected influential and entrenched local networks that enable them to address the needs of the most vulnerable groups more extensively and effectively than international organizations and national government sectors. The following quote from "The Kyoto Declaration: A multi-religious commitment to confront violence against children" is a profound expression of the importance of faith in advocacy and human development: "Our faith traditions take a holistic view of a child's life, and thus seek to uphold all the rights of the child in the context of its family, community, and the broader social, economic and political environment."[9]

International organizations such as the United Nations have esteemed the role of religious organizations in advocating for the well-being of children and families.

Given the shared values and philosophical framework between international organizations and faith communities for the dignity and importance of children, the last ten to fifteen years saw a rise in the concerted efforts of the global evangelical church community to further embrace and implement actions on behalf of children advocated by society at large. At the start of the millennium, as the International Convention on the Rights of the Child and the MDGs were embraced by almost all countries as the foundational instruments and governing frameworks for promoting children's well-being, the evangelical church rose to respond. Three observed factors contributed to the acceleration of the evangelical church's global advocacy efforts for the cause of children. First is an increased awareness of the biblical mandate of the church to minister to children and not just adults. Across the world, leaders of local churches, denominations, and theological institutions participated in vision casting and awareness raising on understanding God's heart for children.

---

9. "The Kyoto Declaration: A multi-religious commitment to confront violence against children," Religions for Peace Eighth World Assembly, Kyoto, Japan, August 2006, quoted in "Partnering with Religious Communities for Children," UNICEF (January 2012), 3.

Second is the local churches' greater understanding and acceptance of their key role in demonstrating the gospel by carrying out holistic ministry models with children and families in their communities. Where children had experienced domestic violence, local churches have increasingly recognized their role as a safe haven and a place where parents and families can reflect on Scripture and understand God's heart for children. In the light of the increased awareness of abuse, exploitation, and violence against children, child protection campaigns were launched in various regions and countries. More local churches and ministries serving children began to adopt and implement child protection policies to make churches and homes safer places for children. Prevention and intervention efforts expanded to children and families who were not part of the church or an organization's usual scope of beneficiaries, but who were in extremely vulnerable situations.

Third is the evidence of the rallying efforts of various Christian NGOs to influence the highest levels of church leadership and promote stronger collaboration to speak and act on issues of child abuse, exploitation, and neglect and children's agency in mission. The last ten to fifteen years saw the birth of networks and movements advocating for children among other global mission movements and among church groups and denominations, sharing experiences and resources on holistic ministry with children and young people.

Embracing Our Biblical Mandate

The 2010 Lausanne Forum for World Evangelization was a defining moment for the global evangelical church. The Lausanne Movement convened 4,200 leaders from 198 countries to frame the Cape Town Commitment (CTC) that provides both a sound and theological framework and practical roadmap of action for global mission including advocating for children at risk. The following are the commitments upon which they agreed:

> The CTC Call to Action on Children identified three specific commitments to fulfill its biblical mandate and holistic mission with children. The church commits to:
>
> 1. Take children seriously, through fresh biblical and theological enquiry that reflects on God's love and purpose for them and through them, and by rediscovering the profound significance for theology and mission of Jesus' provocative action in placing "a child in the midst"

2. Seek to train people and provide resources to meet the needs of children worldwide, wherever possible working with their families and communities, in the conviction that holistic ministry to and through each next generation of children and young people is a vital component of world mission
3. Expose, resist and take action against all abuse of children, including violence, exploitation, slavery, trafficking, prostitution, gender and ethnic discrimination, commercial targeting, and wilful neglect.[10]

Following the Cape Town Forum, in 2012 the Lausanne Movement created two issue groups on children to ensure that the Call to Action would result in practical and sustained implementation. In 2013, a missiology conference on recognizing children and youth as strategic partners in mission was convened by the 4/14 Window Global Movement.[11] Susan Greener of Wheaton College delivered a paper on mission to, for, and with children at risk which later became the framework for developing the "Lausanne Occasional Paper on Children-at-Risk" during the first global consultation of the Lausanne Movement on Children-at-Risk held in 2014 in Quito, Ecuador. This global consultation marked the first time that three influence groups composed of ministry practitioners, senior church leaders, and theologians, missiologists, and academic leaders gathered to commit to stronger unity and collaboration on behalf of vulnerable children around the world.[12]

In November 2013 during the 10th General Assembly, the members of the World Council of Churches (WCC), ecumenical partners, and related organizations affirmed their commitment to recognize the rights and dignity of children and signed a declaration called, "Putting Children at the Centre." In 2015, the WCC and UNICEF signed a partnership to work together to support children's rights with special focus on violence against children and climate change. And in 2016, the outcome of further consultative processes with WCC

10. Quoted in Desiree Segura-April, et. al., "Mission with Children at Risk," https://lausanne.org/content/lop/mission-children-risk-lop-66.

11. 4/14 Window Global Movement seeks to reach, rescue, root, and release children and young people to fulfill their divine purpose and become active partners in global mission. The 4/14 Window refers to a demographic window of opportunity for evangelism and discipleship and signifies the most open and receptive period in a person's life for spiritual transformation and development.

12. John Baxter Brown, ed., "Mission To, For and With Children-at-Risk: A Kairos Moment for the Whole Church Papers from the Lausanne Movement's Consultation on Children-at-Risk," Quito, Ecuador, November 2014, https://lausanne.org/content/statement/quito-call-to-action-on-children-at-risk.

partners and children produced the WCC resource "Churches' Commitments to Children." This document outlines WCC's three commitments to children and presents three specific actions and strategies that any local church can use to respond to the needs and challenges impacting children: (1) Promote child protection through church communities; (2) Promote meaningful participation by children and adolescents; and (3) Raise church voices for intergenerational climate justice, supporting initiatives for and with children and adolescents.[13]

Equipping the Global Church for Holistic Ministry

In sharp contrast to the 1980s and early 1990s when the children's agenda was one of the least discussed topics at mission conferences and holistic and contextual ministry with children was one of the least available ministry resources, there has been a shift of interest in the last two decades. In the last ten to fifteen years, the ministries and organizations listed above formed several partnerships to effectively equip the global church with solid theological grounding and sound knowledge, resource toolkits, and innovative approaches to respond to the needs of children all over the world. Once again, commitment to a shared agenda and intentional collaboration were critical factors that encouraged equipping on a global scale. Here are a few examples.

First, the Global Children's Forum created the Max7 website that contains a massive storehouse of children's ministry resources in various language translations, all open-sourced and easy to access. Second in 2007, leaders of denominations, children's ministry organizations, and theological institutions formed a global alliance to advance programs in holistic child development. This collaboration is more popularly known as the Holistic Child Development (HCD) Global Alliance. The fruit of this global collaboration has been the multiplication of formal education on holistic child development in seminaries and academic institutions around the world. Graduates have implemented various forms of local and contextualized training, curriculum, educational resources, and research with grassroots ministry practitioners. Third, a successful national initiative by Christians began in Ukraine in 2010. They envisioned every orphan child belonging to a permanent family. The combined efforts of participating Christian non-government organizations and thousands of churches from hundreds of denominations resulted in a significant increase in national adoptions and family-based care for orphans

13. "Churches' Commitments to Children: Churches Uniting for Children in the Pilgrimage of Justice and Peace," World Council of Churches, Geneva (March 2017).

and vulnerable children.[14] This national initiative in Ukraine gave birth to the movement World Without Orphans (WWO) which launched in 2015.

Dealing with All Abuse of Children

Beyond vision casting, equipping, and building collaboration, the proof of genuine advocacy is evidence-based practice and strategic and sustained action. The third commitment of the Lausanne Cape Town Commitment Call to Action on Children is to expose, resist, and take action against all abuse of children. Abuse includes violence, exploitation, slavery, trafficking, prostitution, gender and ethnic discrimination, commercial targeting, and willful neglect. And with the continuing global threat posed by the COVID-19 pandemic, more grim realities are being experienced by vulnerable children. The 2020 UNICEF publication "Protecting Children from Violence in the Time of COVID-19: Disruptions in Prevention and Response Services" reports that due to the pandemic, violence prevention and response services have been disrupted, affecting 1.8 billion children in 104 countries.[15] The 2020 study reports that one of the greatest challenges is the inability to carry out assessments of alleged child maltreatment since home visits were stopped due to lockdowns. Furthermore, the lockdowns have largely led to unemployment, significant loss of income, hunger, parental burnout, increase in parental alcohol consumption and accompanying increases in children's mental health issues.

Overall, research has shown that stressed parents are more likely to respond to their children's anxious behaviors or demands in aggressive or abusive ways. A highly stressed home environment is often a major predictor of physical abuse and neglect of children.[16] This risk situation leads to graver risk when children are exploited through child pornography to provide income for the family.

How have the church and society responded? In the example below, we identify critical actions such as research, strategic collaboration, and systematic implementation from global advocacy to local community implementation,

---

14. "World Without Orphans Global Forum for a World Without Orphans 2016 Report" (12 March 2016).

15. "Protecting Children from Violence in the Time of COVID-19: Disruptions in Prevention and Response Services," UNICEF (August 2020).

16. N. Pereda and D. A. Díaz-Faes, "Family Violence Against Children in the Wake of COVID-19 Pandemic: A Review of Current Perspectives and Risk Factors," *Child and Adolescent Psychiatry and Mental Health* 14, no. 40 (20 October 2020).

all of which have contributed to the current global resolve against abuse and violence against children.

Online sexual exploitation of children is a form of abuse that is a grave and growing threat that demands concerted advocacy and urgent action. Research conducted by the International Justice Mission in the Philippines in 2019 found that in three years, 2016–2019, the estimated prevalence rate of Internet-based child sexual exploitation in the Philippines more than tripled.[17] The Philippines is a global hotspot in online sexual exploitation of children. For instance, one woman was arrested and sentenced to twenty years in prison for human trafficking. She had forced her four young children to serve pedophiles from other countries known as Internet "customers." The ongoing and strong partnership of IJM with several governments, many other civil society organizations, Christian ministries, and local churches are all contributing to increasing the number of rescues and restorative services for child victims and bringing perpetrators to justice.

Long Journey Ahead

As we revisit the last ten to fifteen years and acknowledge what has taken place in advocacy for children, our response is gratefulness and hope. We are grateful to the Lord for the milestones. We see hubs of light in the forms of intentional collaborations and sustained actions all around the world. There is fresh inquiry into God's heart for children, and the global church is embracing the biblical mandate to care for children's well-being. A plethora of resources are now available for equipping in holistic ministry to, for, and with children. Children's voices can be heard and are represented in global conferences convened by civil society organizations and faith-based organizations. And there is evidence-based practice to strengthen efforts at child survival, child protection, child development, and upholding children's rights.

But we acknowledge that the sheer number of vulnerable children in the world and the complex sociopolitical issues surrounding them confront us and tell us that much more must be done. The three commitments of the church

---

17. "Online Sexual Exploitation of Children in the Philippines: Analysis and Recommendations for Governments, Industry and Civil Society." International Justice Mission (May 2020). This groundbreaking study was conducted to stop the abuse, heal the scars, end the impunity, and forge a global resolve to end this crime. The study was carried out in partnership with the Philippine government and a variety of stakeholders and under the U.S.-Philippines Child Protection Compact (CPC) partnership between the U.S. Department of State Office to Monitor and Combat Trafficking in Persons and the Government of the Philippines.

for the well-being, protection, and kingdom agency of children reflected in the Lausanne Cape Town Commitment continue to serve as our compass in guiding our mobilization and working together.

Bibliography

Brown, John Baxter, ed. "Mission To, For and With Children-at-Risk: A Kairos Moment for the Whole Church," Papers from the Lausanne Movement's Consultation on Children-at-Risk, Quito, Ecuador, 17–19 November 2014, unpublished. https://lausanne.org/content/statement/quito-call-to-action-on-children-at-risk.

Cameron, Julia, ed. *The Cape Town Commitment: A Confession of Faith and a Call to Action*. Peabody, MA: Hendrickson, 2011. The Cape Town Commitment is available at the Lausane Movement website: https://www.lausanne.org/content/ctcommitment.

"Churches' Commitments to Children: Churches Uniting for Children in the Pilgrimage of Justice and Peace." World Council of Churches, Geneva (March 2017). https://www.oikoumene.org/sites/default/files/Document/CommitmentsToChildren_WCC_ENG.pdf.

"Goal 3: Ensure healthy lives and promote well-being for all at all ages." United Nations Sustainable Development Goals (n.d.). https://www.un.org/sustainabledevelopment/health/.

McConnell, Douglas, Jennifer Orona, and Paul Stockley, eds. *Understanding God's Heart for Children: Toward a Biblical Framework*. Colorado Springs: Authentic, 2007.

"The Millennium Development Goals Report 2015," United Nations (July 2015). https://www.un.org/millenniumgoals/2015_MDG_Report/pdf/MDG%202015%20rev%20(July%201).pdf.

"Online Sexual Exploitation of Children in the Philippines: Analysis and Recommendations for Governments, Industry and Civil Society." IJM International Justice Mission (May 2020). https://www.ijm.org/vawc/blog/osec-study.

"Partnering with Religious Communities for Children." UNICEF (January 2012). https://jliflc.com/resources/partnering-with-religious-communities-for-children/.

Pereda, N., and D. A. Díaz-Faes. "Family Violence Against Children in the Wake of COVID-19 Pandemic: A Review of Current Perspectives and Risk Factors." *Child and Adolescent Psychiatry and Mental Health* 14, no. 40 (20 October 2020). https://capmh.biomedcentral.com/articles/10.1186/s13034-020-00347-1#Sec2.

"Protecting Children from Violence in the Time of COVID-19: Disruptions in Prevention and Response Services." UNICEF (August 2020). https://www.unicef.org/reports/protecting-children-from-violence-covid-19-disruptions-in-prevention-and-response-services-2020.

Segura-April, Desiree, Susan Hayes Greener, Dave Scott, Nicolas Panotto, and Menchit Wong. "Mission with Children at Risk: Lausanne Occasional Paper 66." Lausanne Movement Consultation on Children at Risk, Quito, Ecuador, 17–19 November 2014. https://www.lausanne.org/content/lop/mission-children-risk-lop-66.

"The State of the World's Children 2019: Children, Food and Nutrition: Growing Well in a Changing World." UNICEF (October 2019). https://www.unicef.org/reports/state-of-worlds-children-2019.

"World Without Orphans Global Forum for a World Without Orphans 2016 Report" (12 March 2016). https://wwoforum.org/report.

Biblical and Theological Response:

Children, Advocacy, and the Kingdom of God

Bradley Thompson – Indian

Introduction

When Radha was around ten years old,[18] her parents were tricked by family friends who promised that they would get her a job in the city, but she ended up being trafficked and exploited in Mumbai. Radha was eventually rescued when she was around fourteen years old, but she was diagnosed with HIV and two other sexually transmitted infections. She was taken to meet her family, but they rejected her fearing stigma and discrimination by their local community. Radha was admitted to a government hospital in Chennai for treatment and was later supported by a project implemented by World Vision which focuses on care for women and children affected by HIV and AIDS.

I first met Radha in 1996, and my interactions with her were transformative for me, to say the least. I was amazed at her resilience and inner strength. But she also raised several questions with which I have struggled. Her experience made me think about the role of the church and Christian organizations in preventing the exploitation of children and in responding to issues of children like Radha in India and worldwide. My reflections in this article stem from those questions I had after meeting Radha, and also my work with vulnerable children, families, and communities over the last two decades. This article highlights a biblical basis for "advocated by society" that is focused on the kingdom of God for a framework for advocacy to, for, and with vulnerable children and also reflects on issues related to the church and Christian organizations in advocating for vulnerable children in the Indian context.

Building on a Strong Foundation

Advocacy to, for, and with children must be grounded in the character of God. This point was brought out very clearly in the first volume of *Understanding*

18. Name changed for privacy.

God's Heart for Children. The authors of the biblical reflection for the "Well-being in Society" chapter focus on the theme that love needs to be genuine and relational. Their thesis states, "to achieve this, we need to first understand God's character of love and justice to then understand His call to respond to the issues of vulnerable children."[19] The authors further discuss the need to recognize the God-given responsibility of governments and societal institutions to be just and ensure justice for the weakest and most vulnerable people in society.

Kingdom of God: The Basis of Child-Focused Advocacy

If the vulnerability of children is a concern of the heart of God, then advocacy for, to, and with children is an important expression of the kingdom of God.

Jesus and the Kingdom of God

The kingdom of God was at the core of Jesus's earthly ministry.[20] The revelation of Jesus Christ and his proclamation of God's kingdom are important keys to how we understand and express the theology of transformation in the lives of the most vulnerable children, families, and communities.

If the vulnerability of children is a concern of the heart of God, then advocacy for, to, and with children is an important expression of the kingdom of God.

The reality of God's kingdom is not fully expressed by his people if there is little transformation in the lives of the weak and vulnerable in the society in which they live. Jesus pointed to children as examples to be followed to enter the kingdom of God (Mark 10:13–16). The well-being of children is an expression of God's kingdom on the earth. Advocacy in this context should then be based on strong biblical foundations built on the personhood and revelation of Jesus Christ and his kingdom in which justice and righteousness flow like a river. Advocacy to, for, and with

19. Wendy Sanders, Tri Budiardo, and Paul Stockley, "Let Love Be Genuine and Relational," in *Understanding God's Heart for Children: Toward a Biblical Framework*, eds. Douglas McConnell, Jennifer Orona, and Paul Stockley (Colorado Springs: Authentic, 2007), 135.

20. Arthur F. Glasser, et al., *Announcing the Kingdom: The Story of God's Mission in the Bible* (Grand Rapids MI: Baker Academic, 2003).

the most vulnerable children have their foundational basis in how we as the church understand and apply the principles of the kingdom of God.

This kingdom needs to be the focus of our goals, and we have been given an invitation by God to a three-fold ministry in society – to pray to see the kingdom come, to proclaim the kingdom, and to demonstrate the kingdom (Matt 3:1–2; 4:17; 6:10). We will explore the Bible to see how this kingdom focus can apply in the context of vulnerable children in the majority world.

Praying the Kingdom

The phrase "your kingdom come" from the Lord's Prayer is a heart cry to see the government of God expressed in our lives, homes, families, and communities and to impact societies (Matt 6:10). It is a cry to see justice, righteousness, and peace on the earth through the establishment of God's kingdom. Prayer is central to transformation. Transformation in the lives of the poor does not happen by the mere efforts of people but by God's Spirit working in and through people. As practitioners, we can be easily tempted to "get in there and solve the problems" through our own efforts, forgetting the power that is available to us through prayer.

Prayer is central to transformation.

Second Chronicles 7:14 gives us God's perspective on how problems of the land can be solved: "if my people, who are called by my name, will humble themselves and pray and seek my face and turn from their wicked ways, then I will hear from heaven, and I will forgive their sin and will heal their land." We need the power and blessing of God to heal our communities, society, and countries to be places where children thrive. This blessing comes when the people of God get together, pray, and act!

Proclaiming the Kingdom

Jesus proclaimed that the kingdom of God prophesized in the Old Testament was "at hand" beginning with his ministry. Jesus called people to repentance so they could experience God's kingdom. The kingdom of God is to be proclaimed so that God's rule can be established on the earth. Restored relationships with God and each other are key to the message of the kingdom. The prophetic call is for justice and righteousness to flow like a river (Amos 5:24). The church in particular and society in general have a God-given mandate to

Restored relationships with God and each other are key to the message of the kingdom.

seek justice and pursue righteousness. God is not interested in worship at the neglect of justice and righteousness.

In the New Testament, we see in the Gospels several passages that show the care of Jesus for children and the position he accorded them (Mark 10:14–16; Luke 18:16). Children were not only included in the ministry of Jesus but also treated compassionately. Jesus says in Mark 10:14, "Let the little children come to me, and do not hinder them, for the kingdom of God belongs to such as these." In the Epistles, the people of God are instructed to care for the poor and the needy (2 Cor 9:8–9; Jas 1:27). Caring for orphans was a significant and integral part of the early Christian community.[21]

God calls his people as a community to work together to respond to the needs of the most vulnerable children in society. The church has a prophetic mandate to work with institutions in society to advocate for justice in the lives of the vulnerable children.

Demonstrating the Kingdom

The kingdom not only needs to be proclaimed. It also needs to be demonstrated. Bryant Myers in his book *Walking with the Poor: Principles and Practice of Transformational Development* talks about the importance of witness through "life, word, sign, and deed."[22] The church is called to be salt and light in the world, pursuing a lifestyle that reflects the kingdom of God. This pursuit includes ensuring that the poor, weak, and vulnerable are not oppressed or exploited but are valued and cherished and their basic needs are met. The following passage from the "Oxford Declaration on Christian Faith and Economics" highlights this issue well:

> [Biblical] justice is related particularly to what is due to groups such as the poor, widows, orphans, resident aliens, wage earners and slaves. The common link among these groups is powerlessness

---

21. Josephine-Joy Wright and Glenn Miles, "Holistic Mission to Children," in *Celebrating Children: Equipping People Working with Children and Young People Living in Difficult Circumstances Around the World*, ed. Glenn Miles and Josephine-Joy Wright (Carlisle: Paternoster, 2003), 143–49.

22. Bryant L. Myers, *Walking with the Poor: Principles and Practices of Transformational Development* (New York: Orbis, 2011), 95.

> by virtue of economic and social needs. The justice called for is to restore these groups to the provision that God intends for them.[23]

God's kingdom community is called to live out justice and righteousness. Justice includes dealing with social systems that are broken, particularly in terms of addressing issues faced by the poor and vulnerable, including children. The restoration of broken relationships with God and one other in the context of community is critical to address the poverty and injustice that affect so many children.[24] It is also important to realize that the kingdom of God is not limited to the individual's salvation. The kingdom also encompasses social systems because these systems are created and stewarded by people and need to be restored to God's kingdom order.[25]

Working across social systems is vital to see transformation in practice. The church must engage in collaboration and multi-stakeholder partnerships to restore broken relationships and make this world a better place for children.

Children as Agents of the Kingdom

God sometimes uses children to accomplish his work. The Bible clearly shows children as active agents in God's kingdom and plan. For instance Psalm 8:2 talks about God's strategy to silence the enemy through the praises of babies. He called Samuel, Daniel, Jeremiah, David, and Josiah, all at young ages, to transform nations. If we are to make an impact, we need to think seriously about how we can recognize and empower children as agents of transformation. The church needs to think about strategies to empower children to speak up and use their God-given gifts to bring about change in various arenas of influence – the home, school, community, church, and society.

But how can we effectively mobilize the church to fulfill our kingdom roles in society of being the voice that speaks out, the hands that reach across, and the beautiful feet to find the lost children? Some specific contextual challenges can inform such a venture. But for a glint of the rewards, we only have to be reminded of how often God has used children to reach out and find us.

---

23. "The Oxford Declaration on Christian Faith and Economics," in *Mission as Transformation* (Oxford: Regnum Books International, 1990), 325.

24. Myers, *Walking with the Poor.*

25. Myers.

Indian Christian Theology

A significant proportion (29.5 percent) of the population in India is below fourteen years of age.[26] Though children, the family, and education are held in high esteem from cultural and religious perspectives, the actual status of children seems contradictory.[27] Many children live in conditions of extreme poverty and vulnerability. Efforts have been made to strengthen mission to children through various movements that address basic rights and needs including protection and care. While the church has initiated various responses to serve the most vulnerable children, the needs are still significant.

What will it take to mobilize the Indian church to be a catalyst in society for the well-being of children? Will a contextual approach to understanding the kingdom mandate and engaging the church make a difference in how the kingdom of God is practically demonstrated to enable the fullness of life for vulnerable children? Advocacy efforts to, for, and with vulnerable children need to tap into the contextual understanding of Christian faith and expression of God's kingdom to mobilize the church and societal actors to work together to make a difference.

> Advocacy efforts to, for, and with vulnerable children need to tap into the contextual understanding of Christian faith.

A story is often told of Sadhu Sundar Singh and his observation of a high caste Hindu who refused to drink water from the cup of a Westerner even though he was dying of thirst. The man eventually was given water in his own cup which was lying nearby, and he drank from it.[28] Sadhu observed that though the man needed the water desperately, he was willing to drink it only when it was offered in a cup he recognized. This story has implications for how the church raises and addresses the issues of children and engages in child-focused advocacy in India. Some critical considerations include the following:

- Mobilizing the church to advocate for children in Indian society will require a deeper understanding of children and reflection on

26. "Sample Registration System Statistical Report 2011," Office of the Registrar General India, New Delhi (2011).

27. Chris Gnanakan, "1 Peter," *South Asia Bible Commentary: A One-Volume Commentary on the Whole Bible*, eds. Brian Wintle, et al. (Udaipur: Open Door; Carlisle, UK: Langham Partnership; Grand Rapids: Zondervan, 2015), 1742.

28. Swami Dayanand Bharati, *Living Water and Indian Bowl*, rev. ed. (Pasadena: William Carey Library, 2004).

the kingdom of God in the Indian context and how children need to be cared and advocated for in a pluralistic society.
- The well-being of children is often a great rallying theme. In spite of pluralistic or fundamentalist beliefs, the issues children face can become a mobilizing platform for institutions and governments to work together to address these issues.
- The diverse context of India's existing traditions, the effects of colonization, and the caste oppression will require multiple approaches aimed at embedding and addressing child-focused advocacy issues within existing theological narratives.[29]
- Christ's claims about himself and the kingdom of God and the integration of work and worship must be foundational to effectively address injustice, the exploitation of children, and poverty.[30]
- The importance of engaging across dividing lines needs to be understood. Effective advocacy is achieved through multi-stakeholder engagements and partnerships.

Implications and Potential Strategies

Menchit Wong raises critical issues that require further collaboration to ensure a strategic and sustained response to justice and exploitation issues. The call is for holistic mission to, for, and with children. Listening to children is a global research opportunity, as is exploring opportunities for innovative advocacy in the public square using social media.

As people of faith, we are called to be salt and light, that is to be catalysts in society expressing God's kingdom and addressing issues faced by the children who are often the weakest and most vulnerable citizens. We need to collaborate with global institutions and advocate for and with children, increase allocation of funding for children's ministries, and mobilize the church for holistic mission to and with children. The importance of recognizing the agency of children in

29. See Bharati, *Living Water*; see also Kirsteen Kim, "India," in *An Introduction to Third World Theologies*, ed. John Parratt (Cambridge: Cambridge University Press, 2004), 97.

30. Ken R. Gnanakan, "Biblical Theology in the Indian Context," in *The Bible and Theology in Asian Contexts: An Evangelical Perspective on Asian Theology*, eds. Bong Rin Ro and Ruth Eshenaur (Seoul: Word of Life Press and Asia Theological Association, 1984), 203–16. See also Asian Evangelical Theologians, "The Bible and Theology in Asia Today: Declaration of The Sixth Asia Theological Association Theological Consultation," in *The Bible and Theology in Asian Contexts: An Evangelical Perspective on Asian Theology*, eds. Bong Rin Ro and Ruth Eshenaur (Seoul: Asian Theological Association, 1984), 3–20.

advocacy will include challenging worldviews and exploring what it means to empower children for action.

Conclusion

God's call to the people of faith and society in general is to pray, proclaim, and demonstrate kingdom principles and to empower children to be change agents in preventing and mitigating the negative impacts of the broken social, political, and economic systems that disadvantage them. Opportunities exist and must be sought to strengthen perspectives and approaches to address the issues. The church in India and around the world has a God-given mandate to not only address the needs of the children in their immediate care, but also to collaborate with governments and other institutions to ensure justice and well-being for vulnerable children everywhere.

Bibliography

Amaladoss, Michael. *The Asian Jesus*. Maryknoll, NY: Orbis, 2006.

Bharati, Swami Dayanand. *Living Water and Indian Bowl*. Rev. ed. Pasadena: William Carey Library, 2004.

Glasser, Arthur F., Charles E. Van Engen, Dean S. Gilliland, and Shawn B. Redford. *Announcing the Kingdom: The Story of God's Mission in the Bible*. Grand Rapids, MI: Baker Academic, 2003.

Gnanakan, Chris. "1 Peter," *South Asia Bible Commentary: A One-Volume Commentary on the Whole Bible*. Edited by Brian Wintle, Havilah Dharmaraj, Jesudason Baskar Jeyaraj, Paul Swarup, Jacob Cherian, and Finny Philip, 1741–8. Udaipur: Open Door; Carlisle, UK: Langham Partnership; Grand Rapids: Zondervan, 2015.

Gnanakan, Ken R. "Biblical Theology in the Indian Context." In *The Bible and Theology in Asian Contexts: An Evangelical Perspective on Asian Theology*, edited by Bong Rin Ro and Ruth Eshenaur, 203–16. Seoul: Word of Life Press and Asia Theological Association, 1984.

Kim, Kirsteen. "India." In *An Introduction to Third World Theologies*, edited by John Parratt, 44–73. Cambridge: Cambridge University Press, 2004.

Myers, Bryant L. *Walking with the Poor: Principles and Practices of Transformational Development*. New York: Orbis, 2011.

"The Oxford Declaration on Christian Faith and Economics." In *Mission as Transformation*, 325. Oxford: Regnum Books International, 1990.

"Sample Registration System Statistical Report 2011." Office of the Registrar General India. New Delhi, 2011. https://www.censusindia.gov.in/vital_statistics/SRS_Report/1Contents%202011.pdf.

Sanders, Wendy, Tri Budiardo, and Paul Stockley. "Let Love Be Genuine and Relational." In *Understanding God's Heart for Children: Toward a Biblical Framework*, edited by Douglas McConnell, Jennifer Orona, and Paul Stockley, 135–51. Colorado Springs: Authentic, 2007.

Wright, Josephine-Joy, and Glenn Miles. "Holistic Mission to Children." In *Celebrating Children: Equipping People Working with Children and Young People Living in Difficult Circumstances Around the World*, edited by Glenn Miles and Josephine-Joy Wright, 143–49. Carlisle: Paternoster, 2003.

Case Study:
I Exist, I Am a Citizen

Carmen Alvarez González – Costa Rican

I exist; I want my name to be written in the book of life.

(nine-year-old boy with no birth registration whose words inspired the program)

More than six hundred thousand children and adolescents in Guatemala are being sold for illegal adoption and are trapped in trafficking networks for sexual and labor exploitation. A major contributor to this abuse is that many children lack a valid identity document. Viva Network Guatemala (Red Viva) was confronted by the fact that these children exist and have lives. So in 2012, they started the advocacy program "I exist, I am a citizen." The aim is for each child to have her or his own identity document and thereby gain access to basic services that would normally be their right such as education, health care, and other social programs, services that help them live well, safely, and enabled to develop the potential that God gave each one.

I exist; I want my name to be written in the book of life.

One Girl's Fight to Be Registered

Yolanda is a five-year-old girl who lives with her parents in Ciudad Quetzal, twenty-five kilometers from the capital city in the municipality of San Juan Sacatepéquez, Guatemala. She cannot go to school as she lacks a valid ID.

Yolanda's mother is Felisa, the daughter of a Honduran woman who sold her to a family. Felisa was never registered as a citizen, either in Honduras nor in Guatemala. Over time, Felisa began a relationship and had a daughter, Yolanda. When Yolanda was born, they tried to register her birth but could not. At the Registro Nacional de Personas (RENAP), they told Felisa that she first had to do an extemporaneous registration for herself and that she would need to hire a notary and find two witnesses to her own birth. Such a process was expensive, way beyond the means of their extreme poverty. The RENAP office advised the Felisa to ask Red Viva for support. The process of searching for the family validation began in 2013, and in September 2014, the registration process for Felisa was completed.

Once Felisa was registered, Yolanda's registration could begin. However, it was a process that took a year to complete. Yolanda's birth had been attended by a midwife. So the case had to be done through the courts. The judge ordered DNA and dental tests to establish the legal affiliation between Yolanda and Felisa. The court also had to determine Yolanda's calendar age and thus define a legal age. After four hearings, Yolanda's official registration was finalized in October 2015 in the city of Mixco. In 2016, a place was confirmed for Yolanda to study in the first grade of primary school.

> "I give thanks to Red Viva in Guatemala. If it hadn't been for them, I would have had to pay about US$700 to register Yolanda. We don't have that kind of money. They also helped me with Yolanda's enrolment at school, and now she is going to study. May God bless you."– Felisa

Consequences of Non-Registered Children

Birth registration by itself is the access pass to fundamental human rights. For the child it constitutes the first step toward citizenship, to being identifiably present in society. At the same time, birth registration allows the child to have access to basic services such as education and health care; access to justice, state subsidies, and the ability to participate in social life; access to real opportunities and the ability to exercise their fundamental rights.

In contrast, non-registration of children creates conditions for illegal adoption and for the sale and trafficking of children, violating all the rights that guarantee the development of all the potential that God gave so that they may have life and have it in abundance.

In InnocentiDigest # 9, UNICEF highlights that despite the commitments made by countries at a global level to protect and create safe environments for children, they are still in danger of exploitation and abuse, especially children without birth registration. "A growing trend in the exploitation of children is the trafficking of children into prostitution or other contemporary forms of slavery, often under the false guise of child domestic labor. The trafficking of children has reached alarming dimensions. Several million are currently trapped in the criminal networks of this trade."[31]

Added to this is the emotional impact that non-registration has on children, particularly the impact on their identity, a social violation brought about by the lack of social and governmental sensitivity to their condition. Children who do not have birth registration can usually stay in school for one to three months, then they are expelled. Often their situation is exacerbated by bullying during their short stay in school. There are documented cases of children who have attempted suicide due to unbearable and constant emotional abuse.

In summary, the consequences of missing birth registrations are that children are unprotected by the system and invisible to society and government. They are more likely to be victims of trafficking for sexual exploitation and child labor. They are constantly rejected by society even to the point of attempting suicide because of the emotional damage. These populations are exposed to greater risk and easily fall into the networks of unaccompanied migrant children, children with disabilities, children living on the street, and vulnerable girls.

Overcoming Barriers to Child Registration

The main barriers that prevent children from being registered shortly after birth include a hospital system with limited on-site birth registration resources; registration centers that are a distance away; a cultural attitude that attributes little importance to timely birth registration; and endemic poverty. More than half of Guatemalans live on less than $2 a day, and even when donations are received to pay for the more expensive late registration, the money can get diverted to the costs of everyday living. Moreover, government policies are not particularly supportive. The different offices involved in registration are often poorly integrated, and late registration charges are high.

Faced with this situation, the working group round table between the government RENAP office and the Viva Guatemala team identified five key actions that need to be taken to address the problem and increase timely registration:

1. Lobbying decision makers in the central government to eliminate fines for late registration, to make timely registration a service

31. UNICEF Launch of Innocenti Digest 9 "Birth Registration: Right from the Start", 2002 https://www.unicef-irc.org/media-centre/press-kit/digest9/?article=531&page=11.

without charge to the citizen, and to change public policies to promote interinstitutional coordination.

2. Establishing offices for timely registration in each hospital in the country.
3. Training midwives to facilitate timely birth registration.
4. Creating media campaigns to promote registration and involving both boys and girls (promotion among peers). These campaigns included television spots, radio spots, pamphlets and posters in key places, and targeted meetings with government authorities to express registration needs and the day-to-day reality of the challenges. In addition, awareness forums were held with other decision makers such as directors of schools, health centers, local churches and with presidential candidates so that the registration of children would be included in their operational plans.
5. Accompanying families through the birth registration process to the point where they hold the birth certificate.

This joint effort included the participation of different key players, and UNICEF played a very important role. Round tables were organized, and each participant took on a role to achieve successful results. Viva's role focused on lobbying RENAP authorities to regulate and put policies into practice. Agreements and letters of commitment were signed. Compliance with these commitments was monitored, and Viva was the entity that implemented the program. This has been a very successful joint project. The local church and Viva network played very important roles in the awareness campaign, detecting cases and accompanying families through the process. The central government reviewed and updated registration and under registration policies. Municipal governments defined more efficient mechanisms to expedite procedures. The technical team did a comprehensive job in successfully identifying the families and the appropriate connections to complete the legal registration process.

Lobbying decision makers in the central government to eliminate fines for late registration, to make timely registration a service without charge to the citizen, and to change public policies to promote interinstitutional coordination.

To date, registry offices have been newly established in forty of the forty-three hospitals in the Guatemalan national health system. Three hundred and eighty midwives have been made aware of the problem and trained in timely registration. These community midwives were trained to be able to register a child immediately after birth in the citizen registry and gain the documentation. This action by midwives enables parents to avoid having to return to register their children.

Three hundred and eighty midwives have been made aware of the problem and trained in timely registration.

About 3,784 children and adults without certificates have been registered. Some registration cases involved significant challenges; for example, three generations had to be registered at the same time to achieve the registration of a single child, a process that took one year. An interinstitutional cooperation agreement has been affirmed with RENAP, the National Adoption Council, the Institute of Forensic Sciences (INACIF), and the local courts for the care of unregistered cases. Children with disabilities in the psychiatric hospital and children born to inmate mothers at the women's prison have been registered.

After four years of joint work, RENAP reported 591,478 registered births, of which 422,255 were registered in 2016 and 169,223 in the first six months of 2017. Of these, 79,721 were extemporaneous, 1,069 involved a judicial process, and 12,873 involved a consular process. The report also highlighted that 3,783 registration were carried out by parents who were minors at the time, and 88,987 were at the behest of single mothers.

Engaging Children in Advocacy

This program was the consequence of one child daring to raise his voice, and it was heard. A single "small" act has benefited hundreds of thousands of children in the region. He asked, *"How can I be written into the book of life if I don't have a name?"*

The participation of children in our initiatives adds a perspective that makes decision making closer to reality and improves our practice. Involving them in the analysis, monitoring, and evaluation of the program brings a more dynamic perspective. They can provide leadership and move others, influence their environment, add hope, and believe that success is possible. They also provide a fresh realization of the reality and have clearer ideas of how to work with their peers and how to arrive at simple and achievable solutions. They are critical; they say the straightforward things. All of these benefits were experienced during the implementation of the birth registration program. Listening to the children and taking action were the two key components that motivated relationships between the children, the government, and the Viva team in Guatemala.

Effects of COVID-19 on Child Registration

The COVID-19 pandemic aggravated the registration situation. According to preliminary data published by RENAP, during the pandemic 70 percent of children were not being registered. Government offices including RENAP closed due to the pandemic, as well as the registration offices in hospitals. With the help of the 520 churches that are part of the network, a local survey was carried out, and 13,321 children were identified as not registered.

These children will not be able to enter the school system or have access to health services. They are exposed to trafficking and exploitation. When they become adults, they will not have the same opportunities as others to get a decent job. They will not have the right to integrate into the economic fabric of the country. They will not even have the right to a dignified burial. Faced with this situation, the government and the Viva team have extended their agreement to continue promoting initiatives that help mitigate the impact, promoting timely registration at birth and conducting awareness and promotion campaigns involving other key actors such as parent associations in schools, hospital officials, and organized community groups.

However, this situation will continue to be a challenge for the government. The problem is so serious and the magnitude of its scope so great that it is not a problem that can be solved soon or with a single initiative. Solving the problem requires changes in cultural patterns and in the political will of the government. If this issue is not addressed, the greatest consequence will be to the invisible citizens who cannot exercise their rights, persons who are excluded from the productive life of the country and are excluded from the benefits of public policies. Not having birth certificates, they become ghost citizens.

The Challenge to the Church

Local churches are actively engaged in advocating on behalf of children in Guatemala. They have learned to identify needs and to develop viable strategies and solutions. Their model of collective action can be replicated. Operating as a single body, each participant has a role in bringing about the transformation that is needed. The case study exemplifies Bradley Thompson's comments in reference to the reflection of Sanders, Budiardo, Stockley on the genuineness of love, and their thesis that "to achieve [transformation], we need to first understand God's character of love and justice to then understand His call to respond to the issues of vulnerable children."[32]

First we must understand God's character of love and justice and then understand his call to respond to the problems of vulnerable children. The church needs to advocate with governments and other institutions to guarantee justice and respond to the needs of the most vulnerable, which is fundamental to biblical thinking.

In a society that relies less and less on family commitment and loyalty, the Christian church must restore the value of the family, promote values that restore family health and importance in the culture, and promote integral discipleship. God himself instituted the church as a space from which to work and develop his plan for humanity. The reconstruction of the church, that is the recovery of its essence from its origins and its community character, must take place from both its experience and original tradition. Jesus not only proclaimed life in abundance, he also encouraged people to denounce all those actions that threaten humanity, particularly actions against the most vulnerable and unprotected. We are challenged to be agents of change and to prepare younger generations to live the values of the kingdom of God.

32. Wendy Sanders, Tri Budiardo, and Paul Stockley, "Let Love Be Genuine and Relational," in *Understanding God's Heart for Children: Toward a Biblical Framework*, eds. Douglas McConnell, Jennifer Orona, and Paul Stockley (Colorado Springs: Authentic, 2007), 135.

Discussion Questions for Chapter 4

1. In light of the Lausanne Movement concept of advocacy "to, for and with children," create your own definition of advocacy.
2. The UN Millennium Development Goals (MDGs) have resulted in significant strides in impacting the protection and well-being of children; however, the need is still too great. Thousands of children are still living in extreme poverty, hunger, and various kinds of abuse. How can your own local church, seminary, or NGO act as champions for children? Identify concrete ways.
3. In light of the theological response written by Bradley Thompson, what is your denomination's theological and/or hermeneutical understanding of the kingdom of God as the basis of child-focused advocacy? How can this understanding be translated into concrete undertakings of speaking and acting on behalf of children?
4. How can children themselves be engaged in advocacy? Looking at the case study in this chapter, what are the pros and cons of engaging children to advocate for themselves? What are some developmentally appropriate steps that adults should consider when equipping children to participate in these kinds of initiatives?

5

Secured in Hope

Hope is the essence for survival in children living in difficult situations.

Global Critical Issue:
Spirituality and Hope: The Extraordinary Hidden within the Ordinary

María Alejandra Andrade Vinueza – Ecuadorian

"Hope is when everything goes wrong but you still believe that something good will happen. And, suddenly, you see it!"

José Andrés, my son (seven years old)

In June 2020, the World Health Organization affirmed that globally, an estimated one billion children between the ages of two and seventeen years old experienced physical, sexual, or emotional violence or neglect in the past year.[1] The likeliness that children will experience these types of violence increases in contexts of adversity such as sociopolitical or armed conflict, economic poverty, or forced displacement. Growing in contexts of adversity and violence affects children's mental, emotional, spiritual, and physical health and well-being that can have lifelong impacts. This impact is why individuals and organizations, including faith-based organizations, advocate to include children's protection in the international community's agenda. This call is notably evident in the UN's Sustainable Development Goal targets defined in 2015.

Then in the beginning of 2020, COVID-19 triggered an unprecedented global, health, humanitarian, socioeconomic, and human rights crisis. In many ways this pandemic revealed the fragility of the world's systems, exposed the deep levels of corruption and inequality, and exacerbated the already difficult situation of millions of children and their families. It is estimated that as one of the effects of COVID-19, between forty and sixty-six million children could fall into extreme poverty, adding these millions to the estimated 386 million children already living in extreme poverty in 2019.[2]

1. "Violence Against Children," World Health Organization (8 June 2020).
2. "UNICEF Annual Report 2019: For every child, reimagine," UNICEF (June 2020), 2.

In Venezuela, for example, after six years of consecutive economic contraction, it is now estimated that seven million people inside the country and twelve million on the move are in urgent need of humanitarian assistance; 40 percent of them are children.[3] Similar conditions face children from Syria, Somalia, Myanmar, and South Sudan following years of armed conflict.[4] In places like Yemen, Central Sahel, Sudan, and even in countries like the United Kingdom, food security and malnutrition have increased dramatically in the last months.[5] In terms of education, 91 percent of students around the world face schooling disruptions; and the lack of access to quality, online education for most of these students will magnify the inequality gap. Similarly worldwide, COVID-19 has forced thousands of women and children to be trapped with their aggressors, which has increased domestic and gender-based violence; for many victims, "staying at home" puts them at literally deadly risks.[6]

According to UNICEF, children are fleeing their homes more than ever before. In 2019, approximately nineteen million children were forcibly displaced by conflict and violence; other 8.2 million children had to leave their homes due to natural disaster-related causes.[7] When they leave their countries, displaced children are exposed to gender-based violence, exploitation, abuse, detention, and trafficking: in addition they face discrimination and xenophobia, which makes their life even harder.

In the face of these life-threatening situations, *children need to hope.* All children, regardless of ethnicity, gender, religious affiliation, physical condition, and age need to be assured that whatever they are facing, things can get better. Hope is an intuition, an expectation that something good will happen, that the worst will be over, and a new beginning will dawn. For children facing difficult situations, hope builds patience and imagines possibilities.

Hope is an intuition, an expectation that something good will happen, that the worst will be over, and a new beginning will dawn.

3. "UNICEF Annual Report 2019," 6.

4. "UNICEF Annual Report 2019," 7.

5. "UNICEF Annual Report 2019," 2; Chris Baraniuk, "Fears grow of nutritional crisis in lockdown UK," The BMJ (20 August 2020).

6. Luis Felipe López-Calva, "No safer place than home?: The increase in domestic and gender-based violence during COVID-19 lockdowns in LAC," UNDP Latin America and the Caribbean (3 November 2020).

7. "Child displacement," UNICEF Data (September 2021).

Hope heals.
Hope is the essence of survival.
Hope is the lifeblood of resilience.
Hope prevails when everything else is lost.

In Snyder's words, "Hope is our children's window for a better tomorrow."[8] Because of the hurting and traumatic experiences of inequality, injustice, despair, and isolation, children's hope is often hurt and needs to be cared for. Only then can hope unleash its unstoppable power to transform the environment through inner conviction and determination to keep moving forward despite the darkness that surrounds. In this sense, hope is never passive but all the contrary: it is the fuel that keeps the engine of the will moving.

Children's hope is often hurt and needs to be cared for.

In the first edition of *Understanding God's Heart for Children*, the articles in the chapter dedicated to hope explore how each generation of children hold the promised hope so that through them, the world can be improved. The authors argue that children are conceived as God's promise of hope for every generation,[9] or in Jürgen Moltmann's words, "children are metaphors of hope for all God's people."[10] Tollestrup defines hope as "the expectation of good things to come"[11] and highlights the community dimension of hope: "We cannot really build children of hope without building communities of hope."[12]

Rather than focusing on children as promises of hope, this article raises an awareness that children facing adversity need to hope to resist, to survive, and to flourish. The first section argues that hope is an undeniable ally for children at risk. The second section articulates the relationship between spirituality, hope, and resilience. Finally, the third section proposes that spiritual nurture can engender hope through awareness and intentionality.

---

8. C. R. Snyder, "Measuring Hope in Children," paper presented at the Indicators of Positive Development Conference, Washington, DC, 12–13 March 2003, 3.

9. S. Tollestrup, "Children Are a Promise of Hope," in *Understanding God's Heart for Children: Toward a Biblical Framework*, eds. Douglas McConnell, Jennifer Orona, and Paul Stockley (Colorado Springs: Authentic, 2007), 186.

10. Jurgen Moltmann quoted in L. Wagener, "Hope for Every Generation," in *Understanding God's Heart for Children: Toward a Biblical Framework*, eds. Douglas McConnell, Jennifer Orona, and Paul Stockley (Colorado Springs: Authentic, 2007), 196.

11. Tollestrup, "Children Are a Promise of Hope," 186.

12. Tollestrup, 195.

Hope, an Undeniable Ally for Children at Risk

For many decades, the most common form of poverty alleviation within the relief and development world has been providing concrete and tangible support such as shelter, food, health care, clothing, and education. This practice has partly been built on theoretical proposals like Maslow's hierarchy of needs which argues that physiological needs have to be fulfilled in order to achieve the higher level needs such as safety, love and belonging, esteem, and, finally, self-actualization.[13] However, while frameworks such as Maslow's hierarchy of needs can be helpful for informing relief and development programming, in practice it is now clear that successful strategies for poverty alleviation also need to include providing mental health services, income generation, and community building as part of the basic response. More specifically, child-focused relief and development organizations now acknowledge the importance of including safe spaces for children to play as they recognize how important it is for children's well-being and for building a sense of safety and belonging. Evidence also shows that child friendly spaces can help children to process trauma, engender hope, and build up their resilience. Academic research has proven that these "less-tangible" strategies related to mental and emotional health, hope engendering, resilience, relationship building, and advocacy are crucial to ensuring a holistic, people-focused, and sustainable approach.[14] However, these so called less-tangible strategies do carry intrinsic and particular challenges because they are less easy to control, and crucially for development organizations, less easy to measure. These challenges are particularly the case for strategies focused on securing children in hope; in other words, creating space for hope to be birthed in, to be expressed by, and to thrive in children.[15]

---

13. A. H. Maslow, "A theory of human motivation," *Psychological Review* 50, no. 4 (1943): 370; F. Freitas and L. Leonard, "Maslow's hierarchy of needs and student academic success," *Teaching and Learning in Nursing* 6, no. 1 (January 2011): 9.

14. M. Wessells and K. Kostelny, "Child Friendly Spaces: Toward a Grounded Community-Based Approach for Strengthening Child Protection Practice in Humanitarian Crises," *Child Abuse & Neglect* 37 Supplement (December 2013): 30; A. Ager, L. Stark, B. Akesson, and N. Boothby, "Defining Best Practice in Care and Protection of Children in Crisis-Affected Settings: A Delphi Study," *Child Development* 81, no. 4 (July-August 2010): 1272.

15. Tollestrup, "Children Are a Promise of Hope," 195.

Practical Responses Alone Are Insufficient

In 2012, educator and anthropologist Gillian Mann published an article based on research carried out among Congolese children fleeing war and living in Tanzania. Most of these children had gone through traumatic family and personal experiences ranging from witnessing brutal killings to imprisonments, forced labor, and abduction to fight as child soldiers with all the associated deprivations, losses, and fears. At early ages, most of these children knew how it feels to fear for their life and to wonder if they were going to open their eyes the next day. In contrast with these horrific stories, in Tanzania these refugee children had access to family reunification, rehabilitation, psychological therapy, health care, schooling, and vocational training. Undoubtedly, they still faced limitations, but at least they could feel out of harm's way, safe from the terrors, disorientation, and violence of war.[16] What Mann describes as "shocking" was realizing that all the efforts made by agencies and non-governmental organizations to respond to the "practical and emotional needs of [these] war-affected children"[17] were undoubtedly important but evidently not enough for these children to overcome the adversity they faced and flourish as individuals:

> Most described an overwhelming sense of abjection, a term used . . . to describe the sense of not losing one's place in the world, but the associated feelings of betrayal, humiliation, and having been cast aside. These feelings were exacerbated by a sense of being suspended in a boring and meaningless present in which the future was so uncertain and beyond control that it was at times unimaginable. Boys' and girls' day-to-day lives and futures were contingent on so many different things and people that many found it, both literally and figuratively, painful to think beyond the here and now.[18]

Hopelessness as a Spiritual Death

Listening to these children's narratives, Mann concluded that their illegal status and condition as "refugees," the hostile environment, the lack of access to

---

16. G. Mann, "Beyond war: 'suffering' among displaced Congolese children in Dar es Salaam," *Development in Practice* 22, no. 4 (6 June 2012): 449.

17. Mann, "Beyond war," 450.

18. Mann, 451.

services, the conditions of poverty, and the limited social support resulted in a life characterized by constant fear, isolation, and disappointment. Their situation had a direct impact on how they perceived themselves – as a "lost generation," a "waste" – and how they viewed life as "miserable," "worse than anything ever experienced," "boring and meaningless."[19] In other words, as their present was marked by strong feelings of humiliation, suffering, and hopelessness, children were no longer able to imagine their future, which was undermining their humanity because "it was the very idea of a future that motivated them to make it through the day ahead."[20] This condition is what Mann calls a "spiritual death, in which life has no meaning."[21] United States psychologist Alan Kazdin describes this state of mind as "hopelessness": "negative expectancies toward oneself and one's future."[22]

This situation of Congolese refugee children is an example of how, despite well-intentioned efforts to provide for their basic needs, *these efforts are not enough if they are not able to engender hope*. In other words, wherever they are and whatever they are facing, *children need to hope*. In line with Mann's findings, psychologist Ronnie Janoff-Bulman affirms that traumatic events shatter three inherent assumptions: the overall benevolence of the world, the meaningfulness of the world, and self-worth.[23] In fact, the hardships experienced by the refugee children Mann journeyed with led them to ask very deep questions about the existence of God, the purpose of their life, their sense of being alive, and their worth as human beings.[24] As will be explored in the next section, these children have questions that relate to their spirituality, which is why the present article argues that spirituality and hope are closely linked, and together they can help to build resilience.

Wherever they are and whatever they are facing, *children need to hope.*

19. Mann, 452.

20. Mann, 456.

21. Mann, 458.

22. Alan Kazdin quoted in Snyder, "Measuring Hope in Children," 3.

23. R. Janoff-Bulman, "Assumptive Worlds and the Stress of Traumatic Events: Applications of the Schema Construct," *Social Cognition* 7, no. 2 (June 1989): 117.

24. Mann, "Beyond war," 455.

Spirituality and Hope: Resilience's "Internal Engines"

This story comes from the heart of a dear Brazilian missionary friend, Zaza. It is the story of one young girl – Diba[25] – whom Zaza met in a refugee camp in Uganda.

Love Letters to God

Diba and her family were among the millions of people who were forced to flee their home in Goma due to armed conflict between the government and rebel forces. In their quick rush to escape the violence, Diba's family was separated. When she was able to take some breathe, she found herself with her mother and five-month-old little brother, but her two younger sisters and one brother were lost in the bushes and facing uncountable risks ranging from wild animals and hunger to being recruited by armed groups. Diba was seven at that time.

In the midst of such a great loss, uncertainty, and deprivation, for a period of time thinking and expecting to see her sisters and brother again became Diba's reason to continue her journey. Wherever she went, Diba wrote letters for her sisters to give them news from her. But because they did not know how to read, she sent her letters to God and asked him to read the letters to them. Trusting God to reach her little sisters comforted Diba: God knew where they were. God surely cared for them. So God could read her letters to them. As she did not always find paper and pen, she often wrote her letters on the trees, in the soil, or in the air. Nature became a means for these messages of love. These letters became a source of relief, consolation, strength, and hope, especially in times of solitude and despair. Diba was eventually reunited with one younger sister, but she never saw her two other siblings again. However, her messages written in nature became the source of transcendent hope to a God who reads the letters of a little girl somewhere in Congo.

Spirituality, an Intrinsic Human Capacity

Rick Snyder, creator of the "hope scale" for adults and children, defines hope as "a cognitive set involving the self-perceptions that one can produce routes to desired goals (the pathways), along with the motivation to use those goals (the agency)." The pathways refer to the "perceptual recognition of external stimuli, the acquisition of temporal linkages between events, and the formation of goals." The agency "reflects the child's recognition of him- or herself, along

25. The names in this story have been changed.

with the recognition of the self as the source of actions, and the formation of goals."[26] Diba's love letters to God reflect both of Snyder's key elements of hope: the external stimuli – the pathways – as well as the self-awareness and agency. However, this story evidences the existence of other elements that seem to create the space for hope to emerge: a sense of purpose (being alive and finding her sisters alive), and connections – to God (transcendence), to nature (wider creation), to her family (others), and to herself (through writing her letters). This sense of purpose and these connections relate to spirituality.

Spirituality comes from the Latin *spiritus*, which means "breath of life."[27] Uncountable proposals to explore spirituality have been put forward. However, for the purposes of this article, Christina Puchalski's definition is broad, concrete, and practical. Puchalski defines spirituality as, "The aspect of humanity that refers to the way individuals seek and express meaning and purpose and the way they experience their connectedness to the moment, to self, to others, to nature, and to the significant or sacred."[28] Puchalski's definition highlights two important elements of spirituality: life's meaning and purpose and the sense of connectedness to transcendence, to self, to others and to the environment. Understanding spirituality through this perspective explains Gillian Mann's expression "spiritual death" when talking about the sense of hopelessness that the refugee Congolese children experienced. These children had lost the meaning of their life, and their sense of connections was deeply damaged; thus they were thinking that God is either evil or unable; they are a waste; people are bad; and the world is a dangerous place to be. Together, these definitions and stories suggest that if a broken spirituality leads to hopelessness, then a vibrant spirituality has the potential to instill hope.

Research on Spirituality, Hope, and Resilience

According to research, spirituality is broader than religion and is *inherent to all human beings* regardless of their ethnic origin, gender, social status, or

26. Snyder, "Measuring Hope in Children," 4.

27. D. Elkins, J. Hedstrom, L. Hughes, A. Leaf, and C. Saunders, "Toward a Humanistic-Phenomenological Spirituality: Definition, Description, and Measurement," *Journal of Humanistic Psychology* 28 (1 October 1988): 10.

28. Christina Puchalski is founder and director of the George Washington Institute for Spirituality and Health. C. Puchalski, "Physicians and Patients' Spirituality: Ethical Concerns and Boundaries in Spirituality and Health," *Virtual Mentor* 11, no. 10 (October 2009): 804.

religion.[29] Furthermore, researcher and educator Mariam De Souza affirms that spirituality can be conceived as an intrinsic human capacity, just like the physical, emotional, social, and intellectual human dimensions.[30] This is a powerful truth for all children facing adversity: when everything seems to be taken away – everything that provides physical, emotional, social, and intellectual well-being – spirituality will never go away. Because it is inherent to every human being, spirituality cannot be taken away or be discarded, which means that it will always be possible to heal it, to nurture it, and to benefit from it. Spirituality can always be the "internal engine" that propels the search for connectedness, meaning, purpose, and contribution, which are key to engendering hope and building resilience.

Spirituality cannot be taken away or be discarded, which means that it will always be possible to heal it, to nurture it, and to benefit from it.

Resilience, on the other side, has generally been associated with a sense of purpose, critical consciousness, social competence, autonomy, and problem-solving skills.[31] Within children at risk, resilience relates to the various ways in which children respond to the challenges they face turning from "passive victims" into "active survivors."[32] The relationship between hope, spirituality, and resilience has been investigated in different contexts such as in the face of death, violent trauma, war, and austerity, among other situations.[33] These researchers identify spiritual awareness as a key factor to engender a "realistic hope" and peace because it helps people find meaning in life, make sense of suffering, find a sense of support and protection, feel valued and accepted,

29. M. Rodríguez, M. Fernández, M. y Noriega R. Pérez, "Espiritualidad variable asociada a la resiliencia," *Cuadernos hispanoamericanos de psicología* 11, no. 2 (2011): 28; P. Benson, E. Roehlkepartain, and S. Rude, "Spiritual Development in Childhood and Adolescence: Toward a Field of Inquiry," *Applied Developmental Science* 7, no. 3 (4 June 2003): 208.

30. M. De Souza, "Connectedness and Connectedness: The dark side of spirituality: Implications for Education," *International Journal of Children's Spirituality* 17, no. 3 (2012): 1.

31. M. Raftopoulos and G. Bates, "'It's that knowing that you are not alone': the role of spirituality in adolescent resilience," *International Journal of Children's Spirituality* 16, no. 2 (10 August 2011): 152.

32. M. Ní Raghallaigh and R. Gilligan, "Active survival in the lives of unaccompanied minors: coping strategies, resilience, and the relevance of religion," *Child & Family Social Work* 15, no. 2 (12 April 2010): 227.

33. M. A. Andrade, "The role of spirituality in building up resilience of migrant children in Central America: bridging the gap between needs and responses," *International Journal of Children's Spirituality* 22, no. 1 (9 March 2017): 84.

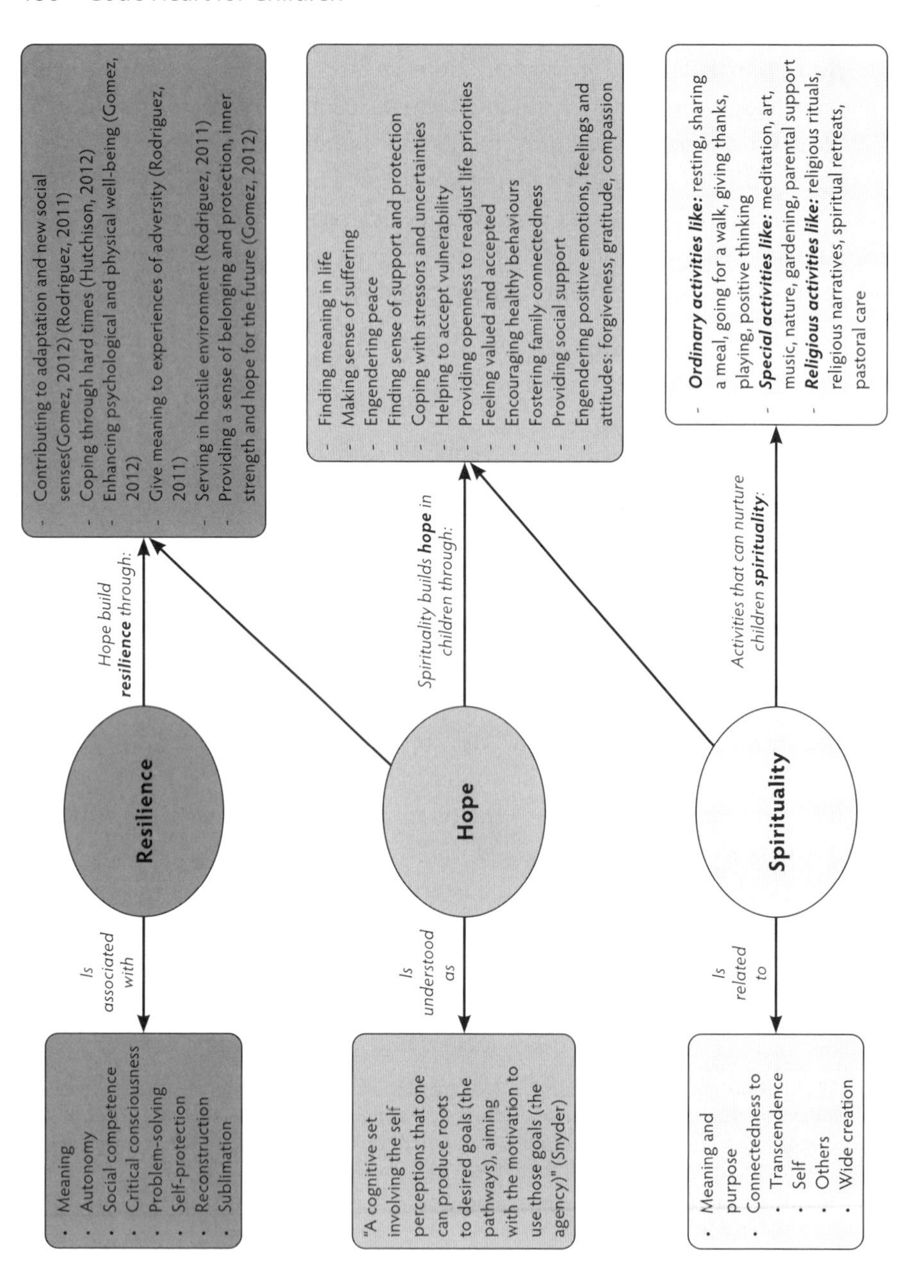

Diagram 1: Spirituality, hope, and resilience according to research[34]

34. Adapted from Andrade, "The role of spirituality."

and cope with stressors and uncertainties. Because spirituality is based on the "conviction that there is 'more' to life than what can be observed materially,"[35] it instills hope in a very natural way because the hope is also based on the expectation than better things are to come. Finally, Mike Dugal proposes the concept of "spiritual resilience" which is "the capacity to respond to stressors, adversity and traumatic events, without . . . losing the vital capacity of the spirit (loving, understanding, forgiving or generously serving others), the mind (to think rationally, objectively and in a balanced way) and the body (to operate healthily)."[36]

A Christian view of spiritual development in children is founded in four affirmations. First, all children are created by God with dignity to experience life in all its fullness regardless of their physical appearance, abilities, economic situation, or social status. Second, children are spiritual beings, so spirituality is one of the development domains along with physical, mental, social, and emotional. Third, children experience a fullness of life when all the domains of development are nurtured to their fullest potential. Fourth, children are meant to thrive as individuals living in communities; therefore, spiritual development is meant to take place individually and in community.

Nurturing Spirituality to Engender Hope

If spirituality has a direct impact on hope and resilience, it seems important to explore how to heal it, to nurture it, and to strengthen it. In the first edition of *Understanding God's Heart for Children*, Linda Wagener refers to resilience as an "ordinary magic."[37] In fact, this characteristic of ordinary magic can be applied to resilience, hope, and spirituality as they can all be fostered through ordinary, daily life activities. As the following section demonstrates, when talking about spirituality, hope, and resilience: *ordinary can be spiritual*; *ordinary can engender hope*; and *ordinary can become extraordinary*.

Ordinary can be spiritual; ordinary can engender hope; and ordinary can become extraordinary.

35. S. Vanistendael, "Spirituality and Resilience," in *Resilience in Palliative Care: Achievement in Adversity*, eds. B. Monroe and D. Oliviere (Oxford: OUP, 2007), 118.

36. Mike Dugal quoted in Rodríguez, Fernández, and Pérez, "Espiritualidad," 27.

37. Wagener, "Hope for Every Generation," 198.

Nurturing Spirituality through Faith

In the biblical and theological response of this chapter, Shake` Geotcherian shares a beautiful and personal story about an eight-year-old girl who found peace during a bomb attack near her camp by repeating Psalm 27, which she had memorized in the days before. According to Geotcherian, the image of God as "light," "salvation," and "stronghold" renewed this little girl's hope. Her faith in her God – which relates to spirituality – built hope in her, and that hope instilled resilience in the face of the adversity she was experiencing. Geotcherian proposes that love, faith and hope work as a triad: hope is founded on faith, and faith comes from experiencing God's perfect love.

As stated in the previous section, spirituality, faith, and religion are three different concepts, but they are still related. As an inherent capacity, spirituality is broader than faith and religion; however, faith and religion – the sacred – play a strong role in nurturing spirituality because they strengthen an individual's sense of meaning and purpose of life as well as his or her sense of connectedness with God, self, others, and creation. In faith-based settings and among religious individuals and communities, activities like prayer, worship, Bible reading and verse memorizing, liturgies, pastoral care, and fellowship can be extremely powerful. In that sense, this article affirms Keith White's words: "Our primary task is to hold the space open for this hope to grow into maturity by creating and maintaining spaces in which children can experience the fullness of God's love with every fibre of their being and soul."[38]

In 2017, I published an article based on a qualitative investigation of adult professionals working with migrant children and adult faith leaders and/or experts in spirituality.[39] Four of the main findings of that research are the following:

1. Spirituality is perceived as an inherent capacity and an integral part of people's lives.
2. Because of spirituality's intrinsic character, it can be nurtured through the sacred (religion and faith) but also through the non-sacred.
3. The ordinary can heal and nurture spirituality if there is awareness and intentionality.

---

38. K. White, "A Child Spells Hope in the Wake of the Tsunami," in *Understanding God's Heart for Children: Toward a Biblical Framework*, eds. Douglas McConnell, Jennifer Orona, and Paul Stockley (Colorado Springs: Authentic, 2007), 205.

39. Andrade, "The role of spirituality," 84.

4. Because spirituality is inherent to all human beings, and because it is broader than faith and religion, it can be nurtured in every culture and every faith and non-faith setting.

The Ordinary Can Be Spiritual

Because spirituality can be nurtured through non-sacred, ordinary, daily life activities and personal attitudes, then spiritual development can take place in any setting, without a particular infrastructure or additional costs.[40] Two elements are, however, necessary for spiritual development: awareness of the spiritual dimension, its importance, and how to strengthen this awareness; and intentionality in connecting daily activities with spirituality and finding the spiritual dimension of the simple things. With the presence of these two elements, *the ordinary can be spiritual.*

In the case of children facing forced migration, very basic activities such as resting, sharing a meal, walking outside (without hiding), or playing can be spiritually nurturing as these activities can help these children "find sense from their suffering, rebuild their identity and connect to themselves, to the moment they are living, to others and to transcendence."[41] The following table proposes ideas for ordinary, special, and sacred/religious activities that nurture migrant children's spirituality, according to empirical research.[42] Although the research was focused on migrant children in Central America, the principles of the findings can be applied to children facing other types of adversities.

Ordinary activities	**Special activities**	**Religious activities (indiv. or in group)**
Welcoming introductions Sharing one's own experiences with newcomers to give them hope and a sense of belonging. Sharing helps to make people feel at home.	**Meditation** Pause from noise and distractions to be in silence and connect with self and/or transcendence.	**Religious rituals** Prayer, Scripture reading, worship, and symbolic liturgies.

40. Andrade, 94.
41. Andrade, 94.
42. Adapted from: Andrade, 95.

Ordinary activities	Special activities	Religious activities (indiv. or in group)
Resting Rest restores the spirit. Migrant children need to get peace back through sleeping and resting.	**Circles of reflection** Time for introspection using child friendly methodologies.	**Fraternal celebration** A weekly meeting in chapel to share thoughts about life, human nature, purpose, challenges, etc. beyond religious beliefs.
Sharing food Food allows migrant children to recover strength but can go beyond to be a special moment of sharing, connecting to others, and exercising gratitude.	**Resources on spirituality** Provision of resources for children that address spirituality through tales, stories, theater, etc.	**Spiritual retreats** Individually or in groups.
Walking outside Going around without hiding and without fear of being detained helps children to connect to their environment and gain a sense of freedom.	**Mutual help role-playing** Role-play stressing mutual help fosters self-esteem, solidarity, humility, and gratitude.	**Pastoral care** Spiritual counselors who provide "psychological first aid" to help children develop coping strategies through making meaning; developing a sense of connectedness, a life purpose, self-esteem, and humor; and developing their own capacities.
Fostering respect Respect can be expressed through every relationship.	**Parental support** Helping parents to help their children through quality time and loving care.	**Religious narratives** Stories can help to explain the causes of disasters and have the potential to strengthen resilience.

Ordinary activities	Special activities	Religious activities (indiv. or in group)
Building relationships and community support Every moment is an opportunity to build trustful and respectful relationships.	**Art, music, nature** Activities that bring harmony and connection to the inner self.	**Dynamics inspired by sacred texts** Choosing texts that tackle issues related to hope, peace, security, courage, solidarity, and God's protection.
Giving thanks For the day, for life, for being alive, etc., giving thanks fosters gratitude and a positive attitude toward life.	**Gardening** Provides an opportunity to reflect on life, renewal, starting again, being useful, and having a sense of responsibility.	
Positive sentences Words have power. Talking positively helps to put stress on opportunities rather than difficulties.	**Capturing places** Young people take pictures of the neighborhood then use them to talk about experiences, feelings, and desires.	
Observing thoughts Asking what are they? Where do they come from? How do they make me feel?		
The nightmare-destroying monster Identifying an ally who takes problems away.		
The sorrow-removing friend Identifying a character who hears problems and takes them away.		
Playing Safe places to play freely and discover through games, stories, or movies.		

Finally, Rebecca Nye, a specialist and researcher on children's spirituality, proposes six criteria for ensuring children's spiritual foundation: space; process; imagination; relationship; intimacy; and trust – S.P.I.R.I.T.:

- Space includes physical and emotional space.
- Process stresses the image of spirituality as a journey in which the present moment is as important as the future outcome.
- Imagination refers to the importance of facilitating creativity, questioning, and inventing answers.
- Relationship recalls the already mentioned component of connectedness within spirituality.
- Intimacy provides a sense of safety to experience.
- Trust refers to the environment that needs to be fostered among children and adults and is expressed through attitudes, actions, and verbal and non-verbal language.[43]

Conclusion

Historically within social sciences there has been a relative lack of attention to issues related to non-tangible aspects of human development such as hope and spirituality because of reasons that include the training, beliefs, and interests of academicians and scientists; the difficulties related to definition and measurement; and considering these topics as potentially "politically sensitive and philosophically difficult."[44] Despite these apparent limitations, stories like those shared in this article provide evidence that traditional development and relief practices are falling short in responding to the holistic needs of individuals, families, and communities. In terms of supporting the millions of children around the world who are exposed to different types of violence and adversity, no response will be successful if it does not help children to experience hope. Unavoidably, promoting hope goes beyond the tangible responses such as providing shelter, food, health care, and even education and psychological support. All of these need to be part of the response, but they are not enough. Fortunately in recent years there has been growing interest among policy makers, practitioners, and researchers in issues related to the very important non-tangible elements which include hope and spirituality. This interest is based on the belief that if more scientific knowledge existed on

43. R. Nye, *Children's Spirituality: What It Is and Why It Matters* (London: Church House, 2009), 41.

44. Benson, Roehlkepartain, and Rude, "Spiritual Development," 206.

the contribution of spiritualty in helping people face adversity, there would be more ways to promote it, measure it, and advocate for it.

The present article demonstrates that children need hope. They need to believe that whatever they are going through, the possibility of a better life exists for them. Without hope, children facing adversity cannot overcome the difficulties they are facing no matter how many programs are available and how much investment is made. Through real-life stories and insights from researchers in different parts of the world, this paper argues that spirituality and hope are like "two sides of the same coin." They are connected and interdependent such that a vibrant spirituality produces hope, and a disconnected spirituality drifts in hopelessness. Therefore, nurturing children's spirituality is key to engender hope regardless of ethnicity, gender, religious affiliation, physical condition, or age. Strengthening children's spirituality is necessary and very important. This nurture is possible because spirituality is an inherent human capacity; everyone has it, and no one can discard it. Spirituality can be nurtured through the sacred – faith and religion – as well as through ordinary, daily activities. The two prerequisites for nurture to happen are *spiritual awareness* and *intentionality*; these two elements have the capacity to build spirituality, hope, and resilience through daily life and *transform the ordinary in the extraordinary.*

Nurturing children's spirituality is key to engender hope.

Finally, thinking about spirituality from a rights perspective, it is important to note that Article 27 of the UN Convention of the Rights of the Child states that, "States Parties recognize the right of every child to a standard of living adequate for the child's physical, mental, spiritual, moral and social development."[45] So nurturing children's spirituality and therefore their hope should not only be the desire of some adults but should be the responsibility of all adults. In terms of children's agency, Nye affirms that childhood is a stage in which spiritual awareness is particularly natural and common.[46] So children can be aware of their spiritual nature; they can be spiritual agents and can develop their spirituality so that it becomes an invaluable ally to build hope and resilience in face of adversity.[47] In this sense, if spirituality is an inherent

45. "Convention of the Rights of the Child," United Nations (20 November 1989), Article 27, https://www.ohchr.org/en/professionalinterest/pages/crc.aspx.

46. Nye, *Children's Spirituality*, 9.

47. Rodríguez, Fernández, and Pérez, "Espiritualidad," 26.

human capacity and children are *full spiritual beings*, then adults can not only nurture children's spirituality but should be especially enriched by it.

Bibliography

Ager, A., L. Stark, B. Akesson, and N. Boothby. "Defining Best Practice in Care and Protection of Children in Crisis-Affected Settings: A Delphi Study." *Child Development* 81, no. 4 (July-August 2010): 1271–86. http://www.ncbi.nlm.nih.gov/pubmed/20636695.

Andrade, M. A. "The role of spirituality in building up resilience of migrant children in Central America: bridging the gap between needs and responses." *International Journal of Children's Spirituality* 22, no. 1 (9 March 2017): 84–101. https://www.tandfonline.com/doi/full/10.1080/1364436X.2016.1278359.

Baraniuk, Chris. "Fears grow of nutritional crisis in lockdown UK." The BMJ (20 August 2020). https://doi.org/10.1136/bmj.m3193.

Benson, P., E. Roehlkepartain, and S. Rude. "Spiritual Development in Childhood and Adolescence: Toward a Field of Inquiry." *Applied Developmental Science* 7, no. 3 (4 June 2003): 205–13. https://www.tandfonline.com/doi/abs/10.1207/S1532480XADS0703_12.

"Child displacement." UNICEF Data (September 2021). https://data.unicef.org/topic/child-migration-and-displacement/displacement/.

"Convention of the Rights of the Child." United Nations (20 November 1989). https://www.ohchr.org/en/professionalinterest/pages/crc.aspx.

De Souza, M. "Connectedness and Connectedness: The dark side of spirituality: Implications for Education." *International Journal of Children's Spirituality* 17, no. 4 (2012): 291–303. https://www.tandfonline.com/doi/abs/10.1080/1364436X.2012.752346.

Elkins, D., J. Hedstrom, L. Hughes, A. Leaf, and C. Saunders. "Toward a Humanistic-Phenomenological Spirituality: Definition, Description, and Measurement." *Journal of Humanistic Psychology* 28 (1 October 1988): 5–18. https://journals.sagepub.com/doi/10.1177/0022167888284002.

Freitas, F. and L. Leonard. "Maslow's hierarchy of needs and student academic success." *Teaching and Learning in Nursing* 6, no. 1 (January 2011): 9–13. https://www.sciencedirect.com/science/article/abs/pii/S1557308710000491?via%3Dihub.

Janoff-Bulman, R. "Assumptive Worlds and the Stress of Traumatic Events: Applications of the Schema Construct." *Social Cognition* 7, no. 2 (June 1989): 113–36. https://guilfordjournals.com/doi/10.1521/soco.1989.7.2.113.

López-Calva, Luis Felipe. "No safer place than home?: The increase in domestic and gender-based violence during COVID-19 lockdowns in LAC." UNDP Latin America and the Caribbean (3 November 2020). https://www.latinamerica.undp.

org/content/rblac/en/home/presscenter/director-s-graph-for-thought/no-safer-place-than-home---the-increase-in-domestic-and-gender-b.html.

Mann, G. "Beyond war: 'suffering' among displaced Congolese children in Dar es Salaam." *Development in Practice* 22, no. 4 (6 June 2012): 448–59. http://www.tandfonline.com/doi/pdf/10.1080/09614524.2012.672958.

Maslow, A. H. "A theory of human motivation." *Psychological Review* 50, no. 4 (1943): 370–96. https://psychclassics.yorku.ca/Maslow/motivation.htm.

Ní Raghallaigh, M., and R. Gilligan. "Active survival in the lives of unaccompanied minors: coping strategies, resilience, and the relevance of religion." *Child & Family Social Work* 15, no. 2 (12 April 2010): 226–37. https://onlinelibrary.wiley.com/doi/abs/10.1111/j.1365-2206.2009.00663.x.

Nye, R. *Children's Spirituality: What It Is and Why It Matters*. London: Church House, 2009.

Puchalski, C. "Physicians and Patients' Spirituality: Ethical Concerns and Boundaries in Spirituality and Health." *Virtual Mentor* 11, no. 10 (October 2009): 804–15. http://journalofethics.ama-assn.org/2009/10/oped1-0910.

Raftopoulos, M., and G. Bates. "'It's that knowing that you are not alone': the role of spirituality in adolescent resilience." *International Journal of Children's Spirituality* 16, no. 2 (10 August 2011): 151–67. https://www.tandfonline.com/doi/abs/10.1080/1364436X.2011.580729.

Rodríguez, M., M. Fernández, M. y Noriega R. Pérez. "Espiritualidad variable asociada a la resiliencia." *Cuadernos hispanoamericanos de psicología* 11, no. 2 (2011): 24–49.

Snyder, C. R. "Measuring Hope in Children." Paper presented at the Indicators of Positive Development Conference, Washington, DC, 12–13 March 2003. https://www.childtrends.org/wp-content/uploads/2013/05/Child_Trends-2003_03_12_PD_PDConfSnyder.pdf.

Tollestrup, S. "Children Are a Promise of Hope." In *Understanding God's Heart for Children: Toward a Biblical Framework*, edited by Douglas McConnell, Jennifer Orona, and Paul Stockley, 185–95. Colorado Springs: Authentic, 2007.

"UNICEF Annual Report 2019: For every child, reimagine." UNICEF (June 2020). https://www.unicef.org/reports/annual-report-2019.

"UNICEF Humanitarian Action for Children 2021." UNICEF (2021). https://www.unicef.org/media/88416/file/HAC-2021-overview.pdf.

Vanistendael, S. "Spirituality and Resilience." In *Resilience in Palliative Care: Achievement in Adversity*, edited by B. Monroe and D. Oliviere, 115–35. Oxford: OUP, 2007.

"Violence Against Children." World Health Organization (8 June 2020). https://www.who.int/news-room/fact-sheets/detail/violence-against-children.

Wagener, L. "Hope for Every Generation." In *Understanding God's Heart for Children: Toward a Biblical Framework*, edited by Douglas McConnell, Jennifer Orona, and Paul Stockley, 196–203. Colorado Springs: Authentic, 2007.

Wessells, M., and K. Kostelny. "Child Friendly Spaces: Toward a Grounded Community-Based Approach for Strengthening Child Protection Practice in Humanitarian Crises." *Child Abuse & Neglect* 37 Supplement (December 2013): 29–40. http://www.sciencedirect.com/science/article/pii/S0145213413003359.

White, K. "A Child Spells Hope in the Wake of the Tsunami." In *Understanding God's Heart for Children: Toward a Biblical Framework,* edited by Douglas McConnell, Jennifer Orona, and Paul Stockley, 204–8. Colorado Springs: Authentic, 2007.

Biblical and Theological Response:
Love, Faith, and Hope

Shake` Geotcherian – Armenian-Syrian

One Night in Lebanon

In 1986 in Lebanon and in the face of an ongoing war, the Armenian Evangelical Christian Endeavor Union of Syria and Lebanon, who organized camps for different age groups, decided to have a camp for underprivileged children. Parents were eager to send their children as they felt the children needed good nutritious food, a change of scenery, some fresh air, and activities. Each morning there was a worship service where the children would sing hymns, learn to memorize a Psalm, and hear stories from the Bible. One night around 1:00 a.m., fighting suddenly broke out on the mountain range in front of our campsite, and we could see and hear the bombs. All of the children in my group were fast asleep and oblivious to what was happening: except one girl. She was eight years old and had previously lost her family when a bomb fell on their home. I was wondering how to keep her calm when in an instant I remembered that during worship, they had memorized Psalm 27. I asked her if she remembered the Psalm, and she said she did. So I asked her, "Would you like to say the Psalm with me?" We started repeating the first three verses that the children had learned so far:

> The LORD is my light and my salvation –
> whom shall I fear?
> The LORD is the stronghold of my life –
> of whom shall I be afraid?
> When the wicked advance against me
> to devour me,
> it is my enemies and my foes
> who will stumble and fall.
> Though an army besiege me,
> my heart will not fear;
> though war break out against me,

even then I will be confident. (Psalm 27:1–3)

After repeating these verses a few times, this little girl was totally calm and ready to go back to sleep, even though the shelling was still going on. She was secure in her renewed hope in God. This is the kind of hope in God which instills resilience in children in the face of sickness, death, destruction, and all the evil forces and is the essence of survival and overcoming. This hope is the key to knowing that in this world there will be extremely bad situations, yet God is with us now, and in the kingdom of God there will be no more pain, crying, or death. Hope is not only for surviving now but also an eschatological hope which provides hope in the kingdom to come.

Introduction

Through hope in God, children can experience his peace, even when turmoil and catastrophe surround them. It is the role of the church, therefore, to help children at risk know and experience God's love by responding to their situations with faith and hope in him. Throughout the Bible, we encounter a God who is active in human history, offering hope for restored relationships. God's love provides the foundation for our hope, which is activated by faith in him.

In the global critical issues section above, María Andrade writes, "hope builds patience and imagines possibilities" and "instills resilience." "Hope is the essence for survival." This article builds on this premise from a theological and biblical perspective, situated in a Middle Eastern context. It presents an understanding of the connection between love, hope, and faith and their impact for nurturing children's spiritually. It is a different perspective on hope than that of Stephen Tollestrup's biblical reflection in "Children Are a Promise of Hope" in the first edition of this book.[48] The aim of this chapter is to help us gain a deeper understanding of our hope in God which is based on God's love and enacted by faith. This hope is different from worldly hope: hope in God helps children to survive in

Throughout the Bible, we encounter a God who is active in human history, offering hope for restored relationships.

48. Stephen Tollestrup, "Children Are a Promise of Hope," in *Understanding God's Heart for Children: Toward a Biblical Framework*, eds. Douglas McConnell, Jennifer Orona, and Paul Stockley (Colorado Springs: Authentic, 2007), 185–95.

the face of troubles, teaches them patience through perseverance, helps them to be creative in imagining possibilities, and instills in them a resilience which is founded on faith in a God who loves them.

God's Love: The Foundation of Hope

Է (ae), one letter from the Armenian alphabet represents God. This letter is found in Armenian churches on top of the altar or inscribed on the pulpit and presents who we worship: the God who is. It contains within it the past, present, and future, a God who was, who is, and who will be, the ever-present One. This is the God who when confronted by Moses' question of who was sending him back to Egypt, responds with אֶהְיֶה אֲשֶׁר אֶהְיֶה, "I am that/who I am," meaning the God who is eternal (Exod 3:14). This is the God who reveals himself to humanity, the relational God, the God who is love. This is the God who loves us so much that he gave his only begotten Son (John 3:16). Throughout biblical history, the main undercurrent of God's revelation as Father, Son, and Holy Spirit is love – love for his creation and love for humanity whom he created in his own image. This is a love for a fallen humanity that needs to be made whole again. In both the Old Testament and the New, God's love is manifested, and hope for a restored relationship is active. What is this hope that is so prevalent in the Bible? A theology of hope has its foundation on faith in God.

Hope in God's Promises

In the Old Testament, the people of God hope in God and in his promises. From Genesis to Malachi, the people of Israel, both individually and as a community, are led by their hope in God. This leading is especially true in times of trouble and tribulation. Whether their hope is for promised children (Gen 15:1–5), or freedom from slavery in Egypt (Exod 3:7–9), or land (Exod 3:17), or for the Messiah who was to come (Isa 53:5), or for return from exile (Ezek 11:14–20), it is always hope that is based on God, his love, and his promises to them.

Hope for the Present and the Future

In the New Testament, the theme of hope is expressed primarily as hope for salvation and for the coming of the kingdom of God. Hope is described by the apostle Paul as essential to enduring suffering for Christ's sake (Rom 5:1–5; 8:35–39; 2 Cor 4:10). Hope is also future oriented, providing the vision of a kingdom where suffering will end, when "He will wipe every tear from their eyes. There will be no more death or mourning or crying or pain, for the old order of things has passed away" (Rev 21:4). In light of this hope, Paul encourages the Roman Christians to "Be joyful in hope, patient in affliction, faithful in prayer" (Rom 12:12). Children who experience great risk or suffering need spiritual guidance to help them to have both hope in the present and hope for the future.

Hope in the Psalms

We see another aspect of hope in the Psalms when the psalmist approaches God, unburdens all of his troubles to him, and ends with a statement of trust that God the Almighty will help, save, or restore him. The Psalms still bring a lot of comfort to those who can relate their hopelessness with the feelings of the psalmists, those who are troubled or in extremely difficult situations, who are pleading with God to listen, and who then find hope in the God they can trust, being reminded of God's faithfulness and love throughout the generations (Ps 55).

The Relationship between Love, Faith, and Hope

Another implication of the theme of hope in the Bible is that God's revelation of himself through the history of humanity brings out a response. Our encounter with the revealed God may result in faith or rejection and a life of unbelief. Those who respond with faith come into an existential experience of being, of being in this world and yet living by the vision of the kingdom of God. "Now faith is confidence in what we hope for and assurance about what we do not see" (Heb 11:1). Faith is what brings living in hope into this trajectory, for hope needs to be firmly founded on faith in the eternal God. Abraham believed God when everything witnessed to the contrary, and under hopeless circumstances, he hopefully believed (Heb 11:8–12).

Faith and hope become this dynamic duality of mutual exhortation: when faith waivers, hope strengthens faith, and when hope falters, faith strengthens hope. Faith and hope are so intertwined that each needs the other to survive. Hope without faith is futile because faith is the foundation for hope, and faith without hope becomes meaningless because Christian hope is based on faith, faith in the resurrected Christ who overcame death.

Faith and hope are so intertwined that each needs the other to survive

God's love gives us hope which is incomprehensible for those who have not experienced God's perfect love. Thus, peace is experienced extensively when we are struggling most with utterly desperate situations which are beyond our control. In these dark periods of the soul, the Christian's total reliance on and belief in God's perfect love sustains and fills her or him with that godly peace and the assurance of being secure in hope in God. God is ever present even when Christians walk in the valley of death, for death has been defeated through the resurrection of Jesus Christ. It is in these dark periods of the soul when total reliance is on God that Christians follow Jesus's example in the garden of Gethsemane, where in full submission, he prays, "may your will be done" (Matt 26:42). This is the ultimate trust in God's perfect love, to put one's life in God's hands and experience perfect peace and perfect hope that comes with doing his will even when evil is at hand and evil has every intention to destroy and bring death. (See Figure 1.)

Hope in God is the foundation for survival in the face of turmoil, war, and the consequences of war. Hope helps children to realize that in this world we will face such situations. But we remember that our Lord, Jesus Christ, overcame death, and that is why we are not hopeless but live with hope in spite of all the difficulties. In Christian faith, hope is the response of the child of God to living in this world where evil reigns and peace seems lost. Hope in God brings a sense of security even when living in an insecure world where nothing lasts, and where persecution and death are daily realities. "Christian hope does not immobilize people, but makes them eager to get to work. It is not escapist hope, but creative hope,"[49] a hope that spurs us on. The book of Acts is a major source of insight on how the disciples and the first church went on preaching, teaching, and baptizing in the face of acute persecution and displacement (Acts 8:1–5). Even though they deeply mourned the death of Stephen, they went about preaching the word. They were not paralyzed by what was happening to them and around them, but these events mobilized them to continue to spread the good news of salvation among the nations.

Hope helps children to realize that in this world we will face such situations. But we remember that our Lord, Jesus Christ, overcame death, and that is why we are not hopeless.

49. D. L. Migliore, *Faith Seeking Understanding: An Introduction to Christian Theology*, 3rd ed. (Grand Rapids, MI: Eerdmans, 2014), 369.

Their eyes were set not on the now but on the then, not on the grim situations but on the eternal glory. They were not in denial about the horrors of persecution but were full of hope that whatever happened, they had a mission to fulfill the great commission (Matt 28:18–20).

Hope in Arabic

In the Arabic language, hope has two words: one is أمل = *amal*, which means to hope, to expect; and the other is رجاء = *rajaa*, which means hope, expectation, anticipation, or urgent request,[50] waiting for something you want with expectation that it will happen and being full of hope and confidence.[51] Thus the term أمل (*amal*) is more of a wishful expectation while the term رجاء (*rajaa*) is more often used to indicate hope in the Bible because it has a deeper theological and spiritual meaning of anticipation, of expectant hope, and of a hope which is confident because its confidence is in God.

The Paradox of Faith and Suffering

Christians living in the Middle East, whether in Iraq, Syria, Lebanon, or Palestine, are living with رجاء (*rajaa*). They are living in both a political and economic collapse and disaster. Theirs is a paradoxical life characterized by faith in the God whom they know is all powerful, yet who seems to remain silent in the face of the atrocities and persecutions they are suffering at the hands of corrupt officials or Islamic militants. They are on their knees, praying like Jesus for God to "take this cup [of suffering] from me" (Luke 22:42), and like Jesus they feel abandoned by God. "The appalling silence of the Father in response to the son's prayer in Gethsemane is more than the silence of death."[52] In such situations, for Christians "hope is faith in action in the face of the empire."[53] That empire is surrounding them like a roaring lion to devour them, and that is why, "to have faith demands a hope that transcends time and

50. Hans Wehr, *Dictionary of Modern Written Arabic*, ed. J. Milton Cowan (London: Macdonald & Evans, 1974), 28, 330.

51. *Al Mounjed Fee Al-loughah Al-Arabieah Al-Mouaseerah* (Beirut, Lebanon: Dar Al-Mashreq, 2000), 259.

52. Jurgen Moltmann, *The Trinity and the Kingdom: The Doctrine of God* (San Francisco: HarperCollins, 1991), 77.

53. Mitri Raheb, *Faith in the Face of Empire: The Bible Through Palestinian* Eyes (Maryknoll, NY: Orbis, 2014), 130.

space."[54] This is a رجاء (*rajaa*) kind of hope, for "Christian faith is expectant faith,"[55] and "Christian hope is resurrection hope."[56]

And this brings us to 1 Corinthians 13:13 where Paul writes, "And now these three remain: faith, hope and love. But the greatest of these is love." Our faith and our hope and the peace which we experience are the direct result of our relationship and encounters with God's love, and love is the greatest of all because in eternity, "when faith and hope are at an end, true charity [love] will burn for ever with the brightest flame."[57] There will be no need for faith or hope in eternity, for we will be fully in the presence of perfect love, the eternal God.

رجاء (*rajaa*) is the kind of hope we want to instill in the generations to come. In the Old Testament, the people of Israel were called to teach their children the commandments of the Lord (Deut 6:4–8), and in the New Testament Christians are also told to bring up their children "in the training and instruction of the Lord" (Eph 6:4b). It is not only knowledge of the Bible that we are called to pass to our children; we are to be living examples of that knowledge, meaning our children watch us before they hear us. Jesus was very particular about this and made a powerful statement that we are to be careful not to let the little ones stumble in their faith (Matt 18:6).

In 2005, I was teaching a Bible lesson to fourth graders, and suddenly we heard a loud explosion. A lot of explosions and assassinations were happening in Lebanon at that time. All my students' faces became worried and anxious, and they could not concentrate because they were extremely worried about their parents and family members who could have been hurt in the explosion. We had no idea where the explosion had been, and I felt quite helpless. So I said, "Let us pray." We all bowed our heads, and I prayed that God protect our loved ones and give us peace. After I finished praying, I looked at their faces again, and I realized these children had experienced a special kind of peace which comes from the knowledge that God is our Father. We took our anxiety about the unknown, our fear of losing a loved one, and we put our hope in his hands. And this is the hope which is foundational for Christian faith. This is the ultimate faith that leads to hope, a hope in the eternal Father, a hope that cannot be crushed even though we are surrounded by chaos, uncertainty,

---

54. Joseph P. Lehmann, "Believing in Hope: A Meditation on Hope, Expectations, and Nature of Faith," *The Journal of Biblical Counseling* 16, no. 2 (Winter 1998): 20.

55. Migliore, *Faith Seeking Understanding*, 347.

56. Moltmann, *Theology of Hope*, 11.

57. Mathew Henry, *A Commentary on the Old and New Testament*, vol. 3 (New York: Robert Carter and Brothers, n.d.), 771.

wars, and plagues, and pandemics because our hope is secure in the one who overcame death, who gave up his life so that we may have life.

This is the kind of hope we want to instill in our children, a hope that is founded on faith. This faith is formed through hearing Bible stories and learning about God as well as forming a relationship with him, being nurtured through biblical knowledge as well as by our example of living the faith that we profess. This is a faith that comes from experiencing God's perfect love. This is a faith that teaches children to come to God even when they are struggling with doubts. The prophet Habakkuk experienced God's peace even when he was surrounded by hopelessness, which is the case especially in the last few decades in the Middle East. His prayer begins –

This is the kind of hope we want to instill in our children, a hope that is founded on faith.

How long, LORD, must I call for help,
but you do not listen?
Or cry out to you, "Violence!"
but you do not save?
Why do you make me look at injustice?
Why do you tolerate wrongdoing? (Hab 1:2–3)

And his prayer ends with an amazing hymn of faith full of hope, a secure hope that did not fail even when everything around him failed.

Though the fig tree does not bud
and there are no grapes on the vines,
though the olive crop fails
and the fields produce no food,
though there are no sheep in the pen
and no cattle in the stalls,
yet I will rejoice in the LORD,
I will be joyful in God my Savior.
The Sovereign LORD is my strength;
he makes my feet like the feet of a deer,
he enables me to tread on the heights. (Hab 3:17–19)

Conclusion

As ministers of the word, Christian educators, and nurturers, it is our sacred duty to instill in children a faith that is so foundational that it will withstand all the trials and the evil that surrounds us, because the hope we have in God is eternal hope. I join my voice with the psalmist and say, "we will tell the next generation the praiseworthy deeds of the LORD, his power, and the wonders he has done" (Ps 78:4).

If we want the generations to come, the children, to have hope in God, then we are to be the examples of that hope lived. We are to be the living testimonies of the hope that is founded on faith in the God who is the God of love.

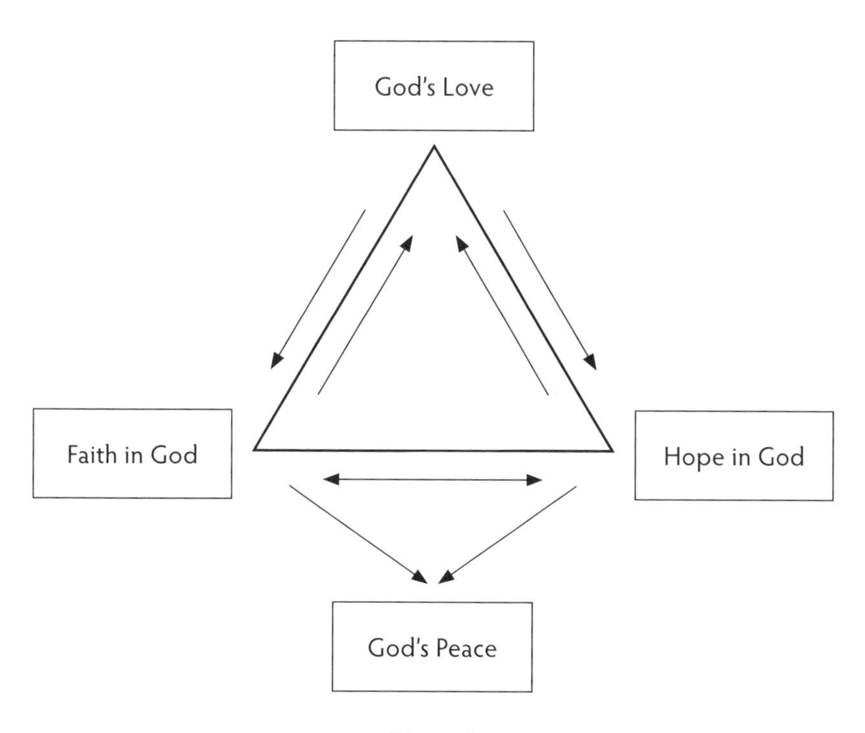

Figure 1

God reveals himself to us because of his love for us, and we respond to his love by faith or non-faith. If we respond by faith, then our hope in God becomes founded on faith in him, and God's peace is the result. As we minister to children, the peace we demonstrate in times of trouble helps them to come to realize that faith and hope in the God of love is the reason. Thus by being live examples, we teach the children how to follow our steps of faith, and they experience God's love in their faith development themselves as we are nurturing them spiritually.

Bibliography

Al Mounjed Fee Al-Loughah Al-Arabieah Al-Mouaseerah. Beirut, Lebanon: Dar Al-Mashreq, 2000.

Henry, Mathew. *A Commentary on the Old and New Testament*. Vol. 3. New York: Robert Carter and Brothers, n.d.

Lehmann, Joseph P. "Believing in Hope: A Meditation on Hope, Expectations, and Nature of Faith." *The Journal of Biblical Counseling* 16, no. 2 (Winter 1998): 14–23. https://www.ccef.org/jbc_article/believing-in-hope-a-meditation-on-hope-expectations-and-the-nature-of-faith/.

Migliore, D. L. *Faith Seeking Understanding: An Introduction to Christian Theology*. 3rd. ed. Grand Rapids, MI: Eerdmans, 2014.

Moltmann, Jürgen, *The Theology of Hope*. New York: Harper & Row, 1967.

———. *The Trinity and the Kingdom: The Doctrine of God*. San Francisco: HarperCollins, 1991.

Raheb, Mitri. *Faith in the Face of Empire: The Bible Through Palestinian Eyes*. Maryknoll, NY: Orbis, 2014.

Wehr, Hans. *Dictionary of Modern Written Arabic*, edited by J. Milton Cowan. London: Macdonald & Evans, 1974.

Case Study:
Child Friendly Spaces: Spaces of Hope

Kezia M'Clelland – British with Subhi Nadhaf – Syrian

Subhi Nadhaf's experience in creating a child friendly space[58] in conflict-affected Syria clearly shows the themes of resilience and hope in practice. Further this experience encourages us to move beyond seeing children as those for whom hope must be restored or given to a wider understanding of their own inherent role as agents of hope.

The Child Friendly Space

In 2015, well into the worst days of the Syrian conflict, Subhi along with a team of friends launched a child friendly space (CFS) in his local town. The team belonged to the same local church and had previously worked together to lead their Sunday school. They were connected to Viva through a local Lebanese partner NGO,[59] and the CFS was established as part of this partnership, with technical support provided by Viva.[60] Around 240 children attended the CFS activities each week, receiving psychosocial support and life skills education; the chance to connect, have fun, and play games with friends; and the regular support of caring adults.[61] The CFS catered to local children as well as those who were internally displaced in Syria, whom Subhi describes as gradually filling the many previously empty buildings in the quiet town: "In the CFS, we had people from everywhere! People would just come down, fleeing from

58. A child friendly space is a safe space set up in an emergency setting to support and protect children. The objective is to restore a sense of normality and continuity to children whose lives have been disrupted by war, natural disaster, or other emergencies.

59. MERATH empowers local churches and organizations to implement relief and development projects for thousands of displaced and vulnerable families in Lebanon, Syria, and Iraq. See https://merathlebanon.org/.

60. Viva hosts an online toolkit at http://learn.viva.org/mobilise/children-in-emergencies/ which provides up-to-date tools and resources to support quality emergency response by churches and NGOs.

61. For more information and guidelines on setting up a child friendly space, see https://childreninemergencies.org/child-friendly-space/.

the war and the violence in that area. They would come here to rent a house in this area."

The CFS was a much needed and much valued intervention which continued to run until 2018. The psychosocial support provided met a pressing need for both local and displaced children in the town. Children coming to the town from the cities often had direct experience of violence and war, and also needed to deal with finding themselves separated from their familiar setting of family, friends, and community. The children who already lived in this relatively "safe" place faced their own challenges of fear and anxiety of an ever near conflict. Subhi recalls, "They were always hearing about stuff – people were killed only just across the neighborhood. There was bombing just across the city beside us. There were people being kidnapped . . . so they were getting anxious – as though that could happen to them any day; that could affect us."

Everyday Resilience

The CFS created a hopeful space amidst these difficult realities where children's resilience was built and strengthened. The CFS provided an extra layer of connection and support that enabled children to flourish and thrive despite their situation.[62] Andrade describes how everyday activities can play a vital part in supporting children's "spiritual" resilience in terms of helping them to "find sense from their suffering, rebuild their identity and connect to themselves, to the moment they are living, to others and to transcendence."[63] This developing of spiritual resilience was evident in the activities at the CFS – simple arts and craft activities, drama, games and sports, and psychosocial support activities served this deeper purpose of helping children to develop inner resilience.

The CFS created a hopeful space amidst these difficult realities where children's resilience was built and strengthened.

One story which particularly touched Subhi was of a five-year-old girl called Naima who was displaced to the town from

62. Qualitative and quantitative evaluation tools used for regular monitoring and evaluation indicated positive change in key areas of psychosocial well-being such as emotional, conduct, hyperactivity-inattention, peer problems, and prosocial behavior as measured by the Strengths and Difficulties Questionnaire (SDQ).

63. M. A. Andrade, "The role of spirituality in building up resilience of migrant children in Central America: bridging the gap between needs and responses," *International Journal of Children's Spirituality* 22, no. 1 (9 March 2017): 94.

a conflict-affected part of Syria.[64] Every day when the children arrived at the CFS, Subhi would greet each child with a smile and a handshake. But each time, Naima would refuse to shake hands and wouldn't meet his eyes. During her time at the CFS each week, Naima wouldn't say a word. After several months of consistent care and building trust slowly, one day Naima shook Subhi's hand, looked him in the eye, and smiled. The story of this CFS is full of seemingly insignificant moments like this which in reality could be life-changing moments for children. The impact of leaders who are rooted in their location and committed to the children who build trust and slowly build relationships is invaluable.

Children as a Source of Hope

The story of this CFS also demonstrates that children themselves can be a source of hope in difficult times. As Andrade mentions, children's resilience means they are "active survivors" and not "passive victims," which leads to an understanding of children themselves *being* a source of hope to others as a component of their resilience.

A clear example of this is the way that children led the way in countering the discrimination and hostility which came from the sudden influx of "outsiders" into the town from different backgrounds and often of a different faith. Despite the atmosphere of antagonism, younger children from all backgrounds were immediately able to play and learn together at the CFS. Subhi remembers that after the hostility shown toward the incoming families, "The [displaced] parents were really happy their kids were coming to the CFS and making friends and having fun. They were so happy."

Older children faced more challenges with integrating together. Subhi states, "We had some sensitive situations, with some children telling others, 'You're not from here,' and staying in their own groups, the people from this town together, that city together. It's sad how adults affect children's way of thinking, 'No you cannot get along with those children, they're immigrants.'" Subhi and the CFS team led the older children in some specific activities targeting the issue of accepting people from different backgrounds, and gradually they saw strong friendships built among children from different backgrounds and different religions. Here children were a vanguard or a going ahead of adults, showing a way where there seemed to be only hatred or intractability.

---

64. Not her real name.

Children are a picture of real hope in situations that seem impossible. This is the 'رجاء' kind of hope that Geotcherian describes: a hope which reveals new life and resurrection reality in the midst of what may appear from the outside as a situation of only darkness and death. The children demonstrated this real hope regardless of their own background and beliefs. The CFS, while led by Christians, was run according to humanitarian principles welcoming children of all backgrounds and beliefs without seeking to proselytize. And yet the new life of the kingdom of God was clearly visible through the lives of these children in this CFS.

Shared Resilience

The resilience of children contributes to the resilience of those around them, opening up another, deeper understanding of where we see hope through children in conflict and emergency situations. Resilience can be seen as something shared and strengthened in a community in which children are active participants. Andrade describes one facet of resilience as spiritual resilience, which includes helping and being aware of others. Children's own agency in creating hope for others, rather than just being individuals who need to be provided with hope, was shown by the way the CFS team found themselves strengthened in their own ability to cope with crisis through their connection with the children. Subhi states, "I don't think I would have survived if I hadn't seen hope across all this. And working with children specifically is one of the things that most gives you hope through these situations. Children can always make you smile; they always impress me with the way they can adjust to new situations, the way they can still have fun, and they can still play – even though everything around them is so bad – they can still laugh and play. And so working with them is the most rewarding thing I have ever done in my life."

Children are part of a shared resilience created through connection, and this mutual agency underscores children's vital role of being hope within the most difficult situations. This role highlights the value of working as the global church to equip and support local people in using their gifts and skills to support children, since this support has the double effect of also building the resilience of the local church.

Are We Making a Difference?

We must be careful, however, not to idealize this work with children in situations of violence and conflict. The inherent fragility and unpredictability of these locations and contexts, and the reality of the pressure local people live under in these situations, is not without impact. We cannot paint work with children in emergencies as a linear narrative of ever increasing impact. All too often setbacks or renewed conflict, or more mundane events such as a key person leaving a project, mean that a project is disrupted or ended. It is easy to feel that any progress made or change observed is totally lost, and hope was not, in fact, real but something transitory and fleeting. In such moments, we feel the Gethsemane silence described by Geotcherian. The CFS project ended after three years. Yet the conflict has continued, and the situation in the town has become arguably even more challenging. Subhi has since left Syria and remembers, "There was some point where I felt like it was all a waste because they're still living in the same conditions and now even it's even getting worse."

Yet the hope we witnessed in the CFS project and in children's lives does not lose its reality or impact because of darkness which may precede or follow it. This reality is clearly shown in another story from the CFS which Subhi shares:

> I remember a little girl called Maha.[65] Maha never missed a session! I remember one day we were having a full day "Fun Day" at the CFS. At the time Maha was at the CFS, her mother was going for some reason to the city, and there was an explosion. There was a bomb, and Maha's mother just happened to be walking beside that bomb, and she passed away that day while we were doing the CFS. When we were at the CFS, we didn't really have connections to the outside world, so we had no idea that when Maha got home after the session, she found out that her mother died. I really remember that because Maha had been brilliant, for some reason I really noticed her. She was enjoying every game, and she was engaged in all the activities we had that day. She seemed really happy in the time she spent with us. It was memorable for us because it was heart-breaking that she went back home to this shocking news. This is one of the times when you feel like just when you think you're doing something, and you're helping, you feel like actually in reality everything is just stronger than you.

65. Not her real name.

> But then after that, as a sign of hope, I remember Maha coming to every session of the CFS we had – she never missed one, not even the one that was a couple of days after the incident. It was actually fulfilling to know that Maha loved the CFS that much, and that was one of the moments when we realized how important we are to this girl and how rewarding it is to know that we were there for her. We realized that we were paying attention, and we were choosing our activities in a very careful and considerate way to help her speak about her trauma. And just having her in all the sessions helped us to feel like we were there and we were helping

Impact in a child's life lasts beyond their circumstances,[66] and hope in a moment is valuable in that it is a sign of God's kingdom then and there. We have not yet seen peace in Syria, but moments of hope seen in and through children point to the reality that the kingdom is already among us (Luke 17:21). Subhi wrestled with this himself, concluding that, "I think somehow the time they spent in that place could be a bit useful for them to be less hurt by everything that was happening around them." So the moments of hope created lasting resilience to equip these children to cope with whatever came next.

Hope in a moment is valuable in that it is a sign of God's kingdom then and there.

In order to sustain work with children in emergency situations, we must hold in tension the desire and push to see total transformation and justice in their situations and believing that impact in a child's life does not depend on this total transformation occurring right now. An investment in a child's life which creates hope is something that endures and is inherently valuable. Subhi speaks of the realism that is necessary for being able to work with children in conflict situations, saying that the team had to think, "It is what it is. We're enjoying it, but we don't know how long it will last. Let's do the best we can." Subhi cautions, "I don't want you to think our team was perfect – our whole Syrian community was going through stress." But this hope, created by and among real people in real situations, was even more powerful given that it took root and grew amidst such fragility.

66. We see this impact in 2 Kings 5:1–6 which accounts the story of a young girl who was kidnapped and violently separated from her family and community. But she demonstrates surprising resilience, courage, and faith when she confidently shares her suggestion for Naaman's healing by Elisha and sees her words taken seriously.

How Should the Church Respond?

Subhi encourages local churches and local communities in conflict-affected areas to make the choice to act on behalf of children. He says,

> Never give up, because no matter how limited your resources, or no matter how few you are, you can make a lot of difference in children's lives. You can do an activity that children are going to talk about for months. You can leave an impression on their lives that they will remember for years. Sometimes it's just those little encounters that you have, those little talks you have with them, that are really going to change you, and they're going to change them. And as long as you're doing that in a church, and you're praying for it, you're not just there alone – there is someone who is guiding and someone who is leading you and blessing this – so never give up.

The global church also has a significant role to play in supporting and being alongside local communities as they work with children in emergencies and fragile locations, sharing resources and ideas, and working together – "doing with" rather than "doing to" so that shared resilience can be strengthened. Recognizing the strengths and capacities of those already present in a location and building on these through meaningful partnership creates the potential for a greater and longer lasting impact than when an external actor simply steps in to meet perceived needs directly and independently.

The story of this CFS is the story of each child who was part of it, each of whom received and created hope through their part in the project. It is the story of Subhi and his team who created a safe, connected space where mutual resilience could grow. It is the story of the "now and not yet" of the kingdom, moments of real hope in the midst of darkness. Children themselves *are* hope in the most difficult situations, and through the support of the global church, they can be part of the transformation of conflict and violence into new life and peace.

Discussion Questions for Chapter 5

1. What is the connection between children's perception of themselves and "hope"?
2. List ways that children can connect spiritually without spending money.
3. How can children in fragile contexts not only be given hope, but also be agents of hope?
4. Child friendly spaces do not completely transport a child out of a war or conflict setting. Are they still worthwhile? Why or why not?

6

Affirmed in God's Church

God welcomes all children fully into the family of faith. Intentional nurture and discipleship of the children allows them to fulfil their vocation as God's people.

Global Critical Issue:
Children on the Move

Enrique Pinedo – Peruvian American

The phrase of children "affirmed in God's church" can be understood as children who attend church regularly must be affirmed in the church – welcomed, integrated, loved, and protected. Or it can be understood as children "outside" the church who also need this affirmation, children who need churches that extend their arms in welcome and take actions to reach them. Both are possible scenarios.

In the first edition of *Understanding God's Heart for Children*, Kara Powell establishes biblical and theological bases from the Old Testament and New Testament to understand how "God welcomes children fully into the family of faith," as well as exploring snapshots of ways children can be involved in communities of faith.[1] In addition, Mazabane and McConnell developed the global critical issue, stating that welcoming children at risk goes with the reminder of Christ's affirmation, "whatever you did for one of the least of these brothers and sisters of mine, you did for me" (Matt 25:40).[2] And it is from these points that we return to and further explore a phenomenon of a group of children at risk who do not have the experience of being welcomed and affirmed in the churches.

Children on the Move in Central America

In December 2015, I had the opportunity to be in Tuxtla Gutiérrez, Chiapas, Mexico at a consultation on children and migration organized by the Nazarene Church in Mexico. Several initiatives were presented there which the churches of the Nazarene denomination had been carrying out on this issue. Likewise,

1. Kara Powell, "God Welcomes Children Fully into the Family of Faith," *Understanding God's Heart for Children: Toward a Biblical Framework*, eds. Douglas McConnell, Jennifer Orona, and Paul Stockley (Colorado Springs: Authentic, 2007), 227.

2. Ndaba Mazabane and Douglas McConnell, "Nature and the Family of Faith," *Understanding God's Heart for Children: Toward a Biblical Framework*, eds. Douglas McConnell, Jennifer Orona, and Paul Stockley (Colorado Springs: Authentic, 2007), 242.

Mexican authorities and specialized organizations on migration participated in that consultation. One of the issues in this event that caught my attention was that on the dangerous "migration route" from Central American countries through Mexico to the US, a large percentage of women and girls end up being raped or transferred to be exploited in Mexican bars and brothels, particularly in Chiapas. One of the suggestions proposed to address this complex reality was that both Central American and Mexican churches work on prevention programs, exposing and raising awareness of this harsh reality of sexual exploitation, especially to women and girls, from the very beginning of the route.

Also shared on that occasion was that many women members of the Nazarene denomination have joined the well-known initiative "Las Patronas" from the state of Veracruz to feed Central American migrants, both children and adults, who transit Mexico to the US on board the train called "The Beast."

The consultation encouraged churches to continue helping migrants despite bad experiences, such as some robberies of church facilities and assets. Churches were advised to take due precautions and work in conjunction with the networks established in civil society and the government. Another topic that was very fresh in those days was the increase since 2014 in the number of Central American minors traveling unaccompanied by adults along this migratory route. The organization Save the Children, in a document titled "Children on the move: A crisis in the Northern Triangle, Mexico and USA," describes this critical situation as an "humanitarian emergency" because during transit, children may be victims of trafficking, violence, physical and sexual abuse, and even death.[3]

These cruel realities are similar around the world. The Mediterranean Sea was the deadliest route from 2013 to 2018, claiming the lives of nearly 18,000 people, including children.[4]

On the other hand, many Central American people and families, including children, decide to stay in Mexico and not continue on the road to the US. This decision is reflected in the increase in the number of asylum applications received by the Mexican Commission for Attention to Refugees (COMAR),[5] which poses a challenge for both the government and the Mexican church. So

---

3. "Children on the move: A crisis in the Northern Triangle, Mexico and USA," Save the Children (2016).

4. "Global migration, by numbers," World Economic Forum (10 January 2020).

5. "Migrantes de Centroamerica: por que Mexico y no EEUU es ahora el destino de muchos de ellos?" BBC News Mundo (2 January 2019).

it is clear that the challenges for the church in Mexico are both with migrants in transit and those who decide to stay and live in Mexico.

Children on the Move around the World

According to the International Organization for Migration (IOM), drawing from United Nations data, "In 2019, the number of migrants globally reached an estimated 272 million, 51 million more than in 2010. International migrants comprise 3.5 percent of the global population."[6] The IOM affirms that approximately fifty million children can be considered "on the move" around the world. And of these children, approximately thirteen million are refugees, 936,000 are asylum seekers, and seventeen million have been forcibly displaced inside their own country.[7] Certainly these huge numbers bring a tremendous challenge to humanity and surely also to the mission of the church.

Save the Children defines children on the move as

> Children moving for a variety of reasons, voluntarily or involuntarily, within or between countries, with or without their parents or other primary caregivers, and whose movement, while it may open up opportunities, might also place them at risk (or at an increased risk) of economic or sexual exploitation, abuse, neglect and violence.[8]

Children are one of the most vulnerable groups in this population displacement and have to face various risks to their survival, health, and education. In addition, they generally travel without documents, do not speak the language of the destination, and are frequently subject to xenophobic discrimination.[9] According to UNICEF, some groups of migrants in the world are more vulnerable than others, and to them greater attention

They generally travel without documents, do not speak the language of the destination, and are frequently subject to xenophobic discrimination.

6. "World Migration Report," International Organization for Migration, United Nations (2019).

7. "What works to protect children on the move: Rapid Evidence Assessment," United Nations (July 2020), 6.

8. "Save the Children's Child Protection Strategy 2013–2015: Making the world a safe place for children," Save the Children (May 2013), 31.

9. "What works to protect children on the move," 7.

should be paid. For example, "an adolescent boy from sub-Saharan Africa with secondary education and traveling in a group along the Central Mediterranean route, faces a 73 percent risk of being exploited, while the risk for a boy from another region drops to 38 percent."[10] In 2014, 28 percent of all detected trafficking victims were children (20 percent girls and 8 percent boys).[11]

IOM's "World Migration Report 2020" states that migration "can be triggered by environmental hazards, conflicts and terrorism, as well as complex emergencies, failures of political and economic management, epidemics and pandemics, and global financial cycles."[12] Examples of recent migration triggers include flooding in Bangladesh and Thailand, conflicts in Libya and Yemen, and the political and economic crisis as in Venezuela.[13] Other triggers include "conflict in countries including Syria, Yemen, the Central African Republic, the Democratic Republic of the Congo and South Sudan, as well as the kind of extreme violence that forced Rohingya to seek safety in Bangladesh, have led to the displacement of millions of people."[14]

> When hundreds of thousands of terrified Rohingya refugees began flooding onto the beaches and paddy fields of southern Bangladesh in August 2017, it was the children who caught many people's attention. As the refugees – almost 60 percent of whom were children – poured across the border from Myanmar into Bangladesh, they brought with them accounts of the unspeakable violence and brutality that had forced them to flee.[15]

Children on the Move and COVID-19

UNICEF states that worldwide, 52 percent of migrant children and over 90 percent of displaced children live in low- and middle-income countries where health systems are often insufficient and do not respond adequately to the demands of the population.[16] Therefore during the COVID-19 pandemic, these children have been among the most vulnerable populations on the globe. "In

---

10. "Children on the Move: Key facts and figures," UNICEF (February 2018), 2.
11. "Children on the Move," 3.
12. "World Migration Report 2020," IOM (2019), 317.
13. "World Migration Report 2020," 317.
14. "Global migration, by numbers."
15. "Rohingya crisis," UNICEF (18 March 2019).
16. "Migrant and displaced children in the age of COVID-19," UNICEF (April-June 2020), 32.

low- and middle-income countries, migrant and displaced children often live in deprived urban areas or slums, overcrowded camps, settlements, makeshift shelters or reception centers, where they lack adequate access to health services, clean water and sanitation. Social distancing and washing hands with soap and water are not an option."[17]

Studies carried out by UNICEF in the countries of Somalia, Ethiopia, and the Sudan

> showed that almost 4 in 10 children and young people on the move do not have access to facilities to properly wash themselves. In addition, many migrant and displaced children face challenges in accessing health care. Half of respondents aged 14–24 years in a UNICEF poll who self-identified as migrants and refugees indicated that they did not see a doctor when needed.[18]

The COVID-19 pandemic is already magnifying the vulnerability of children on the move who suffer discrimination from the local population, aggression, and legal exclusion. If they become ill, it is almost impossible for them to receive medical attention. The COVID-19 pandemic is increasing inequalities among the population, and it is migrants who are the farthest from improving their quality of life and are most exposed to being infected. Many child refugees from Rohingya live in southern Bangladesh in "flimsy bamboo and tarpaulin shelters where the dangers of everyday life remain all too real, including the high risk of the spread of infectious diseases like the coronavirus."[19]

Implementing government policies and urgent actions by civil society, including the church, are required to respond to this great global challenge.

> The pandemic has affected the schools of 1.5 billion students worldwide and is likely to exacerbate the vulnerabilities of the millions of migrant and displaced learners around the world. In many cases, these marginalised children have already missed critical time in the classroom and are at risk of falling even further behind. Even before the COVID-19 crisis, refugee children were twice as likely to be out of school than other children.[20]

---

17. "Migrant and displaced children in the age of COVID-19," 32.
18. "Migrant and displaced children in the age of COVID-19," 32.
19. "Rohingya crisis."
20. "Migrant and displaced children in the age of COVID-19," 36.

Children on the Move Welcome in the Church

Through diverse efforts, denominations, Christian organizations, and ministries are responding to the needs of migrant and refugee families and children. Here are some examples:

> The Refugee Highway Partnership (RHP) was formed as a cooperative network within the World Evangelical Alliance in 2001 and is now a growing worldwide community of Christians who share a commitment to welcome and serve refugees. The RHP facilitates more effective ministry, stimulates strategic initiatives and envisions and equips the Church so that refugee ministries are strengthened, and more refugees are served.[21]

The RHP has guides for "what the church can do," and in this section they propose the following:

- Become informed about refugee realities and biblical perspectives on them, inform others, and raise awareness.
- Pray for forcibly displaced people, and help them overcome challenges refugees face in a new country.
- Determine the greatest challenges that refugees or asylum seekers face. Among them are the great difficulty in finding affordable housing, finding employment that is enough to pay their bills, learning the language in their country of refuge, understanding the school system, and helping their children with homework.
- Make a list of the needs that newly arrived asylum seekers and refugees often have and help with temporary shelter or a safe living space, basic food, climate appropriate clothing and footwear, local transportation, communication with loved ones from whom they are separated, and encouragement.

Even if a local church cannot directly meet these needs, they can often refer refugees to services that might be able to help them.[22]

World Relief also has a series of resources called "Church Leader's Resources on the Refugee Crisis and Immigration" in which they provide guidance to local church leadership on how to respond to various immigration and refugee challenges.[23] One of these resources called "Church Leader's Guide

---

21. "Refugees," World Evangelical Alliance (2021).

22. "Refugee Highway, what the church can do," https://www.refugeehighway.net/what-the-church-can-do.html (2018).

23. "Church Leaders' Resources," World Relief (2020).

to Immigration"[24] was written by several people who have many years of experience working with local churches and denominational leaders in the US. They also work on the biblical and missiological aspects of the subject as well as how to help immigrants in the US with the processes of legal applications. Other valuable resources include the book *Welcome to the Stranger*.[25]

Likewise in 2019, Tearfund Latin America launched a campaign called "As born among us," alluding to Leviticus 19:33–34. They promote a series of initiatives for raising awareness, church mobilization, advocating authorities to uphold migrant rights, integration, welcome, and prayer.[26] This campaign has been promoted by churches and Christian organizations in Latin America and the Caribbean and seeks to join the efforts that already exist to strengthen the capacity of the evangelical community to attend to, protect, and promote the rights of migrants.

Finally Compassion International, the organization I am privileged to serve, has been supporting migrant families and children on the move from Venezuela who are in the city of Cúcuta, Colombia. Cúcuta is one of the official land border crossings between Colombia and Venezuela through which 94 percent of Venezuelan migrants enter. But the number of Venezuelan migrants has caused that city's basic public services to collapse. Compassion International in partnership with several evangelical churches has been providing food and health care services, care for pregnant mothers, support for strengthening child protection practices and policies, and preventing sexual abuse and trafficking. They have also helped to provide beds, cleaning utensils, and materials for educational activities with children as a school replacement as well as emotional and spiritual care for both adults and children.

Summary

Without a doubt the challenge of children on the move is great, both for society and for the mission of the church. The statistics and the conditions of vulnerability and exclusion that have been presented are signs showing that the kingdom of God of welcome, love, and affirmation has not yet "come near" for many of the "little ones" (Mark 10:14). It seems that this harsh reality of the children on the move denies them their longings for fullness of life and the

24. "Church Leader's Guide to Immigration," World Relief (2020).

25. Matthew Soerens & Jenny Yang, *Welcoming the Strangers: Justice, Compassion & Truth in the Immigration Debate World Relief* (Downers Grove: IVP Books, 2018).

26. "Como nacido entre nosotros," Tearfund Latin America (2021).

shalom that the kingdom of God promises, and those characteristics of justice, equity, dignity, love, peace, health, and integral growth seem unattainable.

But on the other hand, we can give thanks to God for the initiatives of hope, solidarity, and welcome that various churches and Christian organizations have developed. They show us that the church can be a community that affirms children on the move and that learns and educates about their challenges and needs. As the church we need to understand that in the Bible, caring for orphans and foreigners is discussed more than thirty times, together with another vulnerable social group, widows. This social triad was considered to be the most vulnerable and excluded in Israel, and in the Old and New Testaments, God calls his people to protect them and raise our voices in their favor. As the church we need to mobilize and extend our arms like Jesus did and say, "Let the little children [on the move] come to me, and do not hinder them, for the kingdom of God belongs to such as these" (Mark 10:14).

This harsh reality of the children on the move denies them their longings for fullness of life and the shalom that the kingdom of God promises.

Bibliography

"Children on the move: A crisis in the Northern Triangle, Mexico and USA." Save the Children (2016). https://resourcecentre.savethechildren.net/node/10107/pdf/factsheet_com_english.pdf.

"Children on the Move: Key facts and figures," UNICEF (2018). https://data.unicef.org/resources/children-move-key-facts-figures/.

"Church Leader's Guide to Immigration." World Relief (2018). http://evangelicalimmigrationtable.com//wp-content/uploads/2018/11/churchleaderguidetoimmigration.pdf.

"Church Leaders' Resources." World Relief (2020).
https://worldrelief.org/church-leaders-resources-download/.

"Como nacido entre nosotros." Tearfund Latin America (2021). https://www.comonacidoentrenosotros.org/.

"Global migration, by numbers." World Economic Forum (10 January 2020). https://www.weforum.org/agenda/2020/01/iom-global-migration-report-international-migrants-2020/.

Mazabane, Ndaba, and Douglas McConnell. "Nature and the Family of Faith," *Understanding God's Heart for Children: Toward a Biblical Framework*, edited by Douglas McConnell, Jennifer Orona, and Paul Stockley, 238–245. Colorado Springs: Authentic, 2007.

"Migrantes de Centroamerica: por que Mexico y no EEUU es ahora el destino de muchos de ellos?" BBC News Mundo (2 January 2019). https://www.bbc.com/mundo/noticias-america-latina-46931134.

"Migrant and displaced children in the age of COVID-19," UNICEF (April-June 2020: 32). https://www.unicef.org/media/83546/file/Migrant-and-displaced-children-in-the-age-of-COVID-19.pdf.

Powell, Kara. "God Welcomes Children Fully into the Family of Faith." *Understanding God's Heart for Children: Toward a Biblical Framework*, edited by Douglas McConnell, Jennifer Orona, and Paul Stockley, 227–237. Colorado Springs: Authentic, 2007.

"Refugees." World Evangelical Alliance (June 18, 2021). https://worldea.org/news/14653/embrace-wea-and-refugee-highway-partnership-encourage-churches-to-observe-world-refugee-sunday-on-june-20-27/ .

"Refugee Highway, what the church can do." Refugee Highway (2018). https://www.refugeehighway.net/what-the-church-can-do.html.

"Rohingya crisis." UNICEF (18 March 2019).

https://www.unicef.org/emergencies/rohingya-crisis.

"Save the Children's Child Protection Strategy 2013-2015: Making the world a safe place for children," Save the Children, Child Protection initiative (May 2013:31). https://resourcecentre.savethechildren.net/node/7434/pdf/cp_strategy_eng_oct1.pdf.

Soerens, Matthew and Jenny Yang, *Welcoming the Strangers: Justice, Compassion & Truth in the Immigration Debate World Relief*. Downers Grove: IVP Books, 2018. https://worldrelief.org/church-leaders-resources-download/.

"What works to protect children on the move: Rapid Evidence Assessment," United Nations (July 2020), 6. https://reliefweb.int/report/world/what-works-protect-children-move-rapid-evidence-assessment-july-2020.

"World Migration Report 2020," IOM (2020). https://publications.iom.int/system/files/pdf/wmr_2020.pdf.

Biblical and Theological Response:

Beyond Welcoming to Engaging Children for God's Kingdom

Shantelle Weber – South African

The 2020 global COVID-19 pandemic highlighted the vulnerability and marginalization of children everywhere. The immediate response of government officials, societal leaders, and even faith communities was to prioritize adult concerns which did not highlight the needs of children on the move. Displaced, uneducated, hungry, orphaned, and refugee children were even further negated in our responses to this pandemic. Above in the global critical issues section of this chapter, Enrique Pinedo focuses on children on the move, migrant children who are further displaced and marginalized during pandemics like this.

In the first edition of *Understanding God's Heart for Children*, Douglas McConnell, Jennifer Orona, and Paul Stockley highlight that our theological response to children should be intentional because God creates children with dignity, and on this basis they need parental love in a broken world; they are gifted to teach adults who have the God-given responsibility to care for their well-being.[27] They also highlighted that God welcomes children fully into the family of faith, and children are essential to the mission of God. This edition highlights our biblical mandate by reminding us of the above mentioned truths and calling for a theological and ecclesiological shift in how we position children in our narratives. Our hope is that a deeper reflection on children on the move in God's word and his mandate for us to engage with and learn from these children will result in a renewed perspective on how we approach children on the move.

27. Douglas McConnell, Jennifer Orona, and Paul Stockley, eds. *Understanding God's Heart for Children: Toward a Biblical Framework* (Colorado Springs: Authentic, 2007).

Being *with* Children on the Move Is Our Biblical Mandate

The Old Testament bears contradictory approaches to children on the move. On the one end, care for the most vulnerable people is a core value in the Hebrew community. Caring for the orphan along with the widow and the resident alien are to be at the ethical center of mercy and piety, care and worship. Esther 2:3–4 and 12–14 portray Israelites who were originally taken into Babylon as prisoners of war experiencing prejudice and sexual exploitation. The Jews were in exile so long that many of their children forgot how to speak Hebrew. Israel also became a land of many refugees like Rahab and Ruth because war and famine scattered people in those days.[28] In Isaiah 10:1–4, God promises to personally intervene on behalf of widows and orphans. The New Testament shows Jesus to be the fulfillment of the right relation of mercy and piety. This example and understanding is critical when journeying alongside children on the move; showing mercy toward fellow human beings without acting out of religious obligation is key. Jesus demonstrates for us how the right relation of mercy and piety is at the center of faith, the sacraments, and discipleship.[29] Jesus became a refugee as a child (Matt 2:13–15). Acts 9:36–41 portrays how the early church fed widows. It is clear that biblical testimony reflects Jesus having a heart for children including those who are oppressed and shunned by society (Matt 18:1–14; 19:13–15). "[A]ll recorded encounters between Jesus and children were kind, gentle and respectful with children seen as central to the new social order that Jesus initiated. By blessing and laying his hands on children, Jesus received children as people in their own right and gave them status, respect and dignity."[30] Many read these texts without considering the context at the time. Jesus was actually being quite radical in his response to children compared to how they were usually treated! Within the Graeco-Roman Empire, children were considered the seed of the future, yet still treated as marginal figures in society. For example, new born babies were inspected by Stoic philosophers at

Caring for the orphan along with the widow and the resident alien are to be at the ethical center of mercy and piety, care and worship.

28. *Africa Study Bible, New Living Translation* (Illinois: Oasis International, 2016), 294.

29. P. D. Couture, *Seeing Children, Seeing God: A Practical Theology of Children and Poverty* (Nashville, TN: Abingdon, 2000), 3.

30. "Ending corporal punishment of children: A handbook for worship and gatherings," Church Network for Non-Violence (2015), 3.

birth resulting in the naming of the child being postponed for a week. If found with some form of defect, these children were not accepted and ended up in rubbish bins or dung heaps. Many of these rejected and abandoned children ended up becoming slaves, prostitutes, or gladiators.[31]

Many cultures around the world today also claim that children are the inheritance of the parents and a blessing from God. Yet the first section of this chapter confirms that the numbers of orphans and displaced migrant children are increasing. Children are orphaned and abandoned as a result of conflict, hunger, HIV and AIDS, unemployment, neglect, substance abuse, and the loss of a loved one. Many become an increased responsibility on older siblings who become primary caregivers of ill parents resulting in child-headed households. These situations are exacerbated by social isolation and the resulting distress, trauma, and depression; psychological trauma through internalized negative feelings; antisocial behavior; and substance abuse themselves. Present-day orphans may become victims of abuse in extended and foster families and receive no or insufficient education; some are caught in prostitution and child trafficking; and others becoming street kids. It is sad knowing that any child experiencing God-given life in these and even more devastating circumstances are not even considered to be a citizen of a particular country. How is it possible that the very life God has ordained and entrusted to us becomes lost in vast numbers? How is it possible that the gospel is being preached and spreading throughout the world but does not liberate these children and their families? Are these children being welcomed in our faith communities? Further still, are we intentional about learning from their lived experiences and by so doing, edifying the body of Christ?

How is it possible that the gospel is being preached and spreading throughout the world but does not liberate these children and their families? Are these children being welcomed in our faith communities?

We ask these crucial questions because our core premise in this chapter is that there needs to be a transformational shift in God's church. A shift from education *about* the marginalized to journeying *alongside* them. A shift from ministry *for* children to ministry *with* children, and a shift from *welcoming*

31. For useful further resources on this topic please see Grobbelaar and Breed, *Welcoming Africa's Children.*

these children through varying programs and even faith-based charities toward *engaging* with the way these children see Christ amidst their daily suffering.[32] All children are exposed to factors that can deter their development, but poor and marginalized children encounter multiple factors that make their lives precarious.[33] Couture argues that caring for vulnerable children is a means of grace, a vehicle through which God makes himself known to us and to them.[34] In their care we (the adults, the church) experience grace, the movement of God in our lives that allows us to give to and receive from others. This mysterious meeting of God in the most vulnerable of children and in ourselves moves us to give thanks. What a missed opportunity to embrace as the church! – to experience God's grace toward us through the least of these. In this sense, spiritual fullness and maturity are dependent upon our care for the most vulnerable of persons, which is central to our biblical witness.

Call for a Theological and Ecclesiological Shift

A theological and transformational shift beyond welcoming to engaging children for God's kingdom requires that we listen to the stories of childhood from the children's perspective; see the children who are in our midst and learn the kinds of practices that allow us to engage them as full members of our religious community; and talk to children at their eye level.[35] Stoller notes that ignoring children's suffering is often shaped by "adultism," seeing faith beliefs from an adult perspective rather than paying attention to whether they are liberating for children.[36] Faith communities can work together to dismantle systematic prejudice and discrimination against children inside and outside the church. This work may involve finding ways to reread sacred texts through a child's lens or reclaim their missing voices.

Biblical perspectives reflect that children, directly or indirectly, are bearers of deep theological truths. God has put children in our midst as a sign or language of God's revelation using real children and sometimes the image of children to communicate the essence of the transformation God wants to

32. During the 2014 Lausanne Consultation on Children-at-Risk, the decision was made to refer to ministry to, for, and with children. "Who are Children-at-Risk?: A Missional Definition." Lausanne Movement Consultation on Children at Risk, Quito, Ecuador, 17–19 November 2014.

33. Couture, *Seeing Children, Seeing God.*

34. Couture, 4.

35. Couture, 1.

36. R. Stoller, "Towards a child liberation theology," https://www.patheos.com/blogs/unfundamentalistparenting/2016/04/towards-a-child-liberation-theology/(April 2016).

achieve in this world. How can we see God as a vulnerable child, not just God as a parent? This seeing is at the heart of the incarnation because God became a child, and "when we receive a child in Christ's name, we receive Christ, we receive God the Child incarnate."[37] God used children at various times and in different ways to communicate theological truths to his people. United Nations Child Protection experts note that "Religious communities are often at the forefront of the care and protection of children as the foundational focus for nearly all religious traditions."[38] Sadly, sometimes children are only important in church and society in terms of what they can become in the future.

Faith communities can contribute at all levels and play multiple roles across the child protection system to both prevent and respond to violence against children.[39] Faith communities can provide low cost but needed support to families and the children within them. Faith leaders can engage official child protection systems and have crucial roles in the prevention and referral of child abuse cases. Faith communities are called to cultivate a series of Christian virtues; patience, kindness, generosity, hospitality, compassion, and joy to create the spiritual space within us to receive these children. The church needs risk prevention strategies that buffer children against risks that may harm them. These strategies should be two fold; children should be taught about basic nutrition, health, safety, sexuality, and the future, but these very children can also teach adults and faith communities what these elements mean and should look like for them, and in this way equip the church on the realities of how to engage with such children.[40] Child-centered approaches are essential in faith communities. Linking child participation and protection improves the children's social status, enables the voices of children to be part of the changes

Linking child participation and protection improves the children's social status, enables the voices of children to be part of the changes that are seen to be needed.

37. Craig L. Nessan, "Child Liberation Theology," *Currents in Theology and Mission* 45, no. 3 (2018): 8.

38. Malia Robinson and Stephen Hanmer, "Engaging religious communities to protect children from abuse, neglect, and exploitation: Partnerships require analysis of religious virtues and harms," *Child Abuse & Neglect* 38, no. 4 (2014): 600–611.

39. Selina Palm, "Spiritual Capital," Ending Violence Against Children Webinar (26 February 2020).

40. Couture, *Seeing Children, Seeing God*, 91–3.

that are seen to be needed, and avoids the rescue and rehab or passive victim lenses.[41]

In terms of pastoral care, church leaders should be equipped on how to deal with the extreme difficulties of a child's life and not solely how to preach to these children.[42]

> where biblical interpretations endorse hatred, abuse, or violence against other human beings created in God's image, especially the most vulnerable and powerless, such readings become acts of blasphemy. They contradict the spirit of the One who taught love for the neighbor, welcome to the child, and special divine concern for "little ones," wherever and whoever they may be. Such acts take God's name in vain, justifying violence against the most vulnerable among us.[43]

Renewing How We Approach Children on the Move

The 2010 Lausanne Commitment says

> The Church exists to worship and glorify God for all eternity and to participate in the transforming mission of God within history. Our mission is wholly derived from God's mission, addresses the whole of God's creation, and is grounded at its centre in the redeeming victory of the cross. We are called to integral mission, which is the proclamation and demonstration of the gospel.

The same commitment calls the church to build "the peace of Christ in our divided and broken world by bringing Christ's truth and peace to bear on racism and ethnic diversity, slavery and human trafficking, poverty, and minority groups such as people with disabilities [children on the move]."[44]

The following statements, articulated by Marcia Bunge, need to move from theological knowledge to exemplified embracing of children on the move

41. Palm, "Spiritual Capital."

42. Couture, *Seeing Children, Seeing God*, 48–9.

43. Troy Troftgruben, "Toxic theology: A pastoral response to Bible passages often used to justify the abuse of children or prevent them from seeking care," *Currents in Theology and Mission* 45, no. 3 (2018): 5.

44. Kevin Smith, "Summary of the Cape Town Commitment," Lausanne Movement (18 March 2011).

irrespective of their race, class, social standing in society, family background, or economic contribution:[45]

- Children are gifts of God and sources of joy, and adults are to delight in and be grateful for them.
- Children are developing beings, and adults are to help teach and guide them.
- Children are orphans, neighbors, and strangers, and adults are to seek justice for children and treat them with compassion.
- Children are fully human and made in the image of God, and adults are to treat them with dignity and respect.
- Children are moral agents who sometimes "miss the mark" (or sin) and who have growing moral capacities and responsibilities, and adults need to help nurture these capacities, be examples of forgiveness, and apologize for their own wrongdoing toward children and others.
- Children are models of faith, and adults are to listen to and learn from them.
- Children are not one-dimensional creatures who are either innocent or sinful, victims or agents.
- Children have intrinsic worth and both rights and responsibilities that correspond to that worth.[46]

The global COVID-19 pandemic challenged what and who we consider to be church. In the church as the *ekklesia*, the gathered ones, the people became a refreshing reminder to anyone who calls themselves Christ's followers. The COVID-19 pandemic has also caused the church to respond beyond welcoming children and move toward doing theology and ministry alongside and with them. We have briefly noted some of the biblical reasons why we should make this move but also highlighted a few barriers for why we are not getting this

---

45. See also further discussion in Marcia J. Bunge, "A more vibrant theology of children," *Christian Reflection: A Series in Faith and Ethics* 8 (2003): 11–19; and Marcia J. Bunge, "Conceptions of and Commitments to Children: Biblical Wisdom for Families, Congregations, and the Worldwide Church," in *Faith Forward (Volume Three): Launching a Revolution through Ministry with Children, Youth, and Families*, edited by David M. Csinos (Wood Lake, 2018), 94–112.

46. Bunge, "Tasks, Sources, and Significances of Theologies of Childhood," 100–101.

right. A theological response engaging children on the move requires a few basic presuppositions:[47]

- Children on the move should be regarded as collaborators in doing theology contextually. Affirming and inviting the agency of children will help us to construct useful and indeed liberating child theologies.
- Children on the move should be engaged as co-researchers in processes that seek to generate knowledge about children. Increasingly there are ethical pitfalls in doing research with children, but we propose that such pitfalls can be overcome in the process of engaging children not merely as objects but as subjects of research and knowledge generation.
- Children on the move articulate their own experiences with God in ways that we cannot afford to miss in our theological deliberations. Children regularly speak of God's presence in their lives. They do this by expressing their faith in God, regularly talking with God, and often associating God with play. Reflections on children's drawings enable verbal expression of how children view God and also how they shape their faith.
- Our understanding of the various biblical imperatives mentioned in this chapter should shift us to listen carefully to and engage with children. Jesus's engagement of rabbinic scholars in the temple at a young age and without his parents being present is very instructive in this regard.
- A shift in scholarship around children is increasingly advocating for intergenerational models of ministry.

Doing theology with children will cause us to wrestle, to create, and to open up innovative spaces in which real children are present offering their real voices, questions, struggles, and hopes, "not as the object of care

Doing theology with children will cause us to wrestle, to create, and to open up innovative spaces in which real children are present offering their real voices, questions, struggles, and hopes.

47. Shantelle Weber and Stephan de Beer, "Doing theology *with* children in a South African context: Children as collaborators in intergenerational ministry," *HTS Teologiese Studies / Theological Studies* 72, no. 1 (25 November 2016): 1–3. This article refers to children in varied contexts including those on the move.

by theology, but as a source of critical and constructive light for theology."[48] What the Child Theology movement affirms is the reality of children's spirituality and how closely it relates to their personal development. What is missing, though, apart from anecdotes, narratives, or metaphors retrieved by the adults, remains the presence, voices, and disruptions of children themselves. We mostly still theologize and theorize over, about, and for children, without children being with us in new and hospitable spaces to share their own experiences, knowledge, and insights firsthand.[49] The utter defenselessness of these children in our midst at first disarms but then disrupts as we with our carefully constructed theological discourses and sophisticated political treatises do not know how to handle the children.[50]

Deuteronomy 24:19–21 admonishes us to welcome and care for refugees. For children growing up differently, exposed to violence from a young age, and often victims of abandonment or neglect, the challenge to negotiate identity and diversity must also be considered theologically. Multicultural churches face the challenge of constructing appropriate language, worship, and practices that are inclusive and just, not allowing dominant language or cultural expressions to dictate, and deeply sensitive to the different life circumstances children bring with them into the worshiping space. How do we accompany children's faith formation in ways that simultaneously foster within them a deep consciousness for social justice and equality rooted in the dignity of all people, and in ways that can help children to socialize beyond the socioeconomic and racial barriers that still keep them apart?[51]

The 2010 Lausanne Commitment calls us toward interfaith partnerships because the church is not the only influential voice affected by the needs of children on the move.[52] Pinedo notes examples of such partnerships in Latin America when highlighting the global critical issue of this chapter.

> Our "neighbors" include people of other faiths. We must learn to see them as neighbors and be neighbors to them. We seek to share the good news in ethical evangelism, and we reject unworthy proselytizing. We accept that our commission includes

48. H. Willmer and K. J. White, *Entry Point: Towards Child Theology with Matthew 18* (London: WTL, 2013), 15.

49. Weber and de Beer, "Doing theology," 3.

50. Stephan de Beer, *The Gospel, Children and the City* (Pretoria: Imagine, 2006).

51. Weber and de Beer, "Doing theology," 9.

52. Smith, "Summary of the Cape Town Commitment," https://lausanne.org/content/summary-of-the-cape-town-commitment.

> a willingness to suffer and die for Christ in reaching out to people of other faiths. We are called to embody and commend the gospel of grace in loving action, in all cultures. We need to respect "diversity in discipleship," and encourage one another to exercise cultural discernment. We recognize global diaspora as strategic for evangelization: scattered peoples can be both recipients and agents of Christ's mission. While being willing to sacrifice our own rights for the sake of Christ, we commit to uphold and defend the human rights of others, including the right to religious freedom.[53]

During the xenophobic attacks in South Africa in 2019, a coalition of ministers under the leadership of Rev. Alan Storey welcomed refugees into the Methodist Church of Cape Town building as a place of safety.[54] This church building became a refuge to many women and their children. We are reminded too of the story of Joseph who being sold into slavery by his own family became a testimony of God's protection and provision. The church needs refugees as exemplars of God's grace and being at work in "the other." Children bring people from all tribes and cultures together because we are called to care for them. The call to an interfaith collaboration which welcomes these children is crucial in our gospel imperative to reaching children and families on the move.

Bibliography

Africa Study Bible: New Living Translation. Illinois: Oasis International, 2016.

Bunge, Marcia J. "A more vibrant theology of children." *Christian Reflection: A Series in Faith and Ethics* 8 (2003): 11–19.

——— "Conceptions of and Commitments to Children: Biblical Wisdom for Families, Congregations, and the Worldwide Church," in *Faith Forward (Volume Three): Launching a Revolution through Ministry with Children, Youth, and Families*, edited by David M. Csinos, 94–112. Kelowna: Wood Lake, 2018.

——— "Tasks, Sources and Significances of Theologies of Childhood" in *Theologies of Childhood and the Children of Africa*, edited by J. Grobbelaar and G. Breed, AOSIS, Cape Town, 2016, 92–112.

Couture, Pamela D. *Seeing Children, Seeing God: A Practical Theology of Children and Poverty*. Nashville, TN: Abingdon, 2000.

de Beer, Stephan. *The Gospel, Children and the City*. Pretoria: Imagine, 2006.

53. Smith, https://lausanne.org/content/summary-of-the-cape-town-commitment.

54. Lucas Nowicki, "Rev Alan Storey fed up with refugee leaders, considering church's options: Methodist Church has provided shelter to hundreds of people for months but the 'hostile and volatile' situation has become 'untenable,'" *Times Live* (10 January 2020).

"Ending corporal punishment of children: A handbook for worship and gatherings." Church Network for Non-Violence (2015). http://churchesfornon-violence.org/wp/wp-content/uploads/2015/03/Ending-corporal-punishment-of-children-A-handbook-for-worship-and-gatherings.pdf.

Grobbelaar, Jan, and Gert Breed. *Welcoming Africa's Children: Theological and Ministry Perspectives*. Cape Town: AOSIS, 2016.

McConnell, Douglas, Jennifer Orona, and Paul Stockley, eds. *Understanding Gods Heart for Children: Toward a Biblical Framework*. Colorado Springs: Authentic, 2007.

Moltmann, Jürgen. *The Power of the Powerless*. New York: Harper & Row, 1983.

Nessan, Craig L. "Child Liberation Theology." *Currents in Theology and Mission* 45, no. 3 (2018): 6–13. https://currentsjournal.org/index.php/currents/article/view/127.

Nowicki, Lucas. "Rev Alan Storey fed up with refugee leaders, considering church's options: Methodist Church has provided shelter to hundreds of people for months but the 'hostile and volatile' situation has become 'untenable.'" *Times Live* (10 January 2020). https://www.timeslive.co.za/news/south-africa/2020-01-10-rev-alan-storey-fed-up-with-refugee-leaders-considering-churchs-options/.

Palm, Selina, "Spiritual Capital." Ending Violence Against Children Webinar (26 February 2020). https://jliflc.com/resources/ending-violence-against-children-webinar-spiritual-capital-with-selena-palm/.

Robinson, Malia, and Stephen Hanmer. "Engaging religious communities to protect children from abuse, neglect, and exploitation: Partnerships require analysis of religious virtues and harms." *Child Abuse & Neglect* 38, no. 4 (2014): 600–611. https://pubmed.ncbi.nlm.nih.gov/24726584/.

Smith, Kevin. "Summary of the Cape Town Commitment." Lausanne Movement (18 March 2011). http: lausanne.org/content/summary-of-the-cape-town-commitment.

Stoller, R. "Towards a child liberation theology" (April 2016). https://www.patheos.com/blogs/unfundamentalistparenting/2016/04/towards-a-child-liberation-theology/.

Troftgruben, Troy. "Toxic theology: A pastoral response to Bible passages often used to justify the abuse of children or prevent them from seeking care." *Currents in Theology and Mission* 45, no. 3 (2018): 56–60. https://currentsjournal.org/index.php/currents/article/view/137.

Weber, Shantelle, and Stephan de Beer. "Doing theology *with* children in a South African context: Children as collaborators in intergenerational ministry." *HTS Teologiese Studies / Theological Studies* 72, no. 1 (25 November 2016): 1–9. http://dx.doi.org/10.4102/hts.v72i1.3572.

"Who are Children-at-Risk?: A Missional Definition." Lausanne Movement Consultation on Children at Risk, Quito, Ecuador, 17–19 November 2014. https://lausanne.org/content/statement/children-at-risk-missional-definition.

Willmer, H., and K. J. White. *Entry Point: Towards Child Theology with Matthew 18*. London: WTL, 2013.

Case Study:
The Lion Is Furious When He Doesn't Know How to Get Back to His Home

Clenir Xavier T. dos Santos – Brazilian

> *"Living with compassion means entering into the other's dark moments. It is to penetrate places of pain; it is not to retreat or look away when someone is in agony. Compassion prevents us from giving easy and light explanations when the tragedy hits someone we know or love."*
>
> Henri Nouwen[55]

Paloma could not understand what was happening that night.[56] One telephone call changed her entire life! Paloma sensed the tension emanating from her parents; their fear was palpable. Her mother, Isabel, hurriedly stuffed some clothes in a backpack, and they fled, trying very hard to do so quietly.

Looking back, Isabel vented, "We were terrified when we discovered they were coming after us." Her eyes widened as she relived the horror of that day. "We had no time to think. We left everything behind. Our daughter would never again see her toys, her room, not even her friends." She continued, "I cut my long hair short and dyed it red. My husband shaved his head. Our daughter perceived our despair, and everything began to change. At every one of the twenty-two military outposts we crossed, we dreaded being recognized. When I finally spotted the Brazilian flag at the border, I burst out in tears of relief. We thought the nightmare was over, but it had only just begun."

Like thousands of Venezuelan families who live in extreme vulnerability, Paloma and her parents took shelter in Boa Vista city in northwestern Brazil. They stayed at four different shelters in the city. Some of these places were

55. Henri Nouwen in Henri Nouwen, Donald McNeill, and Douglas Morrison, *Compassion: A Reflection of the Christian Life* (New York: Doubleday, 1983), 4.

56. The children's names in this article have been changed to protect their identity.

totally unlivable. The family members stood in line for hours just to get a plate of food or a glass of water, enduring 40 C degree (104 F), blistering heat. One of the shelters, housing 3,700 refugees, greeted them by saying, "Welcome to Hell!" At these shelters they witnessed horrors that are seared into their memory. Paloma's parents covered her eyes so that she would not see children being beaten, sexually abused, crying desperately, or being dragged onto the streets to be prostituted.

To her parents' deep distress, Paloma's development halted as she stopped speaking, no longer smiled, was always on edge, would not play, wanted to be alone, reverted to diapers, would not eat, and had frequent fevers. A ray of hope came for Paloma's family when her father managed to find a job in the countryside of Rio de Janeiro. However upon arrival, they discovered they had been tricked and were forced into degrading work. They were in a rural zone, far from everything, with no money to allow them to leave. They were forced into heavy, exhausting labor, seven days a week, and in exchange received only food and a roof over their heads.

The decision to migrate, be it to seek a better quality of life or to flee death threats, changes people's lives completely. Children are especially affected. They have no choice but to follow their parents, grandparents, or uncles and aunts. In these challenging situations, the children witnessed their parents' vulnerability, face unimaginable situations such as the loss of a loved one, and often suffer abuse and neglect. Some children are even left alone at the border by family members in the hope that they will receive better care in the neighboring country. Paloma's case describes the reality many refugee families face, trapped in a situation analogous to slavery. The onset of COVID-19 accentuated the vulnerability of this people group. Daily, they face high danger of the contagion as they live in closed, overpopulated quarters with little or no ventilation and poor hygiene and protection.

In these challenging situations, the children witnessed their parents' vulnerability.

Several Christian organizations have worked to reach out to families and children on the move. Here we mention three organizations and their outreach ministries.

First is Project Nehemiah (Projeto Neemias) founded in Americana, São Paulo and driven by a vision to rescue children like Paloma and her family. The founders are three Venezuelans who endured similar slavery-like experiences when they arrived in Brazil. Ana Graciela Quiva, a cofounder and director of the Nehemiah Project, shares that upon managing to free themselves, they were determined to dedicate their lives to rescuing other families from these inhumane situations. Project Nehemiah seeks to provide the refugees and people on the move with housing and a familiar atmosphere and to promote restoration through a personal relationship with Jesus Christ. The long-term goal is for the refugees and immigrants to regain personal and familiar autonomy through decent work.

Ana Graciela is grateful for the donations that arrive from churches. She muses, "The refugees are not only hungry for food – their hunger is also emotional and spiritual." She understands that aid must be holistic, that the churches need to overcome difficulties such as lack of time and resources and even language barriers in order to present the kingdom of God as the basis of human development. She states, "The Project is committed to helping restore the emotional and spiritual health of our rural people, as all bear deep scars, not only acquired in Venezuela, but also in the country that shelters us." Some local churches have contributed furniture, food, toys, books, and clothes so that more individual refugees and families can experience the Father's care and love in these shelters.

An effusive outpouring of gratitude has come from rescued Venezuelans. One of them stated, "We are so grateful to all those who freed us from the situation of slavery we had to endure. Grateful to those who gave us housing, food, and mainly contributed to our mental and spiritual health. We were like lost children in the streets, without direction or the wherewithal to survive. We hope this project continues; it is very important!"

After six months in this shelter, working with a therapist and a pediatrician, Paloma resumed normalcy and can once again smile, play, and speak. She dreams of a job for her father, and perhaps a new beginning for their family.

Pastor Claudinei Godoi and his wife, Priscila, are volunteers at the Nehemiah Project. They offer pastoral care to the Venezuelans. Every conversation helps these refugees understand more of what it means to lose rights and identity, and the long struggle to redeem basic dignity. Even as these people try to survive in a foreign land, the refugees bear the heavy burden of responsibility for their family members who face extreme deprivation in their country of origin. They send back what little money they can raise, making their own stability even more difficult to achieve.

Pastor Claudinei shared a moving story of his experience at the project. One day when he arrived at the shelter, Pastor Claudinei saw Alicia, a seventy-year-old lady, crying out in pain. She had just learned of her brother's death in Venezuela. Through tears she exclaimed, "Beloved brother of mine, I couldn't help you when you needed me the most, and now I can't even bury you. Woe is me! What shall become of me?" Pastor Claudinei did not know what to do at that moment until a little girl named Inez took him by the hand and guided him to Alicia, her grandmother. Inez remained at his side, waiting for a gesture or a comforting word for her grandmother. Suddenly, Pastor Claudinei felt a powerful prompting that the little girl was trying to communicate to him, "I trust in you! You can comfort my grandmother! Please, do something so that she will stop crying. It hurts me so much to see my grandmother suffering. You can help her!"

As soon as Pastor Claudinei touched the elderly women's shoulders, the little girl Inez moved away and left the pastor to help her grandmother. In the simplicity of a child's act, God communicates, clearly showing the transformation that he desires to carry out in this world, and that is to restore the mission of his church. Many initiatives are ongoing by organizations extending their hands to immigrants and refugees around the world. Sadly, it can be said that God's church has been timid in reaching out to embrace, receive, integrate, and face the difficulties and challenges of the children and their families on the move.

Second, Lifeword's Pavement Project workers have spent twenty years providing assistance to hundreds of churches in twenty-one countries who have accepted the challenge of taking the good news of freedom from oppression and injustice to children and adolescents at risk. The Evangelical Mission of the Portuguese Assemblies of God in Portimão, Portugal (Missão Lusitana) is a Pavement Project partner church and receives immigrants from Angola, Brazil, Cape Verde, and Colombia. Today, 52 percent of the church's active members are immigrants, and 48 percent are Portuguese. The church provides every type of support that is needed for those who arrive in the city and are in vulnerable situations, regardless of whether they are committed to the church. Many of these immigrants are abandoned by their friends or relatives who promised to support them. Hence, they are left with no one to provide them with assistance.

God's church has been timid in reaching out to embrace, receive, integrate, and face the difficulties and challenges of the children and their families on the move.

Although the immigrants easily understand the Portuguese language, cultural differences impose many barriers and separation. The foreigners need a lot of emotional and spiritual help to face their traumas. These traumas include leaving their homes, families, friends, and familiar settings. They also disappointment when their new life does not turn out as they had imagined. The unemployment rate is very high in the region, especially due to the coronavirus pandemic. The work that is available to the immigrants in the city is always heavy labor with very long hours and poor pay. Since they lack work documents, their rights are not respected. The immigrants also run the risk of developing serious health problems.

Missão Lusitana sought Pavement Project training to offer children and their families emotional and spiritual support. The church realized that their members needed to be prepared with knowledge and skills in specialized ministries to the most vulnerable. Only then would the church be able to help these migrants cope with their fears, insecurities, disillusionment, abandonment, rejection, rage, and deep pain. Many times the newcomers blame God for their precarious life, thinking that God abandoned them or does not care.

The children suffer greatly as their parents often end up neglecting them because they have to work excessively long hours. The adolescents encounter prejudice at school and find it difficult to make friends. The churches' ministries offer the migrants an environment where they can feel a sense of belonging and acceptance. Parents and children participate in all the activities alongside the native-born Portuguese. The pastor, Míriam Silveira Miranda, quoted a Portuguese woman who decided to join the community because "heaven will be like this, great diversity in unity!"

Heaven will be like this, great diversity in unity!

Missão Lusitana's vision is to show the migrants who come to the church that they are as welcomed and accepted as all the others, regardless of their place of origin. This ministry involvement with the migrants has changed the church's identity and mission focus. Pastor Míriam affirmed that they now recognize that their task as a church is to embrace this missionary movement.

Third is the Venezuelan Baptist Convention which cares for children and their families who have migrated from Venezuela and who live on the border with Colombia. These families live on the streets and are malnourished, and the children are deprived of education. In a partnership with Pavement Project, the Convention Visión entre Fronteras counsels each child, empathizing with her or his pain and suffering. Using the Green Bag approach,[57] they present Jesus to the children as a friend who can provide relief to their hearts and care for their needs and who views them as important and special. For these children who are suffering from adversity, this encounter is life changing. During the

57. So-called because many of the counselling resources are carried in an attractive green bag that symbolizes hope and healing – though there is now also an app.

counseling sessions, the children can freely share their thoughts without being judged and are fully welcomed and accepted. In this environment, the Holy Spirit has the freedom to bring change in the face of so much misery and to show that God cares for them and wants to walk with them.

Children like Gabriela, Pablo, and Tânia have benefited much from the Pavement Project Green Bag approach. Gabriela, who is thirteen years old, told us that she sees herself as a chameleon, changing her colors so that no one can see her. She was traumatized by her parent's divorce. During a Green Bag activity, she was presented with accounts of characters in the Bible who experienced similar situations. Gabriela said that for the first time, she felt listened to and was able to express herself and her pain, which was a huge relief to her. Now she feels happy and special. Soon after that incident, Gabriela once again compared herself to a chameleon, but this time her attitude was different. She explained, "I am a chameleon, but I no longer need to hide, because I have changed sadness into happiness, and shame into acceptance."

Pablo, a nine year old, is another example of this reality. Living on the streets of Cúcuta, Colombia, he felt rage and sadness. Pablo compared himself to an angry lion. He explained that "the lion is furious when he doesn't know how to get back to his home." Jerameel Linares of the Baptist Convention agreed that "an angry lion" was a perfect description of how Pablo behaved. Anger is a very common reaction to repeated injustices which can cause children to rage when trapped in a vicious cycle of abuse and resentment. When he understood that God helps and receives children as his own, Pablo changed into a happy child. He exclaimed, "Now I am a child of God, and I feel calm because God listens to me."

The Green Bag approach has helped many children like Gabriela and Pablo who suffer in at-risk situations to change how they perceive themselves in light of their circumstances. This perception allows the children to make positive decisions, to dream of a better future, and to once again harbor hope in their hearts. Jerameel shared that in each counseling session, he is surprised at how children begin to experience newness. They find happiness, tranquility, and peace that they did not possess before. He said, "They improve their behavior, become friendlier, more loving toward their colleagues, more willing to learn, and are more self-confident."

Another example of how the Pavement Project has impacted the community is a story from Borlis Chaverra of the PARE Foundation in Medellin, Colombia. This organization works with immigrants and refugees. Children who were already facing so many problems in their native lands usually arrive in Colombia with their family. He said that many children express their fears and worries about other family members who were not able to come with them. Borlis explained that while the parents attempt to find work, they often are not able to do so, and the family ends up living on the streets. This vicious cycle contributes to many of the children on the streets using drugs and committing petty crimes to survive.

For a long time, PARE Foundation struggled to find the best way to help these children. This was before they learned of the Pavement Project and trained to be counselors. Chaverra gratefully affirmed, "Now we see the transformation that occurs when they have an encounter with God." Gently encouraged and affirmed, and singing in their own language, the children worked through the traumas they have suffered. In the healing process, children draw their own conclusions about themselves based on Jesus's love for them. The gospel of Christ is revealed and reflected in the relationship that evolves from the caregiver's effort to understand, identify, listen to, and learn from the child.

Children on the move are persons in development. They possess a deep understanding of life and survival and have great sensitivity to spiritual need and resilience. Rather than being entrenched in acting as the "owners" and "guardians" of truth, knowledge, and power, we as Christian faith communities can reach out to children on the move and develop true dialogue with them. The church can listen with open, empathetic, humble hearts and be willing to learn and allow these children to reciprocate in ministry. In this way, we move away from self-sufficiency and a sense of superiority in the Christian faith and are able to visualize the richness of diversity and bring the children to the center of our conversation.

We as Christian faith communities can reach out to children on the move and develop true dialogue with them.

Christian faith communities face enormous challenges in our efforts to reach out to the migrants, but we also face enormous opportunities to grow as a loving, compassionate expression of Christ's love in the world. By operating from a relationship of equals, the body of Christ can experience a "transformational change" as Shantelle Weber defines in the previous article – seeking to develop its mission of strengthening the identity of the most vulnerable, walking side by side with them, respecting and valuing the richness of their differences, and effectively and integrally contributing so as to enable them to have a life of dignity that is holistic and blessed.

Tânia's self-image reveals a beautiful internal transformation when she described herself: "I am like a bottle full of water to help others who are thirsty."

Discussion Questions for Chapter 6

1. How are children being affirmed by the community where you are residing?
2. What practical steps can the Church make to welcome children on the move?
3. What are the differences or similarities between the way your community and your church affirm children?
4. What are some ways you can raise awareness of affirming children in your church or your community?

7

Included in God's Mission

Children are able to be not only recipients, but also agents of God's mission. Children's participation is essential to the mission of God.

Global Critical Issue: Redeeming Children Is Integral Missions

Sublimé Nyundu Mabiala – Congolese (DRC)

God's mission displays his intrinsic love and purpose to redeem and reinstate the human God relationship broken by disobedience. This salvific plan includes children of every nation, culture, and societal status.

Our generation has experienced massive migratory flux throughout the planet due to natural disasters and human-made tragedies during the last decade.[1] From the persecuted Christian families in restricted regions such as Northern Nigeria, Egypt, North Korea, and the Middle East to internally displaced persons (IDPs) within their own countries, from refugees and asylum seekers fleeing war zones to migrants in general, children remain the most vulnerable "people group" on the planet. Children are increasingly exposed to hostility and cross-cultural mobility on a global scale. In the first edition of this book, Gustavo Crocker and Karissa Glanville consider children both as "the objects" and "the carriers" of God's mission.[2] Glanville in her own article discusses the critical issues of raising children of mission in the twenty-first century by proposing several practical steps to help children and youth become participants in God's mission.[3]

This article takes the work of Crocker and Glanville further by focusing on the thousands of children who are being systemically persecuted because of their identification with the Christian faith. This article highlights the

1. According to the UNICEF statistics in 2019, the number of international migrants reached 272 million, and 33 million were children. "The number of international migrants reaches 272 million," UNICEF (2019), https://www.un.org/development/desa/en/news/population/international-migrant-stock-2019.html.

2. G. Crocker and K. Glanville, "Children and God's Mission," in *Understanding God's Heart for Children: Toward a Biblical Framework*, eds. D. McConnell, J. Orona, and P. Stockley (Colorado Springs: Authentic, 2007), 263–72.

3. K. Glanville, "Raising Kids of Mission in the 21st Century," in *Understanding God's Heart for Children: Toward a Biblical Framework*, eds. D. McConnell, J. Orona, and P. Stockley (Colorado Springs: Authentic, 2007), 273–281.

challenges faced by these children and considers how they are, and can be, included in God's mission. The phrase "included in God's mission" is employed to mean God's intrinsic love and purpose to redeem and reinstate the human God relationship broken by sin. This salvific plan includes children of every nation, culture, and societal status. The following pages cover two issues: First, the religious and societal marginalization, exclusion, and persecution of children due to their faith or ethnic background, and second, how Christian communities have sought to reach out to such children in the midst of these challenges.

Religious and Societal Marginalization, Exclusion, and Persecution

Marginalization, exclusion, and persecution of believers in Jesus Christ has existed from the beginning of the Christian church. Accounts in the book of Acts tell us that adult believers were persecuted, stoned to death, and jailed for their faith.[4] Here we consider the thousands of children who are being marginalized, excluded, and persecuted for their Christian faith. This form of religious persecution is directed at children from Christian families living in hostile environments and who become victims of violence because of their religious beliefs. In 2021 Open Doors, an international NGO that globally advocates for persecuted Christians, reported that between October 2019 and September 2020, approximately 309 million Christians were living in countries with very high or extreme levels of persecution.[5] Ewelina Ochab, cofounder of the Coalition for Genocide Response, reported that "one in eight Christians worldwide live in countries where they face persecution." Ochab highlights the persecution of religious minorities around the globe, particularly on the Daesh genocide in Syria and Iraq, Boko Haram and other jihadist groups in West Africa, and the situation of religious minorities in South Asia. In these contexts, she reports that boys are specifically vulnerable to being recruited

Here we consider the thousands of children who are being marginalized, excluded, and persecuted for their Christian faith.

4. See Acts 4:1–21; 5:17–18; 6:8–14; 9:22–30.

5. "Christian Persecution," Open Doors (2021), https://www.opendoorsusa.org/christian-persecution/.

or killed, and girls are often displaced in informal camps and face a high risk of abduction and forced marriage.[6]

In context of the African church, I now present three examples of the types of marginalization and persecution which children are facing today.

First, Sarah Cunningham of Open Doors tells the stories of Christian children who face persecution in countries hostile to Christianity.[7] The case of Hassan (not his real name) in North Africa who was almost hit by a stone while in the classroom is illustrative of the treatment that children from Christian homes can expect in many communities around the world. The story also shows how Christian parents can strengthen their children's resilience by teaching them that suffering is inherent to following Jesus Christ. Cunningham narrates the conversation of Hassan who asked his father why people throw stones at them. In response, Hassan's father stated that Christians are hated because they follow Jesus (John 15:20; 2 Tim 3:12). In some cases, children who face persecution are encouraged by their parents to participate in Christ's sufferings in spite of this hostility and to love their enemies (Matt 5:43–48). Hassan's story is an example of the persecution faced by Christian children who live out their faith in Christ, or at least their identity as a Christian family, in restricted regions across the globe.

A second type of marginalization, exclusion, and persecution of children, though not necessarily linked to them being Christians, is the allegations of witchcraft. A general definition of witchcraft is "a set of beliefs, structures and shared beliefs by a given population that addresses the origin of misfortune, illness and death, and the set of practices for detection, treatment and punishment that corresponds to these beliefs."[8] The phenomenon of children accused of being witches and harmed continues today in communities around the globe,[9] but is more intense in the African Congolese region. There are many reasons why children are accused of witchcraft. Sometimes the accuser does it out of fear of the supernatural, reluctance to care for a child, or because the

6. Ewelina U. Ochab, "One in Eight Christians Worldwide Live in Countries Where They May Face Persecution," *Forbes* (13 January 2021), https://www.forbes.com/sites/ewelinaochab/2021/01/13/one-in-eight-christians-worldwide-live-in-countries-where-they-would-be-persecuted/?sh=161714315016.

7. Sarah Cunningham, "Children Are the Most Vulnerable Members of the Persecuted Church," Open Doors (1 December 2017), https://www.opendoorsusa.org/christian-persecution/stories/children-persecuted-church/.

8. Marc Auge, "Les Croyances à la Sorcellerie," in *La Construction du Monde*, ed. M. Auge (Cambridge: Cambridge University Press, 1974), 53.

9. D. K. Hanson and D. R. Ruggiero, *Child Witchcraft Allegations and Human Rights* (Brussels: EU Parliament, 2013). It has been evidenced in sub-Saharan African countries.

child has a severe illness. It does not help that even in the churches wrong teachings prevail, the leaders use this situation as a means to earn money through exorcism. Whatever the reason, children who are accused of witchcraft can be ostracized from the community, beaten, imprisoned, or even sometimes set on fire and left to die.

On the global scale, faith-based and human rights-based organizations are increasingly condemning the abusive and inhuman treatment of children accused of practicing witchcraft.[10] In his response article titled, "Christian Pastors and Child Witches in Kinshasa, DRC," Nzash U. Lumeya suggests a community-based hermeneutic approach to this phenomenon drawing from traditional African Congolese kinship and Jesus's model in Matthew 17:14–21.[11] Lumeya draws three implications from this narrative to apply healing to displaced street children who have been abused due to allegations of witchcraft. First, Jesus welcomed the outcast and powerless child (hospitality). Second, Jesus identified the causes of the problem by conversing with the child's parent (sympathy). Third, Jesus rebuked the evil spirit out of the victimized child (opportunity).

A third type of marginalization, exclusion, and persecution which children in Africa are facing today is that many school going children of the Christian faith are subjected to forced labor. These children are forced to work on the

10. J. Ballet, B. Lallau and C. Dumbi, "The Exploitation of Sorcerer Children in Kinshasa (RDC)," in *Child Exploitation in the Global South*, eds. J. Ballet and A. Bhukuth (New York: Palgrave Macmillan, 2018), 132–33; A. Cimpric, *Children Accused of Witchcraft: An Anthropological Study of Contemporary Practices in Africa = Les Enfants Accusés de Sorcellerie: Etude Anthropologique* (Dakar: UNICEF WCARO, 2010), 16–17; F. De Boeck and M. -F. Plissart, *Kinshasa: Tales of the Invisible City* (Leuven: Leuven University Press, 2014); A. Honwana and F. de Boeck, eds., *Makers and Breakers: Children and Youth in Postcolonial Africa* (Oxford, UK: James Currey, 2005); F. de Boeck, 2006, 113–25; F. de Boeck, "At risk, as risk: Abandonment and care in a world of spiritual insecurity," in *The Devil's Children: From Spirit Possession to Witchcraft: New Allegations that Affect Children*, ed. J. La Fontaine (Farnham, UK: Ashgate, 2009), 130, 144–46; J. A. Molina, *The Invention of Child Witches in the Democratic Republic of Congo: Social cleansing, religious commerce and the difficulties of being a parent in an urban culture* (Save the Children, 2006); L. N. Pereira, "Families, churches, the state, and the child witch in Angola," in *Sorcery in Black Atlantic*, eds. L. N. Parés and R. Sansi (Chicago: University of Chicago Press, 2011), 188–90; R. J. Priest, A. Ngolo, and T. Stabell, "Christian Pastors and Alleged Child Witches in Kinshasa, DRC," *OKH Journal: Anthropological Ethnography and Analysis Through the Eyes of Christian Faith* 4, no. 1 (2020): 3; S. Snow, "Explaining Abuse of 'Child Witches' in Africa: Powerful Witchbusters in Weak States," *Journal of Religion and Society* 19 (2017): 5; and Stobart, *Child Abuse Linked to Accusations of "Possession" and "Witchcraft"* (Nottingham, UK: Department for Education and Skills, 2006), 19–20.

11. N. U. Lumeya, "Christian Pastors and Child Witches in Kinshasa, DRC," *On Knowing Humanity Journal* 4 (2020): 81–82.

farms or in the homes of their non-Christian teachers. Because of this forced labor, these children are also denied equal education opportunities.

Standing Alongside Children Who Are Persecuted

In view of the above examples of marginalization, exclusion, and persecution which children face, the local and global church must seriously and vigorously reach out to help strengthen these children and advocate for their well-being. Some ways that the church can and has stepped in to help these children are the following:

a) *Increase the resilience of children and their families.* The reality of Christian persecution of children in hostile environments cannot be denied. Persecution is part and parcel of the Christian faith. I argue that the local and global church needs to do more to prepare children and their parents to endure persecution and provide them with strength to withstand it. Family ministry and education can be carried out in such a way that parents are able to discuss with their children what persecution is about and how they are to respond. Ideally in a home atmosphere of love, protection, and understanding, children can come to a greater appreciation of the Christian faith.

The local and global church needs to do more to prepare children and their parents to endure persecution and provide them with strength to withstand it.

b) *Provide contextual discipleship models* that will equip children for persecution. Jesus made it very clear that the kingdom of God belongs to children, and they form an integral part of the church, not least the African church where numerically children under age fifteen are a large proportion of the congregation. Hence, contextual discipleship which equips children to know God and his word, to be strengthened in the faith, and to be guided to respond when they meet with antagonistic encounters is needed. Contextual discipleship takes into account the political, cultural, and social lenses of the children and their families.

c) *Equip and train the children's workers* to work with children who are persecuted. The church in hostile environments needs Sunday school curricula which incorporate teaching on persecution and Christ-like responses. Also, training is required for children's ministry workers to teach these materials in ways that the children will understand. To strengthen the outreach, children's ministry should go beyond just Sunday school to incorporate listening and counselling services for children who are facing persecution, as well providing protection, care, and shelter for them.

The church in hostile environments needs Sunday school curricula which incorporate teaching on persecution.

d) *Set up a network* to help Christian communities come to terms with the reality of child persecution and to set up support systems that are lacking in local churches. Local churches could connect with the various non-governmental and faith-based-organizations that are working with persecuted children. Within the network should be persons who specialize in treating trauma and who can train local workers. Setting up a network could also improve the advocacy voice of children who face persecution, moving from regional to global platforms.

Conclusion

The article addresses the religious and societal marginalization, exclusion, and persecution of children due to faith beliefs and how faith communities have sought to reach out to them in the midst of these challenges. The three main reasons for the marginalization, exclusion, and persecution of Christian children in the African region are religious beliefs, witchcraft allegations, and forced labor. In these situations, children are physically and sexually abused and denied justice and their human rights. While it is a predicament, the situation presents an opportunity for the African church to rise up and make a difference. The article proposes four main ways to address the challenge: a) increase the resilience of children and their families; b) provide contextual discipleship for children and their families who face persecution; c) equip and train children workers to work with persecuted children; and d) set up a network for collaboration. While these are being enacted, it is hoped that Christians globally will pray, champion the cause, and be involved in empowering, protecting, and caring for these children as part of integral missions.

Bibliography

Augé, Marc. "Les Croyances à la Sorcellerie." In *La Construction du Monde*, ed. M. Augé, 128–136. Cambridge: Cambridge University Press, 1974.

———. "Savoir voir et savoir vivre: les croyances à la sorcellerie en Côte d'Ivoire." *Africa*, 46, no. 2 (1976): 128–36.

Ballet, J., B. Lallau and C. Dumbi. "The Exploitation of Sorcerer Children in Kinshasa (RDC)." In *Child Exploitation in the Global South*, edited by J. Ballet and A. Bhukuth, 125–40. New York: Palgrave Macmillan, 2018.

"Christian Persecution." Open Doors (2021). https://www.opendoorsusa.org/christian-persecution/.

Cimpric, A. *Children Accused of Witchcraft: An Anthropological Study of Contemporary Practices in Africa = Les Enfants Accusés de Sorcellerie: Etude Anthropologique.* Dakar: UNICEF WCARO, 2010. https://www.refworld.org/docid/4e97f5902.html.

Crocker, G., and K. Glanville. "Children and God's Mission." In *Understanding God's Heart for Children: Toward a Biblical Framework*, edited by D. McConnell, J. Orona, and P. Stockley, 263–72. Colorado Springs: Authentic, 2007.

Cunningham, Sarah. "Children Are the Most Vulnerable Members of the Persecuted Church." Open Doors (1 December 2017). https://www.opendoorsusa.org/christian-persecution/stories/children-persecuted-church/.

De Boeck, F. "At risk, as risk: Abandonment and care in a world of spiritual insecurity." In *The Devil's Children: From Spirit Possession to Witchcraft: New Allegations that Affect Children*, edited by J. La Fontaine, 129–50. Farnham, UK: Ashgate, 2009.

De Boeck, F., and M. -F. Plissart. *Kinshasa: Tales of the Invisible City*. Leuven: Leuven University Press, 2014.

"Democratic Republic of the Congo: Intercountry Adoptions and Exit Permits Suspended." Travel.State.gov, U.S. Department of State (4 May 2020). https://travel.state.gov/content/travel/en/News/Intercountry-Adoption-News/democratic-republic-of-the-congo--intercountry-adoptions-and-exi.html.

"Did they plot to steal Africa's orphans of war?" *The Guardian* (n.d.). Retrieved 19 February 2021, https://www.theguardian.com/world/2007/nov/04/france.sudan.

Glanville, K. "Raising Kids of Mission in the 21st Century." In *Understanding God's Heart for Children: Toward a Biblical Framework*, edited by D. McConnell, J. Orona, and P. Stockley, 273–81. Colorado Springs: Authentic, 2007.

Hanciles, J. *Beyond Christendom: Globalization, African Migration, and the Transformation of the West*. Maryknoll, NY: Orbis, 2008.

Hanson, D., and D. Ruggiero. *Child Witchcraft Allegations and Human Rights*. Brussels: EU Parliament, 2013. https://op.europa.eu/en/publication-detail/-/publication/b5c65fff-4145-4891-84ed-f5a43a0d5f87.

Honwana, A., and F. de Boeck, eds. *Makers and Breakers: Children and Youth in Postcolonial Africa*. Oxford, UK: James Currey, 2005.

Jezewski, M., and P. Sotnik. *Culture Brokering: Providing Culturally Competent Rehabilitation Services to Foreign-born Persons*. Buffalo, NY: Center for International Rehabilitation Research Information and Exchange, 2001.

Kraft, C. *Two Hours to Freedom: A Simple and Effective Model for Healing and Deliverance*. Grand Rapids, MI: Baker, 2010.

Kunhiyop, S. *Witchcraft, Beliefs and Accusations*. Jos: Challenge Press, 2020.

Lumeya, N. U. "Christian Pastors and Child Witches in Kinshasa, DRC." *On Knowing Humanity Journal* 4 (2020): 81–82. https://www.researchgate.net/publication/339120067_OKH_Journal_Vol_41_Child_Witchcraft_Accusations_and_the_Church/fulltext/5e3ee248299bf1cdb918ea1c/OKH-Journal-Vol-41-Child-Witchcraft-Accusations-and-the-Church.pdf.

Molina, J. A. *The Invention of Child Witches in the Democratic Republic of Congo: Social cleansing, religious commerce and the difficulties of being a parent in an urban culture*. Save The Children, 2006. https://resourcecentre.savethechildren.net/document/invention-child-witches-social-cleansing-religious-commerce-and-difficulties-being-parent/.

Mukundi, M. "Witchcraft among the Kasaian people of Zaire: Challenge and response." Unpublished PhD diss., Fuller Theological Seminary, 1990. https://www.proquest.com/openview/fb5b6054e9533da4cfc351e3833869b4/1?pq-origsite=gscholar&cbl=18750&diss=y.

Ochab, Ewelina U. "One in Eight Christians Worldwide Live in Countries Where They May Face Persecution." *Forbes* (13 January 2021). https://www.forbes.com/sites/ewelinaochab/2021/01/13/one-in-eight-christians-worldwide-live-in-countries-where-they-would-be-persecuted/?sh=161714315016.

Open Doors, "Christian Persecution" (2021), https://www.opendoorsusa.org/christian-persecution/.

Pereira, L. N. "Families, churches, the state, and the child witch in Angola." In *Sorcery in Black Atlantic*, edited by L. N. Parés and R. Sansi, 188–90. Chicago: University of Chicago Press, 2011.

Pollock, D. C., R. E. Van Reken, and M. V. Pollock. *Third Culture Kids: Growing Up among Worlds*. 3rd ed. Boston, London: Nicholas Brealey, 2010.

Priest, R. J., A. Ngolo, and T. Stabell. "Christian Pastors and Alleged Child Witches in Kinshasa, DRC." *OKH Journal: Anthropological Ethnography and Analysis Through the Eyes of Christian Faith* 4, no. 1 (2020): 1–51. https://www.okhjournal.org/index.php/okhj/article/view/81.

Snow, S. "Explaining Abuse of 'Child Witches' in Africa: Powerful Witchbusters in Weak States." *Journal of Religion and Society* 19 (2017). http://dspace.creighton.edu:8080/xmlui/handle/10504/114375.

Stobart, E. *Child Abuse Linked to Accusations of "Possession" and "Witchcraft."* Nottingham, UK: Department for Education and Skills, 2006. https://liverpoolscp.proceduresonline.com/pdfs/ch_abuse_witchcraft.pdf.

UNICEF "The number of international migrants reaches 272 million," (2019), https://www.un.org/development/desa/en/news/population/international-migrant-stock-2019.html.

Biblical and Theological Response:

Children as Full Members of the Priesthood of All Believers: A Pastoral Paradigm for Including Children in the Mission of God

Harold Segura – Costa Rican

Introduction

In the first edition of *Understanding God's Heart for Children*, Crocker and Glanville explore some of the "biblical premises that place children at the center of God's mission both as the object of his mission and as the carriers of the mission themselves by presenting a biblical survey of children *as* God's mission and *in* God's mission."[12] In this sequel, I will extend this scriptural reflection to confronting and reprising the missionary passion today and update priorities considering the new and challenging conditions of the world. Sublime Mabiala, in the global critical issue of this chapter, identifies various challenges faced by children around the world related to religious and societal marginalization as well as persecution due to their faith or ethnic background. In light of these developments, how should we reflect biblically, zooming in on God's heart to include children in his divine mission as evidenced in various portions of the Bible?

Children: Active Subjects and Full Members of the "Priesthood of All Believers"?

It is necessary to look at children through the lenses of historical and evangelical perspective and consider the scope of the *Missio Dei*.[13] According to the

12. Gustavo Crocker and Karissa Glanville, "Children and God's Mission," in *Understanding God's Heart for Children*, eds. Douglas McConnell, Jennifer Orona, and Paul Stockley (Colorado Springs: Authentic, 2007), 263, emphasis original.

13. The *Missio Dei* is an ancient expression attributed to Augustine of Hippo and addressed in recent centuries by different missiological schools. The intention is to express that the mission belongs to God and not to the church. The Church is an instrument of the mission, but not who

Scriptures, *Missio Dei* is a mission that must be available to all (universal), directed toward all dimensions of life (holistic) and that counts on all (inclusive and participatory). It is at this last point where the question arises about the place of children as protagonists or as *active subjects*.

Missio Dei is a mission that must be available to all (universal), directed toward all dimensions of life (holistic) and that counts on all (inclusive and participatory).

This article will discuss some questions arising from the perspective of Martin Luther's teachings and the Reformed tradition: Are children an active subject of mission? And if they are, in what ways can their participation be understood? Are they the main or secondary actors in the divine drama called mission? Are they part of the "priesthood of all believers" alluded to by Martin Luther and the Reformed tradition? There are other questions which could be addressed, but these will be the focus of this particular discussion.

Luther and the Priesthood of All Believers

It was the German Reformer Martin Luther who, among his well-known theological successes, spoke and wrote about the universal priesthood of all believers. With a brilliant intuition of renewal, he recovered the New Testament doctrine (although there are flashes of it in the Old Testament) that all believers (lay and ordained) are priests and kings in Christ and are called to contribute to the common good in a variety of ways. One of the universal epistles, 1 Peter, declares, "But you are a chosen people, a royal priesthood, a holy nation, God's special possession, that you may declare the praises of him who called you out of darkness into his wonderful light" (1 Pet 2:9). Other texts support the same principle, some in Hebrews and others in Revelation.

Luther exposed the principle of the priesthood of all believers as being in contradiction with the monopoly that for centuries had been exercised by the hierarchy of the church. The priests and bishops, appealing to the sacred honor of their calling, reserved the exercise of the ministry for a few, the ordained priesthood. Contrary to this practice, the Reformer Luther proclaimed the freedom of all people to establish direct communication with God without

defines or configures it. See Charles Van Engen, *Transforming Mission Theology* (Littleton, CO: William Carey Library, 2017), 435.

human intermediaries. He taught that if all people can directly access God, and if the faith that saves is available to all equally, then the mission of God has been entrusted to all. In a famous text written in 1520 and entitled *The Babylonian Captivity*, Luther states,

> This is where the Christian brotherhood has perished, the shepherds have become wolves. . . . If they could be compelled to recognise that all of us baptised are priests in the same degree as they, as we really are, and that their ministry has been entrusted to them only by our consent, they would immediately realise that they do not enjoy any legal domain on us, unless we spontaneously want to grant them. This is the meaning of what is said in the first letter of Peter.[14]

From Luther onwards, other reformers and reform movements have embraced this same principle. Calvin declared it in his own way, and years later, the radical reformers called Anabaptists also did. Luther lived with a passion for the mission of the church, either as spreading the gospel to all the ends of the earth (evangelization of nations) or as working to affect society with the values of the gospel (evangelization of culture), among other dimensions of that same mission.[15]

To respond to Luther's understanding that "through baptism all of us are consecrated to the priesthood,"[16] we in the Christian church today would do well to nurture children in the knowledge of God and use developmentally appropriate avenues to engage children in the *Missio Dei*. Luther wrote catechisms and religious education materials for parents to use in the home, and he emphasized the responsibility of parents to guide and instruct their children in the faith.[17] In the outline "Lutheran Commitments to Children and Youth," Bunge mentions that Lutherans and Protestants hold that "The Holy Spirit has no 'age restrictions' and that all are part of the priesthood of

14. Martin Luther, "La cautividad babilónica de la iglesia," in *Works of Luther*, ed. Teófanes Eguidio (Salamanca: Ediciones Sígueme, 1977), 145–46.

15. Sídney H. Rooy, *Luther and Mission. Theology and Practice of Mission in Martin Luther* (Saint Louis: Concordia, 2014), 109.

16. Martin Luther, *To the Christian Nobility of the German Nation Concerning the Reform of the Christian Estate* (1520) in *Luther's Works* (LW), edited by Jaroslav Pelikan and Helmut Lehmann (St. Louis: Concordia Publishing House, 1955–86), 44:127–30.

17. Jane Strohl, "The Child in Luther's Theology: 'For What Purpose Do We Older Folks Exist, Other Than to Care for . . . the Young,'" in *The Child in Christian Thought*, ed. Marcia Bunge (Grand Rapids, MI: Eerdmans, 2001), 134–59.

believers."[18] As a corollary to this assertion, Bunge adds that Lutherans and Protestants would also admit that children are "full and equal members of the priesthood of all believers, interpreters of the Word; and children have vocations here and now."[19] These assertions imply that children are not merely recipients but are also agents of the *Missio Dei*. Bunge recognizes that children are "gifts of God, signs of God's blessing . . . agents of God . . . moral witnesses, models of faith for adults, sources or vehicles of revelation, and representatives of Jesus . . . and even paradigms for entering the reign of God."[20] In other words, children have the capacity to respond to God, obey his will, and be actors just like adults in the grand scheme of God's plan of reconciling the world to himself (2 Cor 5:19).

> The Holy Spirit has no 'age restrictions'

Children in the Evangelical Missionary Movement

How have the great evangelical missionary encounters and corresponding statements of the last decades answered these questions? The issue of children in mission has been ignored for many years. Mission and social context are historically related in a dynamic way. Sometimes the mission affects the context, but other times, the sociocultural and political contexts define the ministerial actions of the faith community. As for society, it took until 20 November 1989 for the UN General Assembly to approve the Convention on the Rights of the Child (CRC). This historical milestone has deep and logical connotations for mission.

The Lausanne Movement, recognized as a theological and missionary reference of the evangelical world, did not say anything about children in their well-known Lausanne Pact of 1974, although some paragraphs may refer implicitly to work in favor of children, especially those that invite us to carry out holistic mission and be committed to all human needs. Fifteen years after that first declaration another was written, the result of a meeting of more

18. Marcia Bunge, "Lutheran Commitments to Children and Youth: Theological Foundations, Historical Perspectives, and Contemporary Initiatives," Class Handout for The Child in Christian Thought, Asia-Pacific Nazarene Theological Seminary, January 2021, 2.

19. Bunge, "Lutheran Commitments," 2.

20. Marcia Bunge, "The Child, Religion, and the Academy: Developing Robust Theological and Religious Understandings of Children and Childhood," *Journal of Religion* 86, no. 4 (October 2006): 561, 562, 567. Bunge uses Matt 18:2–5 as basis for the assertion "paradigms for entering the reign of God."

than three thousand evangelical leaders in Manila, Philippines. The Manila Manifesto, issued in July 1989, recognizes the place of children in the worship of the church and in extending the faith.[21] These lines show the evangelical movement's new sensitivity toward children.

In 2010, eleven years after the CRC, the Lausanne Movement held another global gathering in Cape Town, South Africa. The final document of this meeting is called "The Cape Town Commitment." One part of this statement reads as follows:

> Children and youth are the Church of today, not just that of tomorrow. Young people have great potential as active agents in God's mission. . . . They represent the "new energy" to transform the world. We must listen to them and not stifle their youth filled spirituality with our rationalistic adult approaches.[22]

This document is a notable advance in the understanding of the universal priesthood of children since it frames children as not only objects of mission (evangelizing, social change, community building, and educating), but also as part of the people of God, subjects and participants in the redemptive project. Thus "The Cape Town Commitment" very much alludes to the priestly functions of children.

This advance in the Cape Town declaration, as well as in other subsequent declarations and in other sectors of the evangelical faith, renders a great service to children and in addition to the rest of the faith community. These commitments help to renew the models of ministry and reject, even a little, the traditional models for fulfilling mission: adult-centered and patriarchal models which revolve around the authority and decisions of adults and almost always the men. *The priesthood of all children* raises eloquent criticism of those models that have characterized the exercise of the mission for many centuries. Children can be teachers of the church and promoters of profound changes. This is perhaps what Jesus was referring to when "He called a little child to him, and placed the child among them. And he said: 'Truly I tell you, unless you change and become like little children, you will never enter the kingdom of heaven'" (Matt 18:2–3).

The Cape Town Commitment very much alludes to the priestly functions of children.

21. "Manila Manifesto," Lausanne Movement (1989).

22. "Cape Town Commitment," Lausanne Movement (2011), IV, 5.

Becoming like children can be humbling, but at the same time liberating. The broad and comprehensive participation of children completes a fundamental change in the mentality of the church, even a profound conversion according to the text of Matthew.

I have presented a new pastoral paradigm for the inclusion of children in the mission of God within the framework of Luther's notion of the priesthood of all believers. On the one hand in this paradigm, children have spiritual, social, psychological, and other needs that the church is called to address. Many children are persecuted, as Mabiala identifies – in Syria, Iraq, Africa, and South Asia. In addition, many children are accused of witchcraft in the African Congolese region. How can faith-based organizations redeem the value of children, bring them to the knowledge of Christ, and equip them to engage in God's mission? On the other hand, children have spiritual, social, psychological, and other capacities that the church is called to recognize and value. For this reason, it is possible to affirm that children are a task and a gift: a task to fulfill (the mission toward children) and a gift to welcome (the mission of children).

Children are a task and a gift: a task to fulfill (the mission toward children) and a gift to welcome (the mission of children).

Urgent Task and Permanent Challenge

Regarding the first task to fulfill children's needs, the fields of need are varied, especially after the COVID-19 pandemic. Children are one of the population groups that have been most affected by the economic and social crisis caused by the pandemic. The level of stress in many homes has also increased. When stress increases, children experience fear and anxiety because of the emotional tension and anxiety of their parents or caregivers and "fear that they may not be able to satisfy their basic needs. These changes pose risks to their well-being and development, especially in the youngest children."[23] The pandemic also caused migrant children in many regions of the world to suffer unsafe living conditions. Migrant minors who are unaccompanied or separated from their families are particularly vulnerable. The International Organization for Migration (IOM) reported the example of children in migrant camps in Greece

23. "Three Ways Children are Impacted by COVID-19," Plan International (23 March 2020).

or France.[24] These camps are some of the new mission fields toward children. The Lord states that the care we give a child is a service we render to him (Matt 18:5). Children are the priestly presence of God and of his kingdom.

These perceived needs of children provide a challenge for the church to mobilize missionary action in diaconal solidarity, providing assistance to the most affected children; prophetic incidence, in favor of their rights; pastoral consolation, psycho-spiritual assistance; and pastoral accompaniment, in favor of hope, resilience, and restoration of the social fabric. Children often suffer so much in silence. But from their pain comes their cry, asking for God and God's people to act. Genesis 21:17 says, "God heard the boy crying." As instruments of God on earth, we in the church need to listen to the cries of children and to act.

Precious Gift from Heaven

Children are not only objects of solidarity, humanitarian assistance, and comprehensive service. Although in many cases they find themselves to be fragile, impoverished, and needy, this situation is not always all there is to reality. Children are missionaries not in potential for tomorrow but in the present for today. Children offer insightful ways of relating to God and understanding his nature which are not clouded by the "enlightened" reason and positivism that have dominated Western theological endeavors for centuries. Children illuminate a new theological epistemology – a new way of knowing God – and a new way of relating to him, or a new spirituality based on sensitive experience and tenderness that comes from the heart (cordial reason). Children are flashes of the new world who announce the kingdom of God, illuminate the darkness of our world, and summon us all to a more humane and fraternal coexistence. This invitation is also a part of God's mission: to give signals now of the world that is coming (Rev 21) and to pass judgment on the inhuman forms of social coexistence that characterize the anti-kingdom. Children as missionary gifts illuminate our ways of enacting theology, living

Children are flashes of the new world who announce the kingdom of God, illuminate the darkness of our world, and summon us all to a more humane and fraternal coexistence.

24. "Analytical Snapshots on COVID-19 # 17: Implications on migrant children and youth," International Organization for Migration, IOM (17 April 2020).

the faith, and rebuilding our social coexistence starting among the smallest and weakest and not, as it has always been, among the greatest and most powerful. Children are evangelizable (task), and they are evangelizing (gift).

Conclusion

This reflection intends to ignite our awareness and encourage reprising the missionary passion today in light of the challenges which thousands of children are facing. Luther challenged his audience in the 1500s to move past the notion that only the church clergy have the power and privilege to exercise priestly duties. He preached that the "priesthood of all believers" encompasses the entire body of Christ and is not limited to the "ordained priesthood." Bunge extends this principle to challenge the church that children are full members of this priesthood of all believers. The Lausanne Movement declared that children are the church of today and *can* participate in the mission of God. This is a new pastoral paradigm. Children come into our midst with various needs, challenges, and evolving capacities. Many children around the world are affected by the pandemic and are marginalized because of their faith and ethnic background, and many of them suffer in silence.

How can the church reach out so these children are healed in Jesus's name? How can the church nurture and equip them so they are ready and willing to engage in the mission of God to the world? If for centuries theologians have used the expression *locus theologicus* to designate the preferred places and sources from which it is possible to speak of God, the expression *locus misionarius* could well be postulated to refer to children as places from which God reveals to us new meanings of mission and from whom we discover God's missionary action in our world. Children are a place of this focus, and recognizing that they are is our challenge.

Bibliography

"Analytical Snapshots on COVID-19 # 17: Implications on migrant children and youth." International Organization for Migration, IOM (17 April 2020). https://www.iom.int/migration-research/covid-19-analytical-snapshot.

Bunge, Marcia. "The Child, Religion, and the Academy: Developing Robust Theological and Religious Understandings of Children and Childhood." *Journal of Religion* 86, no. 4 (October 2006): 549–79.

———. "Lutheran Commitments to Children and Youth: Theological Foundations, Historical Perspectives, and Contemporary Initiatives." Class Handout for

The Child in Christian Thought. Asia-Pacific Nazarene Theological Seminary, January 2021.

———. "The Significance of Robust Theologies of Childhood for Honouring Children's Full Humanity and Rejecting Corporal Punishment." In *Decolonizing Discipline: Children, Corporal Punishment, Christian Theologies, and Reconciliation*. Edited by Valerie Michaelson and Joan E. Durrant (University of Manitoba Press, 2020), 108–122.

"The Cape Town Commitment." Lausanne Movement (2011). https://www.lausanne.org/content/ctcommitment.

Crocker, Gustavo, and Karissa Glanville, "Children and God's Mission." In *Understanding God's Heart for Children*, edited by Douglas McConnell, Jennifer Orona, and Paul Stockley, 263–72. Colorado Springs: Authentic, 2007.

Luther, Martin. *To the Christian Nobility of the German Nation Concerning the Reform of the Christian Estate* (1520) in *Luther's Works* (LW), edited by Jaroslav Pelikan and Helmut Lehmann (St. Louis: Concordia Publishing House, 1955–86), 44:127–30.

Luther, Martín. "La cautividad babilónica de la iglesia." In *Works of Luther*, edited by Teófanes Eguidio. Salamanca: Ediciones Sígueme, 1977.

"The Manila Manifesto." Lausanne Movement (1989). https://www.lausanne.org/content/manifesto/the-manila-manifesto.

Rooy, Sídney H. *Luther and Mission: Theology and Practice of Mission in Martin Luther.* Saint Louis: Concordia, 2014.

Strohl, Jane. "The Child in Luther's Theology: 'For What Purpose Do We Older Folks Exist, Other Than to Care for . . . the Young.'" In *The Child in Christian Thought*, edited by Marcia Bunge, 134–59. Grand Rapids, MI: Eerdmans, 2001.

"Three Ways Children are Impacted by COVID-19." Plan International (23 March 2020). https://www.planusa.org/blog/three-ways-children-are-impacted-by-coronavirus-covid-19/.

Van Engen, Charles. *Transforming Mission Theology*. Littleton, CO: William Carey Library, 2017.

Yong, A. "Children and the Spirit in Luke and Acts." In *Child Theology: Diverse Methods and Global Perspectives*. Edited by Marcia J. Bunge (Maryknoll, NY: Orbis Books, 2021), 108–128.

Case Study:

The Cost for Children Witnessing to Christ in Nigeria

Nathan Hussaini Chiroma – Nigerian

Defining the Issue

The persecution of Christians as a means of witnessing to Christ is as old as the Christian faith. This case study explores the experiences of children who witness to Christ through persecution, focusing on the experiences of children from Northern Nigeria. In most African cultures is the notion that children are supposed to be seen and not to be heard until they become adults. This notion might have contributed in overlooking the experiences of children in relation to persecution of Christians. This case study looks at the role of the church in the face of children being persecuted.

Theological Perspective: Persecution of Christians

The discussion on the persecution of Christians must be properly anchored on a solid theological and biblical understanding. It is not in the scope of this section to discuss the theology of persecution extensively, but rather to provide a brief framework and theological grounding to understand persecution as it relates to Christian children in Northern Nigeria.

Glenn Penner in his book *In the Shadow of the Cross* argues that Jesus expects his followers to walk the pathway of persecution.[25] Penner clearly outlines that Jesus sent his disciples out as sheep among wolves and told them to expect persecution of many forms, and that they might even die in the process of carrying out their ministry. Several Bible passages speak of the reality of persecution for Christians. To be called to follow Christ is to receive a call to suffer (Acts 9:15–16; 14:21–22; 1 Thess 3:2–3; 1 Pet 2:21; 3:9, 17) just

25. Glenn M. Penner, *In the Shadow of the Cross: A Biblical Theology of Persecution and Discipleship* (Bartlesville: Living Sacrifice Books, 2004).

to mention a few. Understanding this expectation, the early church believers thanked God for the honor of suffering for his sake (Acts 5:41).[26]

True Christians must count the cost of discipleship. Persecution is to be expected as seen in various chapters of the Bible. The call to follow Christ is a call to carry our cross to follow him, which may take different forms and shapes depending on our context. Hence theologically, Christians are not expected to be surprised when they face persecution. Persecution is part and parcel of the faith. Children as part of God's fold need to be theologically grounded in understanding the cost of following Jesus.

Children as part of God's fold need to be theologically grounded in understanding the cost of following Jesus.

Christian Children and Persecution in Northern Nigeria

In Nigeria, most of the persecution of Christians has been concentrated in the North. Open Door, a Christian-based religious freedom watch group, describes the level of Christian persecution in Nigeria as extreme and the most severe category of persecution possible.[27] Generally persecution in Northern Nigeria can be broadly categorized into two major divisions; insidious persecution and elevated persecution.

Insidious persecution is endemic in Northern Nigeria.[28] Some examples of insidious persecution of Christians in Northern Nigeria include discrimination in employment opportunities; oppression of various forms in public service such as stagnation of promotion and intentional posting to hostile areas; and discrimination in admission into public tertiary institutions, just to mention a few forms. Persecution undermines people's dignity, their development, and religious freedom.

The second, broader category of persecution of Christians in Northern Nigeria is elevated persecution, which is more dangerous and harmful than insidious persecution. In a nutshell, elevated persecution involves taking pride in the killing and the destruction of believers and their property. Believers become targets and can be framed or set up to find a reason to kill them.

---

26. Charles L. Tieszen, *Re-Examining Religious Persecution: Constructing a Theological Framework for Understanding Persecution* (Johannesburg: AcadSA, 2008).

27. "World Watch List: Nigeria," Open Doors (n.d.).

28. For more details, see Abdulbarkindo Adamu, Alupsen Ben, and Gloria C., "Nigeria: Southern Kaduna and the atrocities of Hausa-Fulani Muslim herdsman," (January 2018), Volume 2.

The persecution of Christian children in Northern Nigeria falls into these two categories but is manifested more as insidious persecution. For the purposes of this article, we will focus more on insidious persecution of children.

Forced Labor

First, Christian children in Northern Nigeria are persecuted through forced labor. Due to their faith, Christian children in primary schools are forced to work on the farms of their teachers. The teachers will select the Christian children and send them to work on their farm without the provision of proper food or water. According to a Catholic priests working in Northern Nigeria,

> Muslim teachers are at liberty to send Christian children to go work on their farms while the other kids remain in class for educational activities. Often they have to walk for long distances in order to get to the farms and no proper food or water is provided.[29]

Another form of forced labor is sending Christian children to work in the homes of their teachers without any compensation. One nine-year-old child lamented, "I will have to work between six and eight hours in my *mallam's* (teacher's) house to wash all the clothes of the family members, wash the dishes, and by the time I get back to school, classes are already done. I have reported to my parents many times but nothing seems to change."[30]

Kidnapping and Forced Marriages

Second, the persecution of Christian children in Northern Nigeria is manifested through kidnapping and forced marriages. There are several documented stories of Christian children being kidnapped and forced into marriage to older Muslim men. The defenselessness of the girl child is mythical in Northern Nigeria where they are forced into marriages at early ages. A large number of these cases have been documented by the Christian Association of Nigeria, the Catholic church, and other human rights groups. Girls as young as twelve years are often taken away from their parents and forced into marriages and later brainwashed to deny their Christian parents. A mother whose daughter was kidnapped and taken into a forced marriage narrates her ordeal,

---

29. Interview on 19 December 2020 in Adamawa. For the safety of the priest, his name and that of the church he belongs to are not revealed.

30. Interview in the presence of the child's care giver at a safety home in Jos on the 14 December 2020. For the safety of the child and the home, all identities are concealed.

> I sent my daughter to school, and she never came back for two days. We reported it to the local police station and were told to write a statement. After two months we were summoned to village chief's house and told that our daughter was found, and she no longer wants to identify with the Christian faith. She had been given in marriage by the local chief because of her new faith. As I speak to you, it has been fifteen years now down the line, and we still don't have access to our daughter. Many Christian lawyers are still working around the clock to help us. We are looking to God for help.[31]

Denied Access to Education

Third, persecution of Christian children in Northern Nigeria is manifested in the denial of Christian religious education in primary schools. Although the teaching of religion is fully embedded in the Nigerian constitution, most public schools in Northern Nigeria do not allow the teaching of Christian religious knowledge in primary schools. Islamic religious knowledge, on the other hand, is found in all the public schools in the North. A concerned parent in Northern Nigeria who requested anonymity regrets that,

> in all our primary schools in this area there is no single CRK (Christian religious knowledge) teacher. Our children are sometimes forced to sit in the Islamic religious knowledge class without their consent. We have tried all our possible means, but things are not working. For those who can afford it, they have taken their children to private schools. This is our country, and our children deserve the right to be taught their faith.[32]

Educational Discrimination

Fourth, persecution of Christian children in Northern Nigeria takes the form of denial of grades and equal education opportunities. Christian children in most public primary schools in Nigeria are often persecuted through the denial of their rightful grades. In many instances, the grades of a Christian child will be

---

31. Anonymous interview with a Borno State Christian missionary, 2020.

32. Anonymous telephone interview with a concerned parent in Yobe state, 30 November 2020.

intentionally swapped and given to a non-Christian. My personal experience as a child in primary school in northwestern Nigeria is an illustration. My high school admission was given to someone else because I am a Christian. Also, sometimes Christian children are made to attend remedial classes even though they have passing grades.

Violence

Sixth, persecution of Christian children in Northern Nigeria is manifested in violent abuse that is unleashed on them by the non-Christian community. They are often accused falsely and are subjected to torture and sexual abuse. Many children have narrated horrible stories of how they were framed by other kids and were severely beaten; some were even left for dead. As a missionary kid growing up in northwestern Nigeria, I was severely beaten by my teachers in primary school because of my faith. I was asked to become a Muslim several times, and when I said no, I was accused of disrespecting the teachers and was beaten. Sometimes I was made to stay outside the classroom until the end of school. Missionaries working in northeastern Nigeria narrate how on many occasions they helped Christian children who were violently abused by the non-Christian community.

The reality of the persecution of Christian children in Northern Nigeria cannot be denied. Several organizations have documented cases of violation of Christian children. The few cases above are just the tip of the iceberg. Unfortunately, many Christian children do not have opportunities to share their experiences because of cultural impediments.

Dream and Design: What the Role of the Church Could Be

The church in Northern Nigeria must vigorously and seriously pursue the issue of child persecution. According to a Christian psychologist working with children in Northern Nigeria, "many Christian children are suffering in silence. Sometimes they don't even tell their parents what they are going through because of the threats they receive from their perpetrators."[33] The church in Nigeria will need to do the following:

Prepare Christian children for persecution from a tender age. The reality of persecution as discussed in the Biblical and Theological Response section

33. Interview at the psychiatrist's office on 13 December 2020 in Bauchi. The identity of this psychiatrist is not revealed for security reasons.

of this chapter cannot be denied. Persecution is part and parcel of the Christian faith; hence the church should prepare children and their parents to deal with persecution. Family ministry must be done in such a way that parents are able to discuss with children what persecution is all about and how they are to respond. Children need to learn the Christian faith. We need to teach, model, and disciple them so they increasingly learn what it means to be a Christian. Bible memorization is an effective way for parents to help their children take on the truths of Scripture in contexts where access to Bibles is limited.

Family ministry must be done in such a way that parents are able to discuss with children what persecution is all about and how they are to respond.

Provide contextual discipleship models that will equip children for persecution. Jesus made it very clear that the kingdom of God belongs to children, and therefore they form an integral part of the church in Northern Nigeria. Contextual discipleship models that will equip children to deal with persecution of various kinds must be considered for children's ministry. The contextual model should include church advocacy against persecution and encourage children to openly communicate.

Implications for Children's Ministry

The church in Northern Nigeria, like other churches, depends heavily on the children's ministry to meet the holistic needs of children in our congregations. Hence, the role of children's workers is crucial in helping children deal with persecution.

Children's workers must be fully equipped and trained to work with persecuted children. First, they need training on how to incorporate teachings on facing persecution in their Sunday school curricula. Second, children's workers must learn to network with various non-governmental and faith-based organizations that are working with persecuted children. The goal of this networking is to help the workers come to terms with the reality of persecution and to establish support systems that sometimes are lacking in the church. Some persecuted children are more comfortable discussing their plights with people who are outside the church setting. Finally, children's workers must provide support for parents at all levels to help them help their children with persecution.

Conclusion

This article considers the persecution of children in Northern Nigeria, briefly outlines the theological understanding of persecution, and argues that the persecution of Christian children is a reality in Northern Nigeria. The article establishes that the most common type of persecution faced by children in Northern Nigeria is insidious persecution, discusses several forms of this insidious persecution, and offers some suggestions to the church and children's workers on how to minister to children facing persecution.

Bibliography

Abdulbarkindo Adamu, Alupsen Ben, and Gloria C., "Nigeria: Southern Kaduna and the atrocities of Hausa-Fulani Muslim herdsman,", World Watch Research Unit/ Open Doors International (May 2016–September 2017) Volume 2 (January 2018). https://opendoorsanalytical.org/wp-content/uploads/2018/01/Nigeria-Southern-Kaduna-Volume-2.pdf.

Eller, Jack David. *Cruel Creeds, Virtuous Violence: Religious Violence across Culture and History*. New York: Prometheus, 2010.

Penner, Glenn M. *In the Shadow of the Cross: A Biblical Theology of Persecution and Discipleship*. Bartlesville: Living Sacrifice, 2004.

Tieszen, Charles L. *Re-Examining Religious Persecution: Constructing a Theological Framework for Understanding Persecution*. Johannesburg: AcadSA, 2008.

"World Watch List: Nigeria" Open Doors (n.d.). https://www.opendoorsusa.org/christian-persecution/world-watch-list/nigeria/.

Discussion Questions for Chapter 7

1. Sublimé Mabiala lists three types of persecution and marginalization happening in Africa. What types of persecution and marginalization of children are evident in your country of ministry?
2. Do you think that churches should include the issues of persecution and marginalization in their children's ministry curriculum? Give reasons for your answers.
3. Children are members of the "priesthood of all believers." How is this teaching expressed in your faith community?
4. "The Cape Town Commitment" states that children, "represent the 'new energy' to transform the world." What evidence can you find in your faith community to support this claim?
5. Nathan Chiroma states that "True Christians must count the cost of discipleship." What do you think is the cost for children to be disciples of Jesus Christ?

8

Engaged in Creation Care

Creation care is a Biblical mandate for the whole Church. Educating and engaging children to play an active role as stewards of God's creation is an essential outworking of this mandate.

Global Critical Issue:
Children and the Global Climate Emergency

Athena Peralta – Filipino[1]

"I want you to act as you would in a crisis. I want you to act as if our house is on fire. Because it is."

Greta Thunberg, young climate activist, Sweden.[2]

Children Are Courageously Declaring a Global Climate Emergency

Children were among the first to form a clear-eyed appraisal of the situation and to declare it as it is: we are living in a time of climate and broader planetary emergency. Despite a slight fall in global greenhouse gas (GHG) emissions linked to the COVID-19 pandemic-induced economic slowdowns, the level of carbon dioxide in the atmosphere still reached a new high in 2020. The year 2020 ties with 2016 as the warmest on record.[3] The six years since 2015 are also the six warmest ever registered. Across the planet, we are witnessing storms of escalating strength and frequency, widespread flooding, unquenchable wildfires, and intense drought.

An emergency "poses an immediate risk to health, life, property, or environment . . . [and] require[s] urgent intervention."[4] Normally in such a situation, we adults would respond with speed and concerted action. Often our first move is to ensure that our children are protected, recognizing that they are vulnerable in part because of their dependence on adults for their safety and satisfaction of basic needs. In the face of global climate change, however, we have not always appreciated the fact that our health and well-being

---

1. The author would like to express gratitude to Frederique Seidel, WCC senior advisor on children's rights, for her suggestions and insights on this text.

2. Greta Thunberg, "Our house is on fire: Greta Thunberg, 16, urges leaders to act on climate," *The Guardian* (25 January 2019).

3. Tylar Greene and Peter Jacobs, "2020 Tied for Warmest Year on Record, NASA Analysis Shows," NASA (14 January 2021).

4. "Emergency," Wikipedia (21 February 2021).

and that of our children are inextricably tied to the health and well-being of the planet. We have sometimes denied the science, and we have been catastrophically slow to act. As today's adult leaders in politics and business, especially in wealthier economies, continue to make decisions that prioritize short-term financial and economic gain but that adversely impact the present and future of the planet, our children are calling for intergenerational climate justice.

Our health and well-being and that of our children are inextricably tied to the health and well-being of the planet.

Importantly, children do not simply see themselves as victims of climate change. Particularly in the age of social media, they are gaining broad awareness of the climate crisis and its causes. Children are also realizing that they have a voice, and many are compelled to take action to protect our increasingly fragile ecosystems. Already they are showing the way. It was at the request of the 144 children consulted in the development of the World Council of Churches' document titled "Churches' Commitments to Children" that the commitment to promote intergenerational climate justice for and with children became a key pillar of this action plan.[5]

Climate Change Harms Children's Rights, Health, and Well-being

> *"I heard strong winds coming in our direction. I closed my eyes. It was scary. I could not see anything outside. I was looking for my other members of the family, I thought they left without me, but then I realized we were all inside the house waiting for the typhoon to calm down. Our small house was lost to floods."*
>
> – child survivor of Super Typhoon Haiyan, Philippines[6]

While no one is entirely shielded from the effects of climate change, children are especially vulnerable because they are typically socioeconomically as well as metabolically less able than adults to respond and adapt to various climate-related exposures. The risks of climate change which confront children range from the direct physical impacts of extreme weather events to impacts on their

5. "Churches' Commitment to Children," World Council of Churches (2017).

6. May Maloney, "See me, ask me, hear me: children's recommendations for recovery three months after Typhoon Haiyan," Save the Children (2014).

health and education (see Table 1). Children in income-poor families and in developing countries are already bearing the brunt of climate change, a burden which will only intensify over time.

Table 1: Survey of Climate Impacts on Children

- Over 500 million children currently reside in areas at extremely high risk of floods due to extreme weather events such as cyclones, hurricanes, and other storms as well as rising sea levels.
- From 2014 to 2018 in the Caribbean alone, around 761,000 children were internally displaced due to extreme weather events, up from 175,000 children displaced between 2009 and 2013.
- An estimated 160 million children live in areas experiencing high levels of drought. By 2040, one in four children will live in areas of extreme water stress.
- Droughts and other weather-related events are causing food shortages. Malnutrition is one of the key adverse health impacts of climate change, especially for children. In climate-impacted La Guajira, Colombia, indigenous children are dying of malnutrition at a rate that is six times the national average. In a medium-high global warming scenario, the world will have an additional 25.2 million malnourished children.
- Nearly 90 percent of the burden of diseases attributable to climate change, such as dengue, is borne by children under the age of five.
- Around 300 million children are breathing toxic air caused by carbon emissions and greenhouse gases – 17 million of them are under age one. This toxic air has immediate and long-term detrimental effects on their health, brain function, and development. Toxic air contributes to the deaths of around 600,000 children under age five every year due to pneumonia and other respiratory problems.[7]

Girl children face additional challenges in the face of climate change.[8] Weather-related disasters heighten the risk for girls to drop out of school or be forced into marriages, trafficking, sexual exploitation, and abuse. Further

7. Alia Sunderji and Hilary Rosenthal, "Colombia's indigenous children are the casualties of climate change," *The Washington Post* (3 December 2020); "Fact Sheet: The climate crisis is a child rights crisis," UNICEF (6 December 2019); Helen Clark, et. al., "A Future for the World's Children? A WHO-UNICEF-*Lancet* Commission," *The Lancet* 395, no. 10224 (18 February 2020).

8. "Climate change: Focus on Girls and Young Women," Plan International (2019).

when food is in short supply due to flooding or drought, girls are more likely than boys to go hungry.

There is also growing evidence that climate change affects our children's mental and emotional health. Post-traumatic stress disorder is common among children who have survived devastating climate events. At the same time, ecological anxiety and grief is an emerging and rising phenomenon among children and youth. In a survey of American teenagers conducted in 2019 by the Washington-based Post-Kaiser Family Foundation, 57 percent of respondents said that climate change made them feel scared, and 52 percent said it made them feel angry – both rates are higher than among adults.[9] Just under 30 percent of these teenagers expressed optimism about the future. Similarly, the results of a poll commissioned by the British Broadcasting Corporation (BBC) in 2020 of two thousand young people ages eight to sixteen years showed that 73 percent were worried about the state of the planet, 19 percent have had a bad dream about climate change, and 41 percent do not trust adults to handle climate challenges.[10] The enormity of the problem of global climate change adds to some children's sense of frustration and futility.

Nearly 90 percent of the burden of diseases attributable to climate change, such as dengue, is borne by children under the age of five.

Children Are Learning, Playing, and Renewing Relationships in and with Creation

> *"They all live here and they feel bad because everywhere is dirty. The children love our planet and they care about the world. These children are from different races. Every child should care about the planet."*
>
> – young child, Poland[11]

9. Jason Plautz, "The Environmental Burden of Generation Z," *The Washington Post Magazine* (2 February 2020).

10. Ashlee Cunsolo, et al., "Ecological grief and anxiety: the start of a healthy response to climate change?" *The Lancet Planetary Health* 4, no. 7 (1 July 2020).

11. Ingrid Engdahl and Milada Rabušicová, "Children's Voices about the State of the Earth and Sustainable Development," https://www.researchgate.net/publication/226714753_Children's_Voices_About_the_State_of_the_Earth (2010).

Children's feelings of anxiety and grief over the current state of the planet and anticipated ecological losses may be a sign of connection to the natural world and can be redirected toward a constructive path. Indeed, their responses could be the "crucible through which humanity must pass to harness the energy and conviction that are needed for the lifesaving changes now required."[12] What is critical here is fostering children's empowerment.

What is critical here is fostering children's empowerment.

Stewardship in the Context of Kinship

Children should learn about actions which protect, care for, or responsibly use environmental resources in and with their community. Educational programs and activities within homes, schools, churches, and communities can play a key role in nurturing ecological stewardship. Often a sense of stewardship emerges initially from care and concern for immediate family, friends, and neighbors, and from a growing understanding that every one of us is utterly dependent on the planet for the air we breathe and for our sustenance. In other words stewardship, which suggests "deep attachments and sense of care and protection," and kinship, which suggests "close relationship, equality, and reciprocal sharing" grow together.[13] Stewardship and kinship flourishing simultaneously can overcome geographical, socioeconomic, racial, and other barriers. For instance, some young climate activists in Europe and North America have expressed recognition of their own privilege living in wealthier families and economies that can better support their development and the differentiated impacts of climate change on other children because of socioeconomic inequalities, geographical circumstances, and their own governments' part in effectively risking the lives of all children through historic and current GHG emissions.[14]

---

12. Cunsolo, et al., "Ecological grief and anxiety."

13. Cathy Dueck and Jacob Rodenburg, "Pathway to Stewardship and Kinship: Raising Healthy Children for a Healthy Planet," Pathway to Stewardship and Kinship (2017).

14. Frank Jordans and Aritz Parra, "Too much of a Greta thing? Activist urges focus on others," *AP News* (9 December 2019).

Churches Empowering, Educating, and Engaging Children

Churches in particular can and ought to be safe, introspective, and creative spaces for children to process feelings of ecological distress, to rediscover Jesus' commandment to "Love your neighbor as yourself" (Mark 12:31), and to tend to creation as well as to learn about concrete ways to practice stewardship as a central expression of discipleship. Sunday schools and other church programs can and ought to impart to children that everyday actions and decisions – about the food they consume, the toys they play with, the clothes they wear, and how they move about – shape, resource, use, and impact the environment and other people. Understanding from an early age that ecology and economy cannot be separated and are in fact deeply intertwined is crucial for getting to the very roots of climate crisis. To this end, the WCC has compiled a toolkit to support churches, church-run schools, Sunday schools, and summer camps in their efforts to promote environmental stewardship and intergenerational climate and environmental justice.[15]

The Importance of Playing

Formal education, however, is not everything. Playing is vitally important for children in their journey of engaging in creation care. Playing in nature allows children to actually experience – not just learn in a structured environment – the concept of stewardship, to build deeper relationships with creation, to better comprehend its interconnectedness, and to encounter God in the joy of playing with other children and creatures as well as in the beauty of creation. A 2017 study by the University of British Colombia found that 87 percent of people who played outdoors as children developed and retained a love for the outdoors; and 84 percent of them considered environmental protection a foremost priority.[16] Furthermore, research indicates that playing in nature not only imparts crea-

Playing in nature allows children to actually experience – not just learn in a structured environment – the concept of stewardship.

15. See "New WCC toolkit empowers churches to work with children and youth for climate justice," World Council of Churches (2020).

16. University of British Columbia Okanagan Campus, "Children who play outside more likely to protect nature as adults," *Science Daily* (17 March 2017).

tive and practical problem-solving skills, it also counters everyday stress and supports children's overall psychological well-being.[17]

Children are Essential Actors in Addressing Climate Change and Caring for Creation

> *"I'm standing here for all the Indigenous people who couldn't be here today. This is my purpose, this should be all of our purposes – to protect our Mother Earth."*
>
> – Tokata Iron Eyes, young environmental activist from the Standing Rock Sioux tribe, United States[18]

While children are disproportionately affected by climate change, they are at the same time essential and effective actors in mitigating and adapting to global warming as well as in preserving and nurturing our precarious environment.

Cases studies of community-based adaptation and resiliency projects in the Philippines and Vietnam found significant benefits in involving and listening to children.

> [C]hildren regularly bring new ideas or creative solutions. They can engage communities and they could potentially break down the barriers on complex and tricky issues. They often have a better understanding of the science of climate change processes than adults in the community due to their school lessons, and they can draw out the implications for local livelihoods.[19]

Moreover, the studies conclude that "[h]arnessing the energies and enthusiasms of children for positive change can have an impact on decision makers at all levels of communities and governments."[20]

Children are gaining a voice. They are doing something to tackle the climate crisis. They are using social media, particularly digital platforms such

---

17. Caroline Piccininni, et al., "Outdoor play and nature connectedness as potential correlates of internalized mental health symptoms among Canadian adolescents," *Preventive Medicine* 112 (July 2018): 168–75.

18. Eilish McDonagh, "Politics and the Pipeline: Tokata Iron Eyes' Fight for Environmental Protection." Emory University (2018).

19. Michael Azucena, et al., "Child-centred Climate Resilience: Case Studies from the Philippines and Vietnam," https://www.comminit.com/la/content/child-centred-climate-resilience-case-studies-philippines-and-vietnam (2015).

20. Azucena, et al., "Child-centred Climate Resilience."

as Twitter, Instagram, and Facebook, to shine a light on climate change and to mobilize other people to their cause.[21] Children are out on the streets calling on leaders and the public to open their eyes to the climate emergency. Remarkably in 2019, several million children and youth all over the world participated in "Fridays for Future" school strikes for the climate and other demonstrations, protesting in front of government buildings and demanding that governments create pathways to ensure that global warming does not exceed the relatively safe threshold of 1.5 Celsius.[22]

Children are even suing their governments for inaction on climate change and fossil fuel corporations for their part in causing global warming. In 2015, twenty-one young people filed a landmark case – Juliana vs. the United States – against the US government for its role in causing climate change and violating their rights to life, liberty, and property, while also failing to safeguard essential public resources.[23] The children asked the court to compel the government to end fossil fuel subsidies and adopt policies that would curtail GHG emissions. Likewise in 2019, sixteen children filed the Children vs. Climate Crisis case, an official complaint to the United Nations Committee on the Rights of the Child.[24]

Children are advocating for divestment from fossil fuels, the banning of single-use plastic bags, and access to clean water. They are engaging in a range of community-based initiatives including keeping vegetable gardens at schools and churches, planting trees and mangroves to protect waterfront structures from storms, cleaning up rivers and oceans, and collecting and recycling plastics.

Hope Lies in Collective Action Now

> *"I want the authorities to take this question of the environment to heart. Because we children are suffering a lot."*
>
> – Junior, fourteen years old, Côte d'Ivoire[25]

---

21. Shelley Boulianne, "School Strike 4 Climate: Social Media and the International Youth Protest on Climate Change," *Media and Communication* 2 (2020): 208-218.

22. V. Masson-Delmotte, et al., "Summary for Policymakers," Intergovernmental Panel on Climate Change (IPCC) (2018).

23. "Youth v. Gov: Juliana v. US," Our Children's Trust (2015).

24. "Children vs Climate Crisis," #ChildrenVsClimateCrisis (2019).

25. "Youth activist speaks up for environmental protection at Human Rights Council," UN News (1 July 2020).

Adults have the main responsibility for transforming our unjust and unsustainable economic systems and must listen to and work with children for a chance of a future. According to the Intergovernmental Panel on Climate Change (IPCC), the next ten years have to be a period of rapid, extensive, and deep-seated mitigation and adaptation efforts to prevent the harshest and most catastrophic effects of climate change.[26] However, notwithstanding mounting scientific evidence and public advocacy, increasingly led by children and youth, some wealthy and powerful governments hindered progress and impeded urgent action at the 25th Conference of Parties of the UN Framework Convention on Climate Change in 2019. The outcomes of the 2019 climate negotiations were a huge disappointment, falling far short of scientific requirements and children's expectations.

Adults have the main responsibility for transforming our unjust and unsustainable economic systems and must listen to and work with children for a chance of a future.

Despite contributing least to GHG emissions, children have stepped up to the climate crisis and demonstrated stewardship and care for the planet, contributing in their own way to awareness building, mobilization, and initiatives to build community resiliency to a warming climate. Sometimes this activity has come at the expense of school and play. But education and playing are not only vital parts of children's lives, they are also basic rights that must be protected and promoted.

As outlined by the IPCC, achieving the goal of carbon neutrality by 2050 entails nothing less than a radical transformation of our systems of production, consumption, distribution, and investment. Children by virtue of being children have limited influence and scope to pursue systemic economic changes, and this is a responsibility we cannot lay on our children's shoulders. As adults, we have the obligation, the power, and wherewithal to make political actions as well as financial and economic decisions for the sake of our children.[27] Indeed these actions are what our children are calling us to do. It is time that we listen to, stand with, and hold hands with our children in jointly building solutions to the climate emergency and in carving out a future together.

---

26. Masson-Delmotte, et al., "Summary for Policymakers."

27. "Cooler Earth, Higher Benefits: Actions by those who care about children, climate and finance," World Council of Churches (2020).

Bibliography

Azucena, Michael, et al. "Child-centred Climate Resilience: Case Studies from the Philippines and Vietnam." https://www.comminit.com/la/content/child-centred-climate-resilience-case-studies-philippines-and-vietnam (2015).

Boulianne, Shelley. "School Strike 4 Climate: Social Media and the International Youth Protest on Climate Change." *Media and Communication* 2 (2020): 208–218. https://www.cogitatiopress.com/mediaandcommunication/article/view/2768.

"Children vs Climate Crisis." #ChildrenVsClimateCrisis (n.d.). https://childrenvsclimatecrisis.org/.

"Churches' Commitment to Children." World Council of Churches (2017). https://www.oikoumene.org/resources/documents/churches-commitments-to-children.

Clark, Helen, et. al. "A Future for the World's Children? A WHO-UNICEF-*Lancet* Commission." *The Lancet* 395, no. 10224 (18 February 2020). https://www.thelancet.com/journals/lancet/article/PIIS0140-6736(19)32540-1/fulltext.

"Climate change: Focus on Girls and Young Women." Plan International (2019). https://plan-international.org/publications/climate-change-focus-on-girls-and-young-women/.

"Cooler Earth, Higher Benefits: Actions by those who care about children, climate and finance." World Council of Churches (2020). https://www.oikoumene.org/sites/default/files/2020-11/CoolerEarth_Web%20PDF.pdf.

Cunsolo, Ashlee, et al. "Ecological grief and anxiety: the start of a healthy response to climate change?" *The Lancet Planetary Health* 4, no. 7 (1 July 2020). https://www.thelancet.com/journals/lanplh/article/PIIS2542-5196(20)30144-3/fulltext.

Dueck, Cathy, and Jacob Rodenburg. "Pathway to Stewardship and Kinship: Raising Healthy Children for a Healthy Planet." Pathway to Stewardship and Kinship (2017).https://campkawartha.ca/pdf/Pathway-to-Stewardship.pdf.

"Emergency." Wikipedia (21 February 2021). https://en.wikipedia.org/wiki/Emergency.

Engdahl, Ingrid, and Milada Rabušicová. "Children's Voices about the State of the Earth and Sustainable Development." https://www.researchgate.net/publication/226714753_Children's_Voices_About_the_State_of_the_Earth (2010).

"Fact Sheet: The climate crisis is a child rights crisis." UNICEF (6 December 2019). https://www.unicef.org/press-releases/fact-sheet-climate-crisis-child-rights-crisis.

Greene, Tylar, and Peter Jacobs. "2020 Tied for Warmest Year on Record, NASA Analysis Shows." NASA (14 January 2021). https://www.nasa.gov/press-release/2020-tied-for-warmest-year-on-record-nasa-analysis-shows.

Jordans, Frank, and Aritz Parra. "Too much of a Greta thing? Activist urges focus on others." *AP News* (9 December 2019). https://apnews.com/article/baa29614a79cbcd2edb83b9e3f7de90f.

Maloney, May. "*See me, ask me, hear me: children's recommendations for recovery three months after Typhoon Haiyan.*" Save the Children (2014). https://resourcecentre.

savethechildren.net/node/8267/pdf/http_mhpss.net_get211_see-me-ask-me-hear-me.pdf.

Masson-Delmotte, V., et al. "Summary for Policymakers." Intergovernmental Panel on Climate Change (IPCC) (2018). https://www.ipcc.ch/site/assets/uploads/sites/2/2019/05/SR15_SPM_version_report_LR.pdf.

McDonagh, Eilish, "Politics and the Pipeline: Tokata Iron Eyes' Fight for Environmental Protection." Emory University (2018). https://scholarblogs.emory.edu/inspiringindigenousyouth/2018/09/18/politics-and-the-pipeline-tokata-iron-eyes-fight-for-environmental-protection/.

"New WCC toolkit empowers churches to work with children and youth for climate justice." World Council of Churches (2020). https://www.oikoumene.org/news/new-wcc-toolkit-empowers-churches-to-work-with-children-and-youth-for-climate-justice.

Piccininni, Caroline, Valerie Michaelson, Ian Janssen, and William Pickett. "Outdoor play and nature connectedness as potential correlates of internalized mental health symptoms among Canadian adolescents." *Preventive Medicine* 112 (July 2018): 168–75. https://www.sciencedirect.com/science/article/pii/S0091743518301312.

Plautz, Jason. "The Environmental Burden of Generation Z." *The Washington Post Magazine* (2 February 2020). https://www.washingtonpost.com/magazine/2020/02/03/eco-anxiety-is-overwhelming-kids-wheres-line-between-education-alarmism/?arc404=true.

Sunderji, Alia, and Hilary Rosenthal. "Colombia's indigenous children are the casualties of climate change." *The Washington Post* (3 December 2020). https://www.washingtonpost.com/opinions/2020/12/03/colombias-indigenous-children-are-casualties-climate-change/.

Thunberg, Greta. "Our house is on fire: Greta Thunberg, 16, urges leaders to act on climate." *The Guardian* (25 January 2019). https://www.theguardian.com/environment/2019/jan/25/our-house-is-on-fire-greta-thunberg16-urges-leaders-to-act-on-climate.

University of British Columbia Okanagan Campus. "Children who play outside more likely to protect nature as adults." *Science Daily* (17 March 2017). https://www.sciencedaily.com/releases/2017/03/170317102447.htm.

"Youth activist speaks up for environmental protection at Human Rights Council." UN News (1 July 2020). https://news.un.org/en/story/2020/07/1067512.

"Youth v. Gov: Juliana v. US." Our Children's Trust (n.d.). https://childrenvsclimatecrisis.org/.

Biblical and Theological Response: Our Beautiful Dwelling Place

Rei Lemuel Crizaldo – Filipino

Introduction

Athena Peralta in the Global Critical Issue article of this chapter outlines serious and pressing ecological concerns together with children-driven responses which are encouraging and a reason to remain hopeful for the future. My task is to spell out the necessary theological grounding that can help sustain action, stir imaginations, and open space for embracing a bit of prophetic critique.

Building a case for engaging children in hoping for a sustainable life on the present planet we call "home" all the more becomes a pressing endeavor. Peralta issues a wise reminder above: "Children's feelings of anxiety and grief over the current state of the planet and anticipated ecological losses may be a sign of connection to the natural world and can be redirected toward a constructive path." For Christians, such a task of redirection requires a recovery of a vision lost, and for churches a mission long neglected:[28] two things that put the best of theology as a discipline to task.

Recovering a Vision of Shalom

Genesis tells an epic story of how God designed life in the world to be lived in all its fullness. It was a beautiful vision of all his creation dwelling in harmony, each interdependent on each other, and everything in its rightful place. God himself cannot but exclaim that indeed the sight "was very good" (Gen 1:31).

28. Douglas Moo and Jonathan Moo refer to three approaches outlined in the book *Greening Paul: Rereading the Apostle in a Time of Ecological Crisis* by David Horrell, Cherryl Hunt, and Christopher Southgate (Waco, TX: Baylor University Press, 2010) by which theologies of creation care have been developed: resistance, recovery, and revisionist. See Douglas Moo and Jonathan Moo, *Creation Care: A Biblical Theology of the Natural World* (Grand Rapids, MI: Zondervan, 2018), 34–35. This article seeks to add a constructive/contextual model as a contribution to *reframing* the present approaches.

The ancient Hebrews had a word to describe this sense of peaceful coexistence between God, human beings, and the rest of creation. They called it *shalom*.

Shalom, however, is not only a vivid picture of beautiful people placed on a beautiful planet. Shalom depicts a God who has created a beautiful dwelling place shared by him, humanity, and all the other living beings.[29] God has built a home! For everything and for everyone. Together with him. The garden of Eden was to serve as the prototype of how everywhere else in the world was meant to be like.

Human beings were given a big share in the task of sustaining this planetary vision of a harmonious home. Created in God's very image (Gen 1:26–28), they were given the authority, and with it the responsibility, to ensure that life on earth would not only flourish but also be dutifully safeguarded (Gen 2:15).[30] Closely intertwined with this task was the development of humane civilizations that would showcase the best of human culture and creativity. This work of carrying on where God left off is often called the "creation mandate" which basically is humankind's part in the project of filling and forming even more the beautiful home God has made.[31]

Shalom depicts a God who has created a beautiful dwelling place shared by him, humanity, and all the other living beings.

It is important to note that the broad task sketched above of working out the potential of the earth through further development means toward its beautification and protection. "Tilling the ground" comes side by side with ensuring its well-being. Immediately this combination indicates that the primal biblical notion of doing further improvements in God's home is intertwined with the goal of seeking the welfare of both human beings and the environment. Anything less, or anything that sacrifices one for the other, is a distortion of the *creative* development that human beings can bring forth.[32]

---

29. T. Desmond Alexander, *From Eden to New Jerusalem: An Introduction to Biblical Theology* (Grand Rapids, MI: Kregel Academic, 2008), 15.

30. If we are to take the suggestion that Gen 2 is the accompanying commentary of Gen 1, then the language of the task in Gen 2:15 supplies the meaning necessary to understand the mandate in Gen 1:26–28.

31. Albert Wolters, *Creation Regained*, 2nd ed. (Grand Rapids, MI: Eerdmans, 2005), 41–42. Some other theologians have suggested calling it the "ecological mandate" (Dave Bookless) or the original "Great Commission."

32. In his book that has been considered a textbook for Christian development work, Bryant Myers articulates a framework that places "healthy and respectful relationship with the environment" as inseparably vital in pursuing a better human future with abundant life for all.

But at the same time, it has to be noted that working toward progress is not necessarily an antithesis to earth keeping especially if pursued within a path that is ecologically sustainable.[33] Suffice it to say that the pursuit of people's well-being has to be closely linked to seeking the welfare of the planet on which they live. Both have to come together and can only be put asunder with fatal consequences tilted primarily toward humanity's loss.

Today's ecological problems brought about largely by years of environmental abuse have uncovered the fragility of human existence. In particular, the coronavirus pandemic of 2020 is a glaring example of what happens when the safe boundaries that are supposed to be maintained and respected between human beings and the other living beings are willfully ignored and violated.[34] Very quickly the viral crisis saw global society spiraling into a crash that included its most advanced economies and industries. A time of reckoning finally came especially for those who have pursued progress unmindful of their responsibility toward the environment and the rest of God's created beings.

It is within this broader backdrop of humanity's *original* mandate, as sketched in the Old Testament, that engaging in creation care can be properly understood. From the very beginning, humanity's task of *overseeing* the rest of God's created order was bound together with the charge to harness its potential for development.[35] Unfortunately, the role of Christians in this endeavor has not been always at the front and center of the church's focus.[36] In fact many, if not all of the ecological crises we are seeing today can be brought to the very

---

Bryant Myers, *Walking with the Poor: Principles and Practices of Transformational Development* (New York: Orbis, 2006), 120.

33. For example Tearfund, a Christian relief and development organization, advocates the fusing together of environmental and economic sustainability (EES) to carry out the ideals of a "restorative economy." This vision works toward a world where extreme inequality is reduced and where everyone can meet their basic needs – and flourish – within their environmental limits. Liu Liu Simpson and Nick Simpson, "Building a Sustainable Future," Tearfund Learn (2019).

34. Ruth Valerio and Gideon Hugh argue that the pandemic of 2020 was not a "natural disaster" but a disaster that human beings brought upon themselves. See Ruth Valerio and Gideon Hugh, "A Christian Perspective on COVID-19," Tearfund Learn (n.d.).

35. Cherith Fee Nordling offers a helpful understanding of the "dominion" God gave to human beings in Gen 1:26 by reordering it according to the cruciform image of Christ wherein one "exercises power on behalf of things" rather than "power over things." See Cherith Fee Nordling, "The Human Person in the Christian Story," in *The Cambridge Companion to Evangelical Theology*, eds. Timothy Larsen and Daniel Treier (Cambridge: Cambridge University Press, 2007), 74.

36. Don Thorsen attributes this neglect to "world-denying theologies" that move Christians to neglect environmental concerns. Such forms of biblical teaching have "considered the earth and its resources something to be exploited rather than cultivated and developed." Don Thorsen, *An Exploration of Christian Theology* (Peabody, MA: Hendrickson, 2008), 114.

doors of Christianity and the roots of the problems traced right straight to the church's teachings and inaction as well.[37] This devastating indictment from outside the walls of the church paints Christianity as the exact opposite of the breathtaking vision of shalom in the Bible.

How did Christians end up in such an awkward position? While there has been much effort to refute the accusation, what is undeniable is the glaring delay, if not altogether lack of collective response, on the part of the global church to prevent the tragic lot that threatens the future of the next generation.

Recapturing a Broader Mission

Part of the current problems can be traced to certain versions of theologizing that developed in the history of the church. This article begins with a reference to an escapist mentality wherein hope is pinned on abandoning earth and looking elsewhere to secure humanity's salvation. It is an eerie comparison, but a very similar spiritual consolation has been what the church has offered. While Elon Musk has his eyes on Mars, the eyes of Christians have been turned away from the earth and tilted toward finally being "home" in heaven.[38] As a popular hymn puts the idea this way:

> This world is not my home
> I'm just passing through
> my treasures are laid up
> somewhere beyond the blue
> the angels beckon me
> from Heaven's open door
> and I can't feel at home
> in this world anymore.[39]

This idea is also reinforced by popular appeals to selected New Testament passages such as Philippians 3:20 on citizenship in heaven; 1 Thessalonians

37. A popular argument for this view is made by the University of California historian Lynn White, "The Historical Roots of Our Ecological Crisis," *Science* 155, no. 3767 (10 March 1967).

38. Richard Bauckham and Trevor Hart are of the conclusion that the legacy of Christianity includes an otherworldly eschatology: "The Christian hope has constantly been understood as hope for human fulfillment in another world ('heaven') rather than as hope for the eternal future of this world in which we live." Richard Bauckham and Trevor Hart, *Hope Against Hope: Christian Eschatology in Contemporary Culture* (London: Longman and Todd, 1999), 129.

39. Jim Reeves, "This World Is Not My Home," https://arnet.pairsite.com/RedEllis/lyr/worldnotmyhome.htm.

4:16–17 on being caught up in the clouds; and 2 Peter 3:10–12 on everything burned up. Isolated from the wider context of the biblical narrative, these verses have been taken to mean that the world is beyond saving for the exact reason that it is meant to be destroyed eventually. The only prospect of hope proclaimed is a mass migration to the heavenlies and making sure that as many people as possible, children included, will secure a ticket to join the blessed evacuation. In some circles of the Christian community, it is even thought that the more planetary devastation happening, the better as it signals that the world is finally coming to an end with Jesus's blessed return looming closely on the horizon.[40]

Not a few theologians have observed the devastating impact this theological perspective has wrought. One of the unfortunate collaterals identified is creation care which results in the gross negligence of Christians to look after the earth.[41] Katsuomi Shimasaki, a Japanese theologian, observes that,

> There might be a theological reason why we Protestant Christians, especially evangelical Christians, have difficulty finding true value in everyday life and in good works. If we believe that the world around us will disappear someday, it follows that we ought not to labor to preserve the planet. If we believe that Christian salvation means the soul would fly away from the world to heaven, our attitude towards life on earth would naturally be indifference.[42]

But it is also very important to place the impact of *escapist* theologies alongside the "evangelistic" work that fueled the colonial era – a period of time wherein Christianity was spread in Africa, the Americas, and Asia. The result was decades of illustrious missionary enterprise which unfortunately was intertwined with painful exploitation of both human and natural resources in the lands colonized by the empires of the Christian West. A curious case

40. Barbara Rossing engages these kinds of teachings made popular by "end times" authors such as John Hagee and Hal Lindsey. See Barbara Rossing, *The Rapture Exposed: The Message of Hope in the Book of Revelation* (New York: Basic, 2004).

41. Hyunte Shin, in her research work tracing the impact of Dispensational theology on Korean Christianity, concludes with this observation, "The tremendous influence of certain brands of Western theology brought by Western missionaries from their home countries are the ultimate root of the apathetic stance of South Korean Christians towards environmental issues." Hyunte Shin, "The Influence of the Bible in Shaping the Negative Viewpoint of Korean Christians towards Nature," *The Expository Times* 132, no. 5 (2021): 222.

42. Katsuomi Shimasaki, "The New Heavens and the New Earth: Our Hope and Motive for Stewardship," in *The Earth is the Lord's: Reflections on Stewardship in the Asian Context*, eds. Timoteo Gener and Athena Gorospe (Manila: OMF Literature, 2011), 18.

of Christian mission was pursued for hundreds of years with the mandate for creation care effectively put somewhere in the brackets.

Both of these theologies, escapist and imperial, are incongruent with a more careful reading of the Bible's teaching about the place of creation care in Christian mission and social responsibility. The apostle Paul wrote in Romans 8:19–22 that the redemption of human beings is closely bound together with the renewal of the earth and everything in it. New Testament theology is quite clear that the gospel is not only about people's liberation from everything that enslaves them but also the liberation of the planet from everything that causes it pain.[43] Furthermore, John the Beloved paints a beautiful portrait of the kingdom of God as a new heavens and a new earth complete with bees, rivers, and trees (Rev 21). Albert Wolters is on point when he says that "God does not make junk, and he does not junk what he has made."[44]

Such is the depth and breadth of the good news sketched in the New Testament that Christians are tasked to proclaim and to live out the implications of in their daily lives. Simply put, the whole of creation defines the expanse of Christian life and ministry. One can only begin to imagine how different history would have been if this breathtaking sketch had been taught as the right path that children were to follow (Prov 22:6). Fortunately, theological developments in history have eventually caught up with this splendid vision of a renewed planet inhabited by redeemed people.

As the Commission on World Mission and Evangelism of the World Council of Churches puts it, "mission in Christ's way must extend to God's creation. Because the earth is the Lord's, the responsibility of the church towards the earth is a crucial part of the church's mission."[45]

Similarly among the ranks of evangelicals, in particular within the Lausanne Movement, a noticeable shift from an anthropocentric to a more cosmological perspective to mission is also evident. "The Cape Town Commitment" drafted during the third global congress of Lausanne in 2010 includes a strong commitment that the whole of creation, not just persons and the societies they live in, is part of the comprehensive mission of God's people. A section of the document reads as follows:

> We cannot claim to love God while abusing what belongs to Christ by right of creation, redemption and inheritance. We care for the

43. Rei Lemuel Crizaldo, "Liberation's Option," Micah Global (11 December 2017).

44. Wolters, *Creation Regained*, 49.

45. Frederick Wilson, *The San Antonio Report: Your Will Be Done, Mission in Christ's Way* (Geneva: WCC Publications, 1990), 54.

> earth and responsibly use its abundant resources, not according to the rationale of the secular world, but for the Lord's sake. . . . Creation care is thus a gospel issue within the Lordship of Christ.[46]

The following year in a global consultation in Jamaica, the Lausanne Movement together with the World Evangelical Alliance issued a strong call for lamentation and repentance for the church's "failure to care for creation."[47]

This growing concern to recover creation care as a missional priority of the church has often revolved around the traditional understanding of Genesis 1:26–28 as the task of "stewardship" – of human beings in the role of "caretakers" or "managers" of the rest of the created order.[48] Gordon Smith's remark is characteristic of this popular notion, "Spiritual formation will mean fostering the capacity to know what it means to be a good steward of creation, as this is inherent in the Creation Mandate."[49]

Proposals to challenge this perspective, however, have been issued which have been brought about by the concern that the language of stewardship implies, albeit unnecessarily, unbiblical ideas of possession and domination, among others.[50] Rather than the posture of being a "steward," the call is to recapture the more intimate relationship shared by human beings and the rest of God's creation.[51] This is an ongoing conversation that can be enriched by considering perspectives on creation care from other cultures other than those of the West.

---

46. Lausanne Movement, *The Cape Town Commitment: A Confession of Faith and a Call to Action* (Peabody, MI: Hendrickson, 2011), 19.

47. "Creation Care and the Gospel: Jamaica Call to Action," Lausanne Movement (November 2012).

48. See Ken Gnanakan's chapter on creation care in the theology textbook by the Asia Theological Association (ATA): "Creation, New Creation, and Ecological Relationships," in *Asian Christian Theology: Evangelical Perspectives*, eds. Timoteo Gener and Stephen Pardue (Carlisle: Langham Global Library, 2019), 116.

49. Gordon Smith, "Spirituality that Takes Creation Care Seriously," in *Walking with God: Christian Spirituality in the Asian Context*, eds. Charles Ringma and Karen Hollenbeck-Wuest (Manila: OMF Literature, 2014), 105.

50. See for example Richard Bauckham's concern that the language of stewardship risks limiting the relationship of humans to nature as purely vertical (nature as a mere object of human rule) and ignores how humans are also horizontally related to nature as one creature among others. See Richard Bauckham, *Living with Other Creatures: Green Exegesis and Theology* (Waco, TX: Baylor University Press, 2011), 3–4.

51. See Ruth Valerio, "Why we are not stewards of the environment," Ruth Valerio blog (18 January 2021).

Reframing Creation Care

The nondualistic cultures and outlook of Asian people have what it takes to develop an approach that addresses the concerns related to the posture of "stewardship." In the Philippines, for example, is a remarkable spirit of hospitality and generosity among the people – celebrated traits that are rooted deeply in a relational sense of being instead of a more individualistic sense of identity. This spirit is mirrored well linguistically in the Filipinos rich vocabulary of *kapwa*, a word that can be roughly translated in English as "fellow" or "neighbor." For Filipinos, the language of *kapwa* opens the possibility of rerooting their creation care theology in the understanding that the rest of the created order are not simply "things" or "resources" to be harnessed or marveled at or much less managed. Instead, they are neighbors with dignity, rights, and well-being that have to be respected. They are "fellow" creatures of God (*kapwa nilikha*) that people need to learn to live with in peaceful coexistence.[52]

Aldrin Peñamora, a Filipino theologian and social ethicist, remarks that it is only within a humble posture such as this that humanity can recover full identity: "Our authentic humanity can only emerge if we identify ourselves as part of the community of creation before the Creator."[53] This perspective from the Philippines suggests a theology of planetary *neighborology* as an alternative framing for creation care – wherein human beings, bees, rivers, and trees form a community of love and support for one another.[54] But this is only one of many possible perspectives that the next generation can be encouraged to pursue and unravel toward the enrichment of the global conversation on a more "relational" theology of creation care.[55]

---

52. In the creation account of Gen 1, Bible commentators have observed a curious and very suggestive play of words and indicate the strong connection between the Hebrew word for human beings (*adam*) and the earth from which they were taken (*adama*).

53. Aldrin Peñamora, "Kapwa-Ethics: Christ-centered Ethics of Responsibility towards the Earth and Neighbor," in *Why, O God? Disaster, Resiliency, and the People of God*, eds. Athena Gorospe, Charles Ringma, et al. (Manila: OMF Literature, 2017), 133.

54. I first articulated this theological perspective in a plenary paper presented at the Creation at the Cross-roads: Lausanne-WEA Creation Care Network Consultation, 10–12 November 2020 in Jamaica. Available online at Rei Lemuel Crizaldo, "An Asian Perspective on Creation Care," half-meant (November 2012).

55. For a brief overview of theological perspectives on creation care from South Asia, see Samuel Richmond Saxena, "Influence of the Bible on Creation Care: Insight from the Indian Context," *Evangelical Review of Theology* 43 (2019): 345–58.

Nurturing a Faith *from* the Future

Ed Brown reminds us that "creation belongs to children in a special way."[56] Certainly they will need a solid foundation upon which they can anchor a confidence that indeed there is more to humanity than just being the unfortunate plague that contributes largely to the devastation of the earth. It does not help that generations of Christians in the past have been largely responsible for the shortcomings of the church to take the lead in providing a suitable response to the ills of the planet. But the good news is that the Bible offers a compelling vision and mission that can inspire a new generation to take up humanity's role of caring for God's creation.

Creation belongs to children in a special way.

"[D]o not hinder [the children]," Jesus told his disciples (Matt 19:14). Today this can mean that they need not be saddled with the baggage of "toxic" theologies of the past and the present – deficient theologies that have been proven and remain incapable of engaging volatile, uncertain, complex, and ambiguous environmental conditions. God forbid that the children will inherit this kind of Christian outlook. But as Athena Peralta points out when she quotes Michael Azucena, children have displayed the capacity for "new ideas or creative solutions" and have potential to "break down the barriers on complex and tricky issues."[57] Indeed, there is no telling how the Spirit of God can infuse hope for the future.

If so, then one of the best things the present church can do is to step out of the way and ensure *free spaces* for today's children to contribute in the church's unfolding journey to recovering creation care. These spaces will demand opportunities for conversations among themselves and will provide not only education designed *for* them but will help the present generation learn to dwell peacefully in the home God has created for human beings. These spaces would make possible a kind of creational spirituality that opens opportunities to delight in what is regarded as God's first book of revelation and be in the presence of God together with their non-human neighbors and

56. Ed Brown, *Our Father's World: Mobilizing the Church to Care for Creation*, 2nd ed. (Downers Grove: InterVarsity, 2008), 118.

57. Michael Azucena, et al., "Child-centred Climate Resilience: Case Studies from the Philippines and Vietnam," https://www.comminit.com/la/content/child-centred-climate-resilience-case-studies-philippines-and-vietnam (2015).

fellow worshippers (see Pss 19:1–6; 96:7–13; 98:4–9; 104; 148). Children need shalom spaces in which to both learn and play!

At the very least, the impending climate catastrophe will make or break the future of the planet depending on the actions, decisions, and policies made in the present, whether political, economic, or even religious. It would do the church of today much good if we would model to a watching world the capacity to listen to voices of the future – the generation of people who will populate earth long after the present has gone. Within the Christian community, hope for engaging in creation care lies in an engaged faith *from* the future to serve as an anchor for collective expressions of a faith *for* the future. Here on earth, and not anywhere else.

Bibliography

Alexander, T. Desmond. *From Eden to New Jerusalem: An Introduction to Biblical Theology*. Grand Rapids, MI: Kregel Academic, 2008.

Bauckham, Richard. *Living with Other Creatures: Green Exegesis and Theology*. Waco, TX: Baylor University Press, 2011.

Bauckham, Richard, and Trevor Hart. *Hope Against Hope: Christian Eschatology in Contemporary Culture*. London: Longman and Todd, 1999.

Brown, Ed. *Our Father's World: Mobilizing the Church to Care for Creation*. 2nd ed. Downers Grove: InterVarsity, 2008.

"Creation Care and the Gospel: Jamaica Call to Action." Lausanne Movement (November 2012). https://lausanne.org/content/statement/creation-care-call-to-action.

Crizaldo, Rei Lemuel. "An Asian Perspective on Creation Care." half-meant (November 2012). https://xgenesisrei.tumblr.com/post/634749462400712704/an-asian-perspective-on-creation-care-theology.

———. "Liberation's Option." Micah Global (11 December 2017). https://micahglobal.wordpress.com/2017/12/11/liberations-option/.

Devlin, Hannah. "Life on Mars: Elon Musk reveals details of his colonisation vision." *The Guardian* (16 June 2017). https://www.theguardian.com/science/2017/jun/16/life-on-mars-elon-musk-reveals-details-of-his-colonisation-vision.

"Elon Musk's plans for life on Mars are a 'dangerous delusion', says British chief astronomer." *Sky News* (15 March 2021). https://news.sky.com/story/elon-musks-plans-for-life-on-mars-a-dangerous-delusion-12243479.

Gnanakan, Ken. "Creation, New Creation, and Ecological Relationships." In *Asian Christian Theology: Evangelical Perspectives*, edited by Timoteo Gener and Stephen Pardue, 101–17. Carlisle: Langham Global Library, 2019.

Lausanne Movement. *The Cape Town Commitment: A Confession of Faith and a Call to Action*. Peabody, MI: Hendrickson, 2011.

Middleton, J. Richard. *A New Heaven and a New Earth: Reclaiming Biblical Eschatology*. Grand Rapids, MI: Baker Academic, 2014.

Moo, Douglas, and Jonathan Moo. *Creation Care: A Biblical Theology of the Natural World*. Grand Rapids, MI: Zondervan, 2018.

Myers, Bryant. *Walking with the Poor: Principles and Practices of Transformational Development*. New York: Orbis, 2006.

Nash, Roderick. *The Rights of Nature: A History of Environmental Ethics*. Madison: University of Wisconsin Press, 1989.

Nordling, Cherith Fee. "The Human Person in the Christian Story." In *The Cambridge Companion to Evangelical Theology*, edited by Timothy Larsen and Daniel Treier, 65–78. Cambridge: Cambridge University Press, 2007.

Penamora, Aldrin. "Kapwa-Ethics: Christ-centered Ethics of Responsibility towards the Earth and Neighbor." In *Why, O God? Disaster, Resiliency, and the People of God*, edited by Athena Gorospe, Charles Ringma, et al., 117–37. Manila: OMF Literature, 2017.

Rossing, Barbara. *The Rapture Exposed: The Message of Hope in the Book of Revelation*. New York: Basic, 2004.

Saxena, Samuel Richmond. "Influence of the Bible on Creation Care: Insight from the Indian Context." *Evangelical Review of Theology* 43 (2019): 345–58.

Shimasaki, Katsuomi. "The New Heavens and the New Earth: Our Hope and Motive for Stewardship." In *The Earth Is the Lord's: Reflections on Stewardship in the Asian Context*, edited by Timoteo Gener and Athena Gorospe, 5–19. Manila: OMF Literature, 2011.

Shin, Hyunte. "The Influence of the Bible in Shaping the Negative Viewpoint of Korean Christians towards Nature." *The Expository Times* 132 (2021): 211–22.

Simpson, Liu Liu, and Nick Simpson. "Building a Sustainable Future." Tearfund Learn (2019). https://learn.tearfund.org/-/media/learn/resources/tools-and-guides/2019-tearfund-building-a-sustainable-future-en.pdf.

Smith, Gordon. "Spirituality that Takes Creation Care Seriously." In *Walking with God: Christian Spirituality in the Asian Context*, edited by Charles Ringma and Karen Hollenbeck-Wuest, 102–11. Manila: OMF Literature, 2014.

Thorsen, Don. *An Exploration of Christian Theology*. Peabody, MA: Hendrickson, 2008.

Valerio, Ruth. "Why we are not stewards of the environment." Ruth Valerio blog (18 January 2021). https://ruthvalerio.net/bibletheology/why-we-are-not-stewards-of-the-environment/.

Valerio, Ruth, and Gideon Hugh. "A Christian Perspective on COVID-19." Tearfund Learn (n.d.). https://learn.tearfund.org/-/media/learn/resources/tools-and-guides/covid-19-tearfund-a-christian-perspective-on-covid-19-en.pdf.

White, Lynn. "The Historical Roots of Our Ecological Crisis." *Science* 155 (1967): 1203–1207. https://www.cmu.ca/faculty/gmatties/lynnwhiterootsofcrisis.pdf.

Wilson, Frederick. *The San Antonio Report: Your Will Be Done, Mission in Christ's Way.* Geneva: WCC Publications, 1990.
Wolters, Albert. *Creation Regained.* 2nd ed. Grand Rapids, MI: Eerdmans, 2005.
Wright, N. T. *Surprised by Scripture: Engaging Contemporary Issues.* New York: Harper One, 2015.

Case Study:
Children and Nature: A Pilot Program of the United Church of Zambia

Jane Travis – British and Damon Mkandawire – Zambian

Creation care is a biblical mandate for the whole church, which includes children. While we cannot off load the responsibility for climate change and ecological destruction onto children, we can encourage them to be good stewards of God's creation.

As Athena Peralta points out at the beginning of this chapter, children and young people are concerned about climate change and the environment. The church needs to be talking honestly about this issue while offering a message of hope and encouraging children to engage positively in caring for God's creation. For children to thrive in the fullness of Christ, they should be enabled to live in connectedness with God and his creation as fully as they can.

For children to thrive in the fullness of Christ, they should be enabled to live in connectedness with God and his creation as fully as they can.

Communities who suffer the worst consequences of climate change and ecological damage are often those who have contributed the least to the problems, which cause disproportionate harm to children, young people, and their communities across the world. For any solutions to climate and environmental degradation to be effective, children and young people must be genuinely empowered as agents of change.[58]

From his Christian faith and deep concern for the environment, Rev. Damon Mkandawire has been piloting an approach in Zambia which seeks to empower children as agents of change by educating and engaging them in

58. "The Climate Crisis, Climate Change Impacts, Trends and Vulnerabilities of Children in Sub Saharan Africa WASH Section," UNICEF ESARO (30 October 2020), https://www.unicef.org/esa/reports/climate-crisis.

playing an active role as stewards of God's creation. In this case study, Jane Travis draws on Rev. Damon's experience and offers inspiration to others who are seeking ways to engage children in creation care.

One Child's Journey Toward Putting Creation Care on the Church's Agenda

Damon's motivation for seeing creation care as a mandate for the church stems from his own experience of environmental injustice as a child. Growing up in the Copperbelt in Zambia, Damon experienced firsthand the impact of contaminated water and toxic air pollution from the copper mines close to his home. His interest in caring for creation comes from "the suffering, from the pain I experienced as a child because of that mining company." It was as if "creation was groaning, and a life of discipleship demanded a response to that wound."[59] Damon continues, "As a young person I asked myself what could I do?"

For any solutions to climate and environmental degradation to be effective, children and young people must be genuinely empowered as agents of change.

Mwambazambi argues that Christians have a "responsibility to stop environmental pollution when the welfare of the population is sacrificed for minority interests."[60] Damon recalls his initial experience of the church in Zambia: "When I went to church, my challenge was that it was situated in a mining town, but the church kept quiet and never said anything about the issue of environmental justice. Yet the people who were most affected were members of the church."

Damon studied environmental management, but he did not feel that he had a voice to mitigate environmental damage. So he decided to study theology and become a minister so he could influence change through the church. "My passion is for environmental justice, and this is connected to my Christian faith. My role is to advocate for the environment and speak for and with the

59. See R. Vellosso, "Presentation Global Connections Creation Care: An Optional Extra?" Global Connections (4 February 2021).

60. K. Mwambazambi, "A Theological View of Environmental Protection in Africa," *Die Skriflig* 45, no. 4 (2011): 864.

people who are affected by environmental degradation." Environmental justice is described as affirming "the sacredness of the earth, (creation) ecological unity and the interdependence of all species, and the right to be free from ecological destruction."[61]

Damon is now an ordained minister with the United Church of Zambia (UCZ). He is also a GreenFaith Fellow, a GreenFaith International Network Founding Partner, and a World Council of Churches Eco-School ambassador who encourages children and young people to adopt active roles as stewards of God's creation.

The United Church of Zambia

> *"Climate change education increases the adaptive capacity of children and their communities, helps to foster environmental stewardship, and develops children's capacity to be agents of change and active citizens."*[62]

The UCZ has begun a strategy of engaging children and young people as essential actors in caring for creation. This strategy involves equipping them with skills to mitigate and adapt to the effects of climate change and environmental degradation as well as protect and nurture fragile ecosystems. The work of UCZ with youth and young adults includes conservation farming, known as farming God's way, sustainable forest management, and exploring renewable energy.

This work with children is conducted nationally through secondary schools under the umbrella of the UCZ. Every child starting secondary school plants a tree and cares for it throughout their time at school. In addition, children attend school environmental clubs where they look at issues such as the science of environmental management and waste management.

Every child starting secondary school plants a tree and cares for it throughout their time at school.

61. Principle 1 of seventeen principles of environmental justice, drafted and adopted in 1991 by the First National People of Color Environmental Leadership Summit. "The Principles of Environmental Justice," NRDC (16 March 2016).

62. "Unless We Act Now: The Impact of Climate Change on Children," UNICEF (23 November 2015).

Children and Nature Pilot Program

> *"It is known that exposure to nature at a young age helps children develop their emotional responsiveness. . . . This highlights the importance of the fact that the children of today will ultimately grow up to become the care-takers of the environment in the future."*[63]

Following his own interest in environmental justice and with the endorsement of the UCZ, Damon has been piloting a program in his local area called "Children and Nature." He developed this program with Greenfaith International[64] and hopes it will eventually be adopted nationally by UCZ. This program is aimed at helping younger children to develop the desire to become active stewards of God's creation. "Children and Nature" is now in its third year, and Damon has been running environmental summer camps with children up to the age of fourteen helping them learn about water science, ecological footprint management, and caring for the environment. Children go on a two-day camp near a waterfall or a lake where they are encouraged to interact with nature, ask questions about what they are learning, and study Bible stories with an ecological lens.

Children go on a two-day camp near a waterfall or a lake where they are encouraged to interact with nature, ask questions about what they are learning, and study Bible stories with an ecological lens.

Damon stresses that "Children and Nature" is a pilot program in its early stages. Here he shares what he has learned so far about helping children understand their role as stewards of God's creation.

Start with Children's Lived Experience

> *"Lived experience of climate change and environmental degradation can provide insights and knowledge that go beyond scientific knowledge."*[65]

---

63. Karen E. Makuch, Sunya Zaman, and Miriam R. Aczel, "Tomorrow's Stewards: The Case for a Unified International Framework on the Environmental Rights of Children," *Health and Human Rights* 21, no. 1 (June 2019): 203.

64. Greenfaith. https://greenfaith.org/.

65. Dina Abbott and Gordon Wilson, *The Lived Experience of Climate Chang: Knowledge, Science and Public Action* (London: Springer International, 2015), 2.

In Damon's program "Children and Nature," drawing on children's lived experience is key. He argues that children are already aware of the damage to their local environment. "Many children are out playing in the streets, and they are choking because of air pollution. Children notice where vegetation does not grow or if they get sick because of contaminated water. These experiences push them to want to know more about these issues." In the summer camps Damon runs, children are able to explore issues facing them locally such as the impact of extractive industries on water and air pollution or the impact of climate change on agricultural practices or the impact of unsustainable fishing practices.

Let Children Interact with Nature

> *"I love nature and trees because they protect me from sunlight and also give me food."*
>
> – A twelve-year-old boy in the "Children and Nature" program.

"Children are born with a sense of wonder and an affinity for Nature. Properly cultivated, these values can mature into ecological literacy, and eventually into sustainable patterns of living."[66] By beginning to interact with and experience nature through the UCZ summer camps, children are encouraged to observe and be grateful for creation, to learn about it, and to ask questions. Children are encouraged to eat wild fruit from the forest and to learn about the trees this fruit grows on, cultivating a sense of gratitude for creation and the benefits it offers. Exploring the benefits of the natural world goes hand in hand with children's Christian spiritual formation. Interaction with the beauty of "creation is seen as a matter of faith."[67]

Exploring the benefits of the natural world goes hand in hand with children's Christian spiritual formation.

At the same time, the UCZ camps help children to learn about the impact of not caring for the environment. Damon explains, "Children are taken to experience the waterfalls in the rainy

66. Zenobia Barlow, "Confluence of Streams: An Introduction to the Ground-breaking Work at the Center for Ecoliteracy Resurgence and Ecologist Ecoliteracy," *Dancing Earth* 226 (September/October 2004): 7.

67. A. E. Orobator, *Theology Brewed in an African Pot* (Maryknoll, NY: Orbis, 2008), 48.

season and then when it stops raining so they can see how the falls change. When they go and the water is falling and the water drops are coming near them, they experience the beauty of that. And then when it is dry, they see the impact on the environment." Based on the children's observations of the waterfalls, Damon and his team are able to relate what children see to the realities of the impact of climate change using simple stories.

Damon stresses that faith and science are not mutually exclusive. Children are taught how water is a gift from God and a precious commodity; they also learn about how water should be managed and how not to pollute water. The camps also provide space for children to study Bible stories and to reflect on water as a giver of life. For example the story of Moses and Aaron turning the water in the Nile to blood (Exod 7:14–24) is used as an example of how water can become contaminated and the damage that can cause to communities. "One thing we encourage from a very early age is that children should not be afraid of asking difficult questions," says Damon.

Build on Indigenous Understanding of Relationship to Creation

"Indigenous peoples' knowledge of sustainable practices and stewardship is a key element in maintaining the world's ecological richness."[68] As well as the joy and spiritual wonder children can experience in nature, Damon stresses the importance of building on traditional knowledge of the local environment as doing so fosters understanding and care for it. He points out that "As Africans the beauty of indigenous knowledge is that we have words to describe the environment which are not found elsewhere."

Those caring for the waterfalls where the children camp are able to share their indigenous knowledge about how to look after the water and the surrounding environment. Damon likes to remind children "that these traditions are not only good for them but are good for creation." He goes on to explain that when the children are learning about caring for creation, "We look at the sacredness of faith and the sacredness of tradition. We remind them that they are Christians and they are Africans. They don't have to be westernized in their thinking about creation. Our view of creation and human beings is that we coexist, and the relationship is mutual." This sense of mutual interdependence is what provokes children to want to take an active role in stewardship.

68. "Unless We Act Now."

Encourage Children to Play an Active Role as Stewards

"Children and young people can play a key role in promoting environmentally sustainable lifestyles and setting an example for their communities"[69] One of the major activities in Damon's region of Mbereshi in Luapula Province is fishing. The use of poisons by some fishing families as a fishing method is an unsustainable practice and causes ecological damage. This damage is increasingly becoming a national concern in Zambia leading to fishing bans during the months of December to February.

Through the summer camps on the lake, the "Children and Nature" program involves children in the discussion of this local way of fishing. Damon uses Bible stories to help them interrogate the practice. He explains, "We are aware that for fishing families the means justify the ends, and they need to put food on the table," but the children are encouraged to think about alternative ways of fishing which are more sustainable. Damon goes on to say, "Children as young as twelve are taken to the lake for fishing, so we want them to ask their parents: Is it ok to do that form of fishing?" In this way, children are encouraged to become agents of change.

Although the ecological footprint of a Zambian child is relatively small compared to a child in the industrialized world, Damon is keen for children to ask the questions, "What am I taking from the earth, and how am I giving back to the earth?" He is profoundly aware that he needs to model what he is asking of others and has developed an initiative called "Payback Sunday." Every Sunday, he picks up litter and makes himself available to talk to others about environmental awareness and the connection between faith and caring for creation.

Children who have participated in "Payback Sunday" are now educating their parents.

Children who have participated in "Payback Sunday" are now educating their parents. One child spoke to her father about throwing litter out of car window, explaining to him that he had committed an ecological sin. Her father came to speak to Damon to understand more. This parent's awareness of caring for the environment has changed as a result of what his daughter pointed out to him.

69. "Environment and Climate Change," UNICEF (3 August 2021).

The Churches' Role

"I love nature because nature is life."

– An eight-year-old participating in the "Children and Nature" program

Damon's dream for the church is that "We raise a generation that is environmentally conscious, a generation that considers the earth to be sacred, a generation that respects creation so that at the end of the day, we will be able to coexist with nature and live in a healthy environment."

Damon suggests that for churches to assist children to become active stewards of creation care, churches must include issues on environmental and climate justice in their Sunday school syllabus as part of teaching about God and creation. "We cannot afford to leave environmental issues only to adults." He goes on to say, "Churches also must invest in training Sunday school teachers and youth pastors about environmental justice. If we invest in people who become passionate about the link between faith and creation care, they will be able to go back to children and teach them."

Finally, Damon suggests that we need to be putting children at the heart of theological education. If ministers and pastors take time to think about children, their thoughts should be led to the future of those children and the world they will inhabit. The church cannot refrain from thinking about children or about its biblical mandate to care for creation because doing so is a risk that future generations will not have a habitable world in which to live.

Bibliography

Abbott, Dina, and Gordon Wilson. *The Lived Experience of Climate Change: Knowledge, Science and Public Action*. London: Springer International, 2015.

Barlow, Zenobia. "Confluence of Streams: A Groundbreaking Work at the Center for Ecoliteracy Resurgence and Ecologist Ecoliteracy." *Dancing Earth* 226 (September/October 2004). https://www.gaiafoundation.org/app/uploads/2018/02/resurgence-issue-226.pdf.

"The Climate Crisis, Climate Change Impacts, Trends and Vulnerabilities of Children in Sub Saharan Africa WASH Section." UNICEF ESARO (30 October 2020). https://www.unicef.org/esa/reports/climate-crisis.

"Environment and Climate Change." UNICEF (3 August 2021). https://www.unicef.org/environment-and-climate-change.

Makuch, Karen E., Sunya Zaman, and Miriam R. Aczel. "Tomorrow's Stewards: The Case for a Unified International Framework on the Environmental Rights of

Children." *Health and Human Rights* 21, no. 1 (June 2019): 203–14. https://cdn1.sph.harvard.edu/wp-content/uploads/sites/2469/2019/07/Aczel.pdf.

Mwambazambi, K. "A Theological View of Environmental Protection in Africa." *Die Skriflig* 45, no. 4 (2011): 849–66. https://www.researchgate.net/publication/267634173_A_theological_view_of_environmental_protection_in_Africa.

Orobator, A. E. *Theology Brewed in an African Pot*. Maryknoll, NY: Orbis, 2008.

"The Principles of Environmental Justice." NRDC (16 March 2016). https://www.nrdc.org/resources/principles-environmental-justice-ej.

"Unless We Act Now: The Impact of Climate Change on Children." UNICEF (23 November 2015). https://www.unicef.org/reports/unless-we-act-now-impact-climate-change-children.

Vellosso, R. "Presentation Global Connections Creation Care: An Optional Extra?" Global Connections (4 February 2021). https://www.globalconnections.org.uk/sites/newgc.localhost/files/codes-and-standards/rosalee_talk.pdf.

Discussion Questions for Chapter 8

1. Looking at your own context, what are some changes in nature you have observed that merit immediate action on the part of the body of Christ?
2. Creation care is a biblical mandate for the whole church. In what ways can you mobilize your local church to take part in being stewards of God's creation?
3. From the example of Rev. Damon Mkandawire, how can you engage the children in your community to become "essential actors in caring for creation," keeping in mind their developmental capacities and limitations?

Epilogue

Two Prayers in Response to God's Heart for Children

A Prayer of Forgiveness

Based on prayers prayed during Viva Global Staff Devotions, February 2022

For failing to care for children well,
Father, forgive us

For not investing in children's education,
Father, forgive us

For ignoring the cries of children who are
living in fear of violence and abuse,
Father, forgive us

For children who are forced to work instead of going to school,
Father, forgive us

For children who are discriminated against
because of their gender, race or abilities,
Father, forgive us

For trashing your creation with our greed and consumption, denying
future generations of children a safe environment to live in,
Father, forgive us

For children whose lives are torn apart by war and conflict,
Father, forgive us

For seeing children as distractions, a cost or a
burden and not as gifts from you,
Father, forgive us

For closing our eyes as children are bought and sold into slavery,
Father, forgive us

For failing to support parents and families as they care for their children
Father, forgive us

For failing to protect children from online abuse and exploitation
Father, forgive us

For making church inaccessible to children and being a
barrier to children coming to know and worship you
Father, forgive us

Save us and help us.
Amen

A Prayer of Commitment

Based on Isaiah 61, adapted by Rosalind Tan

Come Spirit of the Sovereign Lord to be upon us
Anoint us to preach the Good News to children
Send us to bind up their broken-hearts
To proclaim freedom for children captive in fear
To release from darkness children who are imprisoned
To proclaim the year of the Lord's favour
and the day of vengeance of our God
To comfort all children who mourn
and provide for children who grieve
To bestow upon children a crown of beauty
instead of ashes
The oil of gladness instead of mourning
And a garment of praise
instead of a spirit of despair
So that they will be called the "Oaks of Righteousness"
– a planting of the Lord
For the display of Your splendour.

Amen

About the Editors

Lucy A. Hefford is the Theology and Practice Researcher for Viva and Project Coordinator for Theology of Children at Langham Publishing. She is a qualified secondary school teacher and has previously taught religious studies in a number of schools in Oxfordshire, UK. She left teaching to train at All Nations Christian College, UK, in intercultural studies. Lucy has a master's in Applied Theology from the University of Oxford and is currently a PhD candidate at Fuller Theological Seminary, California.

Nativity A. Petallar is Professor of Christian Education and Program Director of Holistic Child Development at Asia-Pacific Nazarene Theological Seminary. Her teaching interests include foundations of Christian education, life-span Christian development, and holistic development of children. Nativity has a doctorate from Asia Baptist Graduate Theological Seminary. She is also a member of the Lausanne Steering Committee for Children at Risk. She is married to Mark, and they have two children.

Rosalind Tan is the Director of Education Programs at Asia Graduate School of Theology Alliance. She also lectures for various institutions. Her areas of interest include academics and instructional theories, Child studies and Community-based research. Rosalind holds a Doctorate from Asia Graduate School of Theology Alliance. Rosalind is married to Sunny Tan and they have two grown-up children.

About the Authors

María Alejandra Andrade Vinueza is an Ecuadorian theologian, sociologist and childhood specialist, with passion for issues related to spirituality, faith and justice. She has spent more than 15 years accompanying Christian communities in engaging with justice and development in different places around the world. Her current research areas include environmental justice, migration, gender and decolonial theologies. She currently serves as Tearfund's Theology and Network Engagement Global Lead. Maria currently lives in Ecuador with her life partner Frank and their two boys Jose and Mati, with whom she is discovering God in new and exciting ways.

Patrick Byekwaso is the Children in Families and Church Partnerships Programme Manager for CRANE (Children At Risk Action Network) in Kampala, Uganda. He is also an Associate Pastor of Lugogo Baptist Church. He holds a BA in Theology from the African International University. Patrick is passionate about working with young people, other leaders, social justice, sports and inspiring a generation of young people to be all that God created them to be.

Nathan Hussaini Chiroma PhD is the Dean of the School of Theology and acting Head of Department of Children and Youth Ministry at Pan Africa Christian University, Nairobi Kenya and a Research Associate, Department of Practical Theology and Missiology, University of Stellenbosch. He has been serving in theological education for the last 30 years, following his work as a pastor spanning different countries. Nathan has a PhD in Practical Theology from the University of Stellenbosch.

Rei Lemuel Crizaldo concurrently serves as the Theological Commission Coordinator of the World Evangelical Alliance (WEA) and as the Theological Education Network Coordinator of Tearfund UK in East and Southeast Asia. In the Philippines, he serves on the faculty of the Asian Seminary of Christian Ministries and as a local author with several books published by OMF Literature, including 'Boring Ba Ang Bible Mo?' (Is Your Bible Boring?), which won a 'Filipino Reader's Choice Award.' He is a licensed professional teacher with a degree in Theology and a master's degree in Mass Communication.

Carmen Alvarez González PhD is the Regional Director for Latin America of Viva – Together for Children. She has a PhD in Health and Social Sciences and has extensive experience working to protect children and develop practical solutions in Latin America and the Caribbean. This experience includes the management of regional teams, the design of strategies, the formulation, monitoring and evaluation of social development projects, public advocacy, and the promotion of justice. Carmen also has a bachelor's degree in Theology with a specialization in Education, and a bachelor's degree in Law and a master's degree in Human Rights and Peace Education from the University for Peace, UN.

Jan Grobbelaar PhD is a retired pastor of the Dutch Reformed Church in South Africa. He served two congregations for 13 years before joining Petra Institute for Children's Ministry in 1996, where he served in various positions contributing to building the leadership capacity of churches and communities to become children-inclusive spaces in various African contexts before his retirement at the end of September 2021. He obtained his PhD in Practical Theology from Stellenbosch University in 2008. His main research interests are the intersection between children/childhood and theology, and intergenerational faith formation and he is still actively involved in doing research in these fields. Jan is a Research Fellow of the Department of Practical and Missional Theology, Faculty of Theology and Religion, at the Free State University in Bloemfontein, South Africa. He is also involved with research at the Theological Faculties of the Universities of Stellenbosch and Pretoria. Over the years he published various articles and chapters in academic journals and books. He is married to Marie and they have three adult children and three grandchildren.

Amberbir Tamire Habtemariam is the Deputy Director of the Child Development Training and Research Centre (CDTRC). He has an MA in Holistic Child Development from the Malaysian Baptist Theological Seminary and a BTh from Evangelical Theological College, Addis Ababa. He lives in Ethiopia with his wife, Tegene Bekele, and their three children – Tinsae, Zekarias, and Melkam.

Saw Law Eh Htoo is the Programme Coordinator for the Pathein Myaungmya Sgaw Karen Baptist Association's Child Ministry. He has a BTh degree from the Kothayu Theological Seminary in Pathein, Myanmar (Burma). He lives in Myanmar with his wife Naw Deeyar Htar and their two children.

Shake` Geotcherian Koujryan Jackson is a lecturer in the field of Practical Theology focusing on Christian Education, Spiritual Formation, Leadership Training, and The Teaching Ministry of the Church. She has recently moved to join her husband in the United Kingdom, after holding the position of Lecturer and Director of the Christian Education Resource Center, at the Near East School of Theology (NEST), Beirut, Lebanon. During her work at NEST, she organised more than 40 trainings for church leaders who came from Iraq, Syria and Lebanon. Shake` has also been an active member of the Union of the Armenian Evangelical Churches in the Near East (UAECNE) and has served in many positions and represented both NEST and the UAECNE in many international conferences. She has a Master of Sacred Theology (STM), from The Near East School of Theology, Beirut, Lebanon.

Jessy Jaison PhD has been a theological educator and training consultant based in Kerala, South India for thirty years. She started as full-time faculty at New India Bible Seminary in 1992 and served there as the Director of Research and Advancement and led the Holistic Child Development Program since 2009 to date. She gained her MTh from the University of Oxford, PhD from the Queen's University of Belfast, UK, and completed postdoctoral writings at Asbury and Fuller Seminaries in the US. She is partnering with the United World Mission (UWM), the Overseas Council, Asia Theological Association-CAED, ICETE Senior Consulting, Re-Forma, LeaderSource and Lausanne Theology Working Group. Jessy resides in India with her husband Dr. Jaison Thomas (Regional Director for Overseas Council, South Asia) and the couple is blessed with two adult sons Abraham and Aquil and their families.

Faith Kembabazi is the Director and Network Development Coordinator of CRANE (Children at Risk Action Network), a Viva partner network based in Kampala, Uganda. Faith holds a Master of Science in Development Management from the Open University and a BA in Social Sciences in Psychology, Sociology and Social Administration. Previously she served with 'True Love Waits', a drive to reduce HIV/AIDS in Uganda, under the Baptist Ministry.

Sublimé Nyundu Mabiala PhD is a Global Educator with Converge International Ministries. In the past, Sublimé has served as a missionary in West Africa, the Arab World and in America with several US-based mission agencies. He completed his PhD in International Development from the University of Edinburgh, Scotland UK. He is currently working on a "Juvenile Mobility & Hostility" post-doc project. Sublimé is married to Rachel and they recently relocated from Detroit, Michigan to Abidjan, Ivory Coast (Cote d'Ivoire), West Africa.

Kezia M'Clelland is the Children in Emergencies specialist for Viva. Over the last fifteen years she has learned from and helped equip local churches and communities to support children and families in crisis situations. This work has spanned Africa, Asia, and the Middle East, and has a focus on child protection and psychosocial support. Kezia has a master's in Violence, Conflict and Development from SOAS University of London. She is passionate about creating opportunities for children affected by conflict and disaster to be safe and fulfill their potential.

Douglas McConnell PhD is Provost Emeritus and Senior Professor of Leadership & Intercultural Studies at Fuller Theological Seminary. The McConnells served as missionaries for 20 years in Australia, Papua New Guinea, and as International Director of Pioneers. McConnell established the program focusing on the mission to children at risk at Fuller Seminary, which engages in research on missional responses to the plight of children globally and equips leaders in this vital field. Doug began his work as a primary school teacher in the US, Australia, and Papua New Guinea. After returning to the US, he served on the international board of Viva.

Damon Mkandawire lives in Mbereshi, Zambia, where he serves as Hospital Administrator for the United Church of Zambia's Mbereshi Mission Hospital. He is a minister of word and sacraments in the United Church of Zambia. He is an environmentalist, young theologian and gender justice activist. Growing up surrounded by copper mines, Damon has first-hand knowledge of environmental degradation and its potentially deleterious impacts on women, children, human health and welfare. Damon spent years as an Environmental Officer at the Konkola Copper Mines, one of Africa's largest producers of copper, and continues to work towards national and international environmental justice and gender justice.

Roseline Olumbe PhD, is Lecturer and Coordinator, Institute of Child Development, Daystar University, Kenya. She has a PhD in Holistic Child Development from the Asia Pacific Nazarene Theological Seminary. She lives in Kenya with her husband Duncan and they have three sons.

Athena Peralta serves as Programme Executive for Economic and Ecological Justice at the World Council of Churches. Previously she worked with the

National Economic and Development Authority of the Philippines as a senior economic development specialist. Her research and advocacy focus on the intersections between economic, ecological and gender justice.

Enrique Pinedo is Compassion International's senior program advisor on strategic alliances for Latin America and the Caribbean. He is a member of the Latin American Theological Fellowship, and he served as President of the Latin American movement "With Children and Youth." He also served as the coordinator of the Global Thematic Forum about Children at the Micah Network and as facilitator of the Global Track "Holistic Children Ministries" at the 4/14 Movement. Enrique was a member of the Children at Risk Committee at the Lausanne Movement, and has a master's in Religious Sciences from the Evangelical University of the Americas in Costa Rica. He is an ordained minister and serves with his wife in the parenting ministry at the Church of All Nations (COAN) in Florida, US. Enrique is married to Miriam, and they have four children – Miriam J., Cesia, Jonathan, and David.

Adnan Azhar Sandhu completed his theological studies at Gujranwala Theological Seminary, Pakistan and Children Bible Ministry, New Zealand. In 2001 he started the Pakistan Sunday School Ministry which focuses on supporting children and building bridges between churches and their communities. In the past twenty years he has trained more than twenty thousand children's workers in South Asia, and he is now in the process of training master trainers who will continue and multiply this work. Over the last nine years he has served alongside international movements including the 4/14 Window Movement and the Global Children's Forum. Adnan is also serving with the Lausanne Movement as a catalyst for children and evangelism. He is married to Neelam, and they have four daughters – Annika, Sabrina, Adelina, and Selena.

Clenir Xavier dos Santos is the Lifewords Pavement Project global director and is part of the Lifewords international executive team. She is a trained social worker and psychologist, and she specializes in marital and family psychotherapy at the Tavistock Clinic, London. Since 1999, Clenir has been in the leadership of the Pavement Project, operating in twenty-one countries. She also founded and spent fifteen years directing a local church's project with street children in Rio de Janeiro. Clenir was elected and served for two years as a member of the Brazil National Children's Rights Council. She currently lives in Rio de Janeiro, is a pastor's widow, and is inspired daily by her three children and grandsons.

Harold Segura PhD is the Director of Faith and Development for World Vision, Latin American and the Caribbean. He is also a Baptist pastor and was previously Rector of the International Baptist Theological Seminary of Cali, Colombia. Rev. Segura completed his doctoral studies at the Javeriana University in Bogotá, Colombia.

Bradley Gabriel Mark Thompson has served with World Vision for over 20 years, including various technical and leadership roles in India and the Philippines. He currently coordinates World Vision's global Child Sponsorship capability and ministry integration team. They are focused on enabling country offices and programme teams to work effectively with partners to achieve sustainable child well-being outcomes through Child Sponsorship. Bradley has a master's in Community Health from Trinity College, Dublin and a master's in Social Work from Loyola College, Chennai/University of Madras, India. He is currently pursuing a PhD in 'Holistic Child Development' at Asia Pacific Nazarene Theological Seminary (APNTS) in Manila, with the goal of utilising his knowledge and experience to create a caring, loving and just world for children. Bradley is based in Hamilton, New Zealand with his wife, Feby, and their two children – Joshua and Tirzah.

Jane Travis is the International Programme Manager for Viva. She leads programme development to equip churches and faith based organisations globally, to engage with and respond to priority issues facing children. Previously she worked in the international NGO sector focussing on emergencies and people affected by conflict. Her roles have included setting up and leading community services in refugee camps in Tanzania, Chad and Zambia. She has also lived and worked in Sudan, India and Rwanda. Her passion is to see the church engaged with issues of our time. Jane is actively engaged with local and national environmental initiatives.

Shantelle Weber PhD has a PhD in Practical Theology from the University of Stellenbosch, where she is currently employed as an Associate Professor in the Department of Practical Theology and Missiology. Her research interests include faith formation of youth and cultural and interreligious studies. Shantelle is also the director of Uzwelo Youth Development, a non-profit organization focused on youth leadership development where her team trains youth workers who cannot study full-time and also mentors young adults. Shantelle is married to Brandon, and they have two daughters – Shannon and Ashleigh.

Menchit Wong currently serves on the International Board of the Lausanne Movement. She also serves in the leadership teams of global mission networks for children and youth, such as the Global Children's Forum and the 1for50 Movement. Since 2018, Menchit's focus of ministry is now in the marketplace, after retiring from 30 years of ministry in child advocacy and holistic child development. She currently serves with the OneCORE Success Center in the Philippines, as a senior consultant, learning facilitator and Gallup-certified Strengths coach for leaders of companies and for-profit organizations. During her 30-year tour of duty with Compassion International, she served as Country Director, and International Child Advocacy Director. Menchit is happily married to Rico for the last 35 years. They are blessed to have three sons, two daughters-in-law and four grandchildren.

Special Tribute

As Viva, we wish to take this opportunity to acknowledge and pay special tribute to Devesh Lal – one of Viva's network consultants in Patna, India. Devesh had been involved in the creation of this publication until he tragically passed away in November 2020.

During his nine years working for Viva in India, Devesh was hugely instrumental in advocating for the rights of girl children; in developing partner networks in Patna, Ranchi, and Shillong; in training church leaders and volunteers about child protection issues; and in mentoring girls about life skills.

The news of his death has come as a terrible shock, and his passing is a devastating loss for his family, church community in Patna, our partner networks in India, and for Viva globally. Devesh served as an inspiration to us all in the way he served children, and we miss him very much.

Speaking on video as part of Viva's Christmas appeal in 2016, which was on the theme of mentoring girls in India, Devesh said –

> *"The church is the only vehicle that can bring a change here in people's mindsets. We love our girls, and we would like to give them opportunities. I have a dream that when people enter Patna – from the railway station, bus stand, road, and airport – they will see that this city is a safe and happy place for girls."*

Subject Index

Scripture Index

OLD TESTAMENT

NEW TESTAMENT

Viva is an international charity dedicated to changing more children's lives to fulfill their God-given potential.

We build and support networks of grassroots churches and organizations to protect and provide for children.

We impact over three million children in twenty-six countries through our thirty-nine partner networks which comprise more than 4,680 local churches and community organizations.

Viva
www.viva.org

Viva's Children in Emergencies toolkit
www.childreninemergencies.org

Viva India
www.viva-india.org

Philippine Children's Ministry Network
www.thepcmn.org

Children At Risk Network – Nepal
www.carnet.org.np

Children at Risk Action Network – Uganda
www.cranenetwork.org

Get in touch with us: **info@viva.org**

Langham Literature and its imprints are a ministry of Langham Partnership.

Langham Partnership is a global fellowship working in pursuit of the vision God entrusted to its founder John Stott –

> ***to facilitate the growth of the church in maturity and Christ-likeness through raising the standards of biblical preaching and teaching.***

Our vision is to see churches in the Majority World equipped for mission and growing to maturity in Christ through the ministry of pastors and leaders who believe, teach and live by the word of God.

Our mission is to strengthen the ministry of the word of God through:

- nurturing national movements for biblical preaching
- fostering the creation and distribution of evangelical literature
- enhancing evangelical theological education

especially in countries where churches are under-resourced.

Our ministry

Langham Preaching partners with national leaders to nurture indigenous biblical preaching movements for pastors and lay preachers all around the world. With the support of a team of trainers from many countries, a multi-level programme of seminars provides practical training, and is followed by a programme for training local facilitators. Local preachers' groups and national and regional networks ensure continuity and ongoing development, seeking to build vigorous movements committed to Bible exposition.

Langham Literature provides Majority World preachers, scholars and seminary libraries with evangelical books and electronic resources through publishing and distribution, grants and discounts. The programme also fosters the creation of indigenous evangelical books in many languages, through writer's grants, strengthening local evangelical publishing houses, and investment in major regional literature projects, such as one volume Bible commentaries like *The Africa Bible Commentary* and *The South Asia Bible Commentary*.

Langham Scholars provides financial support for evangelical doctoral students from the Majority World so that, when they return home, they may train pastors and other Christian leaders with sound, biblical and theological teaching. This programme equips those who equip others. Langham Scholars also works in partnership with Majority World seminaries in strengthening evangelical theological education. A growing number of Langham Scholars study in high quality doctoral programmes in the Majority World itself. As well as teaching the next generation of pastors, graduated Langham Scholars exercise significant influence through their writing and leadership.

To learn more about Langham Partnership and the work we do visit **langham.org**

Paul Bennett is a Solicitor, Mediator and Arb
SRA regulatory, Anti-Money Laundering, emplc
law in the specialist Professional Practice Tean
LLP until the end of February 2019 and then is launching Bennett Briegal LLP with a colleague to support law firms nationally within a niche law firm setting.

Paul's work is national and his experience includes advising hundreds of law firms from High Street, niche firms and City and US law firms on legal issues and regulatory investigatory and enforcement matters. An experienced advocate across a range of Tribunals and Courts he has successfully acted before the Solicitors Disciplinary Tribunal for law firms and individuals.

The majority of Paul's contested cases involve a Queens Counsel on behalf of the other party and Paul's practice is in many ways similar to that of Counsel in terms of the advisory and advocacy work he undertakes. Written advice is regularly given in preference to Counsel and Queens Counsel given his understanding of running a law firm in practice.

A Law Society of England and Wales Council Member since 2017 he Chaired the Small Firms Division Committee in 2015 having previously been a Managing Director who sold the successful niche law firm he had started.

From January 2019 he is the Chair of the Shropshire Business Board and a Member of the Marches Local Economic Partnership (LEP) having previously served as the representative of professional service businesses and the Vice Chair.

Paul writes for and is quoted in the legal press regularly. His book *A Practical Guide to Compliance for Personal Injury Firms working with Claims Management Companies* was published In September 2017 by Law Brief Publishing who also publish this guide.

Paul describes himself as a failed game show host who used to DJ in pubs and clubs. In his spare time he is obsessed with his family, music, football and cycling challenges.

@Law4Professions (Twitter)
07785 623 644

A Practical Guide to the SRA Principles, Individual and Law Firm Codes of Conduct 2019 – What Every Law Firm Needs to Know

A Practical Guide to the SRA Principles, Individual and Law Firm Codes of Conduct 2019 – What Every Law Firm Needs to Know

Paul Bennett
Bennett Briegal LLP
Solicitor Advocate (All Proceedings)
LLB (Hons) LLM PG Dip
Legal and business adviser to Solicitors and Law Firms

Law Brief Publishing

Published 2019 by Law Brief Publishing, an imprint of Law Brief Publishing Ltd
30 The Parks
Minehead
Somerset
TA24 8BT

www.lawbriefpublishing.com

Paperback: 978-1-911035-58-9

This book is dedicated to my beautiful wife Sue and our two daughters, Martha and Nancy, who forgive my absences from family life to write, talk and work far too often. Thank you for your love and patience.

PREFACE

The regulation of solicitors is changing (again) in 2019. The Solicitors' Code of Conduct 2007 was replaced with the SRA Principles 2011. In 2019 we must change again as the Solicitors Regulation Authority (SRA) require compliance with a totally new regime.

As a profession solicitors over the last 18-20 years have been under scrutiny and statutory challenges. The aim of this book is to overview these latest regulatory changes and explain the underlying ethos.

The naturist and scientist Charles Darwin was born in my hometown of Shrewsbury in 1809 and he famously went on to develop the theory of evolution as a scientific model. Law firms can learn much from the theory; the lessons of evolution are a useful guide and demonstrate change continues always. In his seminal work, *On the Orgin of Species*, Charles Darwin wrote:

> *"It is not the strongest of the species that survives, not the most intelligent that survives. It is the one that is the most adaptable to change."*

This book is about helping law firms adapt to the latest regulatory landscape. Expect further changes though.

This is relatively short and guides on each of the core SRA Principles 2019, the Code for Solicitors 2019 (the Individual Code), the Code for Law Firms (the Firm Code) which are due to come into force during the first half of 2019. The SRA standards and regulations alone will not explain the SRA's expectations of you and your law firm – they are too brief. The commentary on these is intended to help you apply the generic wording applying for all firms in England and Wales in practice.

Ethics and regulation are in the legal press daily but for solicitors and the owners of law firms how do they keep up to date and develop their understanding? This book aims to help but it is a living, breathing challenge so expect to listen to podcasts, watch webinars, attend conferences and receive in house training (which I offer to law firms). The combination will ensure the evolving challenge you need to meet can be met in your firm.

Compliance is never static and no doubt this book will be subject to further editions as law firms address the challenge ahead. I hope you find it useful.

With the exception of one footnote about the likely date of introduction of the new regime (April to July 2019) the law and any references to SRA guidance are correct to the 1st December 2018. The exception is expressly stated so assume the 1st December 2018 unless stated otherwise.

Note that this book is not legal advice or a substitute for taking legal advice. It is worth bearing in mind at all times that guidance from regulators can and will change, the Courts will reinterpret points and legislation will be applied. Nothing is certain in the field of professional regulation. You should obtain legal advice on your specific situation if you want it and the factual circumstances arising so these can be assessed and advised on in context as generic commentary is not legal advice.

Paul Bennett
Twitter: @Law4Professions
December 2018

ACKNOWLEDGMENTS

My thanks go to my publishers, Tim and Garry, for publishing this, my second book. They are great to work with and have helped improve the first draft with their experience and insight but any errors are mine alone. Your support is much appreciated.

When I first looked at writing a guide to their rules and expectations the SRA were co-operative and kindly confirmed I could use extracts of their published materials provided the source was acknowledged and you will note this is a the case throughout but the source material can be found on their website www.sra.org.uk. When we have done conference talks together knowing I am writing this book they have been open, transparent and helpful. Chris Handford, Director of Regulatory Policy has been particularly helpful.

Neil Rose, the Editor of the excellent Legal Futures website kindly confirmed I could quote anything from the site with an acknowledgement.

My business partner Mark Briegal at Bennett Briegal LLP our niche professional sector law firm which launches in March 2019 has been understanding as we plan our launch and has picked up some slack as I finish this book and has given his insights in our discussions on various snippets. It is much appreciated.

Colleagues on Law Society Council, the Regulatory Processes Committee and the Law Management Section have through general discussions all contributed indirectly to my thinking and it's always a pleasure to meet with and discuss points with them.

Clients past and present have contributed by ensuring I have seen and done every possible version of most challenges around ethics and running a law firm. My disciplinary work may attract the headlines but the partnership and business efficiency instructions undertaken over many years have probably helped more in writing this book.

CONTENTS

CHAPTER ONE
INTRODUCTION

Law firms, and in particular their senior managers, face a significant logistical and training challenge in 2019 in implementing a totally new approach to solicitors' regulation following policy decisions by the Solicitors Regulation Authority (SRA) to seek to fundamentally simplify the regulation of solicitors for the second time in less than a decade. Firms may rightly ask: "Why this is happening?". We live in an era of regulation and the regulatory models that are preferred are ultimately changing.

The regulation of solicitors, and particular professional conduct regulation, is a hugely complex area subject to significant litigation on a regular basis which is widely reported in the legal press. It is also, as a practitioner I can confirm, widely misunderstood and often when defending professionals, the issue of a lack of understanding of the regulatory regime is either a significant factor, or a contributing factor to disciplinary investigations and disciplinary prosecutions to which I am helping clients address. The ambitious aim of this book therefore is to take the changing ethos and the changing rules and to summarise these neatly in to a user friendly guide aimed at solicitors, both in private practise, and in-house, who have an ethical or professional regulation query.

This book focuses on the SRA Code of Conduct for Individual Solicitors [2019] (Individual Code) and the Code of Conduct for Law Firms [2019] (Firm Code), the two new distinct strands of the SRA Handbook, and the associated SRA Principles 2019. The fundamental shift is not just in the structure, or even necessarily in the simplified rules themselves. It is, however, on the ethos underlying these. Your judgement of your ethical obligations will take centre stage.

In 2017 I took part in a series of conferences organised by two different organisations, firstly, the Law Society of England & Wales, and secondly, the insurance broker, Cox Mahon, at which a senior member of the SRA outlined the SRA's thinking, and I outlined the impact for professionals. It was simplification or "red tape reduction" in action the SRA set out. At the Law Society version, a Law Society Policy Officer also outlined the Law Society's opposition to the changes then proposed. This book is not going to focus on the policy and the rights and wrongs of that policy. Such academic and policy driven debate is neither of use, nor of interest to a busy practitioner, and the emphasis therefore throughout the rest of this text will be on what the rules say now they have been confirmed as coming into force by the SRA's Board (May 2018) and the Legal Services Board (November 2018), and how the rules need to be interpreted, and what you, as a practitioner, need to know.

In July 2018 for the Law Society I took part in an update with their policy team and the SRA lead on this work speaking to solicitors at Chancery Lane. The tone had subtly changed: it is about public protection, about solicitors using their judgement and high ethical standards. The SRA had moved back towards protectionist traits and placed less emphasis on the "red tape reduction".

Why? The policy is catching up with the commentary of the last couple of years. Ethics are back in fashion.

If you are bamboozled by the changes, or if you do want specific personalised legal advice, then of course, as the legal advice disclaimer throughout this book makes clear, you should take that advice, whether from me, or some other qualified professional. The significant ethos change though is this: ethics, by which I mean a return to individual ethical judgement applying the broad brush rules which are to be preferred under the new regime. For those without an ethical background and training, it is going to represent a fundamental challenge, and this is addressed, in part, in the following chapter and, thereafter, throughout the rest of the book. I hope you find it useful and practical.

CHAPTER TWO
LEGAL ETHICS: BACK TO THE FUTURE?

The language and underlying philosophy of legal regulation has, over recent decades, moved from an ethical starting point, from say 1920 onwards, using the language of compliance and the compliance agenda of other regulatory frameworks. The SRA Handbook 2011 owed much to the financial services model then in vogue but which of course had been under intense scrutiny and reform itself following the 2008 financial crisis. The SRA adopted a model which was already behind the curve in 2011.

Compliance is a concept which is based around having and using a set of rules and thereafter putting in place systems and processes to ensure the regulated professional or professionals comply with those rules. Under compliance based regulatory model it is not necessary for the individual professional to understand why the rules exist so long as they simply follow them. You could suggest that this model is one of black and white rules which should be applied irrespective of personal judgement.

By contrast ethical application requires judgment and value decision making.

In the 1980s cult film 'Back to the Future' the main character, Marty McFly, struggled with the unintended consequences of his actions when travelling back to the 1950s. The SRA seek to take us from a compliance model towards an ethical decision model. What will the unintended consequences be? Time will tell.

Since at least Roman times lawyers have been regulated, and not unsurprisingly, the manner of that regulation has evolved and developed over the intervening period. Until the SRA introduced Outcomes Focused Regulations (OFR) on the 6th October 2011 it was arguable that in addition to the regulatory framework there was also an underlying concept which practitioners needed to apply of not just following the rules, but looking beyond the rules and understanding why those rules existed, and thus ensuring they applied them having understood the ethical concept which underpin their role and behaviour as a solicitor.

In fairness to the SRA, the SRA Principles 2011 were clearly intended to underpin, by way of an ethical approach, this concept through the 10 simple rules known as Principles. In a press release from the SRA dated the 13th June 2017 their Chief Executive, Paul Phillip, stated:

> *"Clear, high professional standards are at the heart of public confidence and solicitors, law firms and a modern legal sector. Our consultation confirmed that a shorter, clearer Handbook, with a sharp focus on professional standards, is the way forward."*

The SRA's language for ethics continues to be "professional standards", but practitioners approaching the new SRA Principles and the Code of Conduct for Individual Solicitors and the Code of Conduct for Law Firms should not misinterpret the use of the SRA's language of professional standards as to be anything other than professional ethics.

A Little History

It could be argued as recently as 1960, and arguably still today, that there is a very simple formula to regulating any of the professions, whether that be the legal profession, or indeed any other profession. The Secretary-General of the Law Society of England & Wales, Sir Thomas Lund, wrote in the Guide to the Professional Conduct and Etiquette of Solicitors 1960 as follows:

> *"You may well ask for a short summary of solicitors' duties. I suppose, really, it is the old principle:*
>
> *"Do unto others as you would they should do unto you.". "*[1]

1 A guide to the professional conduct and etiquette of solicitors by Sir Thomas Lund, Law Society, 1960 in the Introduction.

The SRA's 2010 consultation on OFR[2] indicated that the SRA's thinking could be summarised as thus in 2010 ahead of the introduction of OFR:

> *"Our current rulebook is detailed and prescriptive. It tends to lead to the use of resources which could be better deployed on higher risk areas and does not help us to get the best out of our relationship with the profession. Even in the current marketplace it becomes increasingly difficult for detailed rules to keep pace with change. This will be even more so with the liberalised legal landscape starting in October 2011. A rulebook needs to be fit for purpose;"*

This extract from the executive summary of the 2010 document highlights that the SRA's aims, both in 2010 with the introduction of OFR, and in the SRA Regime [2019] with the introduction of the simplified SRA Principles [2019] and the introduction of a Code of Conduct for Individuals [2019] and a Code of Conduct for Law Firms [2019], are, in effect, partly an acknowledgement that the 2011 reform aims have not been met and they need to be met in order to reflect the changing legal services market following the radical regulatory overhaul which occurred through the Legal Services Act 2007.

Ethics in Other Jurisdictions

It is not just the Romans that focused on ethics for legal regulation.

The culture of ethical practise is an integral part of much of the world's common law legal system and whilst the statutory[3] attempts to address professional regulation appear to have moved the jurisdiction in England and Wales away from legal ethics, that is not true of the rest of the world. Legal ethics is taught widely and in detail within the United States regime and is an essential part of the course. Those attending law

---

2 Outcomes Focused Regulation transferring the SRA's regulation of legal services 28th July 2010

3 The Legal Services Act 2007 Section 1 (1) merely states "(h) promoting and maintaining adherence to the professional principles" the details of ethics, standards and professional principles are left by legislators to the regulatory bodies.

school in America have to undertake the essential component parts of the curriculum sitting alongside traditional legal subjects, and every law school has a professor of ethics. In England and Wales the briefest of mentions arises on the Legal Practice Course (LPC) and legal ethics are not a core research activity (with some very notable voluntary academic exceptions).

Why are Ethics Back in Fashion?

The move under the SRA's OFR regime to prosecute individual solicitors for breaches of the SRA Principles 2011 as well as the substantive rules has made ethics key again, whether this is before the Solicitors Disciplinary Tribunal, or indeed to make decisions through the SRA Adjudicators in relation to certain aspects of legal practise such as being a Compliance Officer for Legal Practise (COLP) or Compliance Officer for Finance and Administration (COFA). This means that in practice in recent years the regulatory failures of the recent past are being acknowledged and are being addressed against the existing regime in a manner that was not envisaged and sometimes enforcement is unnecessarily difficult. For that reason the underlying ethos when reading the new SRA Principles [2019] and the new Code of Conduct for Individuals [2019] and new Code of Conduct for Law Firms [2019] stems from principles that Sir Thomas Lund would have recognised back in 1960.

Ethics is a concept which works more effectively when dealing with individual solicitors and their conduct. By contrast, the Outcomes Focused Regulation regime was aimed at introducing an entity based regulatory system (i.e. the firm was responsible for the actions of those within it). It is an approach which has ultimately failed and the revised approach with its separate codes for individuals and firms acknowledges this.

Unethical Shift?

The focus now under the forthcoming regime is to ensure that individual solicitors and also those managing law firms understand that as a member of their profession they have to behave ethically because their work has wider consequences than the individual matter in which they are working. Put simply, the SRA has determined that framing behaviours around ethical rules rather than black and white compliance rules will achieve better outcomes: they are almost certainly right.

Since the SRA started its consultations in relation to the new Handbook in 2016 there has been an explosion of articles, books and webinars focused on ethical practise as a solicitor. Why? The absence of ethics from compulsory academic degree level teachings during the LLB degree and the absence of ethics as the dominant force in practise for many years means that when the SRA first published its proposals, those of us working in the regulatory field immediately recognised the re-emergence of ethics.

The guidance that Sir Thomas Lund gave in 1960, other than its old fashioned language and its inappropriate use of "he" in a profession now dominated by "she", does, however, hold true, and those reading the Principles and the Individual/Firm Code of Conduct moving forward would want to keep these ethical principles at the forefront of their mind. As Sir Thomas Lund put it:

> *"If I had to advise, very briefly, a young solicitor on the guiding principles of conduct when he comes into the profession, I think I should say to him that it is clear that only the very highest conduct is consistent with membership of this profession of ours. Your clients' interests are paramount – that seems to be clear except that you should never do, or agree to do, anything dishonest or dishonourable, even in a client's interests or even under pressure from your best and most valued client; you had better lose them...you should refuse to take any personal part in anything which you yourself think is dishonourable; you should withdraw and cease to act for that client, even if he presses you to go on. So far as you possibly can, consistently with not actually letting your client down, you should be completely frank in all of our dealings with the court, with your brother solicitors and with members of the public generally. Finally, I think I would say that where your word has been pledged, either by yourself or by a member of your staff, you should honour that word, even at*

> *financial cost to yourself, because his reputation is the greatest asset a solicitor can have, and when you damage your reputation you damage the reputation of the whole body of this very ancient and honourable profession of ours."*[4]

Those guiding principles which set out an ethical basis for putting the clients' interests first except where they conflict with public interest and duties to the court remain the same in the SRA Principles and Codes [2019] as the SRA introduce its new ethical code book. Make use of those basic and guiding principles in light of your practise, and your practise will never be too far from appropriate.

Ethics are back. Like the previously mentioned cult film 'Back to Future' the SRA's approach intended or not is changing history by moving away from mere compliance and restoring ethical judgment to prominence.

---

4 Ibid.

CHAPTER THREE
THE SEVEN SRA PRINCIPLES 2019

Introduction

The last chapter explained and explored why ethical thinking is suddenly back in fashion and the practical application of the SRA Principles [2019] is based on the application of ethics to core "principles" or tenets of personal and professional conduct which underpin how each and every regulated person (that is someone working in a law firm regulated by the SRA) should conduct themselves in both their professional and personal lives.

In this chapter we look at the SRA Principles [2019] firstly as a concept as that is central to being able to apply them in practice as a solicitor and/or law firm principal, partner or manager. Thereafter we explore the 7 Principles from 2019.

The Only Way Is Ethics (TOWIE)

TOWIE is not simply a terrible television show (in my opinion) to allow the tabloids to have cheap content and comment pieces and to fill the TV schedule cheaply or even to look at the fictionalised lives of some over the top personalities and attention seeking types. It is what sets out how the SRA are thinking: you have to apply ethics, always and without exception.

In all seriousness the TOWIE link is a key concept, how you practice law must factor in the ethical thinking behind the 2019 professional regime. As the SRA Principles document states:

> *"The SRA Principles comprise* ***the fundamental tenets of ethical behaviour that we expect all those we regulate to uphold****. This includes all individuals we authorise to provide legal services (soli-*

citors, RELs and RFLs), as well ***as authorised firms and their managers and employees****". [Emphasis added in bold]*

In practical terms this means that those of us regulated by the SRA or managing those that are regulated by the SRA have to always start any act, omission or conduct by applying the SRA Principles [2019].

Prior to applying any other rules or guidance the SRA Principles [2019] should be applied.

This means the SRA Principles [2019] apply over and above the SRA Code of Conduct for Individual [2019] and SRA Code of Conduct for Firms [2019]. This means Solicitors seeking to address ethical and compliance challenges after the implementation date (possibly 1st April 2019[1]) will need to start with assessing how the SRA Principles [2019] apply on the facts confronting that solicitor. Then, and only then, should that solicitor seek to move on to the Codes of Conduct rules.

SRA Principles [2019] – What if they conflict?

The SRA Principles [2019] could conceivably conflict with, for example, the duties towards a client (whether that be an individual in a High Street law firm scenario or a Magic Circle firms international client) and towards the Court. In such cases the law firm and/or the individual solicitor should seek to evidence their thinking (in a file note or an email of advice for example) and should demonstrate that the wider public interest obligations prevail over the needs of any individual client.

1 This is the expected implementation date and was alluded to in the SRA June 12 2018 website update, their email of 14th June 2018 to consultee groups and was confirmed by Chris Handford the SRA's Director of Regulatory Policy at an event we both spoke at for the Law Society Small Firms Division on 19th July 2019. The SRA indicated at its Compliance Conference 2018 that the date was fluid but between April and July 2019

The SRA, aware of this challenge, have explicitly set out the prevalence of the public interest aspect in the Introduction to the SRA Principles [2019] themselves by stating:

> *"Should the Principles come into conflict, those which safeguard the wider public interest (such as the rule of law, and public confidence in a trustworthy solicitors' professional and a safe and effective market for regulated legal services) take precedence over an individual client's interest.* ***You should, where relevant, inform your client of the circumstances in which your duty to the Court and other professional obligations will outweigh your duty to them."*** *[Emphasis added in bold]*

Put bluntly the public interest prevails, always.

For the larger City type firms this will present a huge commercial pressure as, whilst it has always been thus in reality, the explicit setting out of the obligation is, in my view, designed to deal with the ambiguity that in the past has allowed larger firms in particular to resist the SRA's intention that public interest factors prevail in finely balanced matters. The clearer emphasis quoted in bold above requires practically that the solicitor and firm demonstrate their thinking (by recording it) and demonstrate that the appropriate weight of public interest factors has been applied. If you do not evidence this you risk sanction. It's a significant shift of simplification to aid the SRA's enforcement options.

The SRA conclude the "Introduction" to their Principles by stating:

> *"The Principles and Codes are underpinned by our Enforcement Strategy, which explains in more detail* ***our approach to taking regulatory action in the public interest."*** *[Emphasis added in bold]*

The enforcement approach is a separate aspect of public interest but the theory behind the reforms is screaming out: public interest prevails over individual client interests.

Most law firms and solicitors, in my experience of advising hundreds of each, focus on a "the client comes first" principle and the potential unintended consequence of these reforms is that balance has shifted because the SRA have not fully appreciated that their statutory duty to focus on the public interest factor is more nuanced for solicitors with other competing factors. The balance has though shifted to public interest prevailing in all aspects not merely the traditional areas of Courts, Tribunal and Oath Administration.

The approach of the SRA is now explicit and therefore the excuses of the past are not intended to work moving forward. Public interest prevails for solicitors and firms because for the SRA the public interest in pursuing enforcement action prevails if they do not act in accordance with the obligation. These may be two distinct elements of public interest but the theme of the 2019 reforms is the wider public interest.

Why is the emphasis changing?

The SRA thinking on the importance of wider public interest and the need for clear, simple ethical rules can be explained in three distinct aims:

1. Rules that focus on what matters – high professional standards;
2. Make it easier for the public to access legal services;
3. Ease the regulatory burden on solicitors and firms to enable them to do business more efficiently.

These are noble aims and unlikely to be contentious yet the reforms will only be effective if the solicitors and firms understand in practice what is expected of them. Alternatively the noble aims are irrelevant. The SRA summarise the position as:

> *"Shorter, simpler rules and standards*

- *A shorter, more accessible Handbook – focussing on the* ***behaviours and principles that support high professional standards.***
- *A separate Code of conduct [sic] for solicitors and one for firms."*[2] [Emphasis added in bold]

The SRA Principles [2019] are by design, as an explicit intention and by the Enforcement Strategy about the behaviours expected and the standards that the public can expect. The profession must adhere to the new standards.

The principles all follow the formula: "You act:" then the principle itself i.e. You act in a way that upholds…..

Principle 1 – in a way that upholds the constitutional principle of the rule of law, and the proper administration of justice.

This applies to conduct both inside and outside of legal practice.

Upholding the law is something that is expected of those working in law firms irrespective of whether or not they are acting in the course of their profession or personally. Any substantive breach of the law, for example, a conviction for committing a criminal offence is likely to breach this Principle.

Upholding the law also applies in the context of client work. For example you cannot be complicit in breaching the law for a client. Therefore if a client of a law firm wanted to pay bribes which breached the Bribery Act 2010 to government officials overseas the firm (its managers and the individual solicitors instructed) would be obliged to assess whether it could continue to act, what obligations arise under the Money Laundering Regulations 2017 and the Proceeds of Crime Act 2002 reporting regimes.

---

2 The SRA Website "Looking to the Future reform" 1st August 2018

The simple sounding "uphold the rule of law" element therefore has multiple impact points and practitioners need to be able to demonstrate that their work meets this principle.

Principle 1 Tips

In practical terms this means the following:

1. Raise awareness of the width of this Principle through training and policy/procedures;

2. Supervise the work for the firm to demonstrate compliance;

3. Report anything which falls short of upholding "the rule of law" to the firms Compliance Officer for Legal Practice (COLP) who should then record whether or not and why the breach is or is not to be reported to the SRA referencing Principle 1 [2019].

By contrast the obligation to uphold "the proper administration of justice" is a simpler statement of our professional obligation to the Court and Tribunal system. As a professional, the obligation to the justice system should be at the heart of what we do. In recent years a series of cases have criticised lawyers conduct[3] and attempts to disengage from the legal system to put the clients wishes first which might include being obstructive.

We must ask: Are our acts or omissions consistent with the proper administration of justice? If not, then Principle 1 is breached. Recording reasons for the decision-making is therefore key. Again, to give this some practical context, in 2018 I realised I had a series of hearings scheduled and limited day's availability. I rarely use counsel but I took a decision to use counsel to ensure my professional commit-

3 See for example legal press reports: https://www.legalfutures.co.uk/latest-news/sdt-berates-careless-disrespectful-approach-sra-solicitors-prosecuting or https://www.litigationfutures.com/news/high-court-judge-criticises-parties-solicitors-attritional-conflict or https://www.lawgazette.co.uk/law/judge-criticises-generally-unhelpful-firm-over-application-in-vw-case/5067110.article

ments did not delay resolution for clients and undermine the "administration of justice". The letters on file to clients, explaining my limited availability and proposal to use Counsel, record my reasoning. This is not difficult if the principle is at the forefront of your mind but for many solicitors and firms it isn't and the SRA Principle [2019] with the renewed emphasis on clearly applying them or being in breach of the rules will, I predict, catch out many professionals.

Principle 2 – in a way that upholds public trust and confidence in the solicitors profession and in legal services provided by authorised persons

In many ways Principle 2 is linked to Principle 1. The SRA acknowledged this in the consultation on the new Principles as follows:

> *"70. We are satisfied that they [the Principles] should apply outside of the practice context as well as within it. This is because they relate to standards of behaviours which, if not met (irrespective of context) would give rise to the need to take action to protect the public or to uphold public confidence in the profession and authorised persons delivering legal services."* [4]

The whole ethos of Principle 2 under the SRA Principles [2019] is that every aspect is focused on upholding public trust and confidence (and not undermining it). In contentious work I have heard solicitors express concern about this but my view of Principle 2 and the Enforcement Strategy is that pursuing your client's legitimate case would never offend the principle.

Obviously, if somewhat controversially, in November 2018 the high profile media solicitor Mark Lewis was successfully prosecuted by the SRA and fined by the Solicitors Disciplinary Tribunal for comments he made on social media in response to anti-Semitic abuse he was the focus of. Many commentators pointed out his Article 10 right to freedom of

4 SRA Our response to consultation: Looing to the future – flexibility and public protection June 2017 page 15 paragraph 70

expression. The mission creep from the SRA's ethical agenda, is already being pursued vigorously, thus you must maintain the confidence of the public in all your actions.

By contrast the Bar Standards Boards (BSB) appear to permit barristers to speak freely and controversially on all topics. We are distinct professions but the contrast is stark and will need to looked at by the oversight regulator the Legal Services Board (LSB) in due course.

As with Principle 1 it is about the wider public and not a specific another member of the public.

Principle 2 was one of the Principles that changed during the SRA consultation from "ensure that your conduct upholds public confidence in the professional and in those delivering legal services" to the current wording. The SRA have explained this change as follows:

> *"We have amended the new Principle 2 to make it clearer that the obligation is to uphold public trust (emphasising the fiduciary nature of the relationship between solicitor and client and public confidence)."*[5]

The wording was completely revised and amended. The real meaning is thus clear from the supporting documents: it is about the trust between a solicitor and client in a fiduciary sense but it will be used by the SRA in the most expansive sense as their pursuit of Mark Lewis demonstrated.

The width of this principle does not immediately occur when reading the revised wording in my opinion and I expect to see challenges on the interpretation before the Solicitors Disciplinary Tribunal (SDT) and High Court (which has appellate jurisdiction) over the next few years. I would hope to act in some of the cases seeking to narrow the remit to ensure a fair playing field with other legal professions such as the Bar Standards Board.

---

5 Ibid at page 16 paragraph 78.

The total rewriting during the consultation of this principle highlights how difficult it is to secure mutual understanding between a pressurised professional, the regulator and the public on matters.

Principle 2 – Tips

In practical terms you should consider the following:

1. Are you able to demonstrate that the fiduciary relationship with clients has been maintained?;

2. Do your files show decision making when public confidence might be engaged? (If not, training and supervision to ensure is essential);

3. The distinction between regulated practitioners and other service providers is clear. How will you ensure your clients are protected if, for example, another party is represented by a non-regulated entity (as is often the case in say employment cases). Do your systems identify the distinction? If not you may wish to amend them given the clear ethical distinction now emerging between regulated and the non-regulated sector.

Principle 3 – with independence

The current obligation to "not allow your independence to be compromised" is a reactive or passive obligation given the language and the implication of it.

By contrast the SRA wording in the SRA Principles [2019] is a much more positive or active wording "You act with independence". It raises the bar beyond passivity and put the professional on notice that their independence must be at the heart of each and every decision, action or omission they make.

Why the distinction? Is it because lawyers love language and syntax? No. It is about the positive, active ethical underpinning set out the previous chapter. The SRA explained their decision:

"We believe it is important to maintain the latter, more positive obligation in the consultation proposal. This reflects the wording in section 1(3) of the LSA [Legal Services Act 2007]."[6]

The SRA's link to the LSA is key to solicitors and firms seeking to comply with the revised obligation. For the SRA you must not do anything which is, or could be seen to be, impinging on your independence. Why? Public interest and public confidence. So yet again the link back to the earlier principles crystallises and confirming the ethical tenets flow together with an increasing emphasis on being able to demonstrate nothing hinders the public interest aspect.

In practice this will mean that you need to demonstrate (and record) your relationships with others including counsel, professional contacts, referral partners (such as Estate Agents or Accountants) does not impact on your ability to act with independence.

Principle 3 – Tips

1. Record each professional relationship you and your firm has and note why it does not create a breach of this principle;

2. Train the staff on the meaning of this principle and supervise to ensure files are managed effectively against it;

3. Ensure that professional relationships are set out in writing to clients and the client has the opportunity to state any preferences.

---

6 Ibid at page 17 paragraph 79.

Principle 4 – with honesty

The first draft of proposals from the SRA proposed to link honesty and integrity into a single principle. The post consultation revised version separates these concepts in to two principles and were approved by the SRA Board on 30 May 2018. Despite the late revision the proposals of the SRA to amend the SRA Principles 2011 merit some rehearsing here because it explains the SRA current thinking and therefore how solicitors and firms will need to apply the SRA Principles [2019] in practice.

The existing version of this Principle has been a moving target for some years and the Courts have repeatedly ruled on contentious application of the concept.

The SRA Principles 2011 state as follows:

> *"2. [You must] act with integrity;"*[7]

The Guidance note to this simple wording reads:

> *"2.6 Personal integrity is central to your role as the client's trusted adviser and should characterise all your professional dealings with clients, the court, other lawyers and the public."*[8]

There is no mention you will note of "honesty". Integrity appears to be used to convey the obligation in some wider sense.

The SRA Consultation launched in June 2016 proposed to revise the wording to:

> *"4. [You must] act with honesty and integrity"*[9]

---

7 The SRA Principles 2011 from the SRA Website as of 01.08.2018.

8 Ibid.

9 SRA Consultation Looking to the future – flexibility and public protection June 2016 page 14

Over the next 12 months or a series of cases occurred in the High Court[10] culminating in a decision of the Court of Appeal[11] in which some guidance is given on the meaning of "honesty" and "integrity" which will apply not just now under the current SRA Principles 2011 but will also continue under the SRA Principles [2019] and the SRA Codes [2019].

Honesty

In the Court of Appeal LJ Jackson gave the leading judgement and observed as follows at paragraph 93:

> *"Let me stand back from the kaleidoscope of the authorities and consider what the law now is. Honesty is a basic moral quality which is expected of all members of society. It involves being truthful about important matters and respecting the property rights of others. Telling lies about things that matter or committing fraud or stealing are generally regarded as dishonest conduct. These observations are self-evident and they fit with the authorities cited above.* ***The legal concept of dishonesty is grounded upon the shared values of our multi-cultural society. Because dishonesty is grounded upon basic shared values, there is no undue difficulty in identifying what is or is not dishonest."*** [Emphasis added in bold]

We can take from this judgment that conduct such as:

- Being truthful;
- Not telling lies;
- Not committing fraud;
- Not stealing.

10 Newell-Austin v SRA [2017] EWHC 411 (Admin); Malins v SRA [2017] EWHC 835 (Admin); Williams v SRA [2017] EWHC 1478 (Admin)

11 Wingate & Anor v The Solicitors Regulation Authority [2018] EWCA Civ 366

In the context of legal practice this would inevitably include a solicitor being open and transparent about their own actions and omissions. For example fabricating letters to clients and for bills. These are fairly typical issues along with misuse of client monies which lead to appearances before the SDT[12]. However, not all acts of dishonesty lead to the same outcome and it is not always clear why. The decision of the SRA using its powers of fining and rebuking as has occasionally occurred[13]. On occasion the SRA has deviated from its apparent policy of always seeking to strike off before the SDT and High Court for any dishonest solicitor. The case of Daniel Smith before the SDT is a rare case were the SRA agreed to a suspension from practice rather than strike off[14].

Honesty then is central, serious and should be identified without "undue difficulty" in the view of the Court of Appeal.

At the same time as the series of cases referred to above before the High Court and Court of Appeal the civil claim of a professional gambler was heard and shifted the tectonic plates of the legal system across civil claims; criminal cases and within professional disciplinary cases as the definition of dishonesty was amended by the Supreme Court in Ivey v Genting Casinos (UK) Ltd (trading as Crockfords Club) [2017] UKSC 67. By the time the Court of Appeal considered Wingate and Anor[15] the dishonesty test was set out as being an objective one which was quoted by LJ Jackson with approval. The test now is:

> *"...When dishonesty is in question the fact-finding tribunal must first ascertain (subjectively) the actual state of the individual's knowledge or belief as to the facts. The reasonableness or otherwise of his belief is a matter of evidence (often in practice determinative) going to whether he held the belief, but it is not an additional requirement*

12 Exemplar Solicitors Disciplinary Tribunal cases: SRA v Welch Case No. 11516-2016; SRA v James Case No. 11657-2017

13 https://www.sra.org.uk/consumers/solicitor-check/457984.article?Decision=2017-12-29

14 http://www.sra.org.uk/consumers/solicitor-check/393067.article

15 Wingate & Anor v The Solicitors Regulation Authority [2018] EWCA Civ 366

> *that his belief must be reasonable; the question is whether it is genuinely held.* ***When once his actual state of mind as to knowledge or belief as to facts is established, the question whether his conduct was honest or dishonest is to be determined by the fact-finder by applying the (objective) standards of ordinary decent people. There is no requirement that the defendant must appreciate that what he has done is, by those standards, dishonest.*** *"* [Emphasis added in bold][16]

For the SRA Principles [2019] therefore the test on the honesty element of Principle 4 will be whether or not the conduct breached Principle 4 and if it does so in the majority of cases this will to strike off unless exceptional circumstances arise which merit an outcome short of strike off.

In November 2018 the High Court in Solicitors Regulation Authority v James & Ors [2018] EWHC 3058 (Admin), decided on a series of dishonesty and exceptional circumstances cases involving mental health factors, alleged extreme working conditions, alleged bullying and an alleged "toxic" working environment. These cases, including one of the author's client cases were being appealed by the SRA after their submissions were rejected by the SDT. These have emphasised the High Court's disdain for any element of dishonesty and even when extreme mitigation exists the High Court is guiding the SDT that dishonesty should lead to striking off a solicitor. The rules which apply to doctors are distinct and far more forgiving.

The High Court approach to solicitors who are ill and commit serious misconduct, as dishonesty is, highlights a disappointing approach. One that the Court of Appeal[17] in the future may need to address given the High Court *approach* contrasts with the empathy shown for doctors guilty of serious misconduct including dishonesty or treatment failing which cause death (see Bawa-Garba in the footnotes) but finding solicitors should be held to a higher standard when a client is misled is the

---

16 Ivey judgment at paragraph 74.

17 Bawa-Garba v General Medical Council [2018] EWCA Civ 1879

current position until the Court of Appeal or Supreme Court has a suitable case to address the High Court's approach.

The Court outlined the high test to avoid strike off for solicitors who are dishonest whether that is about their error or their failure to complete a task for clients as follows:

> *"104. Therefore, whilst the mental health and workplace environment issues in any given case will not exceptional circumstances, they can and should be considered as part of the balancing exercise required in the assessment or evaluation. The problem in the present cases is that the SDT has not engaged in that balancing exercise. Whilst it is correct that in all three judgments the SDT made findings as to the length of time of the dishonesty, its seriousness and the harm caused in earlier passages of the judgments, when the SDT came in each case to its evaluation of whether there were exceptional circumstances justifying a lesser sanction, it did not focus on those critical questions of the nature and extent of the dishonesty and degree of culpability and engage in the balancing exercise which the evaluation requires between those critical questions on the one hand and matters such as personal mitigation, health issues and working conditions on the other. Had it done so, it should have concluded that in none of these cases could the dishonesty be said to be momentary. In James the dishonest conduct extended over 17 months and in Naylor over some 3 months. True it is that in MacGregor, the dishonesty was only for a period of 2-3 days, but that has to be seen in the context of Judgment Approved by the court for handing down. SRA the other misconduct found, the failure of Mrs MacGregor as COLP of the firm to report the fraud and misconduct for another 8 months. Furthermore, in each case the dishonesty was not isolated but was repeated on a number of occasions. In each case, the dishonesty caused harm, in two of the cases to the client (who in one case was vulnerable) and in the other to the LAA."*[18]

18 Lord Justice Flaux at paragraph 104

However the principle of acting with honesty should not be too onerous to achieve. Any examples of dishonesty located in your firm should be reported to the SRA without delay and that as these cases show includes misleading clients.

Principle 4 – Tips (honesty)

1. Record the thinking behind decisions which impact on others (including the client);

2. Train all staff on the meaning of honesty and dishonesty under the case law – it is often not what people think;

3. Think through the actions – could they be misconstrued? If yes the thinking should be recorded in a file note or letter to client to confirm the purpose and its honesty.

Principle 5 – with integrity

As discussed above the separation of honesty and integrity is a relatively recent change of approach from the SRA after the two phases of consultation in 2016 and 2017. It was only confirmed in June 2018.

Integrity

Integrity alone was sufficient in the SRA Principles 2011. The SRA previously tried to say the two concepts and words of honesty and integrity were interchangeable in a series of disciplinary cases. Not every outcome was what the SRA hoped for, hence the splitting into two principles. The concepts may overlap as the SRA have conceded in their June 2017 response to the consultation by stating:

> *"We are comfortable that the terms "honesty" and "integrity" may overlap, but that action can be taken if someone fails to demonstrate one or another.* ***Including them in the same principle does not***

> ***mean they have to be pleaded together.***"[19] [Emphasis added in bold]

The SRA's thinking is clear from their consultation: solicitors should display honesty and integrity and sometimes conduct will be obviously both and sometimes they will from 2019 prefer to plead breach allegations against Principles 4 and 5 of the [2019] regime.

Solicitors and law firms therefore we need to ensure we demonstrate compliance with both concepts individually and collectively.

So what does integrity mean? LJ Jacksons key judgement again helps at paragraphs 96 and 97:

> *"96. Integrity is a more nebulous concept than honesty. Hence it is less easy to define, as a number of judges have noted.*
>
> *97. In professional codes of conduct,* ***the term "integrity" is useful shorthand to express the higher standards which society expects from professional persons and which the professions expect from their own members.*** *See the judgment of Sir Brian Leveson P in Williams at [130].* ***The underlying rationale is that the professions have a privileged and trusted role in society. In return they are required to live up to their own professional standards.*** *"* [20] [Emphasis added in bold]

Integrity is a concept about which solicitors and law firms are held to a higher standard because of professional standards and status. The privileges of the profession (status, income, standing etc.) come with obligations to be held to a higher standard. The reference of LJ Jackson to Sir Brian Leveson P in Williams[21] is a reference to this pertinent clarification of the meaning of integrity:

---

19 As before at page 17 paragraph 80.

20 Wingate & Anor v The Solicitors Regulation Authority [2018] EWCA Civ 366

21 Williams v SRA [2017] EWHC 1478 (Admin) at paragraph 130

> *"....I ought to make it clear that, in the absence of compelling justification, I would reject Mostyn J's description of the concept of want of integrity as second degree dishonesty. Honesty, i.e. a lack of dishonesty, is a base standard which society requires everyone to meet.* ***Professional standards, however, rightly impose on those who aspire to them a higher obligation to demonstrate integrity in all of their work. There is a real difference between them.*** *"* [Emphasis added in bold]

Those in the profession, whether as solicitors, law firms or investors need to understand therefore that the standards that apply from Principle 2 under the SRA Principles 2011 and have increasingly featured as a standalone charge in disciplinary cases will only increase once the SRA have honesty and integrity to choose from. Under Principle 5 with the coming into force of the SRA Principles [2019] the wording may not change from 2011 but expect the SRA enforcement to now ramp up and increase because they have resolved their approach and split integrity from honesty having previously misdirected themselves in a number of high profile cases which have ended before the High Court and Court of Appeal rather than SRA Adjudication or the SDT. The SRA will under the integrity principle seek to hold solicitors and law firms to a higher standard of conduct as they want the profession to display those additional expectations to protect the public and maintain public confidence.

Principle 5 – Tips (Integrity)

1. Record the thinking behind decisions which impact on others (including the client);

2. Train all staff on the meaning of integrity and explain and explore why the professional standards hold them to a higher standard under the case law;

3. Think through the actions – could they be misconstrued? If yes the thinking should be recorded in a file note or letter to client to confirm the purpose and that integrity is not compromised.

Principle 6 – in a way that encourages equality, diversity and inclusion

The SRA are held to account by the Legal Services Board according to statutory criteria set out in the Legal Services Act (2007) Section 1 which includes the rather bland sounding obligation to be:

> *"encouraging an independent, strong, diverse and effective legal profession".*

This has led to a number of controversial aspects including the collection of data collected by the SRA from law firms which requires the diversity data to be collected and submitted to the firms. The characteristics the SRA is monitoring are:

- Age;
- Gender;
- Ethnicity;
- Disability;
- Sexual Orientation;
- State or Public/Private School;
- University education (first to go from family);
- Religion;
- Caring responsibilities for others;
- Transgender.

The Principle is aimed at helping the SRA meeting its statutory obligations under the LSA. For solicitors and law firms they must not undermine equality, diversity and inclusion. These are noble aims but the Principle lack specific enough guidance to have any real meaning.

The aim of the Principle is to encourage diversity of opportunity and respect of diversity which goes beyond the passive and somewhat negative discrimination agenda of employment law not to discriminate. This Principle is reflective of the higher standards that should prevail in the profession and is a positive obligation to act in a manner that is inclusive and promotes equality and diversity.

Principle 6 – Tips

1. Review your work force. Does it mirror your client base and the community you serve in terms of ethnic diversity and social background?

2. Do your suppliers (including Counsel and Expert Witnesses) encounter any equality, diversity or inclusion issues?

3. If asked to justify your equality approach what evidence do you collect to show that you are blind to race, religion, sex, sexual orientation, disability or age factors? An annual review is probably a sensible approach to ensure that those who work in your firm understand you are actively looking at equality and diversity issues and will address any issues that may arise;

4. Training on equality and diversity to staff should be a bi-annual issue. In the employment sphere regular training helps avoid problems arising.

Principle 7 – in the best interests of each client

The SRA Consultation documents are largely silent on this obligation which mirrors the current obligation exactly. Word for word it is the same.

If you go back in time further then acting in "the best interests of the client" was identified as one of five core duties included in the Solicitors Practice Rules 1987. The Solicitors's Practice Rules 1990 added a duty to the Court for the first time but the long engrained ethos of "clients come first" is built into the DNA of the profession and has been for many, many years.

The SRA's notes to accompany the current version of this principle are probably as good a starting point to explore what this really means:

> *"2.8 You should always act in good faith and do your best for each of your clients. Most importantly, you should observe:*
>
> *(a) your duty of confidentiality to the client [....];*
>
> *(b) your obligations with regard to conflicts of interests. [....]"*
>
> [Signifies edited for clarity and brevity]

In addition I would suggest the following are relevant and ought to be considered:

(a) Are your clients best interests served by specific legal action or measures (such as is litigation in the clients best interest having assess the risks, costs and benefit?);

(b) Do the firms interest and the clients diverge? (If so has the firm recorded the potential conflict of interest and followed the guidance on this);

(c) Do you only undertake work you are qualified and experienced to do?

It is my view that the lack of guidance in relation to this principle is reflect that such matters are dealt with in the SRA Codes [2019] and as such the simplicity reflects that it should be obvious whether or not in practice an action is clearly in the clients best interests under the SRA Principles [2019] or it is not.

Principle 7 – Tips

1. Ensure you record your thinking on why an act or omission or commercial compromise is in the clients best interests (in a letter to the client or a file note);

2. Train the team on balancing this Principle 6 against Principles 1 and 2 of the 2019 regime.

Conclusion

The SRA Principles [2019] must become imbedded into each and every one of the 10500 odd law firms and 140,000 practising solicitors in England and Wales. The 2011 regime has been widely misunderstood, hence the dramatic simplification of it for which, in my view, the SRA should be commended as they have acknowledged the regime was ineffective and have sought to be clearer whilst using a focus of high professional standards.

The only way though for firms to imbed the Principles is to:

- Train on them to understand them in context;

- Supervise against them so that all staff know the expectation;

- Take action themselves if the standards are not met including by investing in further training, supervision and support.

The cultural challenge for law firms is to move away from prescriptive rules giving tick box reassurance to move to a model that requires judgement and ethical judgement to be at the heart of all you do. This flies in the face of the last 40 odd years of the compliance model which has evolved as ethical judgement reduced and training across the profession diminished on ethics which the revised SRA Principles [2019] place at the heart of the future of legal practice. It is a sensible step to ask professionals to apply their professional judgement and to increase awareness by focusing on simplified Principles to raise and maintain the standards in practice.

CHAPTER FOUR
SRA CODE OF CONDUCT FOR SOLICITORS, RELS AND RFLS (THE INDIVIDUAL CODE)

Introduction

This Code is for individuals (Solicitors, Registered European Lawyers (RELs) and Registered Foreign Lawyers (RFLs)). Throughout this book I refer to this Code as the "Individual Code" to distinguish it from the Code of Conduct for Firms (aka the "Firm Code"). It would be tedious to write and read the full title each time and whenever I refer to an individual or solicitor obligation please take this mean each individual over whom the SRA has jurisdiction (thus it applies to Solicitors everywhere and non-solicitors working in an SRA regulated practice).

The Code is freely available on the internet. The aim here is to provide practical guidance on it so elements are quoted but if you are looking in this book then realistically you want a practitioner's eye and a regulatory solicitor's guidance, not a copy of something freely available on the SRA's website. Where the wording is lifted from the Code I have identified this by use of quotation marks and italics.

Expect the SRA and Law Society to issue guidance on the Individual Code prior to its implementation. I have seen and heard elements of the discussions of both but at the time of writing these are at a preliminary stage and largely not yet written never mind actually published.

The opening line refers to the standards the SRA "*and the public*" expect of individuals. This emphasises the seismic shift underway in terms of public interest factors being at the heart of the SRA regime to enable the SRA to discharge its public interest obligations more clearly. For individuals the bar of expectation is raised.

The Individual Code is split to various sub-headers (Maintaining trust and acting fairly, Service and Competence etc.) and in this chapter we will examine these sections and their meaning.

Introduction to the Individual Code

Any individual authorised by the SRA to provide legal services is covered. The Individual Code sets out that it *"describes the standards of professionalism"* that the SRA and public expect.

The SRA's intention is that standards include "*conduct and behaviour*" guidance as a *"framework for ethical and competent practice"* which applies irrespective of your role or the workplace model (traditional law firm, In-House, Alternative Business Structure (ABS) etc.).

Personal accountability is stressed in the introduction by stating explicitly that you "must always be prepared to justify your decisions and actions" and stating ominously that a *"serious failure to meet our standards or a serious breach of our regulatory requirements may result in our taking regulatory action against you. A failure or breach may be serious either in isolation or because it comprises a persistent or concerning pattern of behaviour."*

Each Solicitor needs to consider whether or not any breach is serious or not. Patterns of behaviour are more likely to make something relatively minor serious if part of a pattern of risks to a client or a series of clients.

The obligation not to breach:

- The SRA Principles [2019];
- The SRA Codes of Conduct [2019] (consisting of the Individual Code and the Firm Code collectively);

- The SRA Rules more generally (SRA Accounts Rules, SRA Authorisation Rules for Firms, SRA Authorisation Rules for Individuals)[1];

- Referrals fees under section 56 of the Legal Aid, Sentencing and Punishment of Offenders Act 2012 (LASPO) which apply to personal injury, clinical negligence and death related claims;

- The statutory regime relating to AML (Anti-Money Laundering) and counter terrorist funding;

is expressly stated. Stating the obvious is necessary to remove any ambiguity so that when necessary regulatory enforcement action is easier to take so individual solicitors need to be aware of this shift towards being able to take action easier as it is intended to raise standards across the profession by professionals being clearer on their obligations but it will mean in my view things that some individual solicitors have done for their own ease for many years without problem will suddenly be subject to an easier regulatory sanction risk and of course with misconduct prosecutions no losses, harm or detriment need to be shown only a breach of the professional obligation however obtuse.

The key take away points from these bland paragraphs in the introduction is: embedding knowledge of the SRA regime into individuals is essential for all firms (including international, City, High Street and sole practitioner).

Maintaining trust and acting fairly

This is the sub header of the first substantial section of the Individual Code.

---

1 The SRA Rules collectively shall consistent of fifteen sets of rules known collectively as the SRA Handbook [2019]. For brevity therefore only a couple of examples given prior to this footnote.

> *"1.1 You do not unfairly discriminate by allowing your personal views to affect your professional relationships and the way in which you provide your services."*

The obligation to inclusivity and non-discrimination is the first obligation to set expressly set out. You must not allow any personal views to impact on your service delivery to clients (including perspective clients) or in your relationship with third parties such a Counsel or Experts.

> *"1.2 You do not abuse your position by taking unfair advantage of* ***clients*** *or others."*

The status of a solicitor is a privilege and not a right (see Chapter 3 SRA Principles [2019] for detailed analysis of why the Courts have concluded this in relation to honesty and integrity) and therefore you must not use your privileged position by seeking a profit, benefit or advantage.

The obligation to not take unfair advantage of others would include litigants in person or lay opponents. It would not in my view, but this is untested, apply to taking advantage of a solicitor who lacked competence and as every professional knows sometimes other parties legal advisers miss the blindingly obvious. In such situations in the future it would be wise to note on the file your thinking and any efforts to resolve matters by co-operation and or communication.

Any situation which could lead to such an allegation must now be actively managed.

> *"1.3 You perform all undertakings given by you, and do so within an agreed timescale or if no timescale has been agreed then within a reasonable amount of time."*

An undertaking has a special status in the legal profession and having defended numerous solicitors accused of breach undertakings two themes emerge:

(a) It is necessary to consider that an undertaking can be created orally or in writing. The SRA's definition from the SRA Glossary (to the SRA Handbook [2019]) sets out that an undertaking:

"means a statement, given orally or in writing, whether or not it includes the word "undertake" or "undertaking", to someone who reasonably places reliance on it, that you or a third party will do something or cause something to be done, or refrain from doing something"

A common pitfall is therefore not recording the wording in writing, and parties to the undertaking having different expectations as to what will be done or refrained from being done.

(b) The timing expectation of the parties should be the same and realistic given wider factors including availability, workloads, number of persons involved and the systems and processes to be complied with.

As an individual Solicitor who is contemplating giving an undertaking you should consider:

(a) Is the undertaking something I should give and do I control all the relevant parts (such as being in funds, holding a signed document etc.)?

(b) Is it in the interest of justice or the clients best interests to give an undertaking?

(c) What wording would be acceptable to me and what are my red lines of commitments which the other parties may wish to secure but I am unwilling to give;

(d) After any negotiation on wording is it still appropriate to give an undertaking?

(e) After giving an undertaking where am I recording this and the discharge of it by the other parties once fulfilled.

It is worth nothing there is no obligation to give any undertaking and even if it is the practice area's norms this should not influence you unless you are satisfied you can fulfil the undertaking in full in a timely manner. In my career I deliberately seek to minimise undertakings because of the risks that arise of misunderstandings.

> *"1.4 You do not mislead or attempt to mislead your clients, the court or others, either by your own acts or omissions or allowing or being complicit in the acts or omissions of others (including your client)."*

Nothing in your actions or omissions should mislead any client or court. No amount of commercial pressure, client pressure or pressure on you can justify misleading any client or court.

Aim to be: Open and Transparent in all dealings with clients and the court.

Dispute resolution and proceedings before courts, tribunals and inquiries

> *"2.1 You do not misuse or tamper with evidence or attempt to do so."*

Evidence is disclosed only for the purpose of the proceedings and should not be more widely used (i.e. do not disclose it to the media or third parties).

No solicitor should tamper with evidence and seek to make it stronger, weaker or suggest a different context. An unconnected series of recent cases before the Solicitors Disciplinary Tribunal (SDT) appear to show a minority of solicitors willing to tamper with letters and documents. Each case has led to strike off or lengthy suspension from practice. It is career ending and no solicitor should seek to do this or cover it up.

> *"2.2 You do not seek to influence the substance of evidence, including generating false evidence or persuading witnesses to change their evidence."*

Keeping detailed contemporaneous notes is essential and ideally recording any potentially controversial or reluctant witness interviews is a good idea.

The obligation stated is to ensure that the evidence speaks for itself.

Solicitors can clarify and check points and details but it is expressly prohibited to suggest false or misleading evidence. The latter is career ending so if you know the witness is hostile then a witness to the discussions who takes notes or a recording of the meeting will protect you from false allegations made by an aggrieved witness.

> *"2.3 You do not provide or offer to provide any benefit to witnesses dependent upon the nature of their evidence or the outcome of the case."*

No witness should be paid or benefit from any proceedings or evidence. Expert witnesses are exempt from this general obligation for obvious reasons but still they cannot have "skin in the game" in terms of any benefit from the outcome of the case.

The promise of more work for example to an expert witness to seek to influence their evidence would be inappropriate. Witness and evidence providers are to be at arm's length. The iconoclast and polymath Professor Nassim Nicholas Taleb authored the book 'Skin in the Game' which argues without skin in the game an "expert's" view is meaningless. This type of radical thinking has not yet reached the courts system and is unlikely ever to do so but it highlights why non-solicitors might think differently. Taleb stated:

> *"If you give an opinion, and someone follows it, you are morally obligated to be, yourself, exposed to its consequences."*[2]

In the SRA's view such thinking is heresy. Importantly no solicitor can subscribe to it when it comes to witnesses.

> *"2.4 You only make assertions or put forward statements, representations or submissions to the court or others which are properly arguable."*

You should not take points which are clearly devoid of merit.

In the immigration field a number of cases have arisen whereby Judicial Review has been used as a legal means to delay deportation totally without merit[3]. The Law Society has issued a Practice Note on this subject.

Taking points which have no merit undermines the administration of justice and undermines public trust in the profession. Breaching this obligation is likely to be actioned by reference to this rule and the SRA Principles [2019] in terms of Principles 1 and 2.

These points can feel a little like the Thought Police in George Orwell's 1984 saying that a case infringes the good administration of justice but in my view recording your reasons for bringing cases is an essential good habit and most practitioners will be familiar with confirming to the clients their prospects of success after initially assessing them. On this basis, provided legitimate grounds exist, this rule is unlikely to restrict legal activity.

> *"2.5 You do not place yourself in contempt of court, and you comply with court orders which place obligations on you."*

---

2 'Skin in the Game' by Nassim Nicholas Taleb published by Allen Lane 2018 at page 4.

3 A 2018 example can be found online: https://www.lawgazette.co.uk/practice/brothers-sanctioned-over-without-merit-immigration-jr-claims/5064773.article

Court Orders should be complied with. All aspects within a solicitor's control must be complied with. You cannot force a client to comply with a Court Order but you can withdraw if your client is non-cooperative with you in your obligation to comply.

No solicitor should place themselves in contempt of court. Contempt of court is a complex legal area but a 2018 judgement in the criminal law sphere summarises the position as thus:

> "26. ***The law of contempt exists to protect the course of proceedings from interference, to safeguard the fairness and integrity of proceedings and to ensure that orders of the court are obeyed****. It comes in many forms, both statutory and under the common law. Courts may themselves initiate proceedings for contempt in some circumstances when it is necessary to do so to protect the interests of justice in extant proceedings before that court. But the more general practice is for the Attorney General to be invited to initiate proceedings to safeguard the public course of justice. The enforcement of orders made in private proceedings is generally a matter for the parties."*[4] [Emphasis added in bold]

The Court itself may consider contempt has arisen in some circumstances and seek to deal with it or more probably the question should be referred to the Attorney General. In simple terms if a solicitor is accused of contempt of court their actions would need to be serious and the process would inevitable mean the SRA would need to be notified by the solicitor (and their firm separately) and most probably the Attorney General's office.

The wording of this obligation, is in my view, unfortunate in that contempt of court allegations will arise so rarely for solicitors that the emphasis should really be on the compliance with Court Orders which is an issue in courts and tribunals every day.

> *"2.6 You do not waste the court's time."*

4 Yaxley-Lennon (aka Tommy Robinson), Re [2018] EWCA Crim 1856

Solicitors should respect the courts resources and not unnecessarily engage their use. Again this obligation can be linked back to SRA Principles [2019] Principle 1.

> *"2.7 You draw the court's attention to relevant cases and statutory provisions, or procedural irregularities of which you are aware, and which are likely to have a material effect on the outcome of the proceedings."*

This obligation is again linked to the SRA Principles [2019] Principle 1 obligation and effectively is an obligation to ensure you place all material cases and procedural issues with the court to avoid a decision which can then be appealed.

The duty is one to be open and transparent with the court so if a case hinders your argument you must still submit it to the court for consideration, it shows the public interest factors explored in Chapter 3 in action. The public interest of helping the court reach the correct decision prevails over and above the obligation to a client.

Service and competence

> *"3.1 You only act for clients on instructions from the client, or from someone properly authorised to provide instructions on their behalf. If you have reason to suspect that the instructions do not represent your client's wishes, you do not act unless you have satisfied yourself that they do. However, in circumstances where you have legal authority to act notwithstanding that it is not possible to obtain or ascertain the instructions of your client, then you are subject to the overriding obligation to protect your client's best interests."*

The obligation to act for clients only on instruction may seem odd at first but the experience of the SRA and those like me to who defend solicitors accused of misconduct is that certain sectors, notably personal injury and payment protection insurance claims, have been subject to claims from clients that the solicitor and law firm were never instructed and claims have effectively been commenced without the clients' authority. The creation of this obligation explicitly recognises this threat to public confidence in the profession.

In the case of vulnerable persons (children or those who otherwise lack capacity to instruct) you have to put the clients best interests first. In the case of matters involving the Court of Protection therefore it would be the client's best interests and not any family member.

If you find yourself walking the tightrope of competing interests then you should make detailed notes of matters including why each and every action is in the best interests of the client.

> *"3.2 You ensure that the service you provide to clients is competent and delivered in a timely manner."*

Competence is placed as a central obligation under the Individual Code.

This obligation is however about two aspects:

(a) Service competence (i.e. not legal competence which is more difficult to prove given the range of legal opinions that can reasonably exist);

(b) The service should be delivered in a timely fashion. Timescales quoted should be adhered to when practical (or the clients updated – which is good service – and deadlines of the courts and tribunals should be adhered to or you risk cost sanctions in contentious cases and/or Legal Ombudsman sanction for poor service.

The aim is clear: public confidence and interest is protected by individual solicitors delivering a competent and timely service.

> *"3.3 You maintain your competence to carry out your role and keep your professional knowledge and skills up to date."*

Competence in the wider sense is addressed by this follow-on obligation to standard 3.2 above. The emphasis here is on competence for the role (whether or not that be COLP, COFA, MLRO, Partner, solicitor etc.). This is a distinct obligation to the standard above and would be deemed to include supervisory skills and management of others.

The obligation to keep professional knowledge up to date reflects the continuing competence regime in place from the 1st November 2016 which replaced continued professional development (CPD) obligations. The emphasis is on the following:

(a) Reflecting of the quality of your own legal practice;

(b) Identify and address any learning or development needs;

(c) Make an annual declaration that you have done the above.

A solicitor who was, for example, previously a criminal advocate but had for many years focused on running the firm and supervision/management activities would under the 2019 regime have a clear return to practice adopting a plan including training, learning and development and ongoing skills for a return to police stations, Courts and advocacy by refreshing those skills and updating their legal, procedural and evidential knowledge.

The era of "I have done this for years" was supposed to end with this standard. I am sceptical. However each solicitor must therefore be prepared to demonstrate their knowledge, skills and fitness for the role if required to do so by the SRA.

> *"3.4 You consider and take account of your client's attributes, needs and circumstances."*

The client's ability to understand and give cogent instructions is the aim of this standard.

If acting for a vulnerable client what measures have you got in place? Are you following the firm's policy on vulnerable persons?

Again this standard requires a note to be made of the thinking of the individual solicitor. Whilst in most firms this is second nature given the professional indemnity insurance/professional negligence risks of the last 20 years it will place meeting the standard at the heart of things and this is therefore a change of focus for file notes and letters to clients.

3.5 Where you supervise or manage others providing legal services:

(a) you remain accountable for the work carried out through them; and

This standard sets out who is ultimately responsible when a solicitor has supervisory responsibility. This is intended to avoid challenges that "X was doing the work and never brought this to my attention so the SRA cannot hold me responsible".

(b) you effectively supervise work being done for clients.

The operative word in this standard being "effectively". In practice this means you must be able to show your supervision has impacted positively on the client protections.

I expect under the 2019 SRA regime supervisors in cases to become a more frequent focus for professional misconduct investigations.

"3.6 You ensure that the individuals you manage are competent to carry out their role, and keep their professional knowledge and skills, as well as understanding of their legal, ethical and regulatory obligations, up to date."

As a manager or supervisor you supervise by assessing the individuals skills, application and knowledge. As a manager or supervisor you ensure those you supervise think ethically and from a regulatory perspective and do not merely apply the legal position without applying the wider ethical context. As a manager or supervisor you need to ensure others achieve the standard of competency on any reasonable objective basis.

The introduction of "*understanding of their legal, ethical and regulatory obligation*" confirms the need of supervisors to ensure they understand the SRA Principles [2019] and SRA Codes [2019] and their ethical focus. Over the last 40 years or so the focus of legal regulators has been on compliance by evidence rather than the exercise of ethical thinking but this standard confirms that if you manage other lawyers you are responsible for ensuring they understand the revised rules in practice.

This obligation will be jointly exercised with the Firm Code also being engaged.

Client money and assets

> *"4.1 You properly account to clients for any financial benefit you receive as a result of their instructions, except where they have agreed otherwise."*

Solicitors cannot profit from their financial relationship with clients from any third party. This standard is intended to ensure the solicitor declares any "financial benefit" to the client and ordinarily the client should benefit, not the solicitor.

If entering into an exception to this default position the onus will be on the solicitor to explain why the arrangement is in the clients best interest. The guidance under the SRA Code of Conduct 2011 Indicative Behaviours regime states:

> *"IB(1.20) where you receive a financial benefit as a result of acting for a client, either:*
>
> *(a) paying it to the client;*

(b) offsetting it against your fees; or

(c) keeping it only where you can justify keeping it, you have told the client the amount of the benefit (or an approximation if you do not know the exact amount) and the client has agreed that you can keep it;"

The heavily simplified standard of 4.1. under the SRA Code for Solicitors [2019] requires the same process: pay it to the client; offset it against the fees due; retaining it only when justified and with agreement of the client.

As any retention is likely to be controversial it should be the exemption and not the norm. If done it should be expressly authorised, in my view, with sign off by the COLP and the COLP should be taking external legal advice if they feel the circumstances merit retaining the fees. The times it is appropriate are narrow but if the process is robust it becomes an option in a small category of matters were it is appropriate and done with openness and transparency.

"4.2 You safeguard money and assets entrusted to you by clients and others."

It is an essential standard that you protect client money (by use of a client account when appropriate and with careful control of those funds). This standard of care applies to assets such as documents.

The obligation is not just to clients, it's any party who reasonable entrusts you given your professional status (thus includes prospective clients, banks, other professionals etc.).

"4.3 You do not personally hold client money save as permitted under regulation 10.2(b)(vii) of the Authorisation of Individuals Regulations, unless you work in an authorised body, or in an organisation of a kind prescribed under this rule on any terms that may be prescribed accordingly."

This standard is designed to deal with freelance solicitors, a concept being introduced by the same SRA reform agenda. Freelance solicitors will operate on their own, effectively as a sole practitioner, will not be limited liability partnerships or limited companies and may only under the SRA Authorisation of Individuals Regulations [2019] hold clients' money on account of the solicitors own costs and disbursements such as counsel but significantly not court fees or search fees. The Solicitors Accounts Rules [2019] Rule 2(1) (d) also sets out the restrictions.

Solicitors who get their handling of client funds wrong under the freelance solicitor regime risk serious sanction including potentially strike off. Whilst the freelance solicitor model is outside the scope of this book I will write a separate short guide which Law Brief Publishing have agreed to publish early in 2019.

The client must be told, in advance, of where and how the money will be held. This should be done in writing.

Business requirements

Referrals, introductions and separate businesses

> *"5.1 In respect of any referral of a client by you to another person, or of any third party who introduces business to you or with whom you share your fees, you ensure that:*
>
> *(a) clients are informed of any financial or other interest which you or your business or employer has in referring the client to another person or which an introducer has in referring the client to you;*
>
> *(b) clients are informed of any fee-sharing arrangement that is relevant to their matter;*
>
> *(c) the agreement is in writing;*

(d) you do not receive payments relating to a referral or make payments to an introducer in respect of clients who are the subject of criminal proceedings; and

(e) any client referred by an introducer has not been acquired in a way which would breach the SRA's regulatory arrangements if the person acquiring the client were regulated by the SRA."

For many solicitors professional contacts are a key source of work. The revised standards mean that you will need to assess if the terms of 5.1 (a) to (e) are met. The obligation to inform the client of the relationship, its terms and any fee sharing arrangement. Standard 5.1 is not exclusive to referral fees as defined by Legal Aid, Sentencing and Punishment of Offenders Act 2012 (LASPO) i.e. personal injury referrals. It applies to all referral arrangements.

The obligation to record the agreement in writing is key. In my practice I still frequently come across law firms who have had relationships with trusted introducers that are not recorded in writing. Often the contact will be a friend, husband or wife or family member. The obligation could not be clearer: it must be writing irrespective of this.

Criminal proceedings are expressly exempt from this regime and it is a regulatory offence to pay or receive a referral fee. Any solicitor breaching this should expect serious sanction as the prohibition is intended to protect the integrity of the criminal justice system.

When accepting introductions from third parties the solicitor is at risk of sanction if the third party has procured the client through actions which are prohibited for solicitors. This means you must choose any referral partners carefully and monitor how they have been sourced. My book 'A Practical Guide to Compliance for Personal Injury Law Firms Working with Claims Management Companies'[5] explores this in some depth and the expectations are the same whether you are a personal injury firm or a magic circle firm.

5 Published by Law Brief Publishing 2017

"5.2 Where it appears to the SRA that you have made or received a referral fee, the payment will be treated as a referral fee unless you show that the payment was not made as such."

In contrast to Standard 5.1 above this standard applies only to those referrals covered by LASPO because the term referral fee is a defined term in the SRA Glossary [2019].

The SRA have discretion to treat a payment as a referral fee unless you can demonstrate it was not. This is an anti-avoidance mechanism to ensure LASPO compliance.

"5.3 You only:

(a) refer, recommend or introduce a client to a separate business; or

(b) divide, or allow to be divided, a client's matter between you and a separate business;

where the client has given informed consent to your doing so."

The SRA Glossary [2019] guides on the meaning of a separate business as follows:

"means, where you own, manage or are employed by an authorised body:

a separate business which either:

(a) you own,

(b) you are owned by,

(c) you actively participate in the provision of its services, including any direct control over the business or any indirect control through another person, or

(d) you are connected with,

and which is not an authorised body, an authorised non-SRA firm, or an overseas practice."

Effectively where there is shared ownership between the solicitor's business and any separate business then clients can only be transferred or shared when the client has given informed consent. This consent should be clear, unambiguous and demonstrate the informed nature of the consent being given.

The aim of this standard is to protect clients from being partially advised through a solicitor with extensive protections and any separate business where such protections do not apply (no access for the separate businesses actions through the Legal Ombudsman, no solicitors professional indemnity insurance protection and terms and conditions which may be more onerous than the solicitors.

Anytime that clients are being shared between a regulated professional and a non-regulated business care should be taken to evidence that the consent is informed.

Other business requirements

"5.4 You must not be a manager, employee, member or interest holder of a business that:

(a) has a name which includes the word "solicitors"; or

(b) describes its work in a way that suggests it is a solicitors' firm;

unless it is an authorised body."

The word solicitor has special meaning and is a protected term. This standard is intended to help the public distinguish between freelance solicitors and fully functioning law firms.

The standard seeks in (b) to establish clear blue water between the freelance solicitors and regulated firms.

> *5.5 If you are a solicitor who holds a practising certificate, an REL or RFL, you must complete and deliver to the SRA an annual return in the prescribed form.*

Each year as a solicitor you must apply for a practising certificate and the annual return to demonstrate compliance with service and competence (standards 3.1 to 3.6).

> *5.6 If you are a solicitor or REL practising in a non-commercial body, you must ensure that the body takes out and maintains indemnity insurance that provides adequate and appropriate cover in respect of the services that you provide.*

As a solicitor in a non-commercial body (such as a law centre) must ensure their employer obtains and maintains indemnity insurance to cover the services provided.

The obligation is expressly personal to the individual solicitor and who must ensure the body from which they practice has taken out the appropriate insurance.

Conflict, confidentiality and disclosure

Conflict of interests

Before looking at the conflict of interest standards under the SRA Code for Individuals [2019] it is worth clarifying that applying to each conflict situation is the requirement for individual solicitors to make a judgement. The standards are there to guide you on what is, and what is not, acceptable.

The standards under the [2019] regime are deliberately non-prescriptive. The exercise of judgement is crucial in this part of the Code.

If the matter is conscientiously considered by the solicitor then an error of judgement would not amount to professional misconduct. Merely thinking about conflicts in the general sense (evidenced through say a checklist or routine file open process) is unlikely to amount to an effective defence relating to a charge of acting in breach of these standards because the standards that would be applied are likely to be those of an objective and competent solicitor rather than the individual solicitor whose judgement is under scrutiny and inferences may be drawn that any thought to the facts of matter are or could not be deemed to fully address the risks in hand. An inference may be appropriately drawn where the reason given for the solicitor's professional decision is manifestly unstainable[6].

For this reason the evidential requirements on individual solicitors is likely to increase under the SRA Code for Individuals [2019]. The Law Society of England and Wales raised the issue in their response to an SRA Consultation paper by referring to the Connolly judgement as follows:

> *"The decision in Connolly v Law Society [2007] EWHC 1175 (Admin) is relevant here, at [62]:*
>
> *"I accept that generally the honest and genuine decision of a solicitor on a question of professional judgment does not give rise to a disciplinary offence. But* ***that does not mean that for a solicitor to act where there is a significant risk of a conflict of interest cannot be a disciplinary offence. If a solicitor does not honestly and genuinely address the issue, he may be guilty of an offence. And if his decision is one that no reasonably competent solicitor could have made, it may be inferred that he did not (or could not) properly address the issue. That inference may well be appropriate where, as in the present case, the reason given for the solicitor's profes-***

6 See Connolly v Law Society [2007] EWHC 1175 (Admin)

sional decision is manifestly unsustainable."" [7] [Emphasis added in bold]

The obligation is therefore to be:

(a) competent;

(b) to act as a reasonably competent solicitor would;

(c) to properly and full address the risk of conflict;

(d) to evidence the thinking so that any misjudgement cannot be misconstrued into deliberately acting in a conflict of interest situation.

In the SRA Code of Conduct 2011 raised the bar in terms of judgements and in my view the importance of making a judgment is raised significantly by the SRA Codes [2019].

"6.1 You do not act if there is an own-interest conflict or a significant risk of such a conflict."

The prohibition on acting is express and without exception when your interests and a client's conflict. This requires judgment to identify. What is meant by "own interest conflict"? My own interpretation is simple: Your own interest and a current client conflict.

To give an obvious example, a property solicitor could not therefore act in the potential acquisition of a property for client A whilst also being an investor in a competing bid.

The SRA Glossary confirms their meaning of 'own-interest conflict' as:

"any situation where your duty to act in the best interests of any client in relation to a matter conflicts, or there is a significant risk that it

---

7 Law Society of England and Wales Response to SRA Consultation: A Question of Trust, January 2016 page 6

may conflict, with your own interests in relation to that or a related matter"

The prohibition on acting applies not only if there is a conflict of interest but also when there is a "significant risk" of a conflict.

"6.2 You do not act in relation to a matter or particular aspect of it if you have a conflict of interest or a significant risk of such a conflict in relation to that matter or aspect of it, unless:

(a) the clients have a substantially common interest in relation to the matter or the aspect of it, as appropriate; or

(b) the clients are competing for the same objective,

and the conditions below are met, namely that:

(i) all the clients have given informed consent, given or evidenced in writing, to you acting;

(ii) where appropriate, you put in place effective safeguards to protect your clients' confidential information; and

(iii) you are satisfied it is reasonable for you to act for all the clients."

The importance of judgement, outlined in depth above, continues when two or more current clients' interest conflicts. The prohibition here is not absolute as with standard 6.1 but instead at standard the 6.2 grounds of exception are expressly set out. This means the exception only applies when these grounds are met.

The exceptions require the clients to have a substantially common interest. The SRA Glossary [2019] guides on the meaning as follows:

"....a situation where there is a ***clear common purpose between the clients*** *and* ***a strong consensus*** *on how it is to be achieved."* [Emphasis added in bold]

The exception therefore requires the purpose to align and the achievement mechanism to be agreed in every material aspect. This is a high threshold and those individual solicitors seeking to justify acting should record the common purpose and achievement mechanism in writing and take advice on their professional misconduct risk if they are uncertain given the importance of judgement.

In terms of evidencing the clients agreement if the exception terms are potentially met then the following is required:

(a) the informed nature of the consent to you acting should be recorded in writing (whether from you drafting and the clients acknowledging or by the clients own document);

(b) you ensure that client confidentiality is not compromised and ensure effective safeguards are in place;

(c) your judgement is that it is reasonable to act for the clients (and your judgement should, in my view, be recorded in writing in sufficient detail to evidence that your actions were within the bounds of a reasonably competent solicitor's discretion for the reasons set out above standard 6.1 above earlier in this chapter.

Confidentiality and disclosure

"6.3 You keep the affairs of current and former clients confidential unless disclosure is required or permitted by law or the client consents."

Clients are a defined term in the SRA Glossary [2019] and the definition includes prospective clients, current clients and former clients. In simple terms anyone in whom a "client" entrusts confidential aspects therefore triggers the obligation. It is not in contrast to the conflict of interest rule extinguished by the end of the retainer.

Any consent from a client must be informed consent: clear, unambiguous and express consent.

The legal exceptions are narrow and unless they apply consent is required to share any aspect about the solicitor and client relationship (including the fact you have acted).

> *"6.4 Where you are acting for a client on a matter, you make the client aware of all information material to the matter of which you have knowledge, except when:*
>
> *(a) the disclosure of the information is prohibited by legal restrictions imposed in the interests of national security or the prevention of crime;*
>
> *(b) your client gives informed consent, given or evidenced in writing, to the information not being disclosed to them;*
>
> *(c) you have reason to believe that serious physical or mental injury will be caused to your client or another if the information is disclosed; or*
>
> *(d) the information is contained in a privileged document that you have knowledge of only because it has been mistakenly disclosed."*

You need to share all relevant information with clients unless prohibited from doing so. The circumstances where such a prohibition may arise are linked to national security or prevention of a crime (typically a Proceeds of Crime Act 2002 Production Order relating to the affairs of a client for Anti-Money Laundering purposes). Breaching such a prohibition is likely to be a criminal offence in itself hence the subordinate approach of the SRA Code for Individuals [2019].

Clients may prefer not to be engaged in all aspects of a matter. In such a situation they must give informed consent and evidence their wishes in writing.

If a client's health would be adversely affected you may withhold information but only if the harm would be serious.

If a document is inadvertently disclosed but otherwise is a privileged document then you should not disclose it to the client.

Each exemption is distinct and each merits a detailed note of your thinking if relying on any of the exemptions.

> *"6.5 You do not act for a client in a matter where that client has an interest adverse to the interest of another current or former client of you or your business or employer, for whom you or your business or employer holds confidential information which is material to that matter, unless:*
>
> *(a) effective measures have been taken which result in there being no real risk of disclosure of the confidential information; or*
>
> *(b) the current or former client whose information your business or employer holds has given informed consent, given or evidenced in writing, to you acting, including to any measures taken to protect their information."*

The distinction between a conflict of interest and confidentiality situation is again key to standard 6.5. Conflicts of interests arise with current clients only but here the standard requires you to consider if you (or your firm) hold confidential information that is material when a client has an interest in a matter that impacts negatively on another client. It is not clear how the SRA expect to identify or examine large international firms or even multi office firms whose data may be fragmented. I suspect that standard 6.5 is drafted too widely to be of use in such situations to solicitors but this will mean that the SRA will assume that across offices, continents and practice areas individual solicitors can make the connections if clients can do so and raise concerns about the solicitors conduct.

As a practical and public domain example a large bank may have a number of subsidiary entities engaged in property or niche lending. A large law firms acting for the bank will be expected to identify the subsidiary conflict risk if they act for either the bank or the separate entity and are instructed on a deal involving either with a arms length third party. If we use the myriad of companies in The Royal Bank of Scotland Group and the separate but connected entities they used which have attracted publicity over recent year then the scale of the challenge for the larger firms becomes apparent – the systems and the data must be working effectively, must record the link or the risk of acting inadvertently exists.

If acting in a situation in which you know a current client's interest adversely aligns with a current or former client you decline to act or take extensive steps to evidence that the exceptions apply. Firstly, the restrictions on confidential information set out at 6.5 (a) would require the solicitor acting to know that material exists and have access to it. This is probably a data access issue: did you [the individual solicitor] have access? Limiting access to specific solicitors practice area files might reduce the risks. Any safeguards to that data should be taken through a central resource rather than the individual solicitor (you) yourself. In sole practitioner scenarios this will of course be impossible for the exemption favouring the larger firms in practical terms in clear.

Confidential information must be objectively preserved.

Under 6.5 (b) the current or former client whose information the firm holds has given informed consent in writing to you acting include the measures taken to protect their confidential information. In my view in practical terms, unless acting for arm's length corporate clients, this will be impossible to procure in a way that robustly protects confidentiality and client confidence. The barrier to clients given informed consent unless they are sophisticated users of legal services is high. This mirrors the position under the SRA Code of Conduct 2011 at Outcome 4.4 but it is unrealistic to expect every individual solicitor to understand the complex law around the issue summarised in Koch Shipping Inc. v Richards Butler [2002] EWCA Civ 1280 at paragraph 24.

The examples where the court has permitted a solicitor to continue to act have involved sophisticated users of legal services and corporate entities. Unless this is your situation then you should not seek to rely on the 6.5 (b) exemptions given the professional disciplinary risk in my view and if you wish to act then you should take expert legal advice on the ethics and disciplinary risks before taking that step which could have long term implications for your career (and risk it being taken away given the SRA renewed focus on using your judgement as explained earlier in Chapter 3 and in compliance with standards 7.1 and 7.2 below in particular).

It has been said this is a "City Firms Only" exception, it is not quite this but external advice is the only credible way for the law firm, whether city or otherwise, to take a view on the application of the exceptions because the firms internal team inevitably are not independent and have wider commercial responsibilities.

Cooperation and accountability

The SRA have an expectation that solicitors will understand the Code for Individuals fully. Antidotially this is unlikely as for 140,000 odd individuals to significantly up their knowledge of the regulatory system following its simplification is a huge task.

In July 2019 I spoke for the Law Society's Small Firms Division jointly with Chris Handford of the SRA on the forthcoming changes with the SRA to around 100 solicitors. When I asked the question and for a show of hands to confirm if solicitors could answer "How many of you can name all 10 of the current SRA Principles 2011 without looking them up?" Not one solicitor present responded. The laughter in the room highlighted the challenge for the profession under the new regime.

> *"7.1 You keep up to date with and follow the law and regulation governing the way you work."*

This standard like the SRA Principles [2019] is a catch all to some degree but expresses the heightened expectation with the simplification of matters (as expressed here in this the Code for Individuals [2019]) that solicitors will know and apply their obligations in their daily practice.

The obligation to keep up to date with the regulation governing the working environment (which will differ for In-House, Private Practice and the newly created Freelance Solicitors model) is a new obligation. For a busy practitioner the things to consider are:

(a) If required to show a working knowledge of the SRA [2019] regime what would you say? (This book being well thumbed might show something);

(b) Evidence of receipt of training (in-house[8], webinars or in person);

(c) Memos and File Notes demonstrating knowledge;

(d) The COLP and COFA recording in house discussions centrally to see if themes arise in practitioner challenges.

The obligation on the regulatory regime is a continuing on. Would you therefore be able to show continued updating? Reference to the legal press and any briefings received should form part of (c) above.

The other component of standard 7.1 is knowledge of the legal framework for the provision of legal services. The legal services market is complex, more so than at first impression most professionals will appreciate. There are nine (yes – 9!) approved regulators i.e. front line

8 Since 2009 I have offered In House Training to law firms for a fixed fee and since 2008 training for various CPD providers both at conferences, podcasts and in webinars. My experience is that In House training, being personalised, is far superior as it gives multiple key individuals or the whole firm the chance to interact with an expert in an environment they are used to and feels like "their own".

regulators under the Legal Services Act 2007. The SRA is only one of these.

The standard 7.1. obviously requires a working knowledge of:

- The Solicitors Act 1974;
- Legal Services Act 2007;
- The Legal Aid, Sentencing and Punishment Act 2012 (LASPO).

For most Solicitors these are the key pieces of legislation but probably do not need to apply in context within daily practice as a solicitor so the knowledge level of these will be limited. However the legislation is not just these acts but others including, but not limited to, the following:

- Proceed of Crime Act 2002;
- Administration of Justice Act 1985;
- Courts and Legal Services Act 1990;
- Immigration and Asylum Act 1999;
- Senior Courts Act 1981.

For most practitioners the need to apply these pieces of legislation arises infrequently. The knowledge of them needed in practical terms is to know when to look at the legislation and to take a detailed view as to what the position is.

Under Standard 7.1 solicitors should keep up to date as the legislation changes. This requires a commitment that should show in training records of doing so. This could include recording any reading of the legal press when it is on legal services legislation and the framework covered by this obligation.

> *"7.2 You are able to justify your decisions and actions in order to demonstrate compliance with your obligations under the SRA's regulatory arrangements."*

Are you able to justify each and every one of your "decisions and actions" at present? Many solicitors may be able to do so with elements because of the pressures over recent years of the professional indemnity insurance market and the need to manage risk or face higher premiums.

We all make attendance notes, telephone notes, confirm advice in writing.

Standard 7.2 though requires a move from risk management and insurance type thinking into evidencing compliance with the SRA regime. This standard is central to the obligations of each and every solicitor under the new regime.

The short wording of the 7.2 standard needs to be read in conjunction with the introduction to the code which states:

> *"You are personally accountable for compliance with the Code – and our other regulatory requirements that apply to you – and must always be prepared to justify your decisions and actions."*

Understanding the obligation is key: each and every file, decision or action (including non-action) requires reference to the Code for Individuals. The attendance notes, telephone notes and confirmation of advice might need to be a little longer and should in the case of file notes be explicit against the professional obligations in my view.

> *7.3 You cooperate with the SRA, other regulators, ombudsmen, and those bodies with a role overseeing and supervising the delivery of, or investigating concerns in relation to, legal services.*

You must be open and transparent with your regulators (SRA, Legal Ombudsman, Information Commissioners Office etc.). This obligation means if asked for information you supply it, if asked to explain why an action occurred you do so.

Rarely will Legal Professional Privilege prevent this given the unique status of the SRA in being able to access any and all files of the regulated sector and if you think legal professional privilege impacts on you then you should be taking expert legal advice from a regulatory solicitor.

> *7.4 You respond promptly to the SRA and:*
>
> *(a) provide full and accurate explanations, information and documents in response to any request or requirement; and*
>
> *(b) ensure that relevant information which is held by you, or by third parties carrying out functions on your behalf which are critical to the delivery of your legal services, is available for inspection by the SRA.*

See the advice on the standard above (7.3), this is merely an explanation of same obligation in respect of standard 7.4 (a). The standard then goes on in 7.4 (b) to expand on that obligation to co-operate with regulators by confirming you must in respect of the SRA only ensure appropriate records are available for inspection (including but not limited to client files, accounts records, firm policies, supervision records, professional indemnity records etc.).

The reference to "third parties" means if you make use of suppliers or outsourced services your contract with them permits the SRA access to that information. In the case say of a file storage company the obligation would include access to files by the SRA direct if required. This is the case under Chapter 7 of the Code of Conduct 2011 at Outcome 7.10 which makes the obligation explicit by stating "is subject to contractual arrangements that enable the SRA or its agent to obtain information from, inspect the records (including electronic records) of, or enter the premises of, the third party, in relation to the outsourced activities or functions".

My experience of advising those under investigations by the SRA with such arrangements is having addressed the obligation aids credibility in establishing a compliance culture existed and helps mitigate the risk of action being taken against COLPs, COFAs, supervisors and managers.

7.5 You do not attempt to prevent anyone from providing information to the SRA or any other body exercising regulatory, supervisory, investigatory or prosecutory functions in the public interest.

Openness and transparency towards the SRA are essential for every solicitor and anyone seeking to inhibit this risks regulatory sanction.

This simple standard requires openness and transparency not self-flagellation so if you are unsure if you should say something or not to the SRA then take legal advice from a regulatory solicitor. Sometimes information may be supplied without explanation to avoid unnecessary self-incrimination. This is permitted but do not pressurise others or their responses.

7.6 You notify the SRA promptly if:

(a) you are subject to any criminal charge, conviction or caution, subject to the Rehabilitation of Offenders Act 1974;

This obligation relates to new matters (as you should have disclosed these already).

The failure to notify the SRA is often fatal to a career but notification even of serious offences not involving dishonesty may assist in terms of the sanction imposed by the SRA or the SDT.

(b) a relevant insolvency event occurs in relation to you; or

As this is the Individual Code this means bankruptcy according to the Glossary. In my view the omission of IVAs (Individual Voluntary Arrangements) from the Glossary is an error and this may change in the future.

(c) if you become aware:

(i) of any material changes to information previously provided to the SRA, by you or on your behalf, about you or your practice, including any change to information recorded in the register; and

(ii) that information provided to the SRA, by you or on your behalf, about you or your practice is or may be false, misleading, incomplete or inaccurate.

If the information supplied was wrong or changes in a material sense then it must be updated. The standard reflects the need that the SRA assess your regulatory status based on accurate information.

7.7 You ensure that a prompt report is made to the SRA, or another approved regulator, as appropriate, of any serious breach of their regulatory arrangements by any person regulated by them (including you) of which you are aware. If requested to do so by the SRA you investigate whether there have been any serious breaches that should be reported to the SRA.

The standard require prompt reporting of serious regulatory breaches (it is not entirely clear why the SRA use "serious" in this standard and yet used "material" in standard 7.6 (c) (i) above. The SRA has tied itself and the profession in knots with the COLP and COFA guidance on material and non-material breaches since introducing the 2011 regime and this may be why the word material is not used and serious is.

There is an ongoing obligation to report yourself if you have breached the SRA regime in a "serious" manner. If in doubt take advice from a regulatory solicitor.

The obligation to report in the Individual Code applies to reporting others when you are aware of their "serious" misconduct.

The final element is a new obligation to investigate whether or not there have been serious breaches of the SRA by others if the SRA ask you to do so. This is aimed at employers and partners and is included in this, the Individual Code, to ensure you do what is asked of you as an individual (whether as a manager, partner or employee).

7.8 You act promptly to take any remedial action requested by the SRA.

If having had things go wrong the SRA ask you to do something you must do it or you risk breaching this standard. What does "promptly" mean? It is context specific so agree a timetable with the SRA.

7.9 You are honest and open with clients if things go wrong, and if a client suffers loss or harm as a result you put matters right (if possible) and explain fully and promptly what has happened and the likely impact. If requested to do so by the SRA you investigate whether anyone may have a claim against you, provide the SRA with a report on the outcome of your investigation, and notify relevant persons that they may have such a claim, accordingly.

The SRA approach is you are honest and open about clients include what you have done wrong, how a mistake occurred and put it right.

Your professional indemnity insurance may not want you to be so candid but of course the SRA standards prevail and must be your guiding light. Forget what anyone wants: partners, colleagues, insurers, employees or whoever, simply be open with clients and explain what has happened.

Investigations by the firm into actions at the direction of the SRA are means of the SRA controlling its own costs and ensuring firms monitor compliance by its personnel. It is not a soft option, instead it is a serious obligation and if mishandled expect oversight. As a solicitor who has investigated others conduct in the past I expect a boost in those kind of instructions moving forward. Firms will need to ensure they have resources and skills to discharge the investigation request or alternatively flag to the SRA they do not have such resources and skills and fear any attempts to investigation will be inhibited: again the openness and transparency aspect is key.

> *7.10 Any obligation under this section or otherwise to notify, or provide information to, the SRA will be satisfied if you provide information to your firm's COLP or COFA, as and where appropriate, on the understanding that they will do so.*

COLPs and COFAs must report they are the key intermediary with the SRA. If you disclose to them it is enough under the SRA regime but if you know they will fail to report then your obligations go on imply under standard this standard 7.10 that your duties towards the SRA are only discharged if you understand they will report. Failing to report to the SRA will then be a risk if you know a COLP or COFA will not report something they should.

This standard will require a balancing act for individuals: do you have confidence the COLP and COFA are going to report? If not do your concerns require you to report? Each case will turn on its facts but the higher the level of likely non-compliance by the compliance officer the more likely it is you will have to also report the concern because you have grounds to believe they will not report it. For some professionals the knowledge that the Public Interest Disclosure Act 1998 (as amended) is difficult to apply and offers limited protection will cause a personal and professional anxiety but reporting matters yourself is a preferable position to be in than allowing a failure to not report serious misconduct. If in doubt take legal advice from a regulatory solicitor.

Conclusion

The Code for Individuals is a completely new approach – think things over, ensure you have read the Code and get some training on this in the context of your practice.

Good training will include case studies, discussions and an expert course leader.

It gives you freedom to work with less prescriptive rules but you must ensure you demonstrate compliance with the expectations.

CHAPTER FIVE
SRA CODE OF CONDUCT FOR FIRMS (THE FIRM CODE)

Introduction

As in the previous Chapter for individuals, the Code of Conduct for Firms is broken down in this chapter into some introductory thoughts of the author and then extracted guidance in quotations supplemented by some guidance on how practically we as solicitors should seek to manage our firms against the revised SRA regime. The SRA Code of Conduct for Firms (Firm Code) is freely available on the website of the SRA and this book as before seeks to guide on the practical application.

The SRA are, at the time of writing, discussing and consulting on what the new regime should be called. I have adopted the current terminology. For firms the dominant new part of the expected 2019 regime is that firms now know clearly what is expected to be in their sphere of obligations and individuals solicitors know clearly what is expected to be within its sphere of obligation. This is key as the mentality of the new regime, intentional or not, is if a firm fails to meet these then the SRA will have the power to more easily hold the entire firm to account through disciplinary sanction.

The reputational risk is therefore increasing in my view with this regime change.

The Firm Code outlines the "standards and business controls" that the SRA expects, and significantly in my view that they believe that the public should expect, of law firms (including sole practices). The Firm Code only applies to law firms that the SRA licences so does not apply to the smaller number of law firms licenced by the BSB or the CLC or indeed any other legal regulator. This is in stark contrast with the Individual Code which controversially applies irrespective of the entity and whether or not that is regulated at all or by some other regulator.

The standards set out in the Firm Code "aim to create and maintain the right culture and environment for the delivery of competent and ethical legal services to clients" so the standards deal with the working environment in terms of ethical behaviour and conduct, not whether the wallpaper is nice.

It is culturally a significant shift by the SRA in saying if those individuals commit misconduct due to your firms culture the SRA can hold the firm responsible. It looks to me to broaden the risk of law firms in respect of staff and partner misconduct. Over the last few years the SRA has been trying to adopt this approach under the current regime, the trend has increased more recently and the direction of travel is very much about holding the law firm responsible for the oversight it is or should be employing.

The latter standards in the Firm Code relate expressly to the expectations on managers and compliance officers in firms. Those fulfilling those roles – as partners, members, directors or compliance officers – will want to note the clarity comes at a price: the room for excuses is narrowed whilst raising the profile of SRA's expectations.

What happens if firms get it wrong?

The SRA introduction to the Firm Code states:

> *"A serious failure to meet our standards or a serious breach of our regulatory requirements may lead to our taking regulatory action against the firm itself as an entity, or its managers or compliance officers, who each have responsibilities for ensuring that the standards and requirements are met. We may also take action against employees working within the firm for any breaches for which they are responsible. A failure or breach may be serious either in isolation or because it comprises a persistent or concerning pattern of behaviour."*

What does that mean? If it happens on your watch or whilst you are in a specified role (including being a "manager" i.e. partner) then the SRA can look at your contribution including a failure to prevent the actions of others and discipline the firm (the legal entity it regulates) or the post holder (the partner etc.).

The forthcoming regime raises standards by making it easier to take action against individuals therefore. The SRA may not see it in that manner. From my experience I have spoken with them jointly at some events and attended as a delegate some others, it is about holding professionals to account including the firm itself. In reality the enforcement opportunities are widened so it is then about whether or not the SRA choose to use them (under other guidance which is likely to be published nearer to the implementation date). In future editions of this book those matters will be addressed.

Maintaining trust and acting fairly

The first substantive standard set out after the preamble to introduce the Firm Code appear under this heading.

> *"1.1 You do not unfairly discriminate by allowing your personal views to affect your professional relationships and the way in which you provide your services."*

Discrimination is abhorrent and the standard makes this clear but the standard makes clear that a firm or its managers personal views may differ.

In practical terms the expression of views which are discriminatory even in a personal capacity are likely to bring that individual into difficulty. If expressed on social media or some other public forum they should expect to be held to account (see SRA v Daniels[1]).

The aim must therefore be to protect partners, employees, contractors and suppliers (including say self-employed personnel and external ser-

1 http://www.solicitorstribunal.org.uk/sites/default/files-sdt/11752.2017.Daniels.pdf

vice providers such as barristers or expert witnesses) from discrimination of any type and in any manner.

Each firm should therefore ensure there is no unconscious bias or direct bias in its policies and conduct. As the BBC equal pay dispute in 2017/2018 has shown this can be difficult to identify and/or explain.

A law firm managing itself against the standards of the Equality Act 2010 best practice should have no difficulty.

> *"1.2 You do not abuse your position by taking unfair advantage of clients or others."*

The SDT has seen cases in which firms are alleged to have taken advantage of clients whether that is by overcharging, inappropriate referrals or putting the firms' interests above those of clients'. A series of warning notes have been published by the SRA on dubious investments or specific types of claims and conduct. If the firms' systems fail to identify and manage that risk then the SRA have set out the expectation on firms by this simple standard. It raises the question of what is meant by "unfair advantage" as a test? It will be fact specific so if there is any ambiguity expect an SRA Investigation and to be asked to justify the conduct. If your firm is investigated then take expert legal advice, from me or some other suitably qualified and experienced person, because the responses are directly what may lead to enforcement action.

> *"1.3 You perform all undertakings given by you and do so within an agreed timescale or if no timescale has been agreed then within a reasonable amount of time."*

The performance of undertakings is key to public trust in the legal profession. As such firms must have centralised controls in place to ensure the supervision of these is appropriately discharged.

The SRA routinely seek to investigate alleged non-compliance with undertakings and take a dim view when undertakings are not performed and the default position appears to be well established that any breach of an undertaking reported to them is actioned.

Firms should therefore ensure their own records and supervision address this issue to ensure partners and employees do not act in a manner incompatible with this standard and place the firm at risk of sanction.

> *"1.4 You do not mislead or attempt to mislead your clients, the court or others, either by your own acts or omissions or allowing or being complicit in the acts or omissions of others (including your client)."*

If you mislead your clients or the courts (including about your own errors) you should expect serious sanction. For firms therefore they must ensure the supervision of information to clients and the courts is appropriate: including telling clients or the courts when things have gone wrong.

Openness, transparency and honesty in all dealings are essential. Firms must supervise to ensure this culture prevails in their firms.

> ***"1.5 You monitor, report and publish workforce diversity data, as prescribed."***

The SRA want data on diversity shared with them and to the public. You must provide it in accordance with the guidance they issue on this from time to time.

Making the firm responsible for this standard increases the likelihood of enforcement action for non-compliance. The SRA's approach is controversial within the profession as many see it as onerous and unnecessary. Conversely equality campaigners see a lack of diversity in the widest sense, so ethnic origin; religion; sex; disability; social class; private and state schooling, as being a symptom of inertia and recruitment and retention policies failing to deliver a diverse and representative profession.

What should you do? Comply it is not an onerous standard to achieve and frankly probably represents no more than treating everyone as you wish to be treated.

Compliance and business systems

The SRA's focus can be seen from the sub-header above "Compliance and business systems" they link the compliance obligations to the business of being a lawyer. It is a simple observation but it highlights that solicitors who have previously seen a distinction between "their professional obligations" and "the firm" need to evolve their thinking into understanding the regulators perspective of its an all pervasive obligation to do the right thing in each component and overall from a compliance and business perspective.

> *"2.1 You have effective governance structures, arrangements, systems and controls in place that ensure:*
>
> *(a) you comply with all the SRA's regulatory arrangements, as well as with other regulatory and legislative requirements, which apply to you;"*

The firm must comply with all legislation.

All.

It's so wide, what does it mean? The Solicitors Act 1974, Legal Services Act 2007, Legal Aid, Sentencing and Punishment of Offenders Act 2012 are examples but the list is not exhaustive. How you go about marketing your services is also covered. So legislation including the General Data Protection Regulation (GDPR), Privacy and Electronic Communications (EC) Regulations 2003 (PECR) and everything else that impinges on the law firm entity's legal duties from legislation will be caught by this obligation.

The firm must comply with all of the SRA's regulatory arrangements so that includes all their rules and all their guidance. When new guidance is issued the firms obligation is to comply with all of it.

The scope is therefore all-pervasive and onerous. It is also unclear and requires a focus from the firm on ensuring all those who need to know are up to date and know their roles and responsibilities.

In practice appointing someone to oversee this will help but they will be the lead and not the only party responsible. This is a firm – so collective – obligation.

> *"(b) your managers and employees comply with the SRA's regulatory arrangements which apply to them;"*

The firm is responsible for ensuring the partners and staff understand and comply with the entirety of the obligations as outlined above in the commentary on (a). The need for your firm to offer training should be self-evident and it will cover wider compliance.

> *"(c) your managers and interest holders and those you employ or contract with do not cause or substantially contribute to a breach of the SRA's regulatory arrangements by you or your managers or employees;"*

Those that own the firm and provide leadership within it should not seek to motivate, encourage or incentivise others to breach the SRA regulatory regime. This would include in my view turning a blind eye to the actions which amount to a breach.

> *"(d) your compliance officers are able to discharge their duties under paragraphs 9.1 and 9.2 below."*

The firms governance (hence partners/members/director) do not impede the compliance officers in seeking to discharge their duties, this would include not seeking to constrain their duties, investigation of potential breaches of the SRA regime or seeking to stop reports being made about what the compliance officer thinks ought to be reported to the SRA.

> *"2.2 You keep and maintain records to demonstrate compliance with your obligations under the SRA's regulatory arrangements."*

No guidance on what the records are or how to do this are given. You should assess your firms needs and record you decision making. My view is the following would be useful and will be sought by those investigating on behalf of the SRA or defending the firm in the event such an investigation (such as myself or other legal advisers):

- Risk Assessment for the Firm;
- Monthly Compliance Officers reviews;
- File/Fee Earner Review;
- Incident report forms;
- Complaints Register;
- SRA Reporting Log.

If you do not know the content of those core documents then you will need to undergo training specific to being a compliance officer before agreeing to hold such a position.

> *"2.3 You remain accountable for compliance with the SRA's regulatory arrangements where your work is carried out through others, including your managers and those you employ or contract with."*

The firm and its partners/members/directors remain responsible for all work and all conduct undertaken in the firms name. In simple terms you cannot state: "I left X to get on with it, it's their responsibility and not mine". You (as a firm and as individual) are expected to manage the risk of non-compliance.

"2.4 You actively monitor your financial stability and business viability. Once you are aware that you will cease to operate, you effect the orderly wind-down of your activities."

If the firm is going to close down (whether through ill health, death, financial pressures) then you must ensure the closure is orderly and protects clients interest.

"2.5 You identify, monitor and manage all material risks to your business, including those which may arise from your connected practices."

In my view this obligation is aimed at protecting compliance across a range of firms when a group structure exists and the firm is owned and managed as part of a group of law firms. Compliance Officers in, for example, law firm groups which own a number of distinct brands or trading entities will need to be aware of the risk of inappropriate practices spreading across the firms.

Cooperation and information requirements

The SRA, rightly in my view, seek co-operation in an open, transparent and honest manner from solicitors and those involved in the ownership of law firms.

The standards being set within this section are clear, simple and adopt the majority of accepted good regulated sector best practices. We could compare with the standards of other regulated professions and we would see similar standards being set, see similar obligations on other professions across sectors and see the common thread of openness, transparency and honesty being key.

"3.1 You keep up to date with and follow the law and regulation governing the way you work."

You must know and adapt to your changing obligations whether they be legislative driven or set by the regulators collectively (SRA and ICO etc.). For many solicitors this will be a shock and a challenge. My common conference survey on a show of hands of "How many of you can tell me each of the SRA Principles 2011 without looking them up?" has yet to elicit a single raised arm despite being asked to thousands of delegates over a couple of years. When you have a hundred or more people in a room the nervous laughter and relief that no one else knows them either is palpable.

The challenge with the complexity of the legislation and a myriad of regulators and professional bodies seeking to promote good practice, some of whom have jurisdictions which overlap, is how to comply each and every time. By way of an example the SRA, ICO, LeO and Resolution all often feature in the work of say the majority of family law firms to varying degrees.

The average practitioner specialising something other than the provision of legal services itself probably does not have the time or the inclination to become an expert in the nuisances of legal service provision. If I am wrong in your case dear reader, consider applying to me for a job as those of us who are interested are in a minority yet Standard 3.1. obliges everyone to have this working knowledge.

> *"3.2 You cooperate with the SRA, other regulators, ombudsmen and those bodies with a role overseeing and supervising the delivery of, or investigating concerns in relation to, legal services."*

You must assist those investigating your firm: think openness, transparency and honesty. I'm not suggesting self-incrimination in the absence of evidence but a helpful approach.

> *"3.3 You respond promptly to the SRA and:*
>
> *(a) provide full and accurate explanations, information and documentation in response to any requests or requirements;"*

As above you should be helpful, present the information fully and fairly.

> *"(b) ensure that relevant information which is held by you, or by third parties carrying out functions on your behalf which are critical to the delivery of your legal services, is available for inspection by the SRA."*

If the SRA want something it should be in your control or if outside your control you need to ensure the SRA can access it. Off premises storage wise, for example, means you should ensure the documents will be returned to the office upon request in a timely manner to ensure you and your firm can co-operate with the SRA.

> *"3.4 You act promptly to take any remedial action requested by the SRA."*

If the SRA request action to remedy a breach of the standards or to protect a client's interest you do so unhesitatingly and without undue delay. You, of course, may query any genuine concerns about the request but once clarity is established should act as quickly as practicable.

> *"3.5 You are honest and open with clients if things go wrong, and if a client suffers loss or harm as a result you put matters right (if possible) and explain fully and promptly what has happened and the likely impact. If requested to do so by the SRA you investigate whether anyone may have a claim against you, provide the SRA with a report on the outcome of your investigation, and notify relevant persons that they may have such a claim, accordingly."*

This standard is likely to develop into an ongoing irritation from a professional indemnity insurers perspective given the onerous nature of the qualifying insurer rules.

You must tell clients when something goes wrong. It can be embarrassing but not as embarrassing as the SRA taking a statement from them as part of an investigation into why you not have been open and transparent with clients. My experience, personally and through clients, is that openness usually strengthens the client/solicitor relationship and is welcomed by clients.

You (or your insurer) put right any financial losses.

The position if capable of remedying is enhanced by your offer to do so (subject to any objection from the client).

If the SRA ask the firm to investigate any matter and whether or not any member of the firm (partner, employee or consultant) has committed misconduct the firm should do so in a credible manner and report on its findings appropriately. Having been tasked by a number of firms with undertaking independent investigations it can be challenging to get those under suspicion to co-operate but the realisation that non-co-operation will be reported often assists. The SRA will look at the methodology and credibility of such investigations and firms should be under no illusion not being open, transparent and honest will make things far worse.

> *"3.6 You notify the SRA promptly:*
>
> *(a) of any indicators of serious financial difficulty relating to you;"*

Financial difficulty must be reported.

> *"(b) if a relevant insolvency event occurs in relation to you;"*

Bankruptcy, winding up or administration should be reported without delay.

> *"(c) if you intend to, or become aware that you will, cease operating as a legal business;"*

Closure or ceasing practice should be reported. Note the wording "as a legal business" they mean you can be a non-regulated business i.e. non registered SRA entity.

"(d) of any change to information recorded in the register."

Any of the information held about the firm and its ownership should change.

"3.7 You provide to the SRA an information report on an annual basis or such other period as specified by the SRA in the prescribed form and by the prescribed date."

You supply the annual information requested by the SRA.

"3.8 You notify the SRA promptly if you become aware:

(a) of any material changes to information previously provided to the SRA, by you or on your behalf, about you or your managers, owners or compliance officers; and"

What is material? If it may change the SRA's view of the firm or its managers, owners and compliance officers then it is material.

If you are not sure if some change is material, assume it is, transparency being far better than a failure to report or take advice from a regulatory solicitor.

You should therefore update the SRA when information changes about your firm.

"(b) that information provided to the SRA, by you or on your behalf, about you or your managers, owners or compliance officers is or may be false, misleading, incomplete or inaccurate."

Information supplied to the SRA must be accurate. Whatever the cause of misinformation (misunderstanding to something more sinister) should be corrected.

"3.9 You ensure that a prompt report is made to the SRA, or another approved regulator, as appropriate, of any serious breach of their reg-

ulatory arrangements by any person regulated by them (including you) of which you are aware. If requested to do so by the SRA, you investigate whether there have been any serious breaches that should be reported to the SRA."

You promptly report any serious breach of the regulatory arrangements by yourself and colleagues. The need to self-report is critical as it means sole practitioners are not exempt.

If the SRA request an investigation and report then as with standard 3.5 above the firm should investigate whether or not any member of the firm (partner, employee or consultant) has committed misconduct. The firm should do so in a credible manner and report on its findings appropriately.

Having been tasked by a number of firms with undertaking independent investigations it can be challenging to get those under suspicion to co-operate but the realisation that non-co-operation will be reported often assists. The SRA will look at the methodology and credibility of such investigations and firms should be under no illusion that not being open, transparent and honest makes things far worse.

"3.10 You do not attempt to prevent anyone from providing information to the SRA or any other body exercising regulatory, supervisory, investigatory or prosecutory functions in the public interest."

Attempts to prevent reporting are strictly prohibited. The Public Interest Disclosure Act 1998 (as amended) ensures most attempt to do so will fail but the SRA issued guidance on the 12th March 2018 which contained the following introduction from its Paul Philip, SRA Chief Executive Officer, who said:

"The public and the profession expects solicitors to act with integrity and uphold the rule of law. And most do. NDAs have a valid use,

but not for covering up serious misconduct and in some cases potential crimes."[2]

Whilst the publicity and focus of the SRA in this instance focused on sexual misconduct and the use of NDAs (non-disclosure agreements) the press release and the guidance made it clear that any attempts to inappropriately gag those seeking to report misconduct was in itself a serious misconduct issue and risked sanction. The SRA confirmed this again on the 27th November 2018 in their Risk Outlook 2018 Autumn Update which stated:

"Our updated paper, Balancing duties in litigation includes warnings about using non-disclosure agreements to take unfair advantage of someone or to conceal criminal activity. We have received and are investigating more than 50 reports about allegations of harassment by solicitors. We will take action where needed."[3]

Reporting colleagues is an area which has led to confusion as firms battle with the confidentiality they seek to protect their reputation and their professional obligations. It is common in my experience of advising firms for the parties and non-regulatory specialist advisers such as consultants and accountants to fail to appreciate the SRA guidance and at the time of writing it is still common to find employment specialists unfamiliar with the SRA guidance issued and wrongly seeking to fetter reporting believing the confidentiality is appropriate. The SRA guidance could not be clearer: no attempts to fetter reporting are appropriate (see Standard 3.10 here or the NDA guidance from March 2018).

Service and competence

2 SRA Press Release 12 March 2018 see https://www.sra.org.uk/sra/news/press/nda-warning-notice-2018.page

3 SRA Risk Outlook 2018 Autumn Update Integrity and Ethics section see https://www.sra.org.uk/risk/outlook/risk-outlook-autumn-2018-update.page

The standards in this section often seem obvious. They are however expressed due to known problems in this area and common areas of complaints from clients. It is worth all solicitors and managers reading the themes which come out from the SRA's Risk Outcome annually (and the mid-year update) and the Legal Ombudsman's common areas of complaints and specific area guides.

The Legal Ombudsman has recently published a simple guide for consumers aimed at highlighting its areas of work against the SRA's. The guide refers to solicitors who are "dishonest". The consumer protection agenda is front and centre with this and the profession under increasing scrutiny.

The SRA's Price Transparency Guidance of the 5th November 2018[4] indicates the ethos emerging those professionals cannot be trusted from a regulators perspective and that the public should be guided on this risk in each and every matter in the complaints notification which the SRA guide should include the following:

> *"The Solicitors Regulation Authority can help you if you are concerned about our behaviour. This could be for things like dishonesty, taking or losing your money or treating you unfairly because of your age, a disability or other characteristic."*

Given the tiny percentage of solicitors or firms which are dishonest it is extraordinary conduct from the two primary regulators of consumer matters and risks breaching their statutory duties to uphold confidence in the legal profession by implying serious misconduct is widespread rather than a tiny percentage. To put matters into context in 2017 there were 138 cases sent by the SRA to the Solicitors Disciplinary Tribunal in respect of almost 140,000 solicitors on the roll and over 9400 firms. It is likely the SRA will change this wording recommendation given the reception it has received.

---

4 I recorded a Podcast on Pricing Transparency for the Law Society which is available from their website https://www.lawsociety.org.uk/support-services/risk-compliance/price-and-service-transparency/articles/a-practical-guide-to-price-transparency/

The apparently simple standards set out in this section therefore deserve merit and attention simply because the regulatory agenda is to presume the worst case scenario.

> *"4.1 You only act for clients on instructions from the client, or from someone properly authorised to provide instructions on their behalf. If you have reason to suspect that the instructions do not represent your client's wishes, you do not act unless you have satisfied yourself that they do. However, in circumstances where you have legal authority to act notwithstanding that it is not possible to obtain or ascertain the instructions of your client, and then you are subject to the overriding obligation to protect your client's best interests."*

Reports of solicitors and law firms acting without instructions are allegedly rife. Sometimes the focus is on claims for modest sums in the personal injury sector, sometimes it is clients saying they were not asked to provide instructions on some point (material or not) and then raising a complaint. The former can arise when claims are fraudulently brought without or without the firm's knowledge such as when identity theft is used to bring a claim. Checking your client is who they say they are can reduce this risk.

Acting without instructions, due to workload pressures or a presumption of the clients instructions should be something firms seek to eliminate by training staff against this standard and supervision to ensure it does not occur checking staff have obtained specific instructions informally and that it is documented against the file in file reviews.

For corporate, LLP and partnership clients checking the person instructing you has the requite permission to instruct you and recording this on the file is key. It is likely to include an email or letter of authority signed by a duly authorised person unless the person instructing you is by definition that person i.e. the Managing Director of a company with only one Director.

> *"4.2 You ensure that the service you provide to clients is competent and delivered in a timely manner, and takes account of your client's attributes, needs and circumstances."*

The firm must ensure the work it undertakes is within the sphere of expertise of those within the firm i.e. competent.

Firms must ensure the service is delivered in a timely manner which means that deadlines must be achievable both in terms of short term factors and longer term factors.

Vulnerable or disabled or those without a good grasp of the solicitors own language should be dealt with in a manner which enable them to seek advice and does not discriminate. Having and working to a Vulnerable Clients Policy with specific skills and expertise being concentrated in certain personnel can help firms achieve this.

> *"4.3 You ensure that your managers and employees are competent to carry out their role, and keep their professional knowledge and skills, as well as understanding of their legal, ethical and regulatory obligations, up to date."*

Training – it is central to the competency regime. Training on the skills and knowledge required for practice areas is key. Knowledge quickly becomes stale unless it evolves.

Having lectured to thousands of solicitors over many years the level of knowledge is deeply varied in respect of legal, ethical and regulatory obligations. Using this book and making sure it is read widely in the firm, ensuring senior staff get annual ethics training and updates, ensuring all staff I reminded of their obligations around Data Protection, Anti-Money Laundering and Professionals Ethics at least every two years are basic stepping stones towards meeting this obligation.

Managers should be given enhanced training opportunities to ensure their depth of knowledge is appropriate to their management role. This will look different in every firm but the acid test is: how would we show as a firm that we trained our managers to a competent standard to allow them to supervise others against our professional duties?

If scheduling in house training then ensure the level of training is appropriate to the role rather than simply all staff training.

> *"4.4 You have an effective system for supervising clients' matters."*

Supervision should consist of a multi layered approach. Day to day supervision i.e. the work is overseen and checked is one aspect but that alone will not be enough.

Using File Reviews to spot trends in the staff's working methods and any risks arising will be key.

How does your firm take the day to day and File Review lessons back to its staff? How is learning and development from these documented?

Client money and assets

Core to trust in the legal profession is firms protecting client money and assets. These simple standards are on the most high risk area in terms of disciplinary work.

> *"5.1 You properly account to clients for any financial benefit you receive as a result of their instructions, except where they have agreed otherwise."*

If you receive a benefit from any party you must tell the client about it in writing. It would be exceptional to retain it. Why? How is a payment or benefit to the firm of benefit to the client? If you wish to retain some financial benefit then it must be documented clearly (with the third party) and the client to give clients the opportunity to object or to instruct another law firm who would not have such an interest.

This standard requires firms to have in place a notification arrangement at the outset of any such arrangement. If for example your firm receives 5% commission from an After The Event (ATE) Insurer on all policies you would need to explain this and indicate the funds routinely are retained to assist with the running of the law firm and the fixed fee rates charged to the client reflect this cost and are reduced to reflect this. On privately paying matters this would work but not with other funding arrangements.

When considering how to demonstrate you and your firm are compliant with this standard focus on:

(a) Transparency with the arrangement being documented in writing and disclosed to the clients in writing;

(b) Explain the client benefit of such an arrangement;

(c) Seek express consent to retain any such benefit in writing and do not retain the benefit without this.

Always remember that trust in the profession generally and acting in a client's interest are key factors and any decisions on such arrangements should be carefully reasoned and documented in case the SRA, Legal Ombudsman or client raise a query.

> *"5.2 You safeguard money and assets entrusted to you by clients and others."*

The safeguarding of assets entrusted to your firm is essential. This will include databases, money, documents etc.

The basic steps firms should have in place as a minimum included:

(a) vetting, training and supervising staff to ensure everyone is aware of their responsibilities to keep client assets safe;

(b) having strong systems for good management and audit of client assets including the client account generally and any specific clients accounts opened for specified clients;

(c) reconciling client accounts which are thereafter signed off by the COFA at least every five weeks;

(d) ensuring the COFA has sufficient resources including time, staff and training to discharge their duties;

(e) firms must have an effective business continuity plan to enable staff illness or unexpected events do not prejudice the protection of client assets;

(f) have strong IT systems with good backups;

(g) ensure physical and electronic security measures are regularly reviewed and appropriate the work undertaken and assets held.

The issue of protecting assets is a major obligation of the firm. The risks and effectiveness of systems should be regularly reviewed by the COLP and COFA. This review should be periodically documented.

Compliance Officers and Partners of firms should expect the SRA to challenge their approach to this if investigating a complaint or a loss of money or an asset. This is the current approach and the clarity given in the new standards is likely to increase the scrutiny moving forward.

Conflict and confidentiality

The recognising of conflicts of interest for solicitors remains a challenge across the profession – the rules have evolved over many years but each matter is fact specific hence open to interpretation. Get it wrong and the SRA will take a dim view because not acting is appropriate in a wider range of circumstances than may first be clear.

The SRA regime is to a degree misleading because the standards are incomplete. They cannot be read alone. Solicitors are under a legal duty to avoid conflicts which would breach their duties as fiduciaries. The duty as fiduciary is that of single-minded loyalty which is breached if the solicitor owes a conflicting duty to another (whether that is his own firm or another client). You therefore need to apply the factual context to the rules and assess the position: is this a conflict of interest?

Conflict of interests

> *"6.1 You do not act if there is an own interest conflict or a significant risk of such a conflict."*

An own interest precludes your firm from acting.

Own interests once arising are not a debatable position or something which can be managed down in terms of risk. If the solicitor and clients interest conflict the firm must decline to act or continue to act. It is an absolute duty under this standard and the common law.

Firms must assess the ability of anyone within your firm, to act in the best interests of the client and whether or not this is impaired by any financial interest, a personal relationship, the appointment of you, or a member of your firm or family, to public office, a commercial relationship or your employment or partnership.

The phase "significant risk" demonstrates this is beyond whether or not there is an actual conflict to a significant risk occurring. For commercial lawyers the risk of losing a client to a rival firm over a conflict of own interest is always a concern but all firms, including commercially focused ones, need to put the clients first and decline to act unless it is appropriate.

Firms should exercise caution when assessing the significant risk factor. In my day to day practice I offer fact specific guidance on this issue to clients and I have noted over the years that some firms are sometimes blind to the "significant risk" factor dealing only with the actual conflict and other times are seeing risks which are too remote and could not reasonably be interpreted as "significant risk". If you are in any doubt then take expert legal advice.

"6.2 You do not act in relation to a matter or a particular aspect of it if you have a conflict of interest or a significant risk of such a conflict in relation to that matter or aspect of it, unless:

(a) the clients have a substantially common interest in relation to the matter or the aspect of it, as appropriate; or

(b) the clients are competing for the same objective,

and the conditions below are met, namely that:

(i) all the clients have given informed consent, given or evidenced in writing, to you acting;

(ii) where appropriate, you put in place effective safeguards to protect your clients' confidential information; and

(iii) you are satisfied it is reasonable for you to act for all the clients."

The risk of a conflict between two clients relates not just to contentious work. Often property or commercial firms will have clients who are competing for the same asset, property, contract or commercial relationship. In the larger firms the detail required to identify that a conflict may exist across jurisdictions is likely to be purely data or electronic system driven but these systems and the safeguards around data entry are therefore crucial, by contrast in smaller firms the data or electronic input is less material but the detailed knowledge of individuals can be lost on electronic systems. It is vital therefore than conflict training and File Reviews pressure tests the judgements being made.

Training of all staff is vital and should be conducted regularly; the application of that training can then be monitored by all managers (partners) and by the Compliance Officers.

Confidentiality and disclosure

Confidentiality is linked to the other standards in this section 6 of the Firm Code because they each run through the whole of the relationship from pre-instruction (conflict of interest) to post instruction when you cannot use confidentially obtained material.

The duty of confidentiality is wider than Legal Professional Privilege (LPP) meaning even information obtained from clients as a consequence of the solicitor client relationship not directly linked to the instructions in hand or the advice sought is captured. Clients often speak freely to "their" solicitor about matters outside the scope of the retainer and these matters are confidential despite not being about the giving or receipt of legal advice or even the current retainer between the client and the firm.

By contrast LPP is an expression that covers two distinct principles of English law: Firstly, legal advice privilege which covered communications (of any type) about which the dominant purpose is the giving or receiving of legal advice of any kind. This type of privilege only applies to clients and their legal advisers[5]. Secondly, litigation privilege as a distinct type of LPP in relation to documents or reports by third parties prepared on the instructions of a client or lawyer for the purposes of litigation[6]. LPP is far more narrowly drawn.

---

5 The Legal Services Act 2007 does not distinct LPP between the various qualifications of lawyer hence here to be clear it can apply to other qualified legal advisers such as barristers, Patent Attorney etc. It is not a solicitor specific privilege but it does not apply for example to a Chartered Accountant.

6 Litigation privilege therefore applies to non-lawyers in the appropriate circumstances.

> *"6.3 You keep the affairs of current and former clients confidential unless disclosure is required or permitted by law or the client consents."*

The word "affairs" indicate the broad width of this obligation as is set out immediately above. The obligation continues after the end of the solicitor/client retainer and continues without a time limit. If during a retainer your firm acquires confidential knowledge about the affairs of clients the entirety of that knowledge is confidential.

The exceptions to client confidentiality are when a disclosure is permitted by law[7] (typically by way of Court Order or Parliamentary Privilege) or the client consents. Such a consent should always be in writing is my view given the importance of the decision for a client to waive their confidentiality (and it is their confidentiality not your law firms). Clients who seek to waive confidentiality should be clear about the waiver granted and whether or not it will simultaneously waive legal privilege which again is their benefit and should not be waived without clients appreciating the impact on them.

If your client is vulnerable in any way extreme caution is merited from law firms and any credible policy and system about this obligation should in my view require sign off from a small category of lawyers in a firm.

> *"6.4 Any individual who is acting for a client on a matter makes the client aware of all information material to the matter of which the individual has knowledge except when:"*

Firms receive information in their role for clients and should not seek to withhold it from their clients.

---

7 The Proceeds of Crime Act 2002 (POCA) Section 345 permits Production Orders to be issued by the Courts about information requests including of solicitors (only legally privileged documents are usually excluded so, for example, the bulk of a conveyancing file will be disclosable but elements linked to the giving and receipt of legal advice will be protected and must be excluded by the disclosing law firm.

"(a) the disclosure of the information is prohibited by legal restrictions imposed in the interests of national security or the prevention of crime;"

This will by necessity a small residual category.

"(b) the client gives informed consent, given or evidenced in writing, to the information not being disclosed to them;"

Sometimes clients know elements of cases may upset them or distract them from bigger matters and may wish a firm to not share each and every piece of information. In such cases this must be evidenced. I would suggest firms write to clients and develop a consent form to record this carefully and appropriately.

"(c) the individual has reason to believe that serious physical or mental injury will be caused to the client or another if the information is disclosed; or"

Serious concerns for serious physical or mental health factors relating to clients or another person will justify the withholding of material information. A note to justify this should be retained by the firm outside the client file (which of course belongs to the client upon payment of the firm's fees and hence may be disclosed).

"(d) the information is contained in a privileged document that the individual has knowledge of only because it has been mistakenly disclosed."

If your firm receives a document which is legally privileged in error you should not disclose this. This reflects the error and the wider duties to uphold public confidence in the legal system by seeking to protect the information in such circumstances.

"6.5 You do not act for a client in a matter where that client has an interest adverse to the interest of another current or former client for

whom you hold confidential information which is material to that matter, unless:"

The link with conflicts of interest and confidentiality is clearly shown here. Once you hold confidential information material to the adverse interests of another client (including former clients).

The exceptions should be treated as exceptions which on the facts can be justified.

"(a) effective measures have been taken which result in there being no real risk of disclosure of the confidential information;"

Systems are central to this standard. The firms systems must reduce the risk of disclosure effectively to there being no real risk of disclosure.

What on Earth does this mean in practice? Electronic and/or physical restrictions on access should be in place, the personnel involved would need to be distinct (which in effect precludes small firms who cannot establish a separate team without knowledge of the confidential information involved because the existence requires information barriers).

The principles of information barriers are legal rather than SRA based. However these are usefully set out in a case in which a client's right to seek an injunction to protect its confidential information from disclosure through their former solicitors was considered (Koch Shipping Inc. v Richards Butler [2002] EWCA Civ 1280) in which Lord Justice Clarke stated in paragraphs 24 and 25 as follows:

"24. It was, and is, common ground that the relevant principles in this class of case may be stated as follows:

(1) The court's jurisdiction to intervene is founded on the right of the former client to the protection of his confidential information (per Lord Millett at p.234[8]).

---

8 Lord Millet gave the leading judgement in Bolkiah v KPMG [1999] 2 AC 222, HL which the Kock Shipping Inc. judgment relies.

(2) The only duty to the former client which survives the termination of the client relationship is a continuing duty to preserve the confidentiality of information imparted during its subsistence (per Lord Millett at p.235).

(3) The duty to preserve confidentiality is unqualified. It is a duty to keep the information confidential, not merely to take all reasonable steps to do so (per Lord Millett at p.235).

(4) The former client cannot be protected completely from accidental or inadvertent disclosure, but he is entitled to prevent his former solicitor from exposing him to any avoidable risk. This includes the increased risk of the use of the information to his prejudice arising from the acceptance of instructions to act for another client with an adverse interest in a matter to which the information may be relevant (per Lord Millett at pp.235-236).

(5) The former client must establish that the defendant solicitors possess confidential information which is or might be relevant to the matter and to the disclosure of which he has not consented (per Lord Millett at pp.234-235).

(6) The burden then passes to the defendant solicitors to show that there is <u>no risk</u> of disclosure. The court should intervene unless it is satisfied that there is no risk of disclosure. The risk must be a real one, and not merely fanciful or theoretical, but it need not be substantial (per Lord Millett at p.237).

(7) It is wrong in principle to conduct a balancing exercise. If the former client establishes the facts in (5) above, the former client is entitled to an injunction unless the defendant solicitors show that there is no risk of disclosure.

(8) In considering whether the solicitors have shown that there is no risk of disclosure, the starting point must be that, unless special measures are taken, information moves within a firm (per Lord Millett at p.237). However, that is only the starting point. The <u>Prince Jefri</u> case

does not establish a rule of law that special measures have to be taken to prevent the information passing within a firm: see also Young v Robson Rhodes [1999] 3 All ER 524, per Laddie J at p.538. On the other hand, the courts should restrain the solicitors from acting unless satisfied on the basis of clear and convincing evidence that all effective measures have been taken to ensure that no disclosure will occur (per Lord Millett at pp.237-238, where he adapted the test identified by Sopinka J in MacDonald Estate v Martin (1991) 77 DLR (4th) 249 at p.269). This is a heavy burden (per Lord Millett at p.239).

25. It is to my mind important to emphasise that each case turns on its own facts. For example, this is a very different case on the facts from the Prince Jefri case. In the instant case the question is whether there was any risk of a single solicitor inadvertently disclosing confidential information to others within Richards Butler such that it might come into the hands of those conducting Ariadne's case against Koch."

The most high profile example of a former law firm client seeking and obtaining an injunction dates back to 2004 and involved Marks & Spencer, Sir Philip Green and Freshfields[9]. In that case Marks and Spencer secured an injunction which Freshfields sought to appeal to overturn and failed to do so. Earlier in this section I noted that the benchmark for smaller law firms was in practical terms impossible to meet given the limited pool of personnel but the common law position highlights the threshold is high even for City firms and thus the larger regional practices.

The legal position is therefore settled: the duty to preserve confidentiality is unqualified and survives the retainer, if the solicitor holds confidential information which is or might be relevant then the court requires the law firm to show there is no risk of disclosure. The Court will intervene unless it is satisfied there is no risk of disclosure.

9 Marks & Spencer Group PLC & Another v Freshfields Bruckhaus Deringer [2004] EWCA Civ 741

This is wider than the SRA standards and is just one example of the need for law firms to have systems, processes and training to go beyond the SRA regime into practical application. Take a cautious approach and if you are not 100% certain of the facts in hand take expert legal advice from this writer or another legal services expert.

"(b) the current or former client whose information you hold has given informed consent, given or evidenced in writing, to you acting, including to any measures taken to protect their information."

The measures you propose to take above (physical and electronic security and distinct personnel) must be supplemented by informed consent so enable you to act.

Applicable standards in the SRA Code of Conduct for Solicitors and RELs

The Firm Code contains the following to aid interpretation and to make clear you means the firm and individual.

"7.1 The following paragraphs in the SRA Code of Conduct for Solicitors, RELs and RFLs apply to you in their entirety as though references to "you" were references to you as a firm:

(a) dispute resolution and proceedings before courts, tribunals and inquiries (2.1 to 2.7);

(b) referrals, introductions and separate businesses (5.1 to 5.3); and

(c) standards which apply when providing services to the public or a section of the public, namely client identification (8.1), complaints handling (8.2 to 8.5), and client information and publicity (8.6 to 8.11)."

Managers in SRA authorised firms

Managers are wider than many think as a consequence of the SRA Glossary.

The definition used is a member of an LLP; a director of a company; a partner in a partnership; or in relation to any other body, a member of its governing body.

> *"8.1 If you are a manager, you are responsible for compliance by your firm with this Code. This responsibility is joint and several if you share management responsibility with other managers of the firm."*

As an owner or director or partner you share regulatory risk with your colleagues on a joint and several basis.

The clarity of the SRA's drafting is intended to ensure that when a firm acts in a way which is unacceptable and amounts to professional misconduct it can hold the firm and its managers to account. The intention is to remove the finger pointing between managers and avoid others being able to say "Well it was Miss X's our COLP's error not mine!".

Gone are the days when one manager can leave things to a colleague and claim not to be responsible.

Compliance officers

Compliance is led by the COLP and COFA but is not intended as their sole responsibility hence the standard above and the obligations set out in standard 9.

> *"9.1 If you are a COLP you take all reasonable steps to:*

You do not need to be perfect, but you do need to be reasonable and have taken any reasonable steps to comply. This will be different depending on the size of the firm, the risks faced and any unique circumstances.

Do think however that the following are minimum steps so should be reflex actions:

- Training of all personnel (from receptionists to senior partners);
- Processes to manage the known risks;
- Systems to enable monitoring.

(a) ensure compliance with the terms and conditions of your firm's authorisation;

The SRA will have authorised the firm and nothing can deviate from the recorded factors. If you promote someone to be a partner i.e. Manager in SRA speak they must be approved for example.

(b) ensure compliance by your firm and its managers, employees or interest holders with the SRA's regulatory arrangements which apply to them;

As the eyes and ears of the regulator you are expected to ensure compliance by all against the entire SRA regime.

(c) ensure that your firm's managers and interest holders and those they employ or contract with do not cause or substantially contribute to a breach of the SRA's regulatory arrangements;

As the eyes and ears of the regulator you are expected to ensure compliance by all against the entire SRA regime.

(d) ensure that a prompt report is made to the SRA of any serious breach of the terms and conditions of your firm's authorisation, or the SRA's regulatory arrangements which apply to your firm, managers or employees,

> *save in relation to the matters which are the responsibility of the COFA as set out in paragraph 9.2 below."*

The prompt reporting obligation enables the SRA to assess the risk to consumers of legal services. It is therefore a key component in the safeguards in place.

The obligation on COLPs is intended to bite and ensure they feel for their own careers will be adversely impacted if they fail to do so.

Talking to COLPs who I do not act for, they often express a feeling of pressure not to report but sometimes they must do so irrespective of views of other interest holders or managers. To do so takes confidence to know they are right and that the SRA if seeing the right steps being taken often will simply let the COLP get on with things meaning the concerns of those applying the pressure is misconceived.

In practice since it was introduced as a role on the 1st January 2013 the COLP role has caused partnership problems but my advice to COLPs is always: let's assess the situation objectively, based on evidence and if I conclude you should report then let's report.

For firms who relationships internally are damaged two things have proven time and again to be effective: training on the roles and duties to remove the frustrations by building understanding and mediation to rebuild relationships.

> *"9.2 If you are a COFA you take all reasonable steps to:*
>
> *"(a) ensure that your firm and its managers and employees comply with any obligations imposed upon them under the SRA Accounts* Rules;*"*

As with the COLP guidance above the role requires COFAs to be eyes and ears and to ensure compliance is second nature. SRA Accounts Rule breaches are the most frequently cited breaches in disciplinary cases. Therefore compliance should be strictly enforced.

However, you do not need to be perfect, you do need to be reasonable and have taken any reasonable steps to comply. This will be different depending on the size of the firm, the risks faced and unique circumstances.

Do think however that the following are minimum steps so should be reflex actions:

- Training of all personnel (from receptionists to senior partners);
- Processes to manage the known risks;
- Systems to enable monitoring.

"(b) ensure that a prompt report is made to the SRA of any serious breach of the SRA Accounts Rules which apply to them."

The prompt reporting obligation enables the SRA to assess the risk to consumers of legal services. It is therefore a key component in the safeguards in place.

The obligation on COFAs is intended to bite and ensure they feel for their own careers will be adversely impacted if they fail to do so.

COLPs may feel pressure not to report but sometimes they must do so irrespective of views of other interest holders or managers.

In practice since it was introduced as a role on the 1st January 2013 the COFA role has caused partnership problems but my advice to COFAs is always: let's assess the situation objectively, based on evidence and if I conclude you should report then let's report.

For firms who relationships internally are damaged two things have proven time and again to be effective: training on the roles and duties to remove the frustrations by building understanding and mediation to rebuild relationships.

Conclusion

Look beyond the standards set out: consider your common law and statutory legal obligations and think about how you ensure the knowledge of the standards is shared throughout the firm.

Think about daily how would you explain this to the SRA so they can see you and are your team are good solicitors, doing a good job and if something has gone wrong it is not malicious and will be addressed fully, fairly and with the clients interest at the heart of things to ensure the risks of disciplinary action are reduced.

There is no such thing as too much training or too many systems or policy reviews. At least annually look to have someone external assess your firms compliance and know who to call when you are unsure. Most firms do not need regular external compliance support in my experience but they do need to know who to ask.

CHAPTER SIX
HOW TO ADAPT TO THE SRA PRINCIPLES AND CODES OF CONDUCT 2019

You and your law firm will need to change, to evolve in many cases from old fashioned thinking and to adapt to the new focus points in other cases.

You start this process by doing the following:

1. Training on the practical implications of the new SRA regime;
2. Reviewing what you do now and what you need to do moving forward;
3. Ensuring that supervisors understand the obligations on them and discharge that supervision effectively;
4. Recording what you do and why.

Training is the key. I regularly give webinar and podcast talks and they are a good basic starting point but there is no substitute for in-house training which allows you and your team to ask personalised, specific questions unique to a firm. Months ahead of the changes I have bookings for in-house training from City, international and smaller High Street law firms to deliver in-house training with a bespoke question and answer session to make it highly focused on the firm's needs.

Training should be a mix anyway so use the podcasts, webinars, books, magazine articles and supplement them with in-house training. It's not just for large firms with big budgets in that 1-4 partner firms regularly buy a two hour session from me for their smaller firms.

Read the new SRA Principles and Code for Individuals and Code for Firms. These are short, these are only a starting point but they are the core starting point.

Challenge your own understanding. Challenge others understanding and become curious. Have we got this right?

Finally, thumb this book and apply the knowledge in it to help you and if you still need personalised training or advice afterwards then get in touch for bespoke advice or training.

Good luck and do get in touch if you need further support.

MORE BOOKS BY LAW BRIEF PUBLISHING

A selection of our other titles available now:-

'A Practical Guide to Vicarious Liability' by Mariel Irvine
'A Practical Guide to Claims Arising from Delays in Diagnosing Cancer' by Bella Webb
'A Practical Guide to Applications for Landlord's Consent and Variation of Leases' by Mark Shelton
'A Practical Guide to Relief from Sanctions Post-Mitchell and Denton' by Peter Causton
'Butler's Equine Tax Planning: 2nd Edition' by Julie Butler
'A Practical Guide to Equity Release for Advisors' by Paul Sams
'A Practical Guide to Immigration Law and Tier 1 Entrepreneur Applications' by Sarah Pinder
'A Practical Guide to Unlawful Eviction and Harassment' by Stephanie Lovegrove
'In My Backyard! A Practical Guide to Neighbourhood Plans' by Dr Sue Chadwick
'A Practical Guide to the Law Relating to Food' by Ian Thomas
'A Practical Guide to the Ending of Assured Shorthold Tenancies' by Elizabeth Dwomoh
'Commercial Mediation – A Practical Guide' by Nick Carr
'A Practical Guide to Financial Services Claims' by Chris Hegarty
'The Law of Houses in Multiple Occupation: A Practical Guide to HMO Proceedings' by Julian Hunt
'A Practical Guide to Unlawful Eviction and Harassment' by Stephanie Lovegrove
'A Practical Guide to Solicitor and Client Costs' by Robin Dunne
'Artificial Intelligence – The Practical Legal Issues' by John Buyers
'A Practical Guide to Wrongful Conception, Wrongful Birth and Wrongful Life Claims' by Rebecca Greenstreet

'Occupiers, Highways and Defective Premises Claims: A Practical Guide Post-Jackson – 2nd Edition' by Andrew Mckie
'A Practical Guide to Financial Ombudsman Service Claims' by Adam Temple & Robert Scrivenor
'A Practical Guide to the Law of Enfranchisement and Lease Extension' by Paul Sams
'A Practical Guide to Marketing for Lawyers – 2nd Edition' by Catherine Bailey & Jennet Ingram
'A Practical Guide to Advising Schools on Employment Law' by Jonathan Holden
'Certificates of Lawful Use and Development: A Guide to Making and Determining Applications' by Bob Mc Geady & Meyric Lewis
'A Practical Guide to the Law of Dilapidations' by Mark Shelton
'A Practical Guide to the 2018 Jackson Personal Injury and Costs Reforms' by Andrew Mckie
'A Guide to Consent in Clinical Negligence Post-Montgomery' by Lauren Sutherland QC
'A Practical Guide to Running Housing Disrepair and Cavity Wall Claims: 2nd Edition' by Andrew Mckie & Ian Skeate
'A Practical Guide to the General Data Protection Regulation (GDPR)' by Keith Markham
'A Practical Guide to Digital and Social Media Law for Lawyers' by Sherree Westell
'A Practical Guide to Holiday Sickness Claims – 2nd Edition' by Andrew Mckie & Ian Skeate
'A Practical Guide to Inheritance Act Claims by Adult Children Post-Ilott v Blue Cross' by Sheila Hamilton Macdonald
'A Practical Guide to Elderly Law' by Justin Patten
'Arguments and Tactics for Personal Injury and Clinical Negligence Claims' by Dorian Williams
'A Practical Guide to QOCS and Fundamental Dishonesty' by James Bentley
'A Practical Guide to Drone Law' by Rufus Ballaster, Andrew Firman, Eleanor Clot
'Practical Mediation: A Guide for Mediators, Advocates, Advisers, Lawyers, and Students in Civil, Commercial, Business, Property, Workplace, and Employment Cases' by Jonathan Dingle with John Sephton

'Practical Horse Law: A Guide for Owners and Riders' by Brenda Gilligan
'A Comparative Guide to Standard Form Construction and Engineering Contracts' by Jon Close
'A Practical Guide to Compliance for Personal Injury Firms Working With Claims Management Companies' by Paul Bennett
'A Practical Guide to the Landlord and Tenant Act 1954: Commercial Tenancies' by Richard Hayes & David Sawtell
'A Practical Guide to Personal Injury Claims Involving Animals' by Jonathan Hand
'A Practical Guide to Psychiatric Claims in Personal Injury' by Liam Ryan
'Introduction to the Law of Community Care in England and Wales' by Alan Robinson
'A Practical Guide to Dog Law for Owners and Others' by Andrea Pitt
'Ellis and Kevan on Credit Hire – 5th Edition' by Aidan Ellis & Tim Kevan
'RTA Allegations of Fraud in a Post-Jackson Era: The Handbook – 2nd Edition' by Andrew Mckie
'RTA Personal Injury Claims: A Practical Guide Post-Jackson' by Andrew Mckie
'On Experts: CPR35 for Lawyers and Experts' by David Boyle
'An Introduction to Personal Injury Law' by David Boyle
'A Practical Guide to Claims Arising From Accidents Abroad and Travel Claims' by Andrew Mckie & Ian Skeate
'A Practical Guide to Cosmetic Surgery Claims' by Dr Victoria Handley
'A Practical Guide to Chronic Pain Claims' by Pankaj Madan
'A Practical Guide to Claims Arising from Fatal Accidents' by James Patience
'A Practical Approach to Clinical Negligence Post-Jackson' by Geoffrey Simpson-Scott
'A Practical Guide to Personal Injury Trusts' by Alan Robinson
'Employers' Liability Claims: A Practical Guide Post-Jackson' by Andrew Mckie
'A Practical Guide to Subtle Brain Injury Claims' by Pankaj Madan
'The Law of Driverless Cars: An Introduction' by Alex Glassbrook
'A Practical Guide to Costs in Personal Injury Cases' by Matthew Hoe

'A Practical Guide to Alternative Dispute Resolution in Personal Injury Claims – Getting the Most Out of ADR Post-Jackson' by Peter Causton, Nichola Evans, James Arrowsmith
'A Practical Guide to Personal Injuries in Sport' by Adam Walker & Patricia Leonard
'The No Nonsense Solicitors' Practice: A Guide To Running Your Firm' by Bettina Brueggemann
'Baby Steps: A Guide to Maternity Leave and Maternity Pay' by Leah Waller
'The Queen's Counsel Lawyer's Omnibus: 20 Years of Cartoons from The Times 1993-2013' by Alex Steuart Williams

Printed in Great Britain
by Amazon

74185436R00072